TRANSNATIONAL

RADICALS

TRAVIS TOMCHUK

TRANSNATIONAL

RADICALS

*Italian Anarchists
in Canada and the U.S.
1915–1940*

UMP
University of Manitoba Press

CONTENTS

LIST OF
ILLUSTRATIONS

LIST OF ABBREVIATIONS

ACS	Archivio Centrale dello Stato
AdR	L'Adunata dei Refrattari
AAFNA	Alleanza Antifascista del Nord America
ACWU	Amalgamated Clothing Workers' Union
AFL	American Federation of Labor
CCF	Co-operative Commonwealth Federation
CGDCF	Comitato Generale di Difesa Contro il Fascismo
CGL	Confederazione Generale del Lavoro
CNR	Canadian National Railway
CNT	Confederación Nacional del Trabajo
CPC	Casellario Politico Centrale
CPC	Communist Party of Canada
CPR	Canadian Pacific Railway
CPUSA	Communist Party of the United States of America
CS	Cronaca Sovversiva
DKP	David Koven Papers
EGPP	Emma Goldman Papers Project
FA:EGP	Federico Arcos: Emma Goldman Papers
FAI	Federazione Anarchici Italiana
FIOM	Federazione Italiana Operai Metallurgica (Italian Metal Workers' Union)
FSI	Federazione Socialista Italiana

IISH	International Institute of Social History
ILGWU	International Ladies Garment Workers' Union
IM	Il Martello
IWMA	International Working Men's Association
IWW	Industrial Workers of the World
JGP	Jacques Gross Papers
JLCP	Jacob Lawrence Cohen Papers
LC	Labadie Collection
NDP	New Democratic Party
OBU	One Big Union
OFI	Ordine Figli d'Italia (Order of the Sons of Italy)
OGPU	Obedinennoe Gosudarstvennoe Politicheskoe Upravlenie
OND	Opera Nazionale Dopolavoro (National Afterwork Organization)
OVRA	Opera Volontari Repressione Antifascista
PNF	Partito Nazionale Fascista
POI	Partito Operaio Italiano (Italian Workers' Party)
PSAR-FI	Partito Socialista Anarchico Rivoluzionario – Federazione Italiana
PSI	Partito Socialista Italiana
RCMP	Royal Canadian Mounted Police
SFI	Sindicato Ferrovieri Italiani (Italian Railway Workers' Union)
SIA	Solidaridad Internacional Antifascista
SLP	Socialist Labour Party
SLRSI	Società dei Legionari della Rivoluzione Sociale Italiana
SPA	Socialist Party of America
UAWMF	Up Against the Wall Motherfuckers
UIL	Unione Italiana del Lavoro
UMWA	United Mine Workers of America
USI	Unione Sindicale Italiana

INTRODUCTION

If one were to read widely on the subject of Canadian labour and radical history during the first half of the twentieth century, one would be struck by the lack of information on anarchists. There is a large body of works exploring various socialist, communist, and syndicalist groups and movements, biographies on radical unionists, and histories of major labour struggles. Yet, among thousands of pages, there is only passing reference to anarchists if there is any mention at all. Former leader of the Communist Party of Canada Tim Buck mentions briefly in his biography that labour lawyer J.L. Cohen had defended anarchists.[1]

More concrete details of anarchist presence in Canada can be found in the well-known Russian-born anarchist Emma Goldman's biography *Living My Life*, which chronicles her life until the late 1920s. Goldman writes of the anarchists she had met while on speaking tours in cities such as Toronto and Winnipeg. More recently, Theresa and Albert Moritz's *The World's Most Dangerous Woman: A New Biography of Emma Goldman* and its focus on the well-known anarchist's time in Canada, has provided more information on anarchists and their activities in Canada. However, the focus remains on Goldman and not the wider movement. While Mathieu Houle-Courcelle's *Sur les traces de l'anarchisme au Québec (1860–1960)* examines anarchist thought and action in Quebec, it does not explore its existence in other parts of the country.

The lack of historical studies on anarchism in the Canadian context is curious. With so many histories written on other left-wing political movements, a study of anarchism seems like a natural next step in fleshing out the history of the Left in Canada even further. Studying anarchists is no easy task. Anarchists did not keep membership lists, minutes of meetings, or records of important decisions; neither did they organize into a national party as did socialists and communists. To study early-twentieth-century anarchism in Canada, one would find only small groups of Russians in Hamilton and Toronto; Jews in Montreal, Toronto, and Winnipeg; and Italians in Toronto, Windsor, and Sault Ste. Marie. An examination of these groups within the borders of Canada would result in an insignificant and ineffectual "movement." However, by recognizing that these small groups based in Canada were parts of a much larger transnational movement, new possibilities of study are possible.

Take Attilio Bortolotti (a.k.a. Arturo Bartolotti and Art Bertholet), for example. In 1920, at the age of sixteen, Bortolotti left his hometown of Codroipo in the region of Friuli-Venezia Giulia, Italy. Having witnessed first-hand the brutality and senselessness of the First World War, he was determined to avoid the service in the Italian military mandatory for males, beginning at the age of eighteen. His experiences during this conflict also led him to question the religious beliefs of his parents. After he and his mother Maria discovered dead soldiers in a ditch, the young Bortolotti asked, "If there is a God, why does he allow wars and killing like this if he is so powerful?"[2] Bortolotti, who had an older brother, Guglielmo, living in Windsor, Ontario, decided he wanted to go to Canada. When he arrived in Windsor that July, Bortolotti was able to find employment through his brother as an assistant to a blacksmith who worked for a public works contractor. Bortolotti had experience in this trade. As a youth, he had apprenticed to a blacksmith in Codroipo and, after the local blacksmith relocated to Bologna, became the town smith. During his time working and living in Windsor, Bortolotti attended night school to learn English and become a machinist. His training in the latter led to a new position as a lathe operator at the same business. Though Bortolotti was making headway at work, his days in the shop were plagued by the racism of his supervisor, who never called Bortolotti by name—only "wop" or "dago." After nearly two years of abuse, Bortolotti was at the end of his rope. One day, while he was being berated by his supervisor for not repairing the shop's generator fast enough, Bortolotti threw a hammer at the supervisor's leg, knocking him down. This ended Bortolotti's employment with this particular business.[3]

Bortolotti spent his spare time at the Windsor Public Library studying astronomy and the history of religion. He was also reading the works of the naturalist Charles Darwin and the sociologist Herbert Spencer. Bortolotti and his brother Guglielmo would also get together with Italian friends and discuss themes such as religion. The friends would congregate at the apartment of a local grocer, possibly Fortunato Mariotti, an anarchist originally from Fano, Friuli-Venezia Giulia.[4] This personal study and group discussion helped to solidify Bortolotti's anti-religious position and led him to declare himself an atheist in 1921. However, it was not until the following year that Bortolotti became interested in anarchism. He had read a pamphlet on the arrest and incarceration of Nicola Sacco and Bartolomeo Vanzetti, the two Italian anarchists arrested for their supposed involvement in a payroll heist that occurred in Braintree, Massachusetts, in April 1920 that had left the payroll master and a security guard dead. Both men were found guilty and sentenced to death. The pamphlet explained that the two men were innocent of the charges of robbery and murder, and had been convicted on the flimsiest of evidence. At this point, Bortolotti had never heard of Sacco and Vanzetti or anarchism. He wanted to find out more about the two men and the political philosophy to which they adhered, and was given a few anarchist newspapers and some pamphlets by notable anarchist writers Errico Malatesta and Sébastien Faure to read. It took him half a year to fully understand the material but it had a long-lasting influence. The next time he was among friends, Bortolotti stated that he was an anarchist opposed to all government and authority. Two anarchists, most likely Giulio Ghetti and Giuseppe Tubaro, came over to Bortolotti and shook his hand.[5]

Bortolotti's becoming an anarchist coincided with Fascist Benito Mussolini's march on Rome and he was actively involved in antifascist activism in both Windsor and Detroit. Around this time, he met a Friulian bricklayer who had been living in the United States and who had been recently hired by Bortolotti's brother in Windsor. The bricklayer was an anarchist and asked Bortolotti to hand deliver a letter to a comrade in Detroit. The letter was addressed to Fortunato Cernuto, the Sicilian-born owner of a candy store located on Rivard Street.[6] The store also served as an anarchist meeting place and radical library for Il Gruppo "I Refrattari," a local anarchist circle aligned with the New York-based anarchist journal *L'Adunata dei Refrattari*. After Bortolotti had delivered the letter, Cernuto invited him to peruse the anarchist literature and he took some pamphlets. This was Bortolotti's first introduction to Il Gruppo "I Refrattari" and would mark the beginning of his involvement with these Detroit anarchists. From that point on, he would travel to Detroit every Sunday morning to attend meetings. However, Bortolotti continued his interaction with his Windsor comrades and was present for weekly fund-raising dances or performances.[7]

In the oral histories conducted with Attilio Bortolotti, he does not elaborate on the specific antifascist activities he and others were involved in during the early 1920s in Windsor other than his mention of "fight[ing] the Fascists."[8] Bortolotti believed that his difficulty in finding work in Windsor was a direct result of his antifascism which led to local fascists seeking to blacklist him. Bortolotti was able to find employment as a mason with his brother Guglielmo, who by this time had relocated to Detroit and was constructing houses.

Regardless of whether Bortolotti was living in Windsor or Detroit, his anarchist and antifascist activities continued uninterrupted. And, even while living in Detroit, he maintained close contact with comrades in Windsor who would notify him about antifascist actions in that city. For example, Bortolotti was present when the Italian consul to Canada visited Windsor in 1926. At that meeting, Bortolotti raised his hand to speak but the chairman[9] would not recognize his right to do so. As Bortolotti recalled,

Figure 1. Attilio Bortolotti. Busta 772, Casellario Politico Centrale (CPC), Archivio Centrale dello Stato (ACS), Rome.

I called him [the chairman] what he was—a coward. On the platform one of the fascist leaders in Windsor said, "If you have the guts, come here and speak." I got up as fast as I could and in five seconds I was there. I told the consul what they [the fascists] were—a bunch of killers, liars, and the rest. At my shoulder was a picture of the [Italian] king [Vittorio Emanuele III]. I tore it off the wall, crumpled it in my hands, and threw it in the face of the consul. That started a melee. In less than a minute the whole audience was fighting each other. The fascists retreated into one corner. My brother came over with a couple of comrades and said, "Tilio, let's go." We could hear the police sirens coming.[10]

In early 1927, Bortolotti was again living in Windsor after United States immigration officials began to monitor his brother Guglielmo's work sites in Detroit. Still unable to find a job in Windsor, Bortolotti was having difficulties paying rent. However, he was still active politically and had come to the attention of Windsor police. One day while at home, two police officers visited Bortolotti and took him to see the chief of city police for a talk. When Bortolotti arrived at the police station, he saw a number of anarchist pamphlets that had been translated from Italian to English lying on the chief's desk. The police chief told Bortolotti to leave Canada or he would face criminal charges. So, again, Bortolotti was forced to return to Detroit where he found work as a machinist for the Ford Motor Company and resumed his anarchist activities with his Detroit comrades.[11]

Now in the United States, Bortolotti was involved in the distribution of leaflets to commemorate the two-year anniversary of Sacco's and Vanzetti's judicial murder. A comrade with American citizenship did not think it safe for illegal migrants, like Bortolotti, to be involved in the leafleting campaign because of a city by-law that had made the practice illegal. Bortolotti was aware of the risk he was taking and began to hand leaflets to workers as they exited a General Motors factory. A police car happened to drive by and Bortolotti was arrested. He was found guilty of distributing anarchist literature and working in the United States illegally. Admitting in court that he was an anarchist, Bortolotti was ordered to be deported to Italy. Italian comrades were able to raise the $3,000 bail—an enormous sum in 1929—to secure Bortolotti's release from jail. Raffaele Schiavina, then editor of the anarchist journal *L'Adunata dei Refrattari*, arrived in Detroit shortly after bail was secured and counselled Bortolotti to forfeit it. As Bortolotti recalled: "[Schiavina] said to me, 'Tilio, your life is worth more than $3,000. Go back to Canada and get lost.'"[12] Taking Schiavina's advice, Bortolotti returned to Windsor but, because of his previous run-in with local police, made his way to Toronto.[13]

In many ways, Bortolotti's experiences were representative of Italian migrant an-archists. He was part of the mass migration from Italy, one that began in the late nineteenth century. This exodus was due to two important and overlapping fac-tors: the need for unskilled and semi-skilled labour in industrializing nations, and the unification of Italy, known as the Risorgimento, whose leaders had promised but failed to deliver improvements to the daily lives of labourers and peasants. For Bortolotti, the Italian state offered only mandatory military service. Though he did not identify himself as an anarchist prior to leaving his hometown of Codroi-po, anarchist ideas had begun to circulate among Italians during unification and had quickly led to the emergence of a movement. As Italian anarchists migrated to different parts of the globe in search of work, to escape repression because of their political activities within Italy, or to avoid military service (as did Bortolotti), they established sites of anarchist presence in the urban and resource extraction cen-tres, not only in Europe and the Americas, but also in Northern Africa and the Middle East. Often, anarchists did not remain in their first location of settlement and lived in multiple states before finally settling permanently. As anarchists left Italy, they continued to stay in contact with comrades who were yet to migrate. This created transnational links between those anarchists still living in Italy and those living abroad. Thus, when the time came for an anarchist to migrate, a sys-tem of networks—a form of anarchist migration complex—was already in place which provided an important means of settlement within their political and cul-tural milieux. The existence of these anarchist migration networks also provided someone like Bortolotti, who was new to anarchism, access to a pre-existing com-munity of activists. Yet, at the same time, those Italian-born anarchists—many of whom did not become naturalized citizens of the countries to which they mi-grated—were in a precarious position as migrants and as anarchists. Bortolotti's experiences demonstrate these difficulties. When his anarchist activities affected his ability to find work in Windsor, he was forced to seek employment in Detroit. His illegal status in the United States meant having to avoid immigration authori-ties who regularly visited worksites for the very purpose of policing immigrants. Similarly, Bortolotti's inability to claim Canadian or American citizenship made it possible for authorities to expel the anarchist from their respective countries.

Considering that the transnational Italian anarchist movement in which Bortolotti and others were involved was comprised almost entirely of skilled and unskilled workers—people who spent the majority of their time engaged in waged labour—its cultural and political output was significant. Literally, hun-dreds of Italian-language anarchist newspapers were established by anarchists living in Europe and South and North America during the 1870-1940 period, with about one hundred of those newspapers originating in the United States alone. An unknown number of anarchist pamphlets and books were also published by anarchists in their spare time.[14] Italian anarchists wrote their own plays and organized *filodrammatiche* or amateur drama groups to perform them. In place of religious and state holidays, anarchists created their own—replacing Easter with May Day, for instance. Dances, dinners, picnics, and other social functions were other important aspects of the Italian anarchist culture. And it was through this culture that anarchists were able to promote their distinctive values in opposition to hierarchy, government, and religion, and demonstrate their opinions on a whole host of social and political issues—ranging from capitalist society to marriage—to a wider Italian audience.

This study contends that the resiliency of the Italian anarchist movement was due to several factors. First, its transnationalism—"the process by which [migrants] forge and sustain multi-stranded social relations that link together their societies of origin and settlement."[15] The migrant or migrant exile experience of Italian anarchists laid the groundwork for a global movement. These various sites of anarchist presence were in constant contact with people, ideas, publications, and correspondence continually travelling these networks.[16] Though these networks were heavily based on personal relationships—meaning that a rupture between groups or comrades could lead to the breakdown of parts of the complex—this form of organization was remarkably resilient. Not only were Italian anarchists able to maintain their networks despite the difficulties within the movement, but its transnationalism made it more difficult for a state or states to destroy autonomous groups that were spread across wide geographical spaces; although this is not to suggest that national borders were insignificant in the lives of anarchists who, because of their political commitments, were philosophically opposed to nation-states. During the early twentieth century, national boundaries were becoming increasingly defined. Just as crossing a national border could aid an anarchist fleeing political persecution or avoiding military service, the border could also act as a very real physical barrier. And, as nation-states began to police borders more heavily and access to citizenship acquired greater importance, migrant anarchists could find themselves at the mercy of governments and immigration authorities. Emma Goldman, who will be discussed in greater detail in a later chapter, was deported from the United States to Russia in 1919 for her political activities. Unwilling to live in Bolshevik Russia and unable to return to the United States, Goldman spent the remainder of her life moving between France, England, Spain, and Canada. She was able to reside in Canada only because of her marriage to the Welsh anarchist and miner James Colton, which had made her a British citizen.[17] Of course, someone as notorious as Goldman was not going to be able to quietly slip back into the

United States. This posed less of a problem for Italian anarchists. As the experiences of Attilio Bortolotti demonstrate, Italian radicals without Canadian or United States citizenship were vulnerable. Though some Italian anarchists were deported from these countries, a few found their way back, illegally, to continue their activism. Even with a more security-conscious Canada-United States border, Italian anarchists continued to enter these countries illegally with fake or borrowed passports or no official paperwork of any kind; and, in some cases, smugglers were hired to get anarchists across national boundaries. Such drastic measures were the result of a lack of options—anarchists could remain in Europe and face repression or take a chance trying to enter Canada or the United States. But one also gets the sense that, for some anarchists, the border acted more as an inconvenience to be worked around than an impenetrable barrier.

The second factor involved in the resiliency of the transnational Italian anarchist movement was the formation of a strong anarchist identity informed by class, ethnicity, gender, the influence of particular leaders, and specific interpretations of anarchist doctrine. Third, the development of anarchist culture, such as plays, "holidays," and various social events, led to movement retention, reinforcement of movement values, and movement expansion. Fourth, the existence of a well-developed anarchist identity and culture made it possible for the mobilization of the transnational movement and its resources during times of crisis.

This study demonstrates how a transnational approach to the study of anarchist history can provide a more complete picture of these movements in a way that the analysis of anarchists within the boundaries of a nation-state cannot. For instance, there are historical studies on the English, French, and Italian movements, among others. These histories are important contributions to the study of anarchism and have either begun the process of historical inquiry into anarchist formations or built upon them. The nation-state does provide a neat boundary to encapsulate a movement's formation and activity, but this kind of approach has also generated analytical problems of its own.

One issue rising from such national studies is that they tend to focus on native-born anarchists while excluding the contribution of anarchist migrants. Sociologist Michael Mann, for example, has critiqued the assumption such scholars often make "that 'societies' (social formations) are geographically identical with nation states" when no "single bounded society [can be found] in geographical or social space."[18] David Berry's *A History of the French Anarchist Movement, 1917–1945* exemplifies this problem. While examining the French movement's reaction to the Bolshevik Revolution, its relationship with the national labour movement, and its mobilization during the Spanish Civil War, Berry notes the existence of sizeable Italian and Spanish anarchist communities in France and the founding of the Russian-language anarchist newspaper *Dielo Trouda* (The Cause of Labour) in Paris in the 1920s. However, he does not dwell on the activities of these groups or their relationship with the French movement in any significant manner. In one instance, Berry begins a chapter with a quote by Ernesto Bonomini but one would have to read the footnote to know that this Italian-born anarchist spent eight years in prison for assassinating a well-known Paris-based Italian fascist leader in 1924, later fought in Spain, and was a member of the Proofreaders' Union in Paris.[19] As a result, Berry's approach gives the impression that the only anarchist movement of note in France was led by the French, omitting the role and influence of Italians, Spaniards, Russians, and others on the movement in this country. This omission of non-nationals not only excludes some noteworthy activists from the record but also in essence misrepresents the anarchist phenomenon, since so many of its adherents were people who had no secure state identity.

Taking a different approach, Matthew Thomas's 2005 study *Anarchist Ideas and Counter-Cultures in Britain, 1880–1914* likens British anarchists to a political and social sub-culture, instead of a movement. Whereas past histories sympathetic to anarchism tended to focus on organizational histories of anarchist movements, Thomas argues that this strategy is limited because it leads to a discussion of "small sects" of anarchists that flourished briefly and then disappeared with little discernible impact beyond anarchist circles. Therefore, Thomas chooses to measure the success of anarchists not by their numbers, but by their ability to influence public conceptions on issues such as women's rights, educational reform, and labour unrest, as well as the general challenge they posed to Victorian and Edwardian social mores. Thomas has written an engaging study that convincingly demonstrates the importance anarchist ideas can have within a society where a large-scale anarchist movement is not present. However, one issue that crops up, due to the national focus of *Anarchist Ideas and Counter-Cultures in Britain, 1880–1914,* relates to the creation of national anarchisms in states where the movement was comprised of both native-born and migrant anarchists. Thomas acknowledges the existence of Jewish and Italian anarchists among others within this anarchist counter-culture, but these different groupings of anarchist ethnicities all fall under the rubric of "British anarchism," a problematic term which tends to assimilate non-Anglophone anarchists into a wider nationalist identity, not to mention the various strains of anarchism this term is supposed to encompass.[20]

A third critique of a national approach focuses on the tendency to divorce an anarchist movement—within the confines of national borders—from the wider transnational movement of which it is part. Mathieu Houle-Courcelles's *Sur la trace de l'anarchisme au Québec, 1860–1960*, which differs from the Berry and Thomas studies because the "state" in this book is actually a province, attempts to examine anarchist thought and activity in Quebec. Houle-Courcelles, an independent researcher, has written an intriguing book on anarchist traditions in the province. He begins by exploring anti-clerical thought in Quebec and the province's role as a destination of refugees from the Paris Commune of 1871. Houle-Courcelles also discusses visits to Montreal by prominent anarchists such as Emma Goldman and examines the role of the Knights of Labor, the Industrial Workers of the World (IWW), and the One Big Union (OBU) in the province. He then examines the formation, politics, and activities of the autonomists, a group of young artists influenced by libertarian ideals, which took shape in the late 1940s. However, because of the difficulty in tracing this history and the apparent lack of an explicitly anarchist movement in Quebec, only brief glimpses of anarchist presence are given. When discussing Jewish anarchists in Montreal, for example, Houle-Courcelles focuses on their activities in that city while excluding their role in a larger movement that spanned Canada, the United States, and beyond. One leaves Houle-Courcelles's study with an impression of groups that were small, ineffectual, and isolated.[21]

This leads to a fourth and final problem with state-centred studies: they promote the idea that anarchist movements go through periods of proliferation and dissolution. This is apparent in Nunzio Pernicone's *Italian Anarchism, 1864–1892*, where he asserts that the Italian anarchist movement, as it existed within the boundaries of Italy, went through a series of resurgences in the late nineteenth century, which, each time, was met with severe state repression.[22] But, as historian Davide Turcato has argued, a study with a national emphasis cannot effectively examine the realities of movement "continuities and organizational resources." In other words, if one is to explore the rise and decline of the Italian anarchist movement over a long period of time, it is important to take into account the number of its adherents active beyond the boundaries of Italy. As Turcato remarks, "Italian anarchism is best analyzed as a single movement stretching across the Mediterranean Sea and the Atlantic Ocean." Examining the Italian anarchist movement through a transnational lens, then, "reveals forms of continuity and organization unavailable to analyses of national scope, and by broadening our perspective on the anarchist movement, it compels us to look for more sophisticated interpretations of the movement's dynamics."[23] Thus, it is important for scholars to think transnationally when studying radical movements. As the above experiences of Attilio Bortolotti demonstrate, transnationalism was a key component of the Italian anarchist movement. The continent- and ocean-spanning networks that anarchists created meant that their activism was not tied to one particular nation-state but occurred in many. With transnationalism such a prominent feature of this movement, a study focussed solely on a particular country would tell us only part of the story. In the case of Bortolotti, for example, how could a project on anarchism confined to Canada effectively address his activism in both Windsor and Detroit, his links with *L'Adunata dei Refrattari*, or his multiple movements across the Canada–United States border? The Italian anarchists provide an important opportunity to study transnational forms of political activism. Though Italian anarchists active during the interwar period in the United States have received some scholarly attention, their transnational networks have not.[24] And up until this point, there have been no studies dedicated to Italian anarchists in Canada.

To that end, this book focuses mainly on the transnational Italian anarchist movement and its activities in the following six cities: Sault Ste. Marie, Toronto, Windsor, Detroit, Newark, and New York City. These locations have been chosen for two reasons. First, the most influential Italian-language anarchist newspapers were based in New York City—a city that also had a substantial anarchist presence. New York City acted to a certain extent as the movement's theoretical centre. Second, the anarchist circles in cities such as New York and Detroit in the United States had links with those in Toronto and Windsor, Ontario. Sometimes, these links were physical. In other words, Italian anarchists moved between these sites in order to find employment, take part in anarchist activities, or escape legal prosecution even though the changing realities of the border were such that these patterns became increasingly circumscribed. At other times, they could mean financial contributions to an anarchist publication or political cause.

This book examines the transnational Italian anarchist movement between the years 1915 and 1940. This periodization was chosen for the following reasons. First, it was during this period that the anarcho-syndicalist *Il Martello* (The Hammer, 1917–1943) and anti-organizationalist *L'Adunata dei Refrattari* (Call of the "Réfractaires," 1922–1971)[25] newspapers appeared. These publications were important focal points for the dissemination of anarchist activity and local and international news analyzed through an anarchist lens. They also chronicled the antagonistic relationship between the publishers of both *Il Martello* and *L'Adunata dei Refrattari*. This rift often led to the alignment of various anarchist circles in Canada and the United States with one or the other of these newspapers. Second, the interwar period is an important era for the study of transnational Italian anarchists in North America because of the social and political events of that time. Between 1915 and 1940, Italian anarchists felt the full force of the Canadian and American states during the Red Scare, witnessed the rise of fascism in

Italy and within their own neighbourhoods in the urban centres of North America, and mobilized to support the efforts of Spanish anarchists against Franco's coup in the late 1930s. In such historical circumstances, they set themselves the task of building an effective movement.

In *Red November, Black November*, historian Salvatore Salerno describes the challenge of researching the Industrial Workers of the World (IWW), one of the most famous of the radical movements of the early twentieth century: "there is an overwhelming lack of information regarding the activities and way of life of the IWW's artists and worker intellectuals, the floaters and rebel tramps of the jungle, and the activities of the mixed locals when its members were not engaged in strikes or related conflicts."[26]

Researching Italian anarchists has not been an easy task either. Anarchists do not make a habit of keeping records about members and sympathizers, and the information that exists on them and their activities can only be found in archives all over North America and Europe. The anarchist groups which this study focuses on had to be pieced together from various sources. I am indebted to the work done by historian Paul Avrich, especially in his *Anarchist Voices: An Oral History of Anarchism in America*.[27] His interviews with Italian radicals who were active in the northeastern United States and southern Ontario have allowed me to flesh out the individuals involved in anarchist groups such as Circolo Volontà in Brooklyn, New York, and *L'Adunata dei Refrattari* of New York City and Newark. The single most important oral history was the one Avrich conducted with Attilio Bortolotti that gives details on anarchist activities in Detroit, Toronto, and Windsor, Ontario. Federico Arcos and Libera Martignago Bortolotti helped me to identify other important anarchist groups. Arcos is a Spanish-born anarchist who migrated to Canada in the early 1950s and worked and lived in Windsor. Owing to the fact that no Spanish anarchists were active in that city and demonstrating the transnational aspect of the anarchist movement, Arcos went to Detroit and joined a Spanish group there. During that time, he became acquainted with the city's Italian anarchists of Il Gruppo "I Refrattari," and was able to provide me with names of members of that circle. In addition, he was in close friendship with Italian anarchists Attilio Bortolotti and Pietro Beduz, who lived in Toronto and Windsor, respectively, and though hesitant to speak of others, did provide personal recollections of the two men. Federico was also kind enough to put me in contact with Libera Martignago Bortolotti, the daughter of migrant Italian anarchists and partner of the late Attilio

Bortolotti. She spent her childhood living in Sault Ste. Marie and was able to name a number of individuals active in the local anarchist circle in which her parents took part. Interviewing people about the past can have its limitations. Subjects can make errors when recalling events that happened long ago and gloss over particularly difficult periods in their lives. However, the interviews with Arcos and Martignago Bortolotti were conducted to gather the names of Italian anarchists active during the periodization of this study and to get some knowledge about these individuals to assist me in my research. These invaluable conversations, along with Avrich's previous research, helped me decide to focus on particular cities and circles.

The personal information I had gathered on roughly seventy Italian anarchists from the above-mentioned sources helped facilitate my work with the Casellario Politico Centrale (CPC) files which are housed at the Archivio Centrale dello Stato in Rome. The CPC was created by the Italian government in 1894 as a means of surveilling those it "considered dangerous to public order and security." This collection spans nearly fifty years and includes more than 150,000 files on republicans, socialists, communists, antifascists, and anarchists.[28] As much as I personally despise the surveillance of leftist activists by governments, without the CPC files a project of this sort would be even more challenging. This resource allows researchers to follow the movement of their subjects as they travel from Italy to other parts of the world and trace their involvement in anarchist circles abroad. In many cases, the information contained within the CPC files gives important insights into the activism of Italian anarchists that may not appear in movement newspapers or existing oral histories. Of course, one has to be cautious when using security files that have been created and maintained by those who are diametrically opposed to anarchism. It may have been in the interest of the Italian government to have its security apparatus keep the most up-to-date and verifiable information on anarchists around the world, but there is no guarantee that informants were correct in their reporting, that they may not have been purposely misled by those they were spying upon, or "manufactured" evidence to justify their continued employment as informants. Whenever possible, I have referred to other sources to verify the contents of the CPC files.

But what is anarchism? Anarchism is a left-wing and anti-capitalist political philosophy that appeared in the second half of the nineteenth century. It opposed (and still opposes) hierarchy and inequality in all its social and economic forms, including capitalism, the state, and private property. In the place of a hierarchical capitalist society, anarchism envisions one that is stateless, socialist, and self-managed, characterized by cooperation, democratic decision-making processes, and social and economic equality. Anarchist philosophy recognizes the importance of building alternative institutions—such as worker cooperatives—to those that currently exist. An anarchist society is imagined to be one organized as a form of federation that would ensure that everyone's needs were met. Anarchism acknowledges the importance of individual freedom—but that freedom is to be tempered by social responsibility.[29] Anarchism is the idea that people can organize their lives without government; that each individual knows what is best for himself or herself and does not need to be told how to live by an external institution. Anarchism is not dogmatic nor is it a program; it is fluid and adaptive to particular conditions.

Before proceeding further, it is necessary to explain the conceptualization of anarchism from 1915 to 1940, a period commonly known as that of "classical anarchism," although the term "classical anarchism" has begun to fall out of favour. As theorist and historian Jason Adams has argued, part of the problem with this term is its emphasis on a few "great white men" from Europe. The genealogy of "classical" anarchist thought has focussed on the European thinkers—William Godwin, Pierre-Joseph Proudhon, Mikhail Bakunin, Peter Kropotkin, and Max Stirner—with the, perhaps inadvertent, effect of erasing such non-European theorists such as Japan's Shūsui Kōtoku and Mexico's Ricardo Flores Magón. As a result, "classical anarchism" is a misleading term because it does not incorporate all anarchist theorists during the late nineteenth to early twentieth centuries.[30]

Another flaw of the classical definition is the false impression it gives that anarchist thought and practice has undergone a progression from its beginnings to its present.[31] This is not to suggest that anarchist theory and praxis have remained static, but rather, that the term "classical anarchism" also denotes a break in anarchist thought as though the ideas of anarchist theorists in the past have nothing to offer in the present. This is hardly the case. For example, in the early twentieth century, the German-born Jewish anarchist Gustav Landauer called for the creation of socialist institutions and economies that would undercut those of the existing capitalist system, thus eventually rendering the latter obsolete with no need for violent revolution.[32] Landauer's insistence on building socialism alongside capitalism has gained currency among some anarchist theorists today.[33]

In place of "classical anarchism," Adams has divided the history of anarchism into three waves—the late nineteenth to early twentieth centuries, the late 1960s, and the late 1990s—though the periodization of each wave has no specific beginning or end.[34] The reason for such purposefully nebulous historical stages, explains Adams, stems from the difficulty in placing disparate anarchist movements from around the world into a universal period.[35] Avoiding hard-and-fast periodizations—and here I am building upon Adams's idea—also allows us to take note of continuities in anarchist thought from one period to another. By declaring, à la George Woodcock, that a particular era of anarchist history and theory came to an end following the defeat of the Spanish Republic in 1939, we effectively erase the experiences and activities of those who continued in their anarchism well into the later twentieth century.[36] Since this study focuses on the years 1915 to 1940, it is focussed on first-wave anarchism, but it does not assume that this political formation came to an abrupt postwar end.

But is not this book positioned in the "classical" period because of its focus on Italian anarchists who originated in southern Europe? As mentioned above, the classical anarchist canon is often written about so that it is implicitly limited to a handful of individuals identified as the main theorists of anarchist thought and practice. As Adams suggests, in addition to the term "classical" negating the contributions of anarchists living in Asia, Africa, and South America, it has also tended to downplay the theoretical contributions of anarchists active in the states of southern Europe, such as Italy.[37] This marginalization of Italian anarchists in certain treatments of anarchist history may also stem from the peripheral position of Italy, especially its southern regions, with regard to the rest of Europe. The northern parts of the Italian peninsula have generally been considered more European than the regions to the south which were, and still are, seen as inferior and backward.[38] Thus, the written work of Italian anarchists such as Luigi Galleani and Errico Malatesta have often not received the same attention as "northern" English, French, and Russian theorists.

Chapter 1 provides a review of anarchism's main tenets, its different strains, and the historical context surrounding the emergence of this political philosophy. It then turns to a discussion of anarchism's public image and debates surrounding anarchism among the wider Left. This chapter also provides a brief history of Italian anarchism and anarchist thought from the pre-unification period to the rise of fascism in the 1920s. Chapter 2 examines the causes of Italian migration that began in the latter half of the nineteenth century and describes how this process helped establish the transnational anarchist movement. Whether as labourers or political exiles, Italian anarchists' movements to regions of Europe and the Americas led to the creation of transnational networks which in turn provided prospective anarchist migrants with well-travelled paths to anarchist communities abroad. And, unlike their co-nationals, the emigration of Italian anarchists was in part due to their political activities and the resulting consequences—state violence and prison terms.

Chapter 3 explores anarchist culture. Much like that of the wider Left in the early twentieth century, the cultural output of Italian anarchists was remarkable. They produced numerous publications, wrote plays and fiction with anarchist themes, and celebrated anarchist "holidays." Through the anarchist circles that comprised the movement, these publications and plays travelled global networks. Italian anarchists also organized various social events and speaking tours that raised awareness and sought donations to help with political activities. For Italian anarchists, culture was invaluable not only as a means to maintain and expand their transnational movement, but also as a basis for mobilization.

Chapter 4 traces how class, gender, and ethnicity informed anarchist social identities. The Italian anarchist movement in Canada and the United States was largely working class and male. Though women were involved, they rarely held prominent positions of newspaper editor or public speaker as did their male counterparts, and this led to tensions within the movement. In addition, Italian migrant experiences in racist host countries, the reality of life in "lands of promise," and Italian regionalism all played significant roles in identity formation.

Chapter 5 examines the effects of the movement's rank-and-file alignment with a particular strain of anarchism and/or noted figure by exploring the different factions that emerged around Luigi Galleani and Carlo Tresca—two proponents of two different forms of anarchism. It has been argued that the antagonism that existed between these two men and their adherents seriously hindered the effectiveness of the movement to work together to fight fascism in Italian neighbourhoods.[39] However, an examination of this rift through a transnational lens results in a complication of previous assumptions.

Chapter 6 examines how the transnational anarchist movement reacted to the impending deportation of two Italian anarchists—Attilio Bortolotti and Agostino Confalonieri—from Toronto to Italy in 1940. The anarchist movement responded to the legal troubles of Bortolotti and Confalonieri by covering their plight in movement newspapers and organizing various fundraisers to help cover legal expenses. Emma Goldman, who was living in Toronto at the time, was instrumental in this struggle and, as a "key figure," was able to negotiate the factional disputes among the Italian anarchists during this critical period. This case study demonstrates the importance of self-funded political movements in drawing upon resources in a transnational context.

CHAPTER ONE

ANARCHISM AND THE ITALIAN TRADITION

Before delving further into the history of the transnational Italian anarchist movement, an explanation of first-wave anarchism is necessary to help familiarize the reader with anarchism's main tenets, its different strains, and the historical context within which this political philosophy emerged. The public perceptions of anarchism tended towards sensationalism and fear mongering, but in reality the movement was much more complicated than the violent caricature depicted in the press.

During the first wave, there were five identifiable strains of anarchist thought: mutualism, collectivism, communism, syndicalism, and individualism. Mutualism is an economic theory that has been credited to the French writer and philosopher Pierre-Joseph Proudhon, who envisioned a stateless society founded on the principle of federation. In this society, farmers and artisans would organize themselves into local and autonomous communes, which would be part of a much larger federation bound by a single constitution that ensured society would be coordinated by a bottom-up approach. Members of society were to have access to the means of production, were exclusively entitled to what they produced, and could exchange the value of their labour for an equal amount of goods and services offered by others. The means of production, however, were to be held in common. Contracts between autonomous individuals or groups were to ensure that economic interactions were just.[1] Mutualists believed in establishing cooperatives, such as banks and markets, as an alternative to capitalism in order to render the latter useless. Though Proudhon viewed property as theft, private property was not done away with under mutualism. Having a plot of land, mutualists argued, meant that a person was able to work and subsist. Mutualists did, however, object to members of the ruling class owning large amounts of land and exploiting others in order to develop it.[2]

Proudhon may have called himself an anarchist but, in many ways, his political theories could be described as stateless liberalism. Still, his ideas had a strong influence on anarchist thought. The Russian revolutionary and anarchist Mikhail Bakunin, whom I will discuss in greater detail below, helped formulate the collectivist position, which was a synthesis of mutualism and a critical reading of Marx's economic theories. Under a collectivist economic system, society would ideally adhere to a form of federation but there would be no private property—both land and the means of production were to be held in common. And, whereas the mutualists argued that an individual was entitled to everything that he or she produced, collectivists believed that all members of an anarchist society would be entitled to everything that was produced, with the caveat that one's right to take from the commonwealth was based on how much labour one had contributed to production.[3] Fròm Marx was borrowed his analysis of capitalism and its resultant division of society into classes based on their relationship to the means of production. There were, of course, issues that anarchists had with Marx and his political theories but I will address some of those later in the chapter.

In addition, Bakunin and his adherents in the International Working Men's Association (IWMA) have been credited with the emergence of syndicalist ideas that led to the anarcho-syndicalist strain of anarchism.[4] This is due to Bakunin's belief that the role of the IWMA should not be the formation of political parties but the organization of society, "based on the various functions of daily life and of different kinds of labour. It is the organization by professions and trades. Once all the different industries are represented in the International, including the cultivation of the land, its organization, the organization of the mass of the people, will have been complete."

Bakunin argued further that "the organization of the trade sections ... bear in themselves the living seeds of the new society which is to replace the old world."[5] Anarcho-syndicalists, then, believed that by organizing within unions they could radicalize the working class, consolidate it into a mass movement, and move it towards revolutionary goals.[6] They tended to avoid involvement in the formal political processes of political parties and other statist institutions because they did not see this avenue as a way to worker emancipation. Instead, anarcho-syndicalists relied on direct action to fight battles important to workers and did not get involved in elections.[7] For them, direct action meant "every method of immediate warfare by the workers against their economic and political oppressors." This could include actions such as strikes, boycotts, sabotage, anti-war propaganda, and armed resistance.[8] Anarcho-syndicalists also opposed the Leninist proposition of a revolutionary vanguard party taking control of the state. For anarcho-syndicalists, the end of state capitalism was to be achieved by direct action in the workplace, which would ultimately lead to a general strike. This would allow workers to take control of the means of production and organize workplaces along the anarcho-syndicalist principle of unity through decentralized federations.[9]

In North America, the Industrial Workers of the World (IWW), also known as the Wobblies, came the closest of all the large radical bodies to the anarcho-syndicalist position. Formed in Chicago in 1905, the IWW promoted direct-action tactics in place of the ballot box, sought workers' control of society and the abolition of capitalism, and organized workers along industrial lines as opposed to the craft unionism of the American Federation of Labor (AFL). Unlike the AFL during this period, the IWW was open to women, people of colour, and immigrants. The majority of Wobbly unionizing efforts occurred in the resource extraction regions of Canada and the United States, though organizing also took place to a lesser degree in urban centres among factory workers. The union activities of the IWW led to severe violence against the organization and its members by the state as well as by vigilantes acting on the orders of business owners. The repression faced by the IWW appears to have been far greater in intensity in the United States than Canada; however, following the red scares in both countries towards the end of the First World War, the IWW was almost destroyed. Yet, these challenges did not lead to the IWW's immediate demise. The union was particularly strong in Ontario's Lakehead region well into the 1920s and was still a force to be reckoned with in Grays Harbor, Washington, during the Great Depression.[10] The union still exists and continues to organize marginalized workers, though its numbers and profile are not as impressive as those it enjoyed in the early twentieth century.

The role of anarchism in the IWW has been a source of debate among historians. Rudolph Rocker believed that the IWW was Marxist in orientation while historian Melvyn Dubofsky argued that the union was an amalgam of Marxism, Darwinism, anarchism, and syndicalism.[11] Michael Schmidt and Lucien van der Walt have described the IWW as a form of revolutionary syndicalism that shared many aspects of anarcho-syndicalism but cannot be considered explicitly anarcho-syndicalist.[12] Although historian Salvatore Salerno did not identify the IWW as anarcho-syndicalist, in *Red November, Black November* he demonstrates the strong influence that anarchists and anarchist philosophy had on the formation of the union.[13] I do not want to delve too deeply into the debates surrounding the IWW; yet, it is important to note that this syndicalist organization was largely decentralized and democratic in practice and grappled with the issues of leadership, organization, and ideology, not unlike the anarchist movement.[14] It should also be noted that a number of Italian anarchists were members of the IWW, which demonstrates that some anarchists found the praxis of the IWW simpatico. In Paterson, New Jersey, anarchist silk workers affiliated with the IWW in 1906 and the Italian-language anarchist newspaper *La Questione Sociale* featured the union logo on the paper's masthead.[15] In addition, the anarcho-syndicalist Carlo Tresca, who will be discussed in detail in Chapter 5, was actively involved as an organizer with the IWW, though he never became a member.[16]

A third strain of anarchism is anarchist communism—a stateless form of communism. Anarchist communists believe that land, the means of production, and all the necessities of life should be held in common. As an economic and social theory, anarchist communism began to appear in the late nineteenth century. The Russian prince Peter Kropotkin is generally credited with this anarchist philosophy but, as historian Nunzio Pernicone has demonstrated, the Italian anarchist Carlo Cafiero conceived of anarchist communism independently of the Russian. Cafiero was trained as a lawyer but worked as a diplomat. During his travels to London, he saw first-hand the conditions in which the English working class lived, and became a socialist and supporter of the IWMA. While living in the city, he also met the prominent communists Friedrich Engels and Karl Marx, with the latter asking Cafiero to return to Italy and promulgate Marx's form of communism in order to undercut the influence of the republican Giuseppe Mazzini and the anarchist Mikhail Bakunin. Cafiero arrived in Italy in May 1871 and began his work on behalf of Marx, attending conferences and expressing the views of state communism. However, it was not long before Cafiero began to move towards the anarchist position. This impending break with the communism of Marx and Engels was the result of Cafiero's close contact with friends of Bakunin's as well as a resolution passed at the London conference of the IWMA in September of that same year. The resolution called for the International to become a political party, which Cafiero saw as an attempt to centralize the organization—a move that he did not support. In early 1872, Cafiero spent time with Bakunin discussing anarchism, and in a letter to Engels dated 12 June, declared his conversion to anarchism. He wrote for the radical Italian press and was involved with Errico Malatesta and others in an attempt to foment insurrection in the province of Benevento in the Campania region of southern Italy by entering towns, burning tax ledgers, and explaining the principles of anarchism. The exploits of the Matese Band, as they were known, came to a quick end as they were captured by government soldiers and imprisoned. Following his release from prison, Cafiero spent time in France, Switzerland, and England, where he continued his anarchist activities and experienced further state repression as a result. He eventually returned to Italy in the early 1880s but by this time had drifted into paranoia and fits of rage that resulted in his institutionalization at Nocera Inferore, Campania, where he died in 1892 of intestinal tuberculosis at age forty-five.[17]

Cafiero's anarchist communism was adopted at the third national congress of the Italian Federation of the IWMA at Tosi in October 1876, predating that of Kropotkin by six years. Cafiero felt that an anarchist communist economy could be put into practice immediately following a revolution. Under this type of economic system, "material abundance" could be achieved through the following developments: "harmonious cooperation, [the] introduction of new machines, [and the] considerable economy of labour, tools, and raw materials resulting from the elimination of luxury goods and other unnecessary products."[18] Among the Italians in particular, anarchist communism had two distinct branches, comprised of those who believed in organization and those who did not.

In addition to communist and syndicalist strains of anarchism, there is the individualist form. Individualist anarchists were critical of communism, especially the Marxian form, because they believed this political philosophy led to majority rule while negating the individual and his or her desires. According to individualists, in a communist society, social duty becomes of the utmost importance and acts as a new religion. This is anathema to a political philosophy in which the individual and his or her desires are paramount. However, this did not mean that individualists had no use for others or led solitary lives. Some believed that individualists could enter into unions with those who shared the same belief system, in order to organize around areas of mutual interest or need.[19] Though each of these offshoots differed, especially in their economic theories, all shared in common the idea that a life free from oppression, coercion, and hierarchy was not only desirable but possible. Among Italian anarchists, individualism had an insignificant presence in contrast to anarchist communism or anarcho-syndicalism. Yet, it bears mention because it was considered one of the major forms of anarchist thought during the period of the first wave and had an influence within the wider anarchist movement.

Anarchism recognizes that each person is an individual with different temperaments, desires, and experiences; that each person knows best how to govern his or her own life. It aspires to a society based on freedom "in which no one could constrain his [sic] fellow beings without meeting with vigorous resistance, in which, above all, nobody could seize and use the collective force to impose his own wishes on others."[20] This freedom would be extended to all members of society but did not entitle each individual to act in any way. Instead, individual freedom was to be circumscribed by social responsibility; in other words, one's right to behave in a certain manner stopped when it infringed on the rights of another.[21] For first-wave anarchists, the three main impediments to liberty were the triumvirate of oppression known as the state, capital, and religion.

Anarchists have spent a great deal of time criticizing the state. For them, states negate individual freedom because they are administered by a minority that dominates the majority.[22] This minority is often comprised of wealthy elites or those in their service. As a result, the interests of the state are commonly those of the minority and not the wider population. The power of the ruling elites is maintained through laws and more direct means, such as the police or the military, which protect their privileged position and private property, thus reinforcing class inequality. Additionally, the various authoritarian aspects of the state, such as courts, police, schools, and banks, are all in the service of capital. They work to ensure the continued exploitation of workers under capitalism.[23] States are also an affront to the natural solidarity that exists among persons because they encourage nationalism and patriotism.[24] Well in advance of Benedict Anderson's theories of the "imagined community," first-wave anarchists argued that the nation-state relied upon a fiction without any natural foundation.[25] The creation of states is rooted in violence because their formation was often realized through bloody struggles whereby one group subjugated another.[26] States are also inherently conservative and demand conformity from their citizens; respect for the law, obedience, faith in the wisdom of government, and self-sacrifice in times of war are important qualities that need to be fostered within populations to facilitate rule over them.[27] Those who dare to challenge the state are met with laws and/or the physical coercion of state security. In general, states are more concerned with security than with liberty.[28]

Not only do anarchists spurn the state, they are also opposed to government, regardless of political persuasion, whether monarchical, democratic, or totalitarian. Governments, as mentioned above, are either comprised of or controlled by ruling elites who ensure that the function of government is to protect their class interests. It was government that called out the militia or the police to fire upon strikers in industrializing nations from the mid-nineteenth to mid-twentieth centuries. Government has never acted for the benefit of the majority of a population and any positive changes that have occurred within liberal democracies, for example, have been realized through the efforts of grassroots mobilization. For anarchists, this kind of self-mobilization is key.

It is up to the people to work together collectively to initiate social change and not to rely on political parties. As a result, first-wave anarchists generally did not engage in electoral politics.

But anarchism was not simply a philosophy that criticized existing institutions. It also offered some possible solutions. In place of the state system, anarchists proposed a form of federation comprised of autonomous communities.[29] With regards to the organization and planning of society, anarchists had varying ideas regarding forms of direct democracy. Some suggested that each member of an anarchist society would have a say in decisions that affected them, while others envisioned representatives selected by their community. This latter may sound similar to the current electoral system, but in an anarchist society these representatives would be subject to recall and serve short terms to prevent any entrenchment of power. These positions would also be rotated to discourage any such development.

Capitalism is an economic system based on coercion and exploitation, and stands in stark contrast to the principles of anarchism. It is coercive because it forces people to work for a capitalist or starve; it is exploitative because workers create wealth for the bourgeoisie but are not paid the value of what they produce.[30] Capitalism also resulted in changes in who controlled the work process. Previously, skilled workers had far more autonomy when it came to controlling their work. They could establish their own workshops, agree mutually on how much they would produce in a day, set prices for what they manufactured, and set wages accordingly. Under capitalism, employers dictated the pace of work, determined wages and the length of the workday, and controlled how products would be manufactured. This often led to a "deskilling" of work, whereby production would be broken down into a number of smaller steps. For example, prior to the introduction of large factories, a skilled worker would produce a coat in its entirety. They would cut the fabric, sew the various pieces together, attach buttons, make buttonholes and so on. But, under the new factory system, the manufacture of a coat would be broken down in such a way that a worker would not make the entire coat, but would be given one task, such as cutting the pattern out of the fabric. In this way, the industrial revolution transferred the knowledge of manufacturing coats and many other products from skilled workers to managers and widened the pool of unskilled workers, which helped curb craft workers' job actions by making them redundant.[31]

Capitalism is an economic system built on class inequality. And the creation and perpetuation of private property is the definition of this inequality, which is why anarchists have called for its abolition. Anarchists view private property as a form of theft because it prevents all people from enjoying the right to all land or what the land produces naturally or through human intervention.[32] In place of private property, first-wave anarchists called for all land and its resources to be owned in common (as had been the case in the past); every member of an anarchist society was entitled to all the necessities of life.[33]

The third main target of first-wave anarchist critique was organized religion. Anarchists felt that people were free to believe in what they chose, but were quick to explain the oppressive role played by the Christian Church within the capitalist system.[34] The anarchists' focus on Christianity did not stem from their Eurocentrism as much as it did from the negative influence this particular religion has had on populations around the world. Jewish anarchists like Emma Goldman and Alexander Berkman, and the Japanese anarchist Shūsui Kōtoku, all denounced the Christian Church in their speeches and written works. Goldman and Berkman targeted Christianity because of its role as the main religion in countries where they were active.[35] It may be more surprising that Kōtoku was similarly critical of this religion when it was not practised in Japan to the same degree as in Europe or North America. Yet, Christianity appeared to have a growing influence to Kōtoku, who in 1906 commented in a letter to a comrade in California that the "Christian clergy have received considerable funding from the [Japanese] government. Now under State sponsorship, the clergy are going all-out to spread the gospel of patriotism. Prior to the [Russo-Japanese] war, Christianity was the religion of the poor. Now it has turned its coat. Within two years Christianity has turned into a huge bourgeois religion, an adjunct of the State and of militarism."[36] Among anarchists, organized religion was problematic because it taught people to be subservient to authority: "God being master, man is the slave." Organized religion encourages people to put their faith and trust in God's intermediaries on earth, instead of seeking truth and justice on their own. It thus dismisses human reason and freedom. Further, if people believed that God had to be obeyed unconditionally, then it followed that they must passively submit to emperors, kings, and all their functionaries who were viewed as divine authority.[37]

This subservience was also demonstrated in the belief in an afterlife of reward for being a good Christian. The church demanded that persons of the lower classes accept their lot in life, thus persuading "the oppressed to accept oppression meekly."[38] As a result, religion was an important tool used by the state and capital for their own interests. It created a docile population over which to rule. For those who found themselves barely able to afford food and rent or had their wages cut, the church counselled patience and restraint. Of course, anarchists argued that only people had the power to organize and fight for social justice, since no heavenly help would be forthcoming. Indeed, organized religion actually benefited from capitalist society with many denominations amassing great wealth. And, because it profited from the existing system, the church had no interest in changing society for the benefit of the majority. Many anarchists, drawing on this line of reasoning, argued that the church always stood opposed to intellectual and scientific progress, and has persecuted people for challenging ideas contrary to religious dogma.[39]

Free Love

Free love was another significant aspect of anarchist philosophy in the late nineteenth and early twentieth centuries. In his article on Canadian sex radicals Robert Bird Kerr and Dora Forster, Angus McLaren argues that anarchists were the only ones who dealt with the subject of free love and sexuality seriously and explicitly. He bases this assertion on the fact that Forster had to tone down her language on the subject when writing for Canadian socialist newspapers after the anarchist publication *Lucifer: The Light Bearer*, which she had previously contributed to, was censored by American authorities.[40] Free love during this period did not mean sexual irresponsibility, promiscuity, or disrespect for one's partner(s), but rather the right to form and end physical relationships when one was unsatisfied, to express oneself sexually, and to engage in sex for pleasure rather than procreation. However, free love advocates placed more emphasis on the right of women to control their own bodies than they did on the liberation of men's sexuality. Free love was thus directly tied to feminist concerns and became synonymous with calls for access to birth control and abortions, the right to refrain from marriage, and the freedom to have children out of wedlock.[41]

Sex radicals challenged the repressive sexual mores of the patriarchal society in which they lived. During this period, sex and sexuality were subjects largely considered improper to discuss and literature on the subject was considered obscene and illegal to distribute. For instance, Carlo Tresca was sentenced to one year in prison for the distribution of birth-control literature. He had run an advertisement in the paper he edited, *Il Martello,* for a book titled *L'Arte di non fare i figli* (The Art of Not Creating Children) that was available from the newspaper. Though the postal authorities had banned the issue in question and made members of *Il Martello*'s staff cross out the ad with black crayon before it could be mailed, Tresca was still held criminally responsible for its circulation.[42]

Advocates of free love were not interested in a society in which sexual issues were treated with fear, ignorance, and prudery. Instead, they sought a world where the topics of contraception, sexual education, and divorce could be dealt with rationally, scientifically, and non-coercively. They hoped that this approach would put an end to loveless marriage, endless breeding, illegitimacy, prostitution, and venereal diseases.[43] They wanted to demonstrate to both men and women that sexuality was natural and needed to be expressed. But this did not mean that advocates of free love wished simply to satisfy sexual needs. Instead, human sexuality was to be based on self-control and mutual respect for others.[44] Though this may have been the ideal, it was not always the practice. Carlo Tresca abandoned his daughter Beatrice and his wife Helga Guerra, whom he had married in 1904, in order to live with the Wobbly organizer Elizabeth Gurley Flynn in 1913. Later, Tresca would begin an affair with Gurley Flynn's sister Bina and the two would have a son named Peter. When Gurley Flynn found out about the affair and the birth, she fell into a deep depression.[45] Free love, in practice, was not necessarily beneficial to both men and women.

Nor was free love embraced by all anarchists. Emma Goldman may have included this topic in her theories of anarchism, but many of her male comrades did not take this issue seriously, believing it to be inconsequential when compared to such important matters as the social revolution and its aftermath. Some also thought addressing the topic of sexuality would harm the movement.[46] Max Nettlau, for one, argued that the sex question added very little of substance to the anarchist philosophy. Instead, he considered discussions regarding sex to be an issue of personal choice that had nothing to do with the wider anarchist movement.[47] This approach was not confined to male anarchists. As scholar Martha Ackelsberg has shown, anarchist women in Spain generally agreed that sexuality was something worked out between individuals.[48] Debates also existed among anarchists about what "free love" actually meant. Some felt that free love meant having a monogamous relationship with someone you loved. For others, it meant non-monogamy and choosing lovers as one pleased. What was agreed upon was the ability of individuals to leave unhappy relationships.[49]

For the majority of free love advocates and sex radicals of the first wave, discussions of sexuality were framed in a heterosexist discourse that celebrated sex between men and women; homosexuality was almost completely absent from these discussions. But this does not mean that same-sex relationships were ignored within anarchist ranks.[50] Emma Goldman spoke in defence of homosexuality as early as 1890.[51] In her autobiography, she relates her experiences lecturing on the subject and the responses she received. According to Goldman, partisans of same-sex love approached her after her lectures on homosexuality, thanking Goldman for helping them to feel accepted and confident in their sexuality.[52] Significantly, however, Bonnie Haaland has suggested that even though Goldman defended male homosexuality, she did not support lesbianism in the same way. Like the psychoanalysts and sexologists that influenced her thoughts on sexuality, such as Sigmund Freud and Havelock Ellis, Goldman believed male homosexuality to be "a genetic predisposition," whereas lesbianism was predicated upon women's relationships with men—if men could not treat women as equals, then women had no choice but to turn to one another for intimate relations.[53]

Homosexuality was a theme touched upon by Alexander Berkman in his *Prison Memoirs of an Anarchist*, which was originally published in 1912.[54] Berkman is candid about his experiences in prison and describes the emotional bond that formed between himself and another prisoner, Johnny/Felipe, while they were in separate cells in the basement of the prison known as the dungeon.[55] The only human interaction both men have is with each other and, during the course of their time in the dungeon, a strong emotional bond forms between them. Both Berkman and Johnny/Felipe express their love for each other and their desire to kiss when they are among the general prison population.[56]

The second discussion of homosexuality in prison occurs during a conversation between Berkman and his friend George. George is unsure whether to bring up the topic of same-sex relationships with Berkman because he does not know how the anarchist will react. George dislikes the fact that some inmates use their bodies to gain privileges, but is not against homosexuality. He reveals to Berkman that he had been involved in an intense emotional and sexual relationship with another inmate for a year in the recent past. The conversation reveals that both men had an aversion to homosexuals previous to their incarceration, but had changed their opinions based on their prison experiences.[57]

It is possible that Berkman faced criticism because he addressed the issue, but he does not appear to have been ostracized by the wider movement. However, this may be partially due to the fact that he focussed only on describing his desires but never openly admitted to physical intimacy with another man. Furthermore, after Berkman's release from prison, it appears that he formed physical relations only with women, most notably Emmy Eckstein.[58] Goldman, on the other hand, faced criticism for her lectures on homosexuality. Her anarchist comrades, whom she does not name, preferred that she not discuss same-sex relationships because anarchists were already considered by most people to be depraved, and defending "perverted sex-forms" would only harm the movement further. Regardless, Goldman decided to ignore her critics inside and outside anarchist circles and continued to lecture on homosexuality.[59]

Because anarchism is seen as a direct threat to those invested in the status quo, the actual tenets of anarchist political philosophy have largely been obscured by its consistent misrepresentation by governments, monarchies, religious authorities, capitalists, and the mainstream press for the past 150 years. In the late nineteenth century, anarchism was most often portrayed as a violent political creed because of a series of political assassinations carried out by anarchists against heads of state and monarchs in Europe and the United States during this period. The idea that anarchism is synonymous with terrorism still persists today. An article in *The Economist*, for instance, linked anarchism with jihadist terrorism following the London bombings on 7 July 2005.[60] It was also in the late nineteenth century that representations of anarchists began to appear in the media, following acts of political violence attributed to them.

On 4 May 1886, an explosion rocked a strike rally held in Chicago's Haymarket—a bombing that killed both workers and police, and was credited to anarchists.[61] In the weeks following the blast, the New York City–based magazine *Harper's Weekly* published a series of drawings by illustrator Thomas Nast that depicted anarchists as foreign troublemakers who were typically armed and dangerous. Nast appears to have created two types of anarchist agitator: the black-hat-and-trench-coat-wearing anarchist who was a threat to the honest worker, and the more overtly crazed maniac, armed and violent and ready for class war.[62] Both caricatures were characterized by dark clothing, unkempt hair and beards, and a wild look in their eyes.

In one of Nast's drawings (see Figure 2), a worker is sitting with his wife and child in his arms while on his right there stands a capitalist and on his left an armed anarchist. The worker is torn between following his boss, who may fire him, and the anarchist, who may shoot the worker should he fail to join the movement.[63] A second picture (see Figure 3) featured the German-born anarchist Johann Most.[64] This Nast illustration had Most standing in its centre, holding a flag that reads "Socialistic War" in his left hand, while in his right a chipped sabre is held above his head in an imminent striking position. Most is surrounded by at least five rifle-bearing anarchists who are in the process of diving under an equal number of beds. The features of each of the five

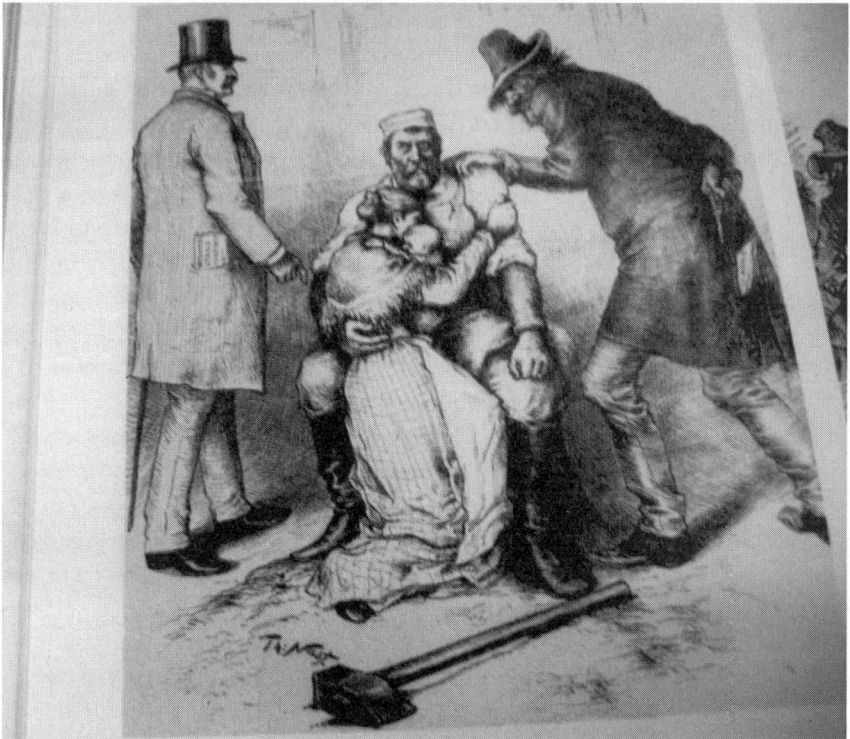

Figures 2 and 3. Illustrations by Thomas Nast, depicting anarchists as foreign troublemakers. From *Harper's Weekly*, c. 1886, reproduced in Carl Smith, *Urban Disorder and the Shape of Belief: The Great Chicago Fire, the Haymarket Bomb, and the Model Town of Pullman* (Chicago: University of Chicago Press, 1995).

are shadowy and impossible to see clearly, and each is clothed in a trench coat and a hat much like the anarchist of the previous Nast illustration. According to scholar Carl Smith, this imaginary Most is leading a drill in which the cowardly anarchists are moving away from their raving and sword-wielding leader.[65] But the drawing could also be a satiric portrayal of the anarchist in American society during the post-Haymarket period or, alternately, a depiction of anarchists as so many monsters under the bed.

It is generally acknowledged that the eight anarchists convicted for the Haymarket bombing had no direct involvement in the attack against police and were instead being tried for their political views.[66] However, as much as the trial resulting from Haymarket led to the railroading of innocent anarchists, there were also cases in the late nineteenth and early twentieth centuries in both Europe and America where acts of political violence or propaganda of the deed were carried out by anarchists. But why this turn to political violence? For some anarchists, disgusted by the inequality they saw in their societies, ones in which extreme wealth was in the possession of a few while the majority of the population starved, attacking symbols of authority appeared the logical conclusion. Political violence was also a means of retaliation against those who persecuted anarchists and workers in general. The period in which first-wave anarchism flourished was a time of brutal and open class war. Governments called out militias to suppress strikes, radicals were thrown into jail for publicly speaking against capitalism and the church, and those of foreign birth were deported for their political activities, while others were executed for the same. By assassinating influential political figures, anarchists were also demonstrating that it was possible to strike against authority. Some who engaged in propaganda of the deed hoped their actions would spark a larger uprising.

On 29 July 1900, Gaetano Bresci, who was living in Paterson, New Jersey, returned to Italy to kill King Umberto I. This was in direct response to events surrounding Italy's colonial wars in northern Africa. Two years before Bresci killed the king, mass demonstrations had been held all over Italy to protest the Italian government's involvement in Ethiopia. In May 1898, General Bava-Beccaris placed the city of Milan under military control to prevent a larger uprising, killing eighty citizens in the process. Afterwards, King Umberto congratulated Bava-Beccaris and decorated the general with a medal. Bresci assassinated the king to avenge those murdered in Milan.[67]

The next year, United States President William McKinley was assassinated by Leon Czolgosz, the Michigan-born son of Polish immigrants, during a public appearance in Buffalo, New York. In his statement to police, Czolgosz stated that he was an anarchist who did not believe in rulers and that killing

McKinley was his duty.[68] Commentators reacted to Czolgosz's actions in much the same way as they did in the aftermath of Haymarket. Many again referred to anarchism as a foreign ideology that had come to North America through European immigration. These "agitators of foreign birth," as one commentator described anarchists, were often thought to have come from countries unused to democratic institutions.[69] As the author of a *Toronto Star* editorial lamented, "It is quite possible that the growth of the United States has been too rapid to be healthy. That country has opened its ports and its fertile acres to immigrants from all climes, and with the good there has come much of the utterly bad. During the past half century, the desperate, the ignorant, the lawless, have found a haven in the United States, and some of them ... have utterly failed to realize the responsibilities that accompany self-government and full personal liberty."[70]

Not only was the Detroit-born and -raised Leon Czolgosz considered a foreign radical with no experience of so-called democratic institutions, but he was also characterized as insane because he chose violence over the ballot box: "The sense of injury in Czolgosz, which has led to his insane resentment against organized society, is, like all delusions, an attempt by a weak and disordered brain to explain a disordered feeling—in this case, a painful feeling, having its origin in the ill-adjustment of the individual and his inability to fit himself successfully into the conditions of life as he found them."[71] Czolgosz's attack was generally seen as the act of a troubled mind. Yet, the assassination of McKinley also occurred following the brutal subjugation of the Philippines after this territory became a United States possession in 1898, and some drew a connection.[72]

The use of propaganda of the deed generated a great deal of debate among anarchists. A few years after the McKinley assassination, the anarchist writer and lecturer Voltairine de Cleyre, citing the existence of Christian and Republican assassins in the past, argued that there was nothing specific to anarchism that led some adherents to commit acts of political violence. Instead, she argued that those who engaged in violence were "react[ing] against the injustices created by the prevailing system of the time." In Czolgosz's case, de Cleyre pointed to a capitalist economic system that literally destroyed lives, polluted the environment, and gave the working class no hope of a better situation. Under circumstances such as these, she felt it was not a surprise that some decided to strike back against an exploitative system.[73]

Debates surrounding political violence were also an important feature of anarchism in Italy in the late nineteenth century. Within the Italian context, anarchism emerged as a movement during the *Risorgimento*, which literally means "The Resurgence," the long and bloody process that led to the country's unification in 1861. Prior to unification, the Italian peninsula was divided among various kingdoms and duchies, which often fell under the control of various European empires, especially the Austrian and the French. Such foreign occupation of and intervention in the region, as well as the influence of the French Revolution, helped to develop ideas of Italian independence and democratic forms of government among the peninsula's educated elite. Over time, revolutionary groups such as the *carbonari* were formed to oust the Austrians, but these attempts ended in failure in the early 1820s. One former member of the *carbonari* was Giuseppe Mazzini, a lawyer originally from Genoa, who became one of the most important figures of the unification movement. He believed that Italy had been created by God Himself to be a united and free nation, which meant that all the reigning monarchs and the Pope had to be dethroned. Mazzini felt that this process could only occur through revolution. Once all the oppressors of the Italian people had been removed from power, a democratic republic could be established. Mazzini published his views and developed a network of liberal supporters who helped finance his Italian endeavours. He also recruited Italians for military service, including Giuseppe Garibaldi, another former *carbonaro* and military leader who had been living in exile in Uruguay.[74]

During the 1848-1849 period, Austrian rule was challenged when the citizens of Milan gained control of the city and established a provisional government. Later, Rome was declared a republic and Pope Pius IX had to flee the city. In both cases, the Mazzinians arrived to take advantage of the situation in the hope that these events would be the catalysts for Italian independence. Yet, this happy outcome remained elusive. The Austrians quickly reasserted their control of Milan and the pope requested the help of the French to restore his rule in Rome. These failed rebellions led to harsh repression, and it was not until the late 1850s that Italy's unification resumed in earnest. An alliance between the Kingdom of Piedmont and France ended in a successful war against Austria, leaving the former in control of northern Italy. During the war, Garibaldi had fought on the side of Piedmont but became disillusioned with the kingdom's prime minister, Camillo Benso, the Count of Cavour. He saw Cavour as a moderate opportunist and opposed his pragmatic cession of Nice, his hometown, to the French. Believing that enough revolutionary sentiment existed in Sicily, Garibaldi organized 1,000 volunteers and sailed to the island to unite the South with the rest of Italy in May 1860. At the outset, Garibaldi claimed his expedition was for Italy and King Vittorio Emanuele of Piedmont; but his real intention, after defeating the Bourbons, was to march on Rome, remove the pope, and proclaim the city as Italy's capital. By doing this, he hoped to challenge Benso and overturn the territorial agreements with France.[75]

Garibaldi's campaign against the Bourbons ended in victory after six months of conflict. He reorganized the government in the Kingdom of the Two Sicilies and proclaimed himself dictator. Cavour and others within the Piedmontese government quickly became concerned with Garibaldi's success and how it might affect that kingdom's plans for the country. To prevent Garibaldi from seizing Rome, the Piedmontese army was dispatched to the Papal States and was able to take control of most of central Italy though leaving Rome in peace to prevent any French intervention. However, when the Piedmontese army met with Garibaldi in the Campanian town of Teano, the revolutionary agreed to hand over all his recently acquired territories. In February 1861, Italy officially became a country and Turin the national capital.[76]

The Risorgimento's broken promises were anarchism's opening opportunities. The Italian state may have been unified in 1861, with Venice and Rome becoming part of Italy in 1866 and 1870, respectively, but the idea of an Italian nation tended to be restricted to relatively few urban-based intellectuals and wealthy elites. For the rest of the peninsula's largely agrarian population, whose loyalties were vested in a particular region or city and not a nation, a centralized government was viewed with suspicion and hostility. During the Risorgimento, the republicans promised Italians, especially those of the lower classes, that a unified Italy would lead to a variety of social reforms. After unification, they largely failed to deliver on them. Instead, peasants confronted a higher tax burden, especially on such necessities as bread. Young men were forced into the army. This not only contributed to a strong distrust of government but also led to peasants, both men and women, to physically resist the state by seizing land and revolting.[77] The social unrest that followed unification challenged the stability of the fledgling nation. It has been suggested by historian Donna Gabaccia that these factors—a weakly reformist state and an unresolved land reform question—influenced the Italian Left's and labour movement's predominantly anarchist character from the 1870s until the turn of the twentieth century.[78] This social unrest led anarchists to view Italian peasants as potential revolutionaries and attempt to channel this discontent.[79] Since anarchists championed direct action and revolution, and believed that people, not governments or political parties, were the initiators of social change, anarchism in some ways simply provided a new name for practices already long in existence. Anarchists such as Mikhail Bakunin, Carlo Cafiero, Andrea Costa, and others did a great deal of work throughout Italy to spread anarchist ideas and organize a movement. This activism ultimately led to the establishment of the first, highly anarchist-oriented Italian branches of the IWMA in the 1870s.[80]

A type of organic anarchism may have been widespread among Italy's lower classes; indeed, anarchism's appeals for liberty and a life free from coercion or oppression would appear to be widely experienced dreams and desires. However, it is difficult to determine how many peasants and labourers, often illiterate people who did not leave a clear record of their ideas, held views that could be described as anarchist or anarchistic. One of the earliest known Italian writers to conceptualize a society on what can be described as anarchist principles was Carlo Pisacane, Duke of San Giovanni. Pisacane was born in Naples in 1818 to a poor noble family and joined the Neapolitan army in 1839. By 1847, he had become influenced by Mazzini's republicanism and spent a short time in both England and France, even serving with the French army in Algeria. Returning to the Italian peninsula during the revolutions of 1848, Pisacane served with Mazzini and Garibaldi, and entered Rome in the fall of that year to take control after political unrest had led to the assassination of Pellegrino Rossi, minister to Pope Pius IX, and the pope's hasty exit from the city. This led to the establishment of the Roman Republic during which Mazzini introduced prison reforms, freedom of the press, and secular education, and redistributed some of the church's landholdings to peasants.[81] In 1849, Pisacane served as chief of staff in Mazzini's army of the Roman Republic, but this position was short-lived; the republic was defeated after four months by the French military under orders from Louis-Napoléon Bonaparte to restore Pius as ruler of the Papal States.[82] Afterwards, Pisacane went into exile, first in London and then later in Genoa, where he supported himself as a teacher.

During this exile, Pisacane came to know the French physician and anarchist Ernest Coeurderoy and the Russian writer and revolutionary Alexander Herzen. It has been suggested that Pisacane's relationship with these two men may have influenced his change in political perspective. He became convinced that Italy was in need of a social—not merely a nationalist and republican—revolution. This led to his break with Mazzini, whom Pisacane had begun to consider an authoritarian and anti-socialist. During this same period, Pisacane was reading the works of French anarchist Pierre-Joseph Proudhon, the French utopian socialist Charles Fourier, and the Italian federalists Carlo Catteneo and Giuseppe Ferrari. Pisacane's political ideology has been described as Proudhonian socialism with a collectivist bent and a precursor to Bakunin's collectivist anarchism. Pisacane, evidently focussed strictly on the Italian peninsula, viewed national and social problems as intertwined and felt that armed struggle had to be carried out, not only against foreign and domestic monarchical rule, but also against the wealthy. He was strongly opposed to private property, the state, and religion, and imagined an ideal Italian society comprised of free communes united by a provisional pact among liberated regions. Within this federation, much as in Proudhon's mutualist anarchist vision, each member would be guaranteed the right to whatever they produced. However, and this appears as a contradiction in Pisacane's thought, both industrial factories and cultivated land would be held collectively. Each individual's "freedom of action" would also be guaranteed under this federation. To achieve his vision of a socialist society, Pisacane believed, much like his radical and nationalist contemporaries, in revolutionary means. Any act of revolt would be useful in sparking the Italian masses to rebel. Among those Pisacane felt were the most open to spontaneous rebellion were the peasants of southern Italy, the region known as the Mezzogiorno. And it was his attempt to put his theories into practice that led Pisacane to sail to Campania in late June 1857 in an attempt to overthrow the House of Bourbon, which ruled Naples at that time. The landing in Campania was a disaster since no widespread support existed for Pisacane's plan, and he and his allies were defeated by Bourbon forces within a few days. It was during that battle that Pisacane decided to take his own life to avoid capture.[83]

Pisacane's political theories were very similar to those of the Russian anarchist Mikhail Bakunin, who lived and organized in Italy following the Neapolitan's death. Bakunin was born in 1814 on his family's estate at Premukhino in the province of Tver. His father was sympathetic to liberal ideas and a cousin of his mother's side had been involved in the failed 1825 Decembrist revolt.[84] Bakunin was educated by private tutors until the age of fifteen, when he was enrolled in Artillery School. After graduating, he left the military and went to study philosophy in Moscow, where he became fascinated with Hegel. This sparked his move to Berlin, which led to his deep immersion in the works of German intellectuals, such as Feuerbach. However, Bakunin did not stay in Berlin indefinitely; he travelled throughout western Europe, meeting Proudhon and Marx in the 1840s and imbibing their political philosophies while radicalizing his own. Not only a philosopher, Bakunin was also a person of action who was more than willing to involve himself in uprisings when the opportunity arose. He went to Paris during the 1848 Revolution and served with the Workers' National Guard. Later that year, he was involved in an insurrection in Prague, and another in Dresden in 1849. The latter led to Bakunin's arrest and eventual deportation to Russia, where he was imprisoned for eight years. Because of his family's appeals to Tsar Alexander II, he was released from prison in 1855 but banished to Siberia. There, he had some freedom of movement and was able to escape, eventually sailing to the United States and then to England. By 1864, Bakunin was living in Italy and inter-mingling with those who shared his political views.[85]

During his lifetime, Bakunin wrote a great deal and contributed much to anarchist theory. A contemporary of Marx, Bakunin is probably best known for his insightful critique of state communism, which he argued would lead to the replacement of the bourgeoisie by a new ruling elite, comprised of edu-cated workers, who would administer the lives of the majority and create a new despotism. It was, for Bakunin, a matter of means and ends: how could a dictatorship of the proletariat end with the eventual dismantling of the state and freedom for all? As he remarked: "They [the Marxists] insist that only dic-tatorship (of course their own) can create freedom for the people. We reply that all dictatorship has no objective other than self-perpetuation, and that slavery is all it can generate and instill in the people who suffer it. Freedom can be created only by freedom, by a total rebellion of the people from the bottom up."[86] In light of the communist revolutions of the twentieth century, Bakunin's reasoning, with respect to state communism, has been viewed as prescient by many scholars.[87]

Of course, Bakunin was critical of all states. They placed the common good, supposedly embodied by the state, over that of the individual. And the com-mon good was not determined by the majority but a minority of legislators, government representatives, religious figures, and capitalists, governing the state to suit their own interests under the guise of representative democracy. States led to working-class exploitation, nationalism, and patriotism, which Bakunin believed was contrary to the natural solidarity that existed among people. Bakunin was against capitalism and private property, and felt that all social wealth should be held collectively. However, one's right to that social wealth depended upon how much labour a person contributed to its creation. Bakunin was also critical of religion because it acted as a tool of the ruling classes and preached subservience to authority. In addition, belief in a god led to the denial of human reason and human liberty.[88]

Bakunin was not only a critic; he also championed more practical ideas about how an anarchist society could be organized. In place of states, Bakunin conceptualized a form of federation, made up of communally organized work-ers' associations, whether industrial, agricultural, scientific, literary, or artis-tic. The commune would then belong to a regional federation, with all regions being part of yet another larger federation. Ideally, these federations would be joined in a truly international union. As much as Bakunin may have wished otherwise, the realization of a federated anarchist society could only occur through social revolution. This would be a violent struggle to overthrow the state and the institutions that supported or benefited from its existence. Even though Bakunin may have spent part of his life travelling around Europe to engage in insurrection, he did write in *Revolution and Revolutionary Violence* that revolutions could not be improvised or made by individuals. Rather, they occurred because the "force of circumstances" led to "the spontaneous action of the masses."[89]

Due to the similarity between the political philosophies of Pisacane and Bakunin, there have been debates surrounding the former's influence on the latter. Why does this matter? Bakunin has generally been given historical credit for introducing anarchism to Italy, especially by T.R. Ravindranathan in his *Bakunin and the Italians*. However, pointing to one specific historical figure as the root of a political movement when similar ideas may already have been widespread before his arrival negates the role of Italians themselves in the creation of anarchist or anarchistic thought. Ravindranathan is adamant that Bakunin was unaware of Pisacane's ideas even though he was friends with two close comrades of Pisacane, Attanasio Dramis and Giuseppe Fanelli, the latter having served with Pisacane during the failed insurrectionary attempt in Campania. He even goes as far as stating that "Fanelli, Dramis, and others who knew Pisacane well and revered his memory never spoke of his writings, let alone his socialist ideas."[90] Only with a Ouija board or a time machine could one be so certain of what people long deceased did or did not discuss throughout their lives. Nettlau, on the other hand, believes that, based on his friendship with Fanelli alone, Bakunin must have known about Pisacane and his political ideas though there is no mention of the Italian in any of Bakunin's writings.[91] Woodcock, for his part, contends that Pisacane's theories and actions were already known among radicals in Italy, which led to Bakunin's friendly reception in the country.[92] In this way, Bakunin acted more as a catalyst than the initiator of the Italian anarchist movement.[93] I err on the side of caution and believe it possible that Bakunin was aware of, and may have possibly been influenced by, Pisacane's socialist views. Tellingly, it was during his time in Italy that Bakunin fully developed his anarchist thought.[94]

After his arrival in Italy in 1864, Bakunin involved himself in what was to be the last phase of the Risorgimento. He believed that the anti-monarchical and anti-clerical republicanism of Garibaldi had revolutionary potential that could spread to the rest of Europe.[95] However, Garibaldi, much like Mazzini, wanted to establish a democratic republic that would maintain the property rights of wealthy landowners and change little for the majority of non-propertied classes. Bakunin's role in Italy, then, was to introduce socialist concepts into debates surrounding republicanism and demonstrate that republicanism would not solve problems of inequality, but simply shift power from the monarchy to the bourgeoisie, much like the American and French revolutions had done previously.[96]

In October 1865, Bakunin was living in Naples and in contact with the circle of disgruntled republicans who wrote and published *Il Popolo d'Italia* (The People of Italy). It was through this channel that he was able to meet a group of radicals from southern Italy that included the revolutionaries Giuseppe Fanelli and Attanasio Dramis, Neapolitan lawyers Carlo Gambuzzi and Alberto Tucci, the former Calabrian priest Raffaele Mileti, and the Sicilian physician and deputy of the Italian parliament Saverio Friscia, among others. These men considered themselves patriotic Mazzinians but had already begun to question how the republican cause, without a well-considered social program, was going to solve Italy's widespread social and economic problems, especially in the Mezzogiorno. But, according to Ravindranathan, these southern radicals were neither willing to challenge Mazzini publicly because of the deep respect they still had for the man, nor able to conceptualize an alternative to republicanism. Thus, Bakunin's meeting with this group was productive for both parties. For the southern radicals, Bakunin's writings in *Il Popolo d'Italia* usefully attacked Mazzini's religious and bourgeois vision of a unified Italy. For Bakunin, the Italian context afforded him the opportunity to advance his anarchist views and provided a nucleus for pan-European revolutionary endeavours. Collectively, the group became known as the Società dei Legionari della Rivoluzione Sociale Italiana (SLRSI; Legionnaire Society for the Italian Social Revolution).[97]

The first action of the SLRSI was to attend a public meeting on 11 February 1866, to protest a new set of government-instituted taxes. The meeting was conducted by a more moderate group of Mazzini and Garibaldi supporters who, while still critical of the new tax regime, were unwilling to denounce it as vociferously as the SLRSI. Alberto Tucci, for instance, declared that the Italian state was created to benefit a privileged minority and called for open revolt. In addition, Carlo Gambuzzi condemned the heavy taxation legislated by the centralized bureaucracy and argued for more regional autonomy in administrative matters. It is unclear how much the intervention of the SLRSI influenced others at the meeting who did not share their views at the outset, but news of the event became a topic of debate in the Italian parliament.[98]

Throughout 1866, Bakunin continued to challenge the Mazzinian cause in republican newspapers open to printing such articles. In the summer of that year, he drafted the *Revolutionary Catechism*, which soon became the political program for the SLRSI. In this document, Bakunin outlined his collectivist form of anarchism: absolute freedom for all except those refusing to work for the common good, political and economic organization from the base to the summit, "[r]eplacing the cult of God by *respect and love of humanity*"[99] (emphasis in original), universal revolution, and the creation of autonomous communes joined in federation as a means of replacing states.[100] Meanwhile, Saverio Friscia had been busy organizing sections of the SLRSI in his native Sicily to great effect. In the fall of the same year, Alberto Tucci and Bakunin collaborated on a pamphlet entitled *La Situazione Italiana* (The Italian Situation), which boldly criticized the actions and motivations of Mazzini and Garibaldi. The pamphlet's appearance came after the latter's failed attempt to wrest control of Venice from the Austrians. *La Situazione Italiana* argued that the efforts of Mazzini and his followers were contrary to the wishes of most inhabitants of the Italian peninsula and that the republican cause had been unable to rectify the whole country's deep social problems. The peasants and workers did not strongly support the republican state because it would not improve their circumstances in any way. On this last subject, Tucci and Bakunin asserted that a bourgeois government would always be opposed to the interests of peasants and workers, and believed that only a "revolution made by the People for their positive and complete emancipation" would truly make Italy free. *La Situazione Italiana* has been credited with laying the groundwork for the inevitable break many republicans made with Mazzini in 1871, following his condemnation of the Paris Commune of that same year.[101]

In early 1867, as the SLRSI and its ideas became more widely known, a new group was formed. It was called Libertà e Giustizia (Freedom and Justice) and it published a newspaper of the same name until the end of that year. This publication continued to disseminate the ideas of the original SLRSI and challenge Mazzinian republicanism.[102] It was this group whose members would comprise the first Italian section of the IWMA in 1869. The IWMA, also known as the First International, was established in London in 1864 in an attempt to unite all leftist political tendencies and labour unions committed to working class struggle. Congresses were held in Switzerland, Belgium, and the Netherlands during the late 1860s and early 1870s. They were highly contentious affairs—inevitably so, given the diversity of socialists from many backgrounds who came to them. Two factions quickly emerged, one headed by Karl Marx and the other by Mikhail Bakunin, divided from each other on questions of revolutionary strategy. Marx and his followers viewed the state as the vehicle for workers' emancipation while Bakunin was openly critical of the centralist and authoritarian aspects of Marx's state communism. In 1872, the IWMA was moved to New York in an attempt to prevent its control by the majority who opposed Marx, but within four years the association ceased to exist.[103] Anarchists, however, would continue to meet at their own congresses following the IWMA's collapse as they had done previously.[104]

The Italian section of the First International was collectivist anarchist in ideology. Its members, such as Gambuzzi and Stefano Caporusso in Naples and Friscia in Sicily, helped enlarge the section's membership to over 3,000 in the first months of 1870. By that time a newspaper, *L'Eguaglianza* (Equality), was being published and section members had begun to involve themselves in labour strikes, leading to their arrests. Within a three-year period, the membership of the Italian section had ranged from between 20,000 and 30,000. The majority of its members were made up of skilled rather than unskilled workers from central and southern Italy, in addition to students and intellectuals. Women were also involved in the early anarchist movement, though only a few of them became prominent within the International in Italy during the 1870s. Women such as Luisa "Gigia" Minguzzi and Vincenza Matteuzi headed the Tuscany Federation and the Marchigian-Umbrian Federation respectively. Most women, however, comprised the rank and file; and by 1876, women's sections had been organized in Florence, Aquila, Imola, Perugia, Carrara, and Prato. These sections were involved in creating their own programs and propaganda, and attending congresses. Women were not immune to attacks by the state. So, they too experienced the same violence as did men.[105]

Post-Risorgimento Italy was far from united and experienced severe social unrest. In the 1860s, peasants in southern Italy resisted conscription and a new tax regime legislated by a government they considered a foreign colonizer. This led to civil war in the southern regions of the country. Disaffection with the Italian government was not limited solely to the south. Rioting broke out in Turin in 1864, following the transfer of the capital to Florence. Insurgents seized Palermo for a short time in 1866. A gristmill tax introduced in 1869, to help pay the debts incurred during the Risorgimento, led to rioting throughout the country.[106] Then in 1873, Italy was hit by an economic crisis due, in part, to its transition from a predominantly agricultural and artisanal to an industrial society as well as rampant inflation caused by the government's issuance of large sums of paper money to balance the budget. Poor harvests that same year led to cost-of-living increases for workers, which caused strikes throughout the peninsula that continued into 1874. Even the government's use of soldiers and the *carabinieri* could not prevent the mass demonstrations in which people engaged.[107]

Under these conditions, the leadership of the International in Italy believed the moment for social revolution and the overthrow of the state was at hand. The Internationalists embarked upon a series of insurrectionary actions which they hoped would provide the revolutionary spark to cause the masses to overthrow the Italian government. The first planned insurrection was to occur in Romagna, the Marches, Tuscany, Rome, Calabria, and Sicily in early August 1874. However, the anarchists miscalculated the support of fellow radicals and the temper of Italian workers and peasants; so, the number of insurrectionists needed for this action did not materialize. In addition, Italian authorities had known about this plan since its outset and the *carabinieri* had been out in full force. The small groups of insurrectionists were, therefore, either arrested or fled in the face of larger numbers of police.[108]

The 1874 insurrection had taught the anarchists that they did not have the resources to take on the Italian state directly. But this did not dampen the belief among anarchists that certain segments of the Italian population, such as landless peasants, were inherently revolutionary due to their exploited and poverty-stricken circumstances, and they only needed a push to outright rebellion. For this plan, the anarchists chose the Matese mountain range south of Naples that straddles Molise and Campania. They felt that the peasants of the Matese had proven themselves to be against the Italian state because they had resisted unification by engaging in armed conflict with Piedmontese soldiers. In a letter to Amilcare Cipriani, Pietro Cesare Ceccarelli explained the anarchist plan for the Matese: "[we will] rove the countryside for as long as possible, preaching [class] war, inciting social brigandage, occupying small towns and leaving them after having accomplished whatever revolutionary acts we [can], and to proceed to that area where our presence would prove most useful." The band of twenty-six poorly armed men, known as the Matese Band, began their activities in early April 1877. When they entered a town free of government soldiers, the anarchists would collect and burn tax registers, distribute arms and money from the local town hall to the peasants, and explain to them the importance of the social revolution. After this was done, the anarchists would move to the next town. The actions of the anarchists did sometimes receive cheers from peasants, but at other times the peasants were suspicious of the Matese Band's motivations. Others were disappointed that the insurrectionists would not collectivize the land, but the anarchists felt that the first priority for the peasants was to defend themselves from the Italian soldiers that were sure to arrive. Unfortunately for the anarchists, their actions in the Matese had no lasting effect. Once they left, the peasants returned to their daily routines. With supplies dwindling and government soldiers on their trail, it was only a matter of time before this action would be forced to cease. Holed up in a farmhouse to escape inclement weather, the anarchists were surrounded by soldiers and eventually surrendered without a shot fired.[109]

These insurrectionary actions did not lead to the successful outcome that the anarchists had envisioned. Yet, it did not quell the militancy among anarchists or their belief that insurrection would eventually bear fruit. According to historian Nunzio Pernicone, the anarchist actions in the Matese Mountains in particular also brought national attention to the anarchist cause and resulted in new adherents of anarchism. But there were negative consequences because of these insurrectionary attempts. The failed uprising in 1874 led to Bakunin's retirement to Switzerland and the Matese action resulted in the eventual Italian outlawing of the International.[110]

As a result of anarchist insurrections in the 1870s, anarchism became synonymous with criminality in the eyes of the Italian government. The movement was often the target of state repression during the frequent periods of social unrest that flared up in Italy during the late nineteenth century. Yet, in spite of such governmental backlash, anarchists continued their activism throughout the 1880s and 1890s. Some, like Luigi Galleani, the law student-turned-anarchist, began organizing workers through the Partito Operaio Italiano (POI; Italian Workers' Party), which was under considerable anarchist influence in the northern regions of the country. At the same time, anarchists in the South were active in the Fasci Siciliani (Sicilian Workers' Leagues), a worker and peasant association that organized around such issues as fairer taxation and land for the poor. The Fasci Siciliani, however, was eventually dissolved and its leaders arrested when Premier Francesco Crispi declared martial law in Sicily and ordered 40,000 soldiers to occupy the island after reports of a planned uprising.[111]

The continual harassment and disruption of the movement and its activities by the Italian authorities caused anarchists to re-evaluate their tactics. Anarchists such as Francesco Saverio Merlino and Errico Malatesta, both of whom had taken part in insurrections, felt that Italian anarchists should organize themselves into a national party that would simultaneously have some legitimacy in the eyes of the state and draw large numbers of supporters amongst the wider population. Merlino was a Naples-born lawyer and writer who began to outline his anarchist ideas in a newspaper he co-published in 1877. After the failed attempts of the Matese Band to foment revolution, Merlino publicly supported their actions and in 1878 defended its arrested members in court. In 1884, he was tried for "conspiracy against state security," found guilty, and given a four-month prison term. However, Merlino went into exile and did not serve his sentence. During this period, he travelled through western Europe and lived in the United States for six months in 1892. While in exile, he continued to write on anarchist themes for various newspapers and when in New York City, he helped his comrades to establish the anarchist newspaper *Il Grido degli Oppressi* (Cry of the Oppressed). In 1894, Merlino returned to Italy but was arrested and forced to serve the prison term that led to his exile. Upon his release from prison, Merlino publicly declared in the pages of the Rome-based conservative paper *Il Messaggero* that he no longer considered himself an anarchist. This led to a year-long debate with his old friend Errico Malatesta, which ended with Merlino describing his political outlook as libertarian socialism, a term which is often used as a synonym for anarchism. Though he was no longer actively involved in the anarchist movement after his time in prison, Merlino continued to represent former comrades in court. In 1904, he was interviewed about anarchism in Italy by a reporter from Turin's *La Stampa*. He declared that the movement was no longer relevant. The article, "La fine dell'anarchismo" (The End of Anarchism), shocked many of Merlino's former comrades and led to a response from Luigi Galleani, which will be explored in greater detail in Chapter 5. Merlino continued to write on socialist topics as well as the rise of fascism in the early 1920s. After the fascists passed a series of laws in 1925 and 1926 that required all political writing to be approved by the government, Merlino was forced to cease publishing. He died in Rome in 1930.[112]

Errico Malatesta, the well-known anarchist communist, was born in the small town of Santa Maria Capua a Vetere in the Campania region in 1853. He was studying medicine at the University of Naples but was expelled after his involvement in a republican demonstration in 1871. Inspired by the Paris Commune, Malatesta became interested in socialism and joined the Naples section of the IWMA. The following year, he met Bakunin and attended the anarchist congress at St. Imier, Switzerland. This was the first meeting of an anarchist international, comprised of groups expelled from the IWMA. Following the congress, Malatesta focussed his energies on anarchist propaganda and insurrection. He was involved in the Matese Band actions of 1877 and was arrested with his comrades. They were imprisoned for over a year and then released. Further repression, following a series of attacks against the Italian monarchy in 1878 and the illegalization of the International, forced Malatesta to go into exile. He lived in a number of countries—Egypt, France, Switzerland, England, Romania, Belgium, Argentina, and the United States—many of which he had to leave due to his political activities. His exile abroad was marked with periodic returns to Italy. However, his notoriety and the ever-present danger of imprisonment meant his visits there were often brief. During his lifetime, Malatesta established a number of anarchist newspapers in Italy, Argentina, and France, and wrote pamphlets such as *Fra Contadini* (Between Peasants), which provided an accessible explanation of anarchist communism. Malatesta returned to Italy for the last time in 1919 and began publishing *Umanità Nova* (New Humanity) but was imprisoned in 1921 for his support of the postwar factory occupations. He was released before the fascists came to power and began to publish yet another anarchist newspaper, *Pensiero e Volontà* (Thought and Will) in defiance of the laws the fascists introduced against any form of independent press. Malatesta spent the rest of his life under house arrest in Rome, where he died of bronchial pneumonia in July 1932.[113]

Anarchists such as Merlino and Malatesta were known as organizationalists. They did not envision a parliamentary political party but rather a movement that would be non-hierarchical in structure and united in action. A clandestine meeting was held in Capolago, Switzerland, in early 1891 to establish an anarchist party that became known as the Partito Socialista Anarchico Rivoluzionario–Federazione Italiana (PSAR-FI; Revolutionary Anarchist Socialist Party–Italian Federation). Two principal resolutions were passed at this congress. One recognized that participation in elections was contrary to anarchist principles and, further, that anarchists should engage in anti-electoral propaganda and voting boycotts. The second resolution condemned any compromise or alliance, no matter how temporary, with republicans and irredentists.[114] Another outcome of the Capolago congress was to call for a general strike in Rome for May Day later that year which, congress attendees hoped, would lead to an insurrection. However, spies within the anarchist movement warned Italian authorities of the May Day plans and the desired uprising never materialized. Many anarchists were arrested and, after being found guilty, were given prison sentences and fines. An even greater crackdown on anarchists and their activities ensued.[115] Ultimately, in the context of the gradual enfranchisement of more and more of the Italian population, the PSAR-FI could not compete with the parliamentary socialism of the PSI.[116]

In opposition to the organizationalists were the anti-organizationalists who, as the name implies, were against organization of any kind. They had two main reasons for their stand. The first stemmed from previous experience with the violence of the Italian state. Above-ground anarchist groups became targets of violence which, in turn, disrupted the anarchist movement. The reasoning of the anti-organizationalists was that if no movement were visible, no movement could be attacked. The second reason was a result of a deeply held mistrust of all organizations because of their perceived authoritarian and bureaucratic behaviour. A given union, for instance, might begin with a handful of workers who coalesced around workplace issues. However, once these workers began to create a union, various hierarchical positions would be needed to oversee its daily affairs. According to anti-organizationalists, these positions would mean too much power in the hands of a minority that is potentially able to act in its own self-interest to the detriment of workers in general. The solution then was for workers to organize spontaneously around specific grievances. Once these grievances were settled with the employer, the workers would return to work and unite in the future if and when it was necessary to do so.

Another important aspect of this strain of anarchism was its embrace of individual acts of political violence. This tactic was called for most ardently by those anarchists who had experienced the brutality of state repression firsthand. Two important adherents of this anarchist approach were Emilio Covelli and Carlo Cafiero.[117] Much like the organizationalists, both viewed true anarchist revolution as a negation of parliamentary politics but, in addition, also believed that constant actions should be carried out against the state to bring about its downfall. These continuous actions would help strengthen the anarchists in "much the same way a gymnast strengthens his [sic] muscles by using them."[118] For Covelli, Cafiero, and other anti-organizationalists, anarchists could not simply wait for the revolution's ideal conditions, nor could they count on the masses to discover anarchism on their own. Instead, a small group of committed revolutionaries would carry out actions that would then, it was believed, motivate others to rebel. In order to conduct acts of violence against the state and avoid reprisals, anarchists were to organize themselves into clandestine cells. As popular as the anti-organizationalist rhetoric surrounding violence was in Italy during the 1880s, most anarchists were unwilling to engage in violent actions. Thus, continuous revolution as a tactic never became a reality among Italian anarchists. As Pernicone has suggested, it was more of a state of mind than a program—a stance that "offer[ed] psychological sustenance to intransigent rebels locked spiritually and morally in unequal combat with the state and bourgeois society."[119] Nonetheless, beginning in the mid-1890s, Italian anarchists were involved in attacks on heads of state or monarchs, such as Sante Geronimo Caserio's killing of French President Marie François Sadi Carnot in 1894 and Gaetano Bresci's assassination of King Umberto I of Italy six years later. Caserio was motivated by Sadi Carnot's execution orders against anarchists Auguste Vaillant and Émile Henry, who themselves were involved in acts of political violence.[120] These attacks may well have demonstrated the vulnerability of their intended targets but they did not lead to mass revolution. In fact, the result of these actions was the introduction of new anti-anarchist laws and the further surveillance and repression of the movement.

As a result of the governmental backlash between 1870 and 1900, the anarchist movement in Italy could no longer sustain a national presence. Nonetheless, it did maintain strongholds in the regions of Tuscany, Umbria, Lombardy, Campania, and Sicily, and in the city of Rome.[121] Despite the constant attempts by the Italian government to suppress their activities, anarchists continued to involve themselves in worker and peasant struggles, as they had since the formation of the First International, through key positions within local chambers of labour. These chambers were originally established in the 1890s as labour exchanges funded by municipal governments but quickly became autonomous. Each chamber represented workers, regardless of skill or vocation, and controlled the labour market in a specific jurisdiction. When labour disputes occurred provincially, such chambers organized boycotts and sympathy strikes, providing a sense of unity among the labouring classes. Chambers of labour also acted as cultural centres, providing a space for social events, educational courses, and regular public meetings where workers would debate issues relating to job actions. Much anti-war and anti-religious organizing was conducted at these chambers as well.[122]

Labour unions did not enjoy the same support within the populace as did the chambers of labour. By 1914, only 10 percent of Italian workers were unionized. Still, anarchists of the organizationalist persuasion who had begun to adopt syndicalist positions became increasingly active in the union movement, joining the socialist-associated Confederazione Generale del Lavoro (CGL; General Confederation of Labour), the Sindicato Ferrovieri Italiani (SFI; Italian Railway Workers' Union), and the Federazione Italiana Operai Metallurgica (FIOM; Italian Metal Workers' Union). Due to the mixed composition of these unions, which included socialists, syndicalists, Catholics, and republicans, in addition to anarchists, each was wracked with internal disagreements on tactics and politics. Anarchists and other syndicalists who became disaffected with the CGL met in Modena in 1912 and established the Unione Sindicale Italiana (USI; Italian Syndicalist Union), which quickly began to organize workers throughout central Italy and Liguria. It also incorporated the chambers of labour in these regions. Within a year, the USI's membership was just over 100,000, about half that of the CGL. The USI advocated direct action in the form of strikes, work slowdowns, and sabotage, as a means of struggle in the workplace.[123]

Anti-militarist campaigns were another important focus of anarchist activity. Italy's invasion of Libya in September 1911 led to anarchists and socialists co-organizing anti-war demonstrations and attempting to stop trains carrying soldiers from travelling to various ports. Anti-militarist activism continued throughout 1913 and 1914 as a European war began to appear inevitable. Anarchists and socialists were constantly being arrested for distributing anti-war literature outside barracks and public meetings were disrupted by police. A demonstration against the military in Ancona on 7 June 1914 resulted in the murder of two protestors and sparked *la settimana rossa* (the Red Week), a week of strikes, street protests, and confrontations with police and nationalists. During this seven-day period, some small towns in the Marche region declared themselves autonomous from Italy. But for all the agitation by the Italian Left against military intervention, within less than a year Italy had entered the First World War on the side of the Allies. This event had repercussions for the Left. Some, including anarchists, believed in the Allied propaganda that the war was being waged to protect the democratic nations of Europe from German authoritarianism. The USI also experienced a serious rift within its ranks over Italy's involvement in the war. Some syndicalists believed that war would strengthen the resolve of the working classes and lead to a proletarian revolution against the bourgeoisie while others maintained their anti-interventionist stance. The union's membership shrank by half during the war, as many were conscripted for the war effort or left the USI because of its position. The internal issues within the USI and the wider Italian Left, however, did not put an end to anti-war activism; anarchists were still distributing literature condemning Italy's involvement, holding anti-war protests, and helping smuggle leftist deserters into neutral Switzerland.[124]

The social unrest that followed the First World War in Italy led to *il biennio rosso* (the Two Red Years), which lasted from 1919 to 1920. Massive social protest, strikes, and the occupation of factories and land were sparked by high unemployment, with 2 million out of work, and by an inflation that caused prices to increase nearly six times their previous value.[125] As a result of the dire economic circumstances, workers voted for the PSI in 1919, which led to 156 seats in the Italian Parliament, the most held by a single party at that time. The following year, the PSI won majorities in a quarter of Italy's *comunes*. During the same period, the CGL membership expanded from 250,000 to over 2 million. The Confederation led many strikes during *il biennio rosso*, including a twenty-four-hour general strike in solidarity with the Russian Revolution that took place in July 1919. Chambers of labour were also active at this time. Following the food riots that erupted in northern and central Italy that same summer, the chambers created food committees that took control of stores and sold the food at reduced prices. In cities like Ferrara and Bologna and its immediate surrounding areas, where chambers of labour had exceptionally strong support, they were able to dictate conditions of work to industrialists and large landowners. USI membership also expanded dramatically and the union led the factory occupations of those workers it represented. During this two-year period, anarchists were heavily involved in protests against high food prices, as well as against the militarism and imperialism that had led to the outbreak of the war. Malatesta's return to Italy from exile in London in late December 1919 led to a speaking tour of the country from January until the summer of the following year. His lectures were very popular and drew large crowds, not only of peasants and workers, but also of police who disrupted these gatherings. The violence unleashed by the state only increased tensions between it and the wider public. In June 1920, two divisions of Italian soldiers mutinied at Ancona. In order to come to the aid of the soldiers and take advantage of a revolutionary moment, Malatesta led members of the USI and a group of anarchists to the city. Shortly thereafter, Ancona was in open revolt as the local armoury was seized and its contents distributed to strikers and the general populace. However, the rebellion fizzled out rather quickly after the CGL refused to call a general strike.[126]

The climax of *il biennio rosso* came in September 1920, when more than 400,000 workers across the country seized control of their places of work. This action was a result of solidarity with Fiat plant workers in Turin, locked in a wage dispute with their employer. For four weeks, workers controlled factories, set up kitchens to feed themselves and, in Turin, continued to manufacture cars, reportedly faster and more efficiently than before the strike. The seizure of factories panicked industrialists who called on Prime Minister Giovanni Giolitti to restore order. However, Giolitti ignored the calls to use violence and decided to allow the workers to realize that their situation could not last indefinitely because they did not control the banks, post offices, the telephone system, and other important institutions. Conflicts within the Italian Left also played their part in ending the factory occupations. While the USI believed that Italy was on the brink of revolution, the CGL viewed the workers' control of their workplaces as a response to grievances with employers. The confederation also felt that a revolution in Italy would lead to intervention and sanctions by other countries. Thus, the CGL refused to accept the USI and PSI position that workers' power was the first step in overthrowing the capitalist system. However, the PSI was unwilling to allow the CGL to control the strike. In early October, workers, lacking support from the wider Italian Left and with a vague promise by the prime minister that workers would have more control in matters relating to their industries, began to leave the factories.[127]

––––––––––––––––––––

As a result of the militant working class uprisings during *il biennio rosso* and because of Prime Minister Giolitti's refusal to use violence to end the factory occupations, Italian elites, fearing that Italy was in danger of its own socialist revolution, decided that they would take it upon themselves to destroy any threat that the Left still posed to their interests. To that end, they helped form *squadristi* in regions where socialists, broadly defined, were most numerous and influential. The *squadristi*, or blackshirts, were comprised of ex-soldiers, university students, and anti-socialist peasants who used violence to destroy leftist organizations and institutions in the two years following *il biennio rosso*. They often acted with the approval or cooperation of local prefects, police, or military. Within six months of the formation of the *squadristi*, it was responsible for the destruction of 119 chambers of labour, 107 cooperatives, and 83 peasant league offices. In the place of destroyed leftist organizations and institutions, these fascists created their own alternatives.[128]

At first, Benito Mussolini, the former socialist who gradually turned to fascism during the course of the First World War, did not ally his fascist movement with the *squadristi* but chose instead to run for parliament on a platform that was almost identical with that of the PSI. Mussolini had tried to form an alliance with the Unione Italiana del Lavoro (UIL), a nationalist syndicalist union. And, much like Mussolini and his followers, the UIL was wary of a premature revolution led by the proletariat and thought Bolshevism was the greatest threat to Italy. However, the UIL, keeping true to the syndicalist position that rejected parliamentary action, was unwilling to accept a merger with any political party.[129] Mussolini's political fortunes improved once he abandoned the socialist parts of his platform. He fed on bourgeois fears of a Bolshevik revolution in Italy, formed an alliance with the *squadristi*, and convinced Italian elites to financially support his newspaper, *Popolo d'Italia*.

In order to curb the growing influence of Mussolini, Giolitti hoped to co-opt the fascists by including them in the government, a tactic he had used with the socialists prior to the First World War. He invited the fascists to be on the government ticket during the 1921 elections, which they accepted, and won thirty-six parliamentary seats.[130] The prime minister's plan appeared to be working and, within a few months, Mussolini had proposed a truce with the socialists. This action on Mussolini's part raised the ire of the *squadristi* leaders and almost led to his downfall within the fascist movement, demonstrating the precariousness of Mussolini's position within the party. The future Il Duce quickly began to endorse the violent tactics of the blackshirts and, in the fall of 1921, after the Partito Nazionale Fascista (PNF) was created, the *squadristi* became the movement's private army.[131]

By the middle of 1922, PNF membership was over 300,000. In the summer of that year, the blackshirts targeted towns in northern Italy, mainly socialist strongholds. A general strike in Genoa was forcibly halted, with the city then falling under fascist control. Milan was the next and last socialist city to fall into the hands of the fascists. After a few hours of fighting leftists in the streets, the fascists had succeeded in smashing the printing presses of the local socialist daily *L'Avanti* (Forward) and setting fire to movement buildings. Mussolini and the fascists were now too powerful to be stopped. An offer made to the PNF to join a coalition government was dismissed by Mussolini. With the Italian parliament dissolved, the Italian king refused to declare martial law and, instead, invited Mussolini to form a new government. Mussolini arrived in Rome by train in October 1922, to assume his position as Italy's dictator.[132]

The rise to power of the fascists was a monumental blow to anarchists and the wider Italian Left. The constant attacks and continual repression made it difficult for anarchists to maintain their organizing activities. According to historian Carl Levy, anarchists most likely experienced the greatest violence, in comparison to other tendencies on the Left between 1921 and 1926, which forced many to leave Italy or live in poverty.[133]

The success of anarchism in Italy was related to the particular patterns of its state formation. Prior to unification in 1861, the Italian peninsula was fragmented into a series of kingdoms and city-states, and, in the aftermath of the Risorgimento, the Italian state could hardly be considered united. For the overwhelming majority of the peninsula's population, unification meant marginalization and exclusion. It was under these conditions that Italy's anarchist movement flourished. It also laid the groundwork for what would become its transnational North American component. It was in Italy, after years of experimentation with other forms, that the two most influential strains of anarchism, anti-organizationalist anarchist communism and anarcho-syndicalism, developed and were put into practice. As Italian anarchists began to migrate to Canada and the United States, they carried with them their anarchist politics and experiences as activists. In effect, they embodied and expanded this intricate history. Once in North America, they were able to recreate the anarchist milieu they had been part of in Italy with its newspapers, *circoli*, and antagonisms.

CHAPTER TWO

MIGRANT ANARCHISTS

Migration among the peoples of the Italian peninsula can be traced to the early sixteenth century when peasants began sojourning as a means of economic survival.[1] But it was not until the late nineteenth and early-to-mid twentieth centuries that a truly mass migration of Italians occurred. From 1876 to 1942, around 18.5 million Italians migrated to other parts of Europe, North and South America, the northern and southern coasts of Africa, Australia, and the Middle East.[2] Most of the historical works concerning this process focus on the experiences of Italians from certain regions of Italy or the history of Italian migrants more generally.[3] The picture of Italian migration that emerges from these studies is of one that was typically seasonal and temporary. As we have seen, some would migrate to urban centres within Italy or to other countries to find work in the winter, and return to their home villages in the summer to resume working in the fields. In this way, incomes received from migrant labour supplemented local livelihoods and allowed families to avoid reliance on one specific source of income, thus reducing the negative impacts of periods of economic crisis.[4] Migrants abroad often sent remittances home to family members or tried to save their earnings to buy their own land upon their return to Italy. However, financial considerations were not the only impetus for migration; Italians also left home for other reasons, ranging from failed courtship and the avoidance of military service to environmental devastation. Migrants from Italy were usually young, single peasant men in their early twenties. Sojourning Italians travelled through established migration networks created by those family members, friends, and *paesani* who had previously migrated.

The sojourns of Italian anarchists are relatively unstudied in the histories of Italian migration. Studies exist on the other elements of the Italian Left, such as the socialists, communists, and syndicalists. They explore how these well-established Italian political cultures were transplanted to the United States.[5] But there is no parallel monograph-length study for anarchists in America or elsewhere. This has left a hole in the existing scholarship on Italian migration history in general, and radical migration history in particular. Did it mean something different to be an Italian anarchist migrant, as opposed to a communist or socialist one? Were an anarchist's reasons for leaving Europe the same as those of other Italians? How did the experience of the non-anarchist migrant compare to that of the anarchist? During the closing decades of the nineteenth century, various sites of anarchist settlement outside of Italy were established in countries like France, Switzerland, Argentina, Brazil, Canada, and the United States. Like other elements of the Italian left, anarchists who migrated to distant parts of the world brought with them a distinct political philosophy and culture. These transnational radicals continued their political activities against the state, created anarchist newspapers, and kept their comrades abreast of events, both locally and internationally. In the 1920s and 1930s, they also took to the streets to combat fascism within the contested neighbourhoods of the various "Little Italies." Though the migrant experiences of Italian anarchists share similarities with those of other non-anarchist Italian migrants, political activism and its consequences—state violence and prison terms—played as significant a role in the decision of anarchists to migrate as did the need for waged labour. Yet, not all Italians emigrated as anarchists. For others, it was the migrant experience that led to their politicization. Dangerous working conditions, low pay, crowded tenements, and racism could quickly dispel preconceived notions of what life would be like in Canada or the United States after arrival. In his study of Italian and Jewish migrant anarchists, historian Kenyon Zimmer suggests that "American conditions ... usually forged migrants into anarchists, rather than Euopean ones."[6] However, I would argue that in the case of the Italian anarchists, politicization could have occurred prior to migrating or as a result of experiences in a new country.

The Casellario Politico Centrale (CPC) files at the Archivio Centrale dello Stato in Rome were a major resource for this book. CPC files can be located with the help of an online database that allows the researcher to search by name, place of birth, place of residence, political persuasion, or *busta* (folder) number, if known.[7] For the Canadian-based subjects of this book, I entered the terms "anarchist" and "Canada" into the database and was given a list of thirty-nine names, thirty-six of which I was able to access while in Rome. A link for each name opened a page that listed the *busta* number (necessary for ordering files on site), the dates the file was active, as well as personal information on the subject such as place and year of birth, place of residence, and occupation. A general database search for anarchists living in the United States resulted in a list of more than 5,000 persons, too great a number to sift through for this project. It then became necessary to search the database for the names of specific subjects who were involved in the anarchist circles of Detroit, New York City, and Newark. Through this method, I was able to obtain forty-five security files on Italian anarchists who had lived in America.

CPC files come in a light brown cardstock folder, with a file number in blue in the upper left-hand corner. The subject's name is written in pen across the top of the folder. Below the subject's name appears the Ministry of the Interior, which oversaw the CPC files, followed by the various subdepartments within the ministry that are responsible for security matters. These included the General Directorate of Public Security and the Reserved and General Affairs Division. Below this last appears Casellario Politico Centrale, followed by a series of columns. The two columns on the left side of the folder were reserved for inputting the dates of each report while a third column on the right with the heading *"Richiamo ad altri fascioli"* (Refer to other documents) had information on the subjects' political persuasion and whether they lived in Italy or abroad. The right column on the front of Windsor, Ontario's Egidio Artico stated that he was an anarchist who lived in North America, was considered *pericoloso* (dangerous), and went by the name "Jack." If a subject had died, *"Morto"* was stamped in red on the front of the file folder. On the inside cover of the folder was listed Artico's full name (Egidio Domenico Artico), the names of his parents (Giovanni Artico and Carrissima Flumiani), his place and date of birth (Mereto di Tomba, Udine, on 3 September 1906), his vocation (worker), his place of residence (North America), and his political identification (listed once again).[8] Below this was a section titled *"Connotati"* or Distinguishing Marks. This section of Artico's file was left blank but there were three columns beginning on the left side that allowed for a very detailed physical description of the subject, including their height, build, hair (colour, style, and thickness), face (complexion, shape, and dimensions), forehead (shape, protrusion, and dimensions), eyes (shape, dimensions, and colour), nose (shape and dimensions), ears (shape and dimensions), moustache (shape, thickness, and colour), beard (shape, thickness, and colour), jaw, chin, wrinkles, mouth (shape and dimensions), neck (length and width), shoulders, legs, hands, feet, gait, countenance, usual clothing, and identifying marks (scars, tattoos, deformities, etc.). Below *"Connotati"* there was space for a photograph and most files usually contained at least one of the subject. The pictures could be a mug shot showing front and side profiles or a studio portrait. The appearance of the latter in these files leads me to believe that the parent or parents of anarchists were approached by Italian security for this purpose. In some of the files I examined, a picture of the anarchist's wife was also included, as was the case with New York City's Donato Carrillo, whose file contained a picture of his partner Agata Pesce.[9]

Personal information on subjects was sometimes compiled into a handwritten or typed biography, describing the personality of the individual in question. The authors of these biographies, often the prefects of the anarchists' hometowns, commented on their subjects' educational backgrounds, familial relationships, run-ins with the law, and so on. A description of Vincenzo Capuana, who was born in the commune or municipality of Fezzano in the Liguria region and migrated to the United States in 1924, provides an example:

> [Capuana] has a bad public reputation, has little [formal] education, has a shrewd intelligence, [and is] of mediocre cultivation. He is a weak worker. [Towards] his family he behaves badly. He is frequently in the company of subversives and previous [criminal] offenders. He is a member of the anarchist party and no evidence exists to show that he had belonged to any other parties. He has taken part in all subversive gatherings and meetings of the anarchists. During his time in Spezia he engaged in propaganda among comrades at work. He had never held an administrative position in the movement. He collaborated with subversive newspapers and maintained correspondence with subversives abroad. He holds little reverence for authority. He is of a hard-headed and impetuous character. He served in the military and during WWI was declared a deserter two times. He is a persistent antifascist and dangerous element who is watched attentively.[10]

These biographies also traced the activities and movements of their subjects as the information was gathered by the Italian state's security apparatus in Italy and abroad. Below is an excerpt from Dulio Giorgini's CPC file:

> 18 Jan. 1909: Took part in a meeting held in Fano by the noted anarchist Cesare Naldini, where he was side by side with Naldini during his stay there.

> 28 Feb. 1910: Because of previous conduct and because he is considered dangerous, Giorgini is being surveilled.

> 26 June 1910: Giorgini leaves Fano for unknown destination in search of work.

> 31 July 1910: Giorgini found at Cattolica where he found work with the builder Pio Basetta.

22 Aug. 1910: He returns to Fano from Cattolica.

23 Aug. 1910: Giorgini leaves Fano for Rome to look for work.

2 July 1911: He returned home to interact with his family at Fano, where he stays now.

20 Feb. 1912: Supplied with a passport for Canada he leaves for Genoa from where on the night of the 23rd he will board the steamer "Duca D'Aosta" direct from Napoli to New York.

14 Apr. 1912: On 7 Mar 1912 Giorgini arrived in New York and then was found living with Oddo Ghiandoni in Sudbury, Ontario.

17 June 1928: Giorgini immigrated to Canada in 1912.

8 Aug. 1929: Giorgini still believed to be living in Canada but exact whereabouts unknown because he has not written to his relatives in many months.

25 Feb. 1931: The house of Giorgini's mother, Rosa Carradorini, was searched in order to confiscate letters from her antinational son or to ascertain his address. Nothing was found.

29 May 1935: [Giorgini] resides in Detroit, Michigan. He is still [an] anarchist but limits his involvement in political activity. He takes part in an antifascist league in Detroit.[11]

As this excerpt indicates, Giorgini was watched attentively by Italian security while still living in Italy. Authorities also knew his departure date to Canada and what steamship he was going to take. After Giorgini's arrival in Sudbury, Ontario, in 1912, there is a sixteen-year gap in his file. This absence may be due to Italian security losing track of Giorgini, a lack of resources for surveillance in Sudbury, or Giorgini being of low priority for Italian authorities. It does appear, however, that once the Fascists came to power in Italy in the 1920s, locating and reporting on Giorgini's activities became important once again—so much so that local police paid a visit to the anarchist's mother in an attempt to discover a current address.

CPC files can also contain correspondence between anarchists. Nicola "Nick" Di Domenico, the manager of *L'Adunata dei Refrattari*, corresponded with his nephew Giuseppe De Luisi, also an anarchist, who was imprisoned at Pozzuoli near Naples.[12] The majority of correspondence in these files, however, is between consul generals in various North American cities and the Ministers of the Interior and Foreign Affairs in Rome. The contents of these letters included the most recent addresses and political activities of their subjects.

The files also included mailing lists for certain anarchist publications, reports on interactions between different anarchist circles, the events they held, and sometimes provided the names of anarchists involved in a particular group.

The amount of information contained in each CPC file depends on who the subject was and where that person lived. For instance, the file of Raffaele Schiavina, editor of New York City's *L'Adunata dei Refrattari* contains 304 pages, while that of Domenico Moscardelli of Il Gruppo Libero Pensiero in Sault Ste. Marie, Ontario, has only eleven pages.[13] As a result, some CPC files are more complete than others. However, even in the files of anarchists who did not generate a great deal of paperwork, important information can still be found. These sources do not record the experiences of Italian anarchists as migrants, the racism they may have encountered, or the exploitation they faced as workers. Instead, I have had to rely on existing oral histories and interviews in order to flesh out the migrant experience of Italian anarchists. Although holes do exist within these sources, general conclusions can be drawn from them.

Figure 4. Raffaele Schiavina (Max Sartin). Busta 4690, CPC, ACS.

The picture that emerges from these sources reveals a movement largely made up of men ranging in age from the mid-teens to the mid-forties, with the majority in their twenties and thirties. Most of those who migrated to Canada tended to come from the northern and central regions of Italy whereas those who came to the United States often originated from both northern and southern Italy. Why did so many migrate? Their reasons included poverty, military conscription, political persecution, and various combinations of all three. Italian anarchist migration was often facilitated either through familial migration or anarchist networks. Regardless of the exact channels, Italian anarchists settled in areas where previous anarchist migrants had already established themselves. Some anarchists did not remain in the same place indefinitely. For example, those who originally came to Canada may have crossed into the United States for better employment opportunities. And, in contrast with the majority of Italian migrants, most anarchists in this study were trained in some kind of trade, whether as bakers, bricklayers, electricians, or typographers, to name but a few.

Where the CPC collection leaves a gaping void, at least within the North American context, is in regards to the lack of files on women in the anarchist movement. This absence could be due to the nature of Italian migration, since it often entailed single men crossing the Atlantic, which in turn was reflected in the gender composition of the Italian anarchist movement in Canada and the United States. It is also in part due to my reliance on Paul Avrich's *Anarchist Voices* to provide names for Italian anarchists, especially in the United States, when the majority of Italians he interviewed were men. He did conduct oral histories with Concetta Silvestri, Jenny Salemme, and Catina D'Amico Willman, but could have gone much further. For example, during his interview with Dominick Sallitto, a Sicilian-born anarchist who was almost deported from the United States in 1934, Avrich mentions the presence of Sallitto's partner Aurora Alleva, who provided the men with lunch. Alleva was an anarchist militant in her own right, speaking publicly and writing articles for *L'Adunata dei Refrattari*, but, possibly because he was unaware of this fact, Avrich did not record Alleva's reminiscences. Curiously, Sallitto does not mention his partner once in his interview.[14] Studies by historians Caroline Merithew and Jennifer Guglielmo have further demonstrated that the Italian anarchist movement was not exclusively male.[15] The existence of CPC files on women anarchists, such as the New York City–based poet Virgilia D'Andrea and Maria Vecile of Sault Ste. Marie's Il Gruppo Libero Pensiero, shows that Italian authorities were aware of women as political actors.[16] If the Italian state was so concerned with the surveillance of anarchists living in North America, then why did it focus predominantly on the movement's men? Guglielmo has stated that it was typical for anarchist *circoli*, or circles, to be largely male in composition while women were more likely to form their own women's groups.[17] Male migration numbers aside, it seems that a gender bias on the part of Italian authorities can also explain the dearth of CPC files on women.

A second important source for fleshing out the experiences of Italian anarchists has been the Italian-language newspapers *L'Adunata dei Refrattari* and *Il Martello*. Both were published in the United States and are readily available on microfilm. Not only do these publications provide the researcher with articles explaining different anarchist theories and viewpoints on local and international events, but they also track the activities of anarchist circles. Each issue of these respective newspapers had a page dedicated to listing events and printing the names of groups and individuals who contributed funds to a particular paper or cause. For example, if Detroit's Il Gruppo "I Refrattari" held a benefit for comrades persecuted in Europe, they would advertise this event in the "*Communicazioni*" section of *L'Adunata dei Refrattari*. Once the event had taken place, Il Gruppo "I Refrattari" would place another notice in the paper, listing their costs in putting on the event, how much money was raised, and the total amount to be donated after expenses. The movement of individuals can also be traced in this way, since it was common for names of subscribers and their cities of residence to be published.

From 1870 until the outbreak of the First World War, 4 million Italians migrated to Canada and the United States, with the overwhelming majority settling in the latter.[18] During the 1890-1920 period, for instance, roughly 126,647 Italians arrived in Canada as opposed to more than 14.5 million in the United States. Even during periods of migration restriction, the United States always experienced greater numbers of Italian migrants than did Canada.[19] This disparity in numbers was due, in part, to the scale of rapid industrialization that occurred south of the Canadian border, and the dire need of capital for cheap immigrant labour to maintain this process. Canada also needed immigrants at the turn of the twentieth century, but the official line of the Canadian government placed emphasis on the need for agricultural workers to settle in the Canadian West. Basing his opinion on what he perceived to be the case in the United States, Clifford Sifton, the Canadian Minister of the Interior from 1896 to 1905, felt Italians did not make good immigrants because they were far more likely to settle in urban centres instead of agricultural regions.[20] Thus, the Canadian government did not actively encourage Italian settlement. In addition, the Italian Commissariat of Emigration, under the Ministry of Foreign Affairs, published a series of discouraging bulletins on Canada, arguing that only wealthy peasants would be able to settle there successfully.[21] But even this lack of support from the Canadian and Italian governments did not prevent a system of seasonal migration from being established between the two countries in the early twentieth century.[22] The official line on immigration coming from Ottawa may have been that Canada required agricultural workers, but the realities of Canadian immigration were quite different. Capitalists needed unskilled labour for their businesses in the ever-expanding industrial sector. This meant that the thousands of mostly male Italian labourers who migrated to Canada in the years before 1914, expecting to engage in farm labour, were often channelled into factories, resource extraction, and building such infrastructure projects as railways, bridges, canals, and dams.[23] If labourers were in short supply, the United States became a site of recruitment. Migrants would typically arrive in Canada during the early summer to do seasonal labour, with the intention of returning to Italy in the fall. However, the trip home did not always materialize. Low wages and high costs of living could mean having to delay one's return to Italy, forcing some migrants to spend winter months existing precariously in Canada.[24] Those migrants who could not return home, or who eventually chose to stay in Canada, gravitated toward the urban centres of Montreal or Toronto, with their more favourable employment opportunities. Cities were generally favoured by Italian migrants because of the urban need for labourers to construct and maintain roads and sewers. Such centres could also provide an opportunity for Italians to go into business for themselves and open their own modest grocery stores or shoe repair shops.[25]

Italians who migrated to the United States found themselves working in resource extraction and infrastructure construction as they did in Canada, especially in the western states. They also came to the United States as replacement labour for freed slaves.[26] In addition to constructing roads, sewers, and buildings, Italian migrants would also be employed in the textile mills of Massachusetts and New Jersey and the steel mills of Pennsylvania. As in Canada, the majority of Italians tended to settle in America's larger urban centres such as New York, Boston, and Chicago, where employment opportunities tended to be greatest. Cities could also provide an escape from the brutal working and living conditions of isolated labour camps.[27]

The majority of Italian migrants were males, but women also migrated, though often in the company of family. While it may have been more likely for women to travel with family members than make the sojourn alone, one has to keep in mind that they, too, were labour migrants. Their ability to contribute to the household income would be just as important as male earnings.[28] Between 1876 and 1915, women comprised 19 percent of all migrants from Italy, while in the 1916–1945 period, 33 percent of the migrants were women. Employment options for women were more restricted than for men, but jobs could be found in the garment or service industries. Another option, especially among married women, was to take in boarders to supplement family incomes. Boarders could be relatives or *paesani* from Italy who paid low fees for accommodation, meals, and laundry service. The money brought in from boarders was only a third of what could be earned working outside the home, but such income could be a blessing for mothers struggling to raise children. Additionally, taking in boarders might well be the only type of work available to women in smaller resource extraction centres.[29]

Even with the low wages that Italian migrants received in North America, their earnings made a real difference to families in Italy. Sending remittances in Canadian or American funds was easier than having one's family travel to North America, where the reality of the low wages meant it was difficult to support a family. Migrants would usually save money by boarding, foregoing entertainment, and being thrifty when buying food.[30] In some cases, migrants planned to work a season in Canada or the United States and earn enough money to return to Italy and buy land. They might therefore make many trips to North America. A male sojourner could migrate as a youth to help support his immediate family; then, with a family of his own, spend a season abroad; and make yet another voyage later to support ailing parents.[31]

Italian migrants were often exploited in North America. They worked in dangerous conditions for low pay, may have had part of their wages kept by a foreman or *padrone*, could be forced to pay inflated prices for goods at company stores, and, as manual labourers, had no job security as they moved from one workplace to another. Sometimes they acted as strike-breakers.[32] Italian workers, however, did not always quietly accept their exploitation. Forms of resistance included work slowdowns, refusal to work, or quitting. As migrants, Italian labourers were in a precarious situation, especially if a *padrone* was holding their wages until the end of the season. *Padroni* were men who acted as labour agents, selling jobs to migrants who wanted them for a fee and, thus, facilitated the migration of single labourers or whole families from Italy to the Americas and elsewhere. *Padroni* are often viewed as corrupt exploiters of immigrant labour who made their money by cheating migrants of their wages. Labour agents of this sort, such as Montreal's Antonio Cordasco, the self-crowned "king of Italian labourers," definitely existed. Cordasco had a monopoly on providing the Canadian Pacific Railway with unskilled workers during the early twentieth century. He would charge migrants for their voyage across the Atlantic, finding them employment, as well as transporting them to the work site. Food for Italian labourers was provided by the labour agent's travelling commissary service, whereby the cost of items was deducted from the migrants' wages. In order to ensure the good behaviour of workers in the field, wages were kept by Cordasco in Montreal until a worker's term of employment expired. Not all *padroni* wielded as much power as Cordasco. However, Italian migrants were dependent on *padroni* and this could lead to exploitation and manipulation.[33] The need for a *padrone* was eventually circumvented through chain migration, whereby a migrant would travel to a destination outside of Italy with a prepaid ticket, with friends and/or family eventually following the same route.[34]

In North America, during the late nineteenth and early to mid-twentieth centuries, the Italian migrant was viewed in a very complex and contradictory manner. This was in part due to the racism of the time as well as the formation of national identities in Canada and the United States. Within this context, the Italian migrant was constructed as the exact opposite of what it meant to be a Canadian or an American.[35] Thus, Italians were portrayed as criminals and anarchists by employers and strikebreakers by non-Italian co-workers. Italians also had a complex relationship with whiteness—that complex set of socially-constructed privileges derived from defining the non-white Other, one so normalized in North America that its daily existence is unmarked. The benefits of whiteness include living relatively free of police harassment, being favoured in job interviews, learning white history in school, and seeing whites represented predominantly in all forms of media.[36] In both Canada and the United States, whiteness became the criterion by which all other peoples were judged. For Italians, whether they were considered white or non-white by the host societies of Canada and the United States or their respective governments depended on context and location. In the United States, for example, Italian migrants could be considered black in the southern states and white in the northern states.

Racist ideology has had a long history as a means of justifying one group's brutality over another. It has also played an important role in creating national or ethnic identities. During the nineteenth century, attempts were made to prove scientifically the racial superiority of one group over another. Those who sought scientific proof for their racial superiority were given great impetus with the publication of Charles Darwin's research on natural selection. Intellectuals, who became known as Social Darwinists, began to apply Darwin's theories on nature to humankind, arguing that there was a correlation between race and progress. Because the majority of Social Darwinists[37] were men from countries located in northwestern Europe, it was not surprising that the white male European/Caucasian was viewed as the apex of evolution. As the German biologist Ernst Haeckel wrote, "The Caucasian … man has from time immemorial been placed at the head of all the races of men, as the most highly developed and perfect."[38] Eastern and southern Europeans, not to mention the peoples of other continents, did not fare well in this hierarchy. And, according to historian Michael Miller Topp, southern Italians were often deemed the lowest of the European races.[39]

The idea that the various peoples of the earth could be ranked hierarchically, based on their supposed progress, enjoyed a great deal of currency during this period of mass migration. These prejudiced views informed the treatment, often entailing discrimination and violence, that Italian migrants and others received from the host societies of Canada and the United States. In some cases, the justification for classifying Italians as an inferior race, or to limit the number of Italians admitted by Canadian or American immigration, was actually provided by Italian "scholars" who were involved in the racist construction of their co-nationals.[40]

The study of Italy's citizens began in earnest following the Risorgimento. During this period, positivism, a philosophy that bases itself on the premise that "actual sense experience" is the only means of gathering "authentic" knowledge, flourished within the country's universities, and scholars attempted to convert certain disciplines, such as sociology, anthropology, and criminology, into precise sciences. The "scholarship" that resulted tended to argue in favour of the supremacy of northern Italians over their southern counterparts. For instance, the Italian sociologist Alfredo Niceforo, who wrote such books as *La Deliquenza in Sardegna* (1897) and *Lo Studio Scientifico delle Classi Poveri* (The Scientific Study of the Poor Classes; 1907), asserted that Italians from the northern regions of the country were Teutonic Aryans while those of the south were a mixture of Europeans and Africans. In addition, the research conducted by the Italian criminologist Cesare Lombroso further denigrated the inhabitants of southern Italy. He argued that delinquency was an inherited trait that could be identified by physical characteristics, such as high cheekbones, among others. In an article he wrote in 1902 entitled "The Last Brigand," Lombroso asserted that southern Italians were genetically predisposed to criminal behaviour.[41]

The "scholarship" of Niceforo and Lombroso contributed, inadvertently or otherwise, to the ill treatment of Italians as they migrated abroad.[42] In 1911, the United States Immigration Commission's *Dictionary of Races of People* quoted Niceforo when it divided Italians from the North and the South into two distinct ethnic groups, claiming that the Italians of these two regions "differ as radically in psychic [sic] characters as they do in physical."[43] In Canada and the United States during the late nineteenth and early twentieth centuries, Italians, especially those with darker complexions—originating in southern

Italy—were not always considered to be white.[44] More research needs to be conducted on the implications of this pattern within the Canadian context. The United States situation has been more completely explored. In the southern states, southern Italians, considered to be on the lowest rung of Europe's evolutionary ladder, confronted a racism that at times shared similarities with that oppressing African Americans. The United States government went as far as to make a distinction between northern and southern Italians in its immigration statistics, beginning in 1899.[45] During this time, the term "guinea," which was used as a racist term for African Americans, began also to be directed against Italians. Though the racism experienced by Italians in the southern states was never as pervasive or systemic as the racism experienced by blacks, Italians were segregated and barred from streetcars, schools, theatres, and churches. In a few well-known cases, Italian migrants even became victims of lynchings.[46]

In the southern United States, Italian migrants were also labelled as blacks because of the types of labour they performed. Italians were employed by plantations to pick crops, such as cotton, a form of labour that had traditionally been done by blacks. Italians also intermingled with African Americans who were working on the cotton fields, which, according to scholar Joseph Cosco, resulted in Italians being equated socially and economically with blacks.[47] In Canada, work was racialized by nativist workers. "Black" labour was considered the most dangerous, poorly paid, and vile available—jobs often taken on by Italians and other southern or eastern European and Asian migrants. In the eyes of some Anglo-Celtic labourers, the fact that Italians and others would work in such wretched conditions was proof of their racial inferiority.[48]

In the context of the United States, however, the experiences of Italian migrants differed between the northern and southern states. Though Italians were more likely to be considered black in the South and at times were treated in a fashion similar to blacks, Italians who settled in the northern states tended to benefit from whiteness. Historian Thomas Guglielmo's study of Italians in Chicago from 1890 to 1945 shows that Italians were "white on arrival" and had access to all the advantages of whiteness. For example, Italian migrants were not targeted by restrictive covenants nor were they singled out during Chicago's 1919 race riot that erupted between Irish Americans and blacks. Italians were still considered an inferior people in the North but they did not face the same barriers as did African Americans.[49]

The United States Immigration Commission's *Dictionary of Races of People* went on to characterize southern Italians as having a genetic predisposition to "excitable, impulsive, [and] highly imaginative" behaviour. In addition, southern Italians were deemed to be too individualistic, which made them incapable of adapting to highly organized society. The northern Italians, on the other hand, were considered "cool, deliberate, patient, practical and capable of great progress on the political and social organization of modern civilization."[50] Lombroso's ideas regarding the criminality of Italians also spread and gained acceptance, especially among those who opposed Italian migration to Canada and the United States. By the late nineteenth century, not only were racial distinctions being made between northern and southern Italians, but diagnoses of the supposed criminal and impassioned nature of Italians in general were also firmly upheld. Italians were often described as "stiletto-wielding criminals," anarchists, or members of the mafia.[51]

According to immigration historian Robert Harney, the media stereotypes and popular misconceptions to which Italians were subjected were similar to the portraits of "bad natives" in more straightforwardly colonial settings. Italians were described as animalistic, shiftless, likely to engage in violent behaviour, and peculiarly susceptible to the influence of a leader. The Canadian and American popular presses often made a point of reporting on violence within Italian communities, thus reinforcing negative stereotypes about Italian migrants. Violence among Italians was often attributed to their passionate nature or involvement in organized crime and, though physical confrontations did occur and some Italians were involved in illegal activities—as happens in all communities everywhere—these portrayals made it seem as though violent behaviour was peculiarly Italian. Unfortunately, with the host societies of Canada and the United States already believing Italian migrants to be inherently violent, the actions of Gaetano Bresci, the Italian anarchist who assassinated King Umberto I of Italy in 1900, could only have strengthened this opinion in the minds of Canadians and Americans.[52]

Conceptions of Italians as labourers were many and various. Employers who relied on the guest worker program to fill their need for workers viewed Italians as a docile and malleable workforce. However, once Italian workers began to assert themselves, disrupt production, or go on strike, employers began to label them as radical troublemakers. Nativist elements among Canadian and American labour viewed the arrival of Italian migrants as a threat to job security. Various businesses did hire immigrants in order to depress wages or break strikes, leading to a widespread misconception that most Italians were scabs. However, a wide body of literature on Italian labour radicals in North America has challenged this stereotype.[53]

During the interwar period, Italian migration to North America declined due to a series of restrictive immigration policies targeting "less desirable" immigrants, implemented by both the Canadian and American governments at the behest of capital. These restrictions were deemed necessary by both countries in order to address economic crises, xenophobia/racism, and social unrest. The United States tended to spearhead these anti-immigrant initiatives, with Canada following suit.

After the First World War ended, the massive output of wartime economies slowed down dramatically. In Canada and the United States, jobs were in short supply and unemployment was on the rise. Many of the unemployed were migrants who, in times of boom, were considered a necessary element of capitalist prosperity. Once the economy faced a serious downturn, they became expendable.[54] At the same time, veterans began returning home and looking for work. In Canada especially, they felt jobs should be their reward for the fulfillment of their patriotic duties. Many Canadian or British-born veterans believed that migrants should be removed from places of work to make way for returning soldiers. Xenophobia and outright racism prevailed in many places. This was coupled with an already-entrenched nativism among the majority of Canada's dominant Anglo-Celtic population. Anti-immigrant sentiment was also an issue in the United States. According to the elites of both nations, southern and eastern Europeans were the least desirable migrants after the Chinese. Not only were these groups considered alien in appearance and custom, but they also lived in crowded migrant neighbourhoods, areas of perceived criminal and morally unacceptable behaviour, and home to the foreign radical.[55]

The success of the Russian communists in overthrowing the tsar in 1917 fired the imaginations of socialists around the world and caused more than a few North American capitalists to fear a possible communist-led revolution in Canada and/or the United States. Measures had to be taken to protect the interests of Canadian and American ruling elites and capital. The image of the bomb-wielding foreigner was dusted off and used, as it had been following the 1901 McKinley assassination. Both states unleashed the full might of their respective security forces: strikes were crushed by police, the offices of left-wing newspapers ransacked, and various socialist, communist, and anarchist groups were infiltrated, though the intensity of this repression was greater in the United States than it was in Canada.[56] Show trials sentenced those guilty of "Bolshevik" tendencies to prison terms. Those unable to claim Canadian or American citizenship were often deported to their countries of birth.

These were the issues that led the United States to introduce a literacy bill that came into effect in 1920, which prevented illiterate migrants from entering the country. As literacy among Europeans increased, this legislation became less effective and led to an immigration quota in 1921. The law restricted European immigrants to 3 percent of the 1910 census, which meant that only 355,000 migrants would be allowed entrance into the United States. For Italians, who tended to have lower rates of literacy than northern Europeans, migration numbers dropped from 204,000 to 42,000 per year. This was still considered too high, so another restriction quota was introduced in 1924 that further limited the number of Italian migrants to the United States to less than 4,000 annually.[57] The introduction of restrictions to Italian immigration in North America led to more families migrating to join partners and simultaneously saw rates of migrant return to Italy increase between 1921 and 1945, with 83 percent of returnees moving from Canada and the United States.[58] Restrictions in North America did not lead to a decrease in the number of Italians leaving Italy. Rather, they simply travelled to other nations such as France, Argentina, and Brazil. In fact, following the First World War, Italian labourers were more likely to travel to other European nations, with France being the most popular destination, even more so than the United States.[59]

Canadian legislation tended to mirror that of its neighbour to the south, and also included the introduction of literacy laws and quotas to curb the number of migrants allowed into the country. Though it has been suggested that Canada did not enforce its anti-immigration laws to quite the same degree as the United States, the fact remains that these laws were in effect and implemented.[60] A quota law was passed in Canada in 1920, in part due to postwar depression and social unrest; additional pressure came from the United States after its own quota law came into effect. This new legislation included the requirement that each migrant carry a minimum of twenty-five dollars and hold a ticket to their final destination. They would only be allowed into Canada if they had arrived on a continuous journey ticket and, once landed, underwent strict health and literacy tests. In addition, only migrants who were farmers, farm workers, or domestic servants gained entrance.[61] As a result of this general Canadian quota, only immediate family members of resident immigrants and agricultural labourers were allowed into the country.[62] This legislation had the desired results. Between 1911 and 1920, 62,663 Italians migrated to Canada; but following the introduction of quotas, the number of Italians declined to 26,183 in the 1920s.[63] It must be noted, however, that in the mid-1920s, large numbers of immigrants were again entering Canada due to pressure from the private transportation companies, the Canadian Pacific Railway (CPR) and the Canadian National Railway (CNR), whose role in immigration and the settlement of migrants was a profitable aspect of operations. As a result, both the CPR and CNR signed the Railway Agreement with the federal government in 1925. This agreement allowed the railway companies to circumvent anti-immigration legislation and recruit farm labourers from southern and eastern Europe. During this period, the CPR and CNR definition of farm labourer was loosely interpreted. The Great Depression of the 1930s would again seriously restrict the entrance of migrants to Canada.[64]

United States and Canadian immigration restrictions were one reason for declining numbers of Italian migrants; Italian emigration rules were another. The Fascist government in Italy had its own ideas about migration and felt that its citizens were needed at home to work the land, build infrastructure, and serve in the military.[65] In fact, migration historian Franc Sturino asserts that Fascist regulation outweighed North American restrictions in curbing Italian immigration.[66] Following the Fascist immigration law of 1927, long-standing patterns of family reunification were disrupted. First, it denied the cousins of migrants permission to emigrate. Eventually, it also prevented in-laws, aunts and uncles, and unmarried siblings from doing so. One of the few ways that Italian migrants could leave Italy was by adding their name to a governmental list of workers guaranteed work abroad.[67] Preventing the movement of Italian migrants became moot when the global economy collapsed in 1929. Job opportunities in Canada and the United States dried up and, in order to avoid having to care for unemployed immigrants, both nations resorted to more restrictions.[68] During the 1930s, fewer than 4,000 Italians arrived in Canada.[69]

Who was an anarchist? In the eyes of the political theorist, as we have seen, an anarchist might be anyone supporting a political philosophy that holds the state to be harmful and replaceable, and supports and works for a stateless, free society. The Casellario Politico Centrale (CPC) files,[70] which monitored the Italian regime's enemies in the 1920s and 1930s, applied a somewhat different standard—one based on reputation, documented activism, and adherence to particular groups and leaders. Seventy files of such "anarchists" were examined for the purposes of this book. From these files, one can derive some fascinating impressions that greatly enrich our understanding of the anarchist movement in North America. One important theme they raise is that not all of these people arrived in North America as fully formed anarchists. Based on the CPC files, Italian authorities had twenty-one migrants listed as anarchists prior to their arrival in Canada while four became anarchists at some point after migration. (When exactly the remaining eleven migrants assumed their political identity is unknown.) For those anarchists in the files pertaining to the United States, the breakdown is as follows: nineteen were anarchists upon leaving Europe, seventeen became anarchists after their arrival in America, and the stories of nine are unknown. For some, particularly noticeable in the Canadian files, conversion to anarchism occurred prior to migration; for others, more prominent in those files relating to the United States, the opposite would be true.

These files suggest that the ages of anarchist migrants to North America tended to vary from the mid-teens to the mid-forties. The majority of them were in their twenties and thirties upon arrival in North America, which differs from the typical age of the early twenties among non-anarchist migrants. Eleven anarchists came to Canada between the ages of twenty and twenty-nine while seven arrived between thirty and thirty-four. Thus, eighteen Italians who were anarchists, or who would eventually identify as such, came to Canada between the ages of twenty and thirty-four. Five migrated to Canada in their teens (between the ages of fourteen and eighteen) while four arrived in their forties (between the ages of forty-one and forty-six). The ages of the remaining nine Italian anarchists are unknown because either their dates of birth were not recorded in their CPC files or their dates of arrival in Canada were unknown, or both. In the United States, thirteen arrived between the ages of twenty and twenty-eight while seven came between the ages of thirty and thirty-nine. Six migrated as teenagers (between the ages of seventeen and nineteen), while only five arrived in their forties (between the ages of forty and forty-four). Among this sample group, the age of fourteen individuals at the time of their arrival in the United States is unknown. With the exception of two women, all in this group are male.

Italian migrants who travelled to Canada came from all over the Mezzogiorno, from the regions of Lazio and Marche in central Italy, and Friuli and Veneto in the country's Northeast.[71] These findings generally correspond with those of anarchist migrants who came to Canada in the years between 1901 and 1940. Much like the wider non-anarchist migrant Italian population, the majority (fourteen) of those thirty-six individuals who were identified as anarchists in Canada came from the Marche region in central Italy. Twelve originated from northwestern Italy and six from the Mezzogiorno. An exception to the migration trend would be the two anarchists, Giuseppe Rolle and Agostino Confalonieri, who came from the northeastern regions of Piedmont and Lombardy, respectively.[72]

According to immigration historian Rudolph Vecoli, the vast majority of Italians who migrated to the United States were originally from the Mezzogiorno and, based on the CPC files, nineteen United States–bound anarchists, almost half, came from southern Italy.[73] However, twelve anarchists from this corpus originated from northern Italy while another eight migrated from the central part of the country. Again, this group is quite small and a wider study would have to be conducted to reach a definitive conclusion. Nonetheless, these initial findings suggest that Italian anarchists who migrated to the United States may have had more varied regions of origin than non-anarchist Italians.[74]

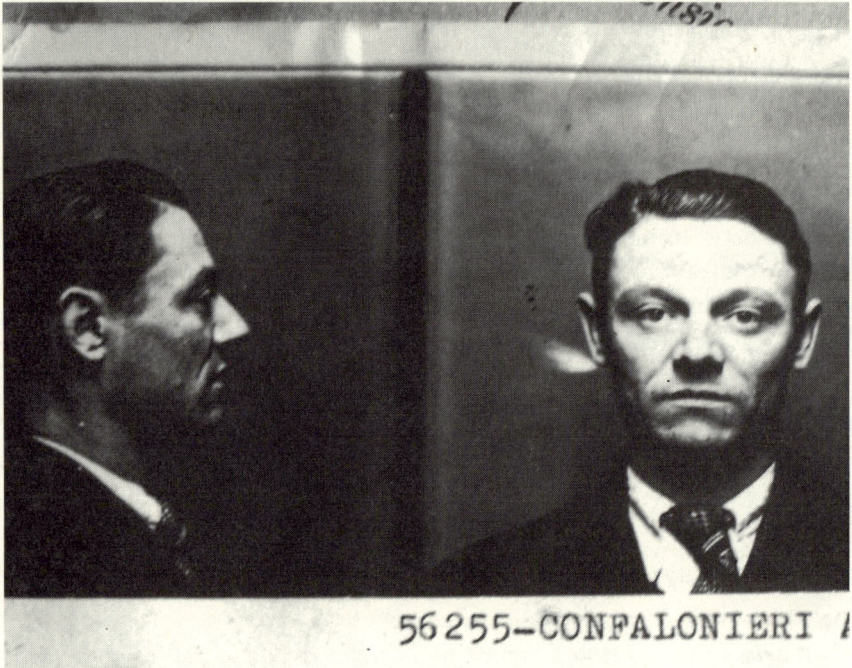

Figure 5. Agostino Confalonieri. Busta 1438, CPC, ACS.

Among the corpus of Italian anarchists migrating to Canada and the United States, there is not a significant difference in the numbers who came to North America before the First World War and after. In the Canadian context, fifteen anarchists arrived between 1901 and 1914 while fourteen migrated during the 1920–1940 period. The fourteen years prior to the war saw eighteen anarchists travel to America. After 1918, another twelve arrived. The immigration restrictions of the 1920s in both Canada and the United States do not appear to have played that great a role in preventing Italian anarchists from migrating to each country. During that period, nine anarchists arrived in Canada while thirteen went to the United States. The 1930s were a different story. The Great Depression and the resultant restrictions placed on immigration by receiving countries meant that anarchist migration in those years was seriously reduced. In the 1930s, only two anarchists, Ruggero Benvenuti and

Agostino Confalonieri, came to Canada.[75] In that same period, only Ernesto Bonomini travelled to the United States.[76] At no point during the First World War did any of the anarchists from this corpus migrate to North America.

The overwhelming majority of those who migrated from Italy did so in order to work. According to migration historian Donna Gabaccia, during the period 1876-1914, more than 14 million migrants travelled abroad for employment, as opposed to members of the elite, the second group she identifies, which numbered only 565.[77] This trend continued into the 1915-1945 period, when almost 4.5 million Italian migrants left their country, including only 188 elite members.[78] It is difficult to know the exact reason for Italian anarchist migration, due to the lack of definitive sources on the subject. However, what is evident is that anarchists, like their Italian co-nationals, often migrated to work abroad. For example, Vincenzo Gabbani arrived in Canada in 1912 and worked for a number of years on the construction of a power station, possibly located near Ottawa. By 1929, he had moved to Cobalt, Ontario, where he worked as a manual labourer and operated a boarding house.[79] Giulio Russiani settled in Sault Ste. Marie, Ontario, in 1921 and may have been employed by Algoma Steel, the town's main employer during this period.[80] Among the Canadian-based anarchists, five migrated for work while three living in the United States did so. Some anarchists, though not identifying as such while still youths, migrated with their families. Maria Vecile came to Canada along with her mother, in either 1902 or 1903, to reunite with her father, who worked in Sault Ste. Marie.[81] This only occurred in one other instance in the Canadian context and was more common with the Italian anarchists who migrated to the United States, where seven migrated with their families.

Other motives, such as war resistance or avoidance of the draft, could influence anarchist migration. Giuseppe Rolle left Italy before the outbreak of the First World War because he did not want to be forced to fight.[82] While in his mid-teens and living in his hometown of Codroipo, Attilio Bortolotti experienced the war first-hand. The senseless violence he witnessed convinced him that he never wanted to fight for any government. Bortolotti contacted his brother living in Canada in order to obtain the proper forms to initiate the migration process.[83]

State repression played a much larger role in anarchist migration than did the fear of military service. Vincenzo Capuana had been under heavy surveillance while living in Italy because of his anarchist activities. He served in the military during the First World War but deserted twice. On one of those occasions, he was sentenced to four months in jail. After the Fascists came to power, Capuana, committed to the antifascist cause, was "watched attentively" because he was considered dangerous by authorities. Employed as a merchant mariner, the anarchist jumped ship while in New York City, ostensibly because life in Italy was becoming too difficult.[84] Capuana was not the only anarchist to jump ship to avoid a return to Fascist-controlled Italy. Giovanni "John" Vattuone, a native of Carloforte, Sardinia, was a member of the Maritime Union and sailed on a cooperatively controlled ship bearing the musical name *Il Giuseppe Verdi*. When he arrived in New York City in 1920, a letter was waiting for him from his sister who still lived in Carloforte. She warned Vattuone about returning to Sardinia because local Fascists were aware of his radical views and activism. However, it was not until the Fascists became more powerful that Vattuone decided Italy was no longer safe for him. In September 1922, he, like Capuana, left his ship while docked in New York City.[85] In total, in our corpus of files, persecution resulted in three anarchists migrating to Canada and eight to the United States.

In at least one example, an anarchist had to leave Italy because of criminal activity that had nothing to do with anarchist activism. Efisio Constantino Zonchello was found guilty of embezzlement while living in Cagliari, Sardinia, in 1908. His security file is vague on the details surrounding this charge, but Zonchello was fined 250 lire, banned from holding any type of public office, and sentenced to ten months in jail. Not wanting to serve the time, he left Italy and later made his way to the United States.[86]

For Italian anarchists, there were two forms of migration: the standard familial or regional pattern and one that was specifically anarchist. Attilio Bortolotti, for instance, migrated to Windsor, Ontario, where his older brother Guglielmo had settled and was able to find his first job through an Italian contractor known by his sibling.[87] Such networks were crucial when anarchists needed to escape persecution in Italy or abroad. They played a key role in helping Italian anarchist fighters in the Spanish Civil War find their way to Canada and the United States.

The majority of the Italian anarchists from this group were trained in some kind of skilled labour, through which they became bakers, bricklayers, typographers, electricians, among other professions. But this did not necessarily mean that they were able to find work in their fields of expertise. Giulio Ghetti, who was a cobbler by trade and lived in Windsor, actually made his living as a delivery driver for a local bakery.[88] In many cases, it is hard to tell how many of these anarchists found their jobs in North America. Before the First World War, many may have used the *padrone* system and/or familial migration networks. Employment could also be secured through fellow anarchists. When Agostino Confalonieri arrived in Montreal in the fall of 1939, comrades there offered him work as a painter. However, because he was in Canada illegally, he declined the offer and stayed on the move.[89]

Italian anarchists migrated to towns and cities all over Canada and the United States, but a few cities in both countries deserve special attention. Sault Ste. Marie's Little Italy was in the city's west end, with James Street as the neighbourhood's commercial centre. The local Italian anarchists formed a circle known as Il Gruppo Libero Pensiero and had a hall on Albert Street West. At least three of the circle's members lived on the same street as their hall while others lived on Queen Street West, Rome Street, and Toronto Street, which were also located in the city's west end.[90] Algoma Steel was the main industry in Sault Ste. Marie and some of the anarchists from Il Gruppo Libero Pensiero worked in the mill.[91] The group was aligned with Carlo Tresca and his newspaper *Il Martello*. In 1919, Il Gruppo Libero Pensiero brought Tresca to Sault Ste. Marie, where he delivered a series of lectures.[92]

Toronto had more than one area of Italian settlement though it appears as though most anarchists lived near the Little Italy neighbourhood at Dufferin Street and Davenport Road, with Brandon Avenue being the focal point.[93] The neighbourhood began to coalesce in the 1890s, as Italian migrants settled in the area to work on maintaining the railway, constructing sewers, and building roads. In 1905, a foundry was opened by Canadian General Electric at the corner of Lansdowne Avenue and Davenport Road, which attracted more migrants to the area. Some of the earliest Italians to live in this neighbourhood came from the town of Terracina in the Lazio region. However, beginning in the 1920s, the migrants from Terracina were joined by others from the regions of Friuli-Venezia Giulia and Abruzzi. According to immigration historian John Zucchi, the Dufferin and Davenport Little Italy was primarily home to both skilled and unskilled labourers who worked in construction. The neighbourhood had numerous boarding houses operated by Italian migrants.[94] The boundaries of this Little Italy were Davenport Road to the north, Dufferin Street to the east, Dupont Street to the south, and the Canadian National Railway line to the west.[95] Addresses in the CPC files show Italian anarchists living on Brandon Avenue, which falls within these boundaries, but also on St. Clarens Avenue, just south of Dupont, to the east of Lansdowne Avenue; and on Gladstone Avenue, which lies one street east of Dufferin Street and runs south from Dupont Street.[96] The active anarchists in this neighbourhood were known as Il Gruppo Libertario and published a newspaper under the title *Il Libertario*.[97] Later, some of the Italians involved in this group joined the Libertarian Group, organized by Emma Goldman during her time in Toronto in the mid-1930s.[98]

Windsor was the site of another Little Italy. However, this Little Italy did not begin to form in earnest until the construction of St. Angela Merici Church on Erie Street in 1939, which acted as a focal point for the Italian community. Prior to 1939, Italians settled on Wyandotte Street and in the city's downtown.[99] By the 1920s, the number of Italians living in Windsor was quite small, with only 271 living in the city in 1921. This number would increase to more than 1,100 by the 1930s, as a result of a construction boom in the 1920s and jobs in the automobile manufacturing sector. Work in these occupations meant that Windsor's Italian community was predominantly working-class.[100] Windsor was also the third site of considerable anarchist presence in the province, with most of the anarchists living within the Wyandotte and Erie area. Italian anarchists resided on Howard Avenue and Mercer, McDougall, and Assumption Streets. It is unknown whether this group was identified by a name, but, during the 1920s, they did meet above a grocery store operated by Fortunato Mariotti, located at 500 Mercer Street. The store also had a modest anarchist library.[101] The Windsor anarchists organized regular social events and were active in antifascist struggle. They would also travel to Detroit to fight fascism and attend social events held by their comrades in that city.[102]

Detroit did not have a Little Italy. There were areas of Italian concentration but no specifically Italian neighbourhood. Italians initially settled in the city's downtown and later near Gratiot Street, in neighbourhoods that had previously been home to German migrants.[103] Information on the addresses of Detroit-based anarchists is scarce, but at least two still lived in the Gratiot area in the 1930s. Three more anarchists lived in Oakwood Heights, southwest of Gratiot and closer to Dearborn, which was a typical area for Italians to move once leaving Gratiot. Detroit's Italian anarchists were known as Il Gruppo "I Refrattari" and they organized numerous social events in and around Detroit to raise money for various anarchist causes. This group was an adherent of the New York City–based newspaper *L'Adunata dei Refrattari*.

As was the case with Windsor, Newark, New Jersey's Little Italy centred around a church, the Church of St. Lucy, which was built at 118 Seventh Avenue in 1891. Seventh Avenue acted as the community's hub, with Italians living in the surrounding area. The boundaries of this Little Italy were Parker Street to the west, Stone Street to the east, 8th Avenue to the south, and Park Avenue to the north. The community was comprised of Sicilians, Calabrese, and Neapolitans, as well as others from the Mezzogiorno. The Italians from these regions brought their religious customs with them and each town or *comune* celebrated its own saints, weekly, between June and October.[104] Newark was also the home of L'Adunata dei Refrattari, the anarchist circle responsible for writing, editing, and publishing the New York City–based anarchist newspaper of the same name. Others involved with the group did not have a "hands on" role with the production of the newspaper. L'Adunata may have had a meeting place at 8 Garside Street, which was located within Newark's Little Italy.[105]

Italian settlement in New York City was widespread, with migrants living in neighbourhoods all over the five boroughs. The city's well-known Little Italy was located on Mulberry Street in Manhattan, but it is not clear whether any Italian anarchists from this study lived in that community.[106] The office for Carlo Tresca's *Il Martello* was located in Manhattan but far north of Mulberry Street. A group of the same name was formed around the newspaper though where exactly its members lived in the city is unknown. Italian anarchists also resided in Brooklyn, which was home to Circolo Volontà and the South Brooklyn Group who were allied with *L'Adunata dei Refrattari*. Circolo Volontà was known to meet at 112 Troutman Street, but records did not reveal a meeting location for the South Brooklyn Group.[107]

The anarchists in these six cities comprised a part of the transnational network created by Italian anarchists on both sides of the Atlantic Ocean. Within North America, Italian anarchists travelled this network to find work, engage in activism, conduct speaking tours, or escape the authorities. In addition to the movement of anarchist militants, ideas, newspapers, and personal correspondence travelled between cities and across the Canada–United States border.

The Italian anarchist migrant experience shared some similarities with that of their non-anarchist co-nationals. Anarchist migrants were mostly men who travelled, via migration networks, to pre-established sites of Italian settlement in Canada and the United States. In the Canadian context, anarchist and non-anarchist migrants came from a variety of Italian regions. The greatest Italian migration to the United States was from the Mezzogiorno, but, at least judging from our small sub-population, anarchist migrants tended to come from all parts of Italy. As was the case for Italian migrants generally, anarchists also faced discrimination and outright racism. For the majority of Italian migrants, leaving home to find work was part of a long-standing pattern of sojourning. Yet, among anarchists, political persecution could also play as significant or greater a role in determining migration. As a result of their political activities, anarchists could be arrested, charged, and given long-term prison sentences. Under fascist rule, conditions worsened for anarchists, who increasingly found themselves targets of state violence. There were other differences between anarchist and non-anarchist migration. Anarchists tended to be of a wider range of ages than the average Italian migrant and were often trained in some type of skilled trade, although there was still no guarantee that they would find employment in these trades after arriving in North America.

The existing scholarship on Italian migration focuses on the process in a general way—why and where Italians migrated and their experiences migrating and living in non-Italian host countries. What has not received the same amount of attention is the migration of radical political movements. By examining the specific aspects of anarchist migration and how it compares with that of their co-nationals, a clearer picture of Italian migration begins to emerge. The push and pull factors that initiated migration were not necessarily the same for all Italians, especially when such traits as political identity are taken into consideration.

As Italian anarchists moved beyond Italy's borders, they brought not only their political philosophy but also their anarchist culture. While living in Canada or the United States, they organized themselves into *circoli* as they did in Italy, created *filodrammatiche* or amateur drama societies that performed anarchist-themed plays, and established Italian-language anarchist newspapers. This rich cultural output and its importance to movement expansion and retention is the subject of the next chapter.

CHAPTER THREE

ANARCHIST CULTURE

The late nineteenth and early twentieth centuries constituted a period of intense cultural output by the Left. Socialists, communists, and anarchists created an enormous diversity of artistic and cultural forms to challenge capitalism, unite activists, and direct political action. These forms included newspapers, political cartoons, folk dancing troupes, drama societies, choirs, and radical "holidays" among others. Whether it was the radical songs of the Industrial Workers of the World (IWW) or the mandolin orchestras of the Communist Party of Canada–affiliated Ukrainian Labour Farmer Temple Association, the Left used art and culture to resist the role of government and capital in creating patriotic and hard-working citizens committed to the perpetuation of the status quo. These forms were also "a means of unifying workers and ... a basis [from which] to move against the repressive social conditions of industrial development that extended beyond the point of production."[1] As "oppositional ideologies," socialism, communism, and anarchism not only had to demonstrate that there were alternatives to the capitalist liberal democratic order, but were also required to develop strategies for building and maintaining these movements.[2]

As Marcella Bencivenni has shown in her study on Italian immigrant radical culture in the United States, Italian migrants brought their radical cultural practices with them as they made their transnational journeys. These cultural practices would then be adapted to the new realities of life in a different country.[3] For Italian anarchists, these cultural practices manifested themselves in a variety of ways. Newspapers were an important means of communicating anarchist theories and views on current topics to the movement's faithful as well as to potential adherents. Paul Avrich has suggested that between 1870 and 1940 as many as 500 anarchist periodicals were produced in the United States, with Italian output comprising one-fifth of that total.[4] Publications like *Il Martello* and *L'Adunata dei Refrattari* also acted as a form of historical memory by printing commemorative obituaries to well-known radicals or featuring articles on aspects of anarchist history, such as the Paris Commune of 1871. But newspapers were not the only form of anarchist literature. Many pamphlets and books were published, either by those responsible for movement newspapers or by others in their spare time.[5]

Social events, such as dances, dinners, and plays performed by *filodrammatiche*, generally open to the wider Italian neighbourhood, also provided a way to attract new adherents. These social events combined entertainment and fundraising.[6] The plays were often local productions, though some *filodrammatiche* groups did tours of Italian communities to a limited extent. Plays dealt with anarchist themes, such as workers' exploitation under capitalism and the hypocrisy of religion, among others. The plays of anarchist songwriter and poet Pietro Gori were a popular choice among *filodrammatiche* groups, though the performance of plays written by less well-known anarchists was also common. Gori's plays were transnational and were performed by Italian anarchists in Canada, the United States, and other countries where Italian anarchists settled.[7] Events of this nature could be organized to raise badly needed funds for the movement or coincide with an anarchist "holiday."

Another way to reach prospective members was through public speaking. Prominent anarchists would tour Italian communities, speaking on a wide variety of subjects, from anarchism to Italian literature. If anarchist comrades found themselves in trouble with authorities, these speaking tours were an invaluable means of raising awareness and support for their cause. In addition to tours, anarchists also spoke publicly during strikes and antifascist rallies.

Anarchist groups were a central component in the promotion and maintenance of radical culture. Anarchist circles, where aspects of anarchist thought and literature could be discussed, provided an alternative to nationalist or religious associations. They also organized social events and made arrangements to host anarchist lecturers.[8] These groups, in all their remarkable diversity, made up Italian anarchism's vibrant transnational cultural network. Of equal importance was their ability to fundraise, not only for anarchist causes abroad but also to maintain their own institutions, such as halls and newspapers. Like IWW locals, anarchist circles used social and cultural events to educate, entertain, and mobilize their members.[9] As McCarthy and others have argued, mobilizing structures are "those collective vehicles ... through which people mobilize and engage in collective action."[10] In this way, the specifically radical culture of Italian anarchists can be considered a mobilizing structure. This culture was invaluable, not only as a means for Italian anarchists to maintain, reinforce, and expand their transnational movement, but also as the basis for mobilization. Yet, at the time, the focus upon Italians and little interaction with other migrant populations or with the host societies of Canada and the United

States meant that Italian anarchists' organizing efforts were largely limited to their own communities.

The most influential anarchist newspapers in North America during the 1920s and 1930s were the anarcho-syndicalist *Il Martello* (The Hammer) and the anti-organizationalist anarchist communist *L'Adunata dei Refrattari* (Call of the "Réfractaires"). Both papers were based in New York City and travelled Italian anarchist networks throughout Canada, the United States, South America, and Europe. Each newspaper was packed with numerous articles as though the publishers wanted to include as much information as possible in the available space. In keeping with anarchist principles, these publications were devoid of advertising for businesses or appliances, as a way of ensuring that the editorial direction remained free of external influence.[11] The modest advertisements that did appear focussed on anarchist speakers' tours and literature sales. *Il Martello* was four pages in length while *L'Adunata* was eight.

Both *Il Martello* and *L'Adunata dei Refrattari* were text-heavy publications, with their mastheads often being the most aesthetically interesting parts of each newspaper. *Il Martello* had at least three different mastheads during its existence. The first was simply a hand holding a hammer to the left of the paper's logo.[12] The second had three men, just below the logo, holding a large battering ram, charging to the left, where sat a large shaded humanoid creature wearing a helmet. This Goliath-like figure actually sat between the *Il* and *Martello*.[13] The third masthead was a return to a more simplistic form and had a worker, pictured from the forehead down to the torso, looking forward while holding a hammer in his right hand. The figure was inside a circle, with lines radiating from behind him as though he was standing in front of a bright light. This illustration also appeared to the left of the paper's logo.[14]

The *L'Adunata dei Refrattari* masthead was quite plain during the 1920s. The original version had *L'Adunata* written in large letters at the top left of the front page, with *dei* and *Refrattari* in smaller print to the right.[15] In the late 1920s, the masthead simply had *L'Adunata* across the top, with *dei Refrattari* centred underneath.[16] Things became a little more creative in the early 1930s when a new masthead was developed that featured a revamped logo and an illustration. The drawing, to the left of the paper's logo, featured a waterfall in the background feeding a pool below, with a single tree to the left of the waterfall. In the foreground was the left profile of a young woman who was in the act of drinking water from her left hand.[17] The waterfall and pool possibly represented *L'Adunata dei Refrattari* and suggested, perhaps, that reading the newspaper was like drinking from a pool of knowledge.

Figure 6. *Il Martello* masthead, 19 April 1919.
Figure 7. *Il Martello* masthead, 9 July 1921.
Figure 8. *Il Martello* masthead, 12 January 1924.
Figure 9. *L'Adunata dei Refrattari* masthead, 15 September 1923.
Figure 10. *L'Adunata dei Refrattari* masthead, 6 July 1929.
Figure 11. *L'Adunata dei Refrattari* masthead, 17 January 1932.

Both *L'Adunata dei Refrattari* and *Il Martello* included photographs and political illustrations within their pages, especially in the 1930s. Political cartoons were sometimes published with articles. A drawing in the 27 January 1923 issue of *Il Martello* pictured a male Italian fascist in black shirt with rifle slung over his left shoulder, holding hands with a member of the Ku Klux Klan (KKK) dressed in white robes and hood. Both the fascist and klansman were each standing on top of a man who represented workers (see Figure 13). The political cartoon corresponded with an article titled "Fascismo e Klu Klux Klan [*sic*]" that demonstrated the similarities between both groups and the threat they posed to Italian workers in North America.[18] Drawings were also often printed without relating specifically to an article or column. An illustration by Robert Minor, the American-born artist and journalist who turned from anarchism to communism, following the Bolshevik Revolution, appeared in *Il Martello* in 1924.[19] It showed a sitting worker, with "*Lavatore Italiano*" (Italian Worker) written on his torso, hunched over a lever connected to a machine that read "*Produzione Capitalista.*" The drawing's subject was surrounded by bayonets (see Figure 14). To the right of the drawing was added in Italian: "Under the Fascist government, with salaries reduced and hours increased, the worker must produce even more for ... the fatherland and the coffers of their bosses."[20]

Il Martello was purchased by Carlo Tresca in 1919 and appeared bi-monthly until 1921, when it was published on a weekly basis. The newspaper continued publication until Tresca was murdered in 1943. *Il Martello*'s circulation began with 2,500 copies per issue and increased to 10,500 in 1924. By 1929, however, only 8,000 copies were printed due to financial constraints and it is likely that the circulation number dropped further once the Great Depression was in full swing.[21] *L'Adunata dei Refrattari* first appeared on 15 April 1922, established by adherents of Luigi Galleani, to campaign on behalf of Sacco and Vanzetti, fight fascism locally and globally, and continue the propagation of anti-organizationalist anarchist communism.[22] It too began as a bi-monthly publication but in less than a year began to appear weekly. *L'Adunata*'s circulation during the 1922–1943 period was around 5,000 copies per issue.[23] However, it has been gathered that, during the 1930s, as many as 15,000 anarchists supported the paper; which means that the circulation number may have spiked dramatically in those years.[24] The last issue of *L'Adunata* appeared in 1971, as the paper folded up due to lack of subscriptions. Ironically, although the paper was maintained by anti-organizationalists, *L'Adunata dei Refrattari* was published for almost fifty years.

Figure 12. Illustration from Il Martello, 27 January 1923.
Figure 13. Illustration from Il Martello, 26 April 1924.

The distribution of anarchist newspapers occurred in a few different ways. An individual could act as a distributor for a publication within a particular anarchist group or community. Such a person would receive a certain number of issues and sell them or give them away to comrades.[25] Newspapers could also be shared and passed around, meaning multiple anarchists could read the same issue.[26] Anarchists who had their own stores might also have radical libraries inside. Detroit's Fortunato Cernuto had a modest anarchist library in his candy store on Rivard Street.[27] Similarly, Ninfa and Firmino Gallo's newsstand in Paterson, New Jersey, was the site of one of the most extensive anarchist libraries in the United States, known as the Libreria Sociologica (Sociological Bookstore).[28] Individual subscriptions were another means through which anarchist newspapers were distributed among movement networks. Since *Il Martello* and *L'Adunata dei Refrattari* spurned advertising in their publications, they relied heavily on subscriptions and donations from cash-strapped supporters to keep their papers viable.[29] But this could be a challenge. Before the outbreak of the Great Depression, *Il Martello* was already $5,300 in debt. The financial crisis only exacerbated matters. This meant that Tresca could not earn any money nor pay his staff. Loans, benefits, and cutting back to bi-weekly publication helped get *Il Martello* back into the black.[30]

Since most of anarchist newspapers were shipped through the mail, they were often at the mercy of American postal censors, who could remove mailing privileges. *L'Adunata* does not appear to have been disrupted in this way, but *Il Martello* did occasionally run afoul of the New York Post Office. The 8 September 1923 issue was seized because of a small advertisement for a book on birth control. Members of the *Il Martello* staff were required to scratch out the offending advertisement from every issue with a black crayon before postal authorities would agree to deliver it. Unfortunately, the entire edition had to be remailed, meaning that *Il Martello* was forced to spend twice the amount on postage.[31] A less dramatic issue related to sending newspapers through the mail could be the delivery of a newspaper to the wrong address. However, in at least one instance, this led to a positive outcome. In 1927, John Vattuone's copy of *L'Adunata dei Refrattari* was mistakenly delivered to the home of another anarchist by the name of Antonio Ciminieri, who lived a few blocks away. Ciminieri brought the paper to the bakery where Vattuone was employed but Vattuone was on a delivery run. When Vattuone returned, he was informed that Ciminieri had been by. After work, Vattuone paid a visit to Ciminieri's home to thank him for re-delivering the issue of *L'Adunata*. There, Vattuone met Ciminieri's daughter Elvira and the two became lovers.[32]

Both *Il Martello* and *L'Adunata dei Refrattari* acted as an instrument of social change, both as a form of education and a means of direct aid. These newspapers were important sources of information about social, political, and labour issues in North America, Italy, and the world through an anarchist lens. Articles were often attacks against government, capitalism, and religion, not to mention other anarchists. In addition, these newspapers promoted their own particular forms of anarchism among their readership.

L'Adunata dei Refrattari tended to have a greater focus on international news than local reporting. In the 17 January 1932 issue, of the nine articles published, four reported on events in Europe and South America, two were ideological in nature, and two focussed on historical subjects. No articles appeared regarding news in the United States. The majority of international articles discussed issues directly related to anarchists. For instance, one article discussed the expulsion of three Italian anarchists from Spain for their involvement in a strike led by the Confederación Nacional del Trabajo (CNT), the Spanish confederation of anarcho-syndicalist unions, in September 1931. The author condemned the Republic for sending the men to Portugal, then under the fascist rule of António de Oliveira Salazar. Another article, "Agli anarchici e simpatizzanti dell'Argentina" (To the Anarchists and Sympathizers of Argentina), explained the decline of the anarchist movement in that country and demonstrated *L'Adunata*'s presence there. The piece was co-signed by seventy Argentine anarchists and explained that the problems facing the movement were due in part to the repression of the government but also were derived from the infighting among the country's anarchists. The way forward, according to the undersigned, was "Concord in the libertarian family; union in the struggle against all the enemies of liberty. Only in this way can we give life to a strong movement, prepared to give battle to the regime of privilege and of authority, capable of destroying it. To do the contrary would be ... the ruin of our movement, and, the consequence [would be] to postpone indefinitely the day of human emancipation."[33] Two other features pertained specifically to Italian fascism but were actually lists and not articles in the traditional sense. The first, titled "Vive pericolosamente" (Living Dangerously), listed a number of attacks against Italian consular officials between 1927 and 1931 in cities such as Paris, Buenos Aires, Nice, Tunis, Zurich, and Pittsburgh.[34] The second, called "Al Tribunale Squadrista" (At the Squadrista Court) was a weekly column that printed the names of antifascists and the political crimes for which they were charged in Italian courts.[35]

In keeping with *L'Adunata*'s anti-organizationalist position, the anarchist journalist and poet Luigi "Gigi" Damiani wrote an article entitled "Per la nostra rivoluzione: Dall'esperienza spagnuola di oggi and quella possible, di domani, in Italia" (For Our Revolution: From the Spanish Experience of Today and that Possible Tomorrow in Italy) in which he critically examined the CNT. Damiani explored the ability of the confederation to thrive in an environment hostile to revolutionary union activity. He also explained that anarchists were numerous in the organization and claimed that anarchist philosophy was widely supported within it. However, as an anti-organizationalist, he did not believe in large unions. As Damiani wrote, "We who distrust syndicalism, gigantic organizations, who [ascribe to] the classic conception of [spontaneous] revolution ...can attribute to the CNT all the inconsistencies ... that are, for us, consequences of syndicalist methods." Damiani felt that the CNT, even with its large anarchist membership, was still susceptible to the influence of non-anarchist syndicalists and political parties who wished to use the confederation as a means to electoral ends. However, he did recognize the importance of the CNT in disseminating anarchist ideas and its work towards a post-capitalist society. Damiani also admired the CNT for "its tenacity, for its long life, [and] for its resistance." Still, as he concluded, "[In] our point of view, we lament that the Spanish comrades have not yet given life to an independent anarchist movement."[36]

L'Adunata dei Refrattari also included a review section. In this particular issue, a pamphlet called *Guerra alla guerra imperialista* (War against Imperialist War), a 1930 reprint regarding the Allied intervention in Russia during the country's civil war, was critiqued. The pamphlet's author condemned the counter-revolutionary presence of the Allies who sought the overthrow of the Bolsheviks and the end of the social revolution. However, the reviewer from *L'Adunata*, unsurprisingly, had a much different view on the subject. Taking issue with the pamphlet's title, the reviewer stated, "To be against war means to be against the war of all the governments, the Russian government included." Furthermore, the review's author did not have much sympathy for the Bolsheviks: "I well understand that for the communists the Russian government is the social revolution. And here is the root of the misunderstanding. The Russian government is a government like all the others, and like all the others hates social revolution."[37]

Il Martello placed greater emphasis on local reporting than did *L'Adunata dei Refrattari*. In the 1 August 1931 edition of *Il Martello*, four articles on news in the United States were printed with only one international story. This issue also contained six pieces of ideological writing and one focussed on a historical event. Of the "local" stories, two focussed on a series of miner strikes in the states of Illinois, Kentucky, Pennsylvania, and West Virginia. Both were highly critical of the United Mine Workers of America's (UMWA) role in selling out the workers. In the Illinois coalfields, the officials of the UMWA had ordered striking miners back to work—a move that, according to the author, demonstrated the union was an "accomplice of the Peabody Coal Company."[38] In light of the UMWA's conduct in these strikes, Carlo Tresca described the union officials as the "lieutenants of capital" and appealed to workers to "struggle against the criminal union."[39]

The ideological reporting in this issue of *Il Martello* focussed on revolution and the debate between organizationalists and anti-organizationalists. In the weekly column "Fatti e Commenti" (Facts and Comments), the author explained the conditions under which revolutions occurred: "One knows that revolutions are not the result of devious propaganda or the malevolent influence of a few agitators. Revolutions are inevitable historical phenomena that appear ... when the social system demonstrates itself incapable of holding the mass of people in intolerable conditions of life and when the beneficiaries of the system lose ... every confidence."[40] Writing almost two years into what would become known as the Great Depression, the author believed that the time was now opportune for the creation of an "intelligent and audacious" working-class army of "militant strength ... ready to act, to be the guide, to destroy and reorganize; ... ready to carry every revolutionary situation by speeding up the death of capitalism, to transform every revolutionary situation, local or international, in an intense general movement to eliminate capitalism and capable of organizing the new society, a society of free men [sic], when the revolution will have triumphed."[41]

The other ideological article of note, "Sullo stesso argomento" (On the Same Argument), was written by Giusto Volcelo and revisited the debates surrounding tactics. The author was responding directly to Luigi Damiani, Luigi Bertoni, and Luigi Fabbri (the three Gigis, in Volcelo's satirical expression), all European-based anti-organizationalists. Volcelo took the three Gigis to task for their criticism of those anarchists willing to work within union structures or other forms of political organization—anarchists whom the anti-organizationalists regarded as revisionists. Volcelo stated that the three Gigis want to keep anarchism on "the old path" characterized by spontaneity, a lack of concrete plans, a rigid theory and practice, and a chasm separating it from the rest of the population. He then asserted that the methods used by anarchists up until the 1930s had led to a movement with members "very few [in number], isolated, unprepared and impotent."[42] Volcelo felt that anarchists needed to be more open-minded when it came to activism: "We must act according to the existence of the struggle and use the most effective means for arriving at our end.... We do not share completely the maxim 'All or nothing.' We will attempt to make the greatest leap towards anarchy; if we will not arrive at its extreme edge, we will pause where we will arrive, maintaining that position with all means, resuming the advance only when it is possible."[43]

Both *Il Martello* and *L'Adunata dei Refrattari* included writings on anarchist history. These articles could be biographies of notable anarchists, as was the case in the 17 January 1932 issue of *L'Adunata* which featured a piece on the life of Luigi Galleani, who had died the previous year.[44] Historical writing could also explore an important event or an anarchist movement in a particular country, such as Spain.[45] These newspapers would also place the odd quote by Bakunin, Malatesta, or another anarchist within their pages, often in the lower right corner following an article.

In light of the kinds of reporting and writing that appeared in *Il Martello* and *L'Adunata dei Refrattari*, we can surmise that the faithful readers of these publications were militant anarchists dedicated to the social revolution, interested in the debates surrounding theory and practice within the movement, and attentive to the movement's history. Supporters of *Il Martello* were well informed about labour issues in the United States while readers of *L'Adunata* were more aware of the plight of anarchist comrades abroad.

Both newspapers were involved in direct aid. It was often in the pages of these papers that news of arrested comrades was first reported, with appeals for readers to give generously to help fellow anarchists. In these instances, the newspapers became the main avenues for donations. As money was received for a particular individual or individuals, *Il Martello* and *L'Adunata* would record this information on the last page of the paper and, as will be shown in a later chapter, forward the funds to the necessary group or defence committee. The treasurers of the newspapers were responsible for sending the money so gathered to the proper recipients. Osvaldo Maraviglia held this position with *L'Adunata dei Refrattari*. As his Casellario Politico Centrale (CPC) file glumly observes, Maraviglia sent lots of money to Italy "to help the anarchist cause."[46] A few examples include Maraviglia sending funds in 1928 to Giuseppina Cola, of Rome, whose husband Stagnetti, an anarchist militant, had recently died, and to Giuseppe De Luisi and Alfredo Franzini, who were both imprisoned, the former at Soriano nel Camino near Rome and the latter on the penal island of Pantelleria.[47] He also forwarded money raised by the newspaper to Errico Malatesta and his partner Elena Melli to help with living expenses during the early 1930s. At this time, Malatesta, who was in his late seventies, was making a meagre living as an electrician.[48] In addition, Maraviglia sent Melli 100 lire to help cover the costs of Malatesta's tomb when the well-respected anarchist died in July 1932. As late as 1936, Maraviglia was still sending Melli money, ostensibly to help her meet her needs.[49]

Figure 14. Osvaldo Maraviglia. Busta 3017, CPC, ACS.

Additionally, the last pages of *Il Martello* and *L'Adunata* were reserved for anarchist circles around North America to advertise social and cultural events in various localities. These groups tended to be most concentrated in the eastern United States, in cities such as East Boston, Needham, Newark, Paterson, Brooklyn, Pittston, Pennsylvania, and Manville, Rhode Island. *Circoli* also existed in Detroit, Chicago and Gary, Indiana, and on the west coast in San Francisco and Los Angeles. In Canada, groups in Toronto, Sault Ste. Marie, and Windsor were the most active during the 1920s and 1930s. If the events advertised by these circles were fundraisers, which they often were, each group would give an account of the money raised, the cost of holding the event, how much money remained after costs were covered, and the cause for which the money had been collected. For example, a notice from Il Gruppo "I Refrattari" was placed in the 6 January 1940 issue of *L'Adunata dei Refrattari*, stating that Filodrammatica Aurora would be performing two plays at Detroit's Carpathia Hall on 20 January 1940. The first was written by W.C. Wentworth, entitled "Spose di Guerra" (Brides of War) and the other, a comedy, "I Due Sordi" (The Two Deaf People) written by G. Moineaux. The plays were to be followed by a dance with the music performed by an orchestra. Food and refreshments were also to be available. The price of admission for the event was thirty-five cents per person, and the money that remained after expenses was to be donated to political prisoners.[50] Four weeks after this event was held, a follow-up notice posted by Il Gruppo "I Refrattari" in *L'Adunata* stated that $411.40 had been made at the door while expenses totalled $272.10. The remaining $139.30 was to be divided among three different funds for political prisoners as follows: the Bortolotti-Confalonieri defence fund in Toronto (the subject of Chapter 6), received $50; $44.65 each was given to Political Victims in Italy and to the Persecuted of Europe, respectively.[51] It was more difficult for anarchists in smaller centres to raise the same amount of money as comrades in large cities. In 1922, an unnamed group in Timmins, Ontario, held a dance to raise money for Sacco and Vanzetti, and *Il Martello*. Though ticket and refreshment sales of $28.15 was realized, after expenses only $20 remained. These funds were then divided as follows: $15 was sent to the Sacco and Vanzetti Defence Fund and $5 given to *Il Martello*.[52] In addition to advertising events, the last page could also be an inexpensive way for comrades to communicate with one another by posting a notice. Umberto Martignago, who had previously lived in Sault Ste. Marie, Ontario, sent a brief letter to *L'Adunata dei Refrattari*, notifying them and his many comrades who read the newspaper that he had a new address in Rouyn, Quebec.[53]

The last page would also feature a list of all those who had paid for subscriptions and/or donated money to help cover the deficits these newspapers often had. Again, a full account of the funds the paper received were printed, totalled, and subtracted from the remaining deficit. A surprising aspect of these subscriber and contributor lists was the amount of information published about each. If comrades gave money to a newspaper or a cause, the first initial of their first name was printed along with their surname, as was the city or town in which they lived, and the amount they had forwarded. This kind of publicity is hard to imagine in contemporary anarchist publications concerned with personal security. In this period, it was plainly very important for Italian anarchists, whether they published newspapers or held fundraisers, to report to fellow comrades on money-related matters and demonstrate that funds were going to their intended recipients. This way, there could be no accusations of theft from within the movement. Honesty was a highly regarded attribute among Italian anarchists, and so, perhaps in this case, honesty trumped security. Alternately, in light of the considerable surveillance on the part of Canadian, American, and Italian security forces, the publication of the names and locations of adherents could also be interpreted as a form of defiance.

Anarchist circles were the life's blood of the Italian movement. It was these groups that supported movement newspapers and sometimes established their own, organized social and cultural events, hosted lecturers, and engaged in various kinds of activism within Italian communities. They also provided a space for anarchists to meet and discuss anarchist philosophy and tactics, social and political issues, as well as maintain existing social ties and develop new ones. Anarchist circles were usually titled by words that reflected the philosophy's ethos: *volontà* (will), *libertà* (liberty), *pensiero* (thought) and *libertario* (libertarian). Groups were also named after anarchist newspapers. Both *Il Martello* and *L'Adunata dei Refrattari* had groups comprised of those involved in each newspaper's publication as well as others who were not. Among the Italian anarchists in North America, it does not appear to have been a common practice to name *circoli* after anarchists. Yet, some groups did pay homage to well-respected or martyred anarchists. Il Gruppo Femminile Luisa Michel, which will be discussed in the next chapter, was named after the French anarchist and communard. A group bearing the name of Michele Schirru, the would-be anarchist assassin of Mussolini, was formed in New York City in the 1930s, following Schirru's execution by Italian authorities.[54]

Unfortunately, Italian anarchists did not leave behind much information regarding the creation and history of the particular *circolo* to which they belonged. Many who migrated to North America during the 1920s and 1930s joined groups that were already in existence and, because the majority of the anarchists in this study have long since passed away, their memories are lost forever. Still, we can get a sense of how these circles may have formed, based on the little information that does exist.

When Attilio Bortolotti moved from Windsor to Toronto in 1929, he did not have much contact with the Italian Left in that city, though he had met a number of Jewish and Russian anarchists. In August 1934, a young anarchist from Pennsylvania, Nicola Leone, came to Toronto to visit his sister and sought out Bortolotti, whose address he was given by the publishers of

L'Adunata dei Refrattari.[55] That month marked the fourth anniversary of the execution of Sacco and Vanzetti, and the two anarchists decided to print 1,000 leaflets to commemorate the Italian martyrs. It was while handing out this literature, most likely in the Dufferin Street and Davenport Road area, the Little Italy where Bortolotti lived, that Bortolotti and Leone met an Italian socialist who informed them of another anarchist, Ruggero Benvenuti, who also lived in the community. Soon after Bortolotti and Benvenuti became acquainted and started to attend meetings at the Matteotti Club, named after the Italian socialist and parliamentarian assassinated by fascists in 1924, in the hope of finding others open to anarchist ideas. The club was mostly comprised of socialists, but Bortolotti often expressed his anarchist views at their gatherings. After a few months, one of the socialists challenged Bortolotti to a debate, presumably to prove which of the two political philosophies had the most merit. There is no description about the debate itself but, after it ended, six men approached Bortolotti and shook his hand. The consensus among the group was that they should start their own anarchist circle and this was how Il Gruppo Libertario was formed.[56]

Anarchist *circoli* ranged in size. Toronto's Il Gruppo Libertario, for instance, had only twelve members while Il Gruppo Libertà from Needham, Massachusetts, numbered thirty.[57] However, given the lack of membership lists, it is difficult to know the size of other anarchist circles in North America, and trying to recreate them through available materials leads to an incomplete picture. It is quite likely that groups could number less than twelve and others in excess of thirty. Though anarchists were not a large demographic within Italian communities in North America, they still had an influence stronger than their numbers might suggest. As Jennifer Guglielmo has argued, this was due to the establishment of "quite visible alternative cultural and political spaces in their neighbourhoods, which became popular centres for immigrant education, political discussion, labour organizing, and recreation."[58]

Anarchist groups typically met every week in a variety of different locations.[59] Sault Ste. Marie's Il Gruppo Libero Pensiero either purchased or rented a 150-person capacity hall on Albert Street West, located in the predominantly Italian community of the West End. The size of the building made it an ideal location for holding social events like dances and plays.[60] It was at this hall, presumably, that Giuseppe Coleffi, the director of the local Società Guglielmo Marconi *filodrammatica*, staged plays.[61] Another option could be for groups to construct their own meeting place, though it is uncertain how frequently this occurred among Italian anarchists. According to Evaristo Ricciardelli, a member of Il Gruppo Libertà, the Needham-based anarchists built what he described as "a clubhouse" on Sachem Street.[62] Building, renting, or buying a space was an expensive proposition for a working-class movement; meeting in members' homes was a less costly alternative.[63] Brooklyn's Circolo Volontà enjoyed, rent-free, a large meeting place with a stage. Some of the group's Sicilian members had links with the Mafia, which owned this Cook Street building. As a result of this relationship, the anarchists used the space rent-free and were never interfered with.[64] This interaction between anarchists and organized crime is quite surprising, considering the very different philosophies of each group. Mafia members were often paid by employers to prevent union-organizing attempts in various factories and disrupt strike picket lines in New York City during this period.[65]

As with the wider Left, autodidacticism was common among anarchists, with literature being read in one's spare time. Anarchist circles were a good source for radical reading material and an important means of education for a movement comprised mostly of people who, having to begin working at a young age to help contribute to family incomes, had received very little in the way of formal education.[66] Some even had their own modest libraries, such as the Il Gruppo "I Refrattari" from Detroit.[67] Members were free to borrow books, pamphlets, and newspapers, which in turn led to discussions. As the Toronto-based anarchist Marie Tiboldo recounted, the group her father belonged to discussed anarchist philosophy, articles from *Il Martello*, and even Henry George's Single Tax Movement.[68]

Anarchist *circoli* also published small-scale newspapers. In 1934, Toronto's Il Gruppo Libertario embarked on the time-consuming work of publishing *Il Libertario* on an old mimeograph machine. This process required the use of a typewriter to cut a stencil in waxed mulberry paper, which was then placed around an ink-filled drum. Once a blank sheet of paper was placed in the mimeograph, a hand crank located on the side of the machine put the drum and a pressure roller into action, drawing the sheet forward. The process would force the ink through the stencil and onto the paper. It is unclear how many years this newspaper was produced, the total number of issues released, or its circulation, but it did range in size from four to six pages.[69]

In addition, anarchist groups were responsible for organizing a wide variety of social and cultural events. Dances, dinners, plays, concerts, and picnics were often held on weekends and these provided anarchists the opportunity to socialize. These *feste* were advertized among, and open to, the wider Italian community in an attempt to recruit new adherents as well as make contacts with those outside the anarchist movement. As historian Salvatore Salerno has shown in his study of the IWW, such happenings helped extend the movement's criticism of "industrial society beyond the confines of the factory gate."[70] Social events also helped contribute to unity and solidarity, in addition to reinforcing one's commitment to activism.[71] Often, these events were held in tandem, and a dinner could be followed by a dance or a play. In most cases, these gatherings would mobilize resources through fundraisers to support movement newspapers, political prisoners in Italy and elsewhere, and defence funds, among others. A door fee was usually charged for these events to cover costs and raise money. In some cases, there was a general admission and, in others, men would pay a higher entrance fee than women. In January 1929, Il Gruppo Autonomo of East Boston held an event for a *Festa della Frutta*, for which men were charged one dollar to enter but women could attend for free.[72] This may have been an attempt to draw more women to anarchist events or ease the financial burden on couples when both were anarchists. It was rare, however, for those who could not afford the cover charge to be turned away.[73] Efforts were also made to include the children of adherents in these activities. The advertisement for the annual *Il Martello* fundraising picnic and dance had "Bring your kids" written in English, followed with this explanation in Italian: "[Carlo] Tresca will speak in English, as in the preceding years, to make them [the kids] know the faith that animates their parents."[74]

In keeping with their anti-nationalist and anti-religious views, anarchists created their own "holidays," a tradition that had begun in Italy.[75] In place of national birthdays, such as Dominion Day, and religious holidays like Easter, anarchists would celebrate May Day and commemorate 23 August, the date that Nicola Sacco and Bartolomeo Vanzetti were executed. To that end, there were commemorative reprints of paintings made in honour of these two anarchists. *Il Martello* ran an advertisement for reproductions of a Sacco and Vanzetti painting done by Totò Tamburrino that would become available on 22 August 1931. The four-colour reprints were 20 x 17 inches in size. A caption from the advertisement reads: "Decorate your home with the image of the two great martyrs."[76] A radical calendar, known as the *Almanacco Sovversivo*, was created to keep track of these important days as well as note significant revolutionary moments in history, such as the fall of the Bastille and the Paris Commune.[77]

Radical holidays were a time for militants to wear red ties or carnations, and were observed in different ways—from local events that might include a meal and a speech to large convergences[78] that would draw anarchists from various cities.[79] On 2 September 1923, a public park in Detroit was the site of the commemoration of Gaetano Bresci's assassination of Italy's King Umberto in 1900.[80] According to one witness, more than 2,000 were in attendance—most of them Italians, though some Spaniards and Americans were also present.[81] The gathering was chaired by Umberto Martignago of Sault Ste. Marie's Il Gruppo Libero Pensiero and featured speakers living in the United States and Canada. Windsor, Ontario's anarchist circle was also present, with Giulio Ghetti saying a few words on this occasion. No detailed record of the proceedings appears to have survived, but speakers did explain who Gaetano Bresci was and why he killed King Umberto I.[82] Though links existed between Detroit and Sault Ste. Marie anarchists, it was uncommon for the members of Libero Pensiero to travel to the United States with much frequency due to costs, time off work, and possible problems while crossing the border. A trip of this sort would only occur for special events.[83]

May Day was another significant date on the anarchist calendar and anarchists had different ways of observing it. May First was an international demonstration for the eight-hour workday as well as a commemoration for Chicago's famous Haymarket martyrs.[84] For some Italian anarchists, like Luigi Galleani, Primo Maggio was a time to celebrate the day's historic origins and reinforce revolutionary militancy in adherents.[85] These anarchists became concerned over time that May Day was turning into a symbolic event, divorced from its radical roots. They did not want it to become just another social occasion during which people ate food, danced, and got drunk; nor did they want Primo Maggio to be a state-sanctioned holiday. Instead, some anarchists "insisted that it should be a day of real solidarity with the dispossessed, a day of unyielding militancy, such as the May 1886 strike had been."[86] However, even with these criticisms, many anarchists still viewed it more as a workers' holiday.

It was not uncommon for anarchist groups and circles to have their own *filodrammatica*. Plays were generally performed weekly and were an integral part of the Italian anarchist culture. As Bencivenni has shown, the *filodrammatiche* provided a number of important functions. They provided a space for radicals and non-radicals alike to socialize and briefly escape from the challenges of daily life. As an educational tool, the performances of *filodrammatiche* could help shape the opinions of audience members, create social consciousness, and introduce the audience to anarchist philosophy and ideals, as well as social issues. But just as important for radicals themselves was the melding of artistic and political expression.[87]

The *filodrammatica* of Detroit's Il Gruppo "I Refrattari" was organized by Ugo Baldi,[88] an anarchist considered to be a gifted actor.[89] While in Toronto, Attilio Bortolotti was the coordinator of Il Gruppo Libertario's *filodrammatica*.[90] There were also *filodrammatiche* comprised only of women, such as Paterson, New Jersey's Femminile di Musica e di Canto (Women's Club for Music and Song).[91] Like other cultural events, theatrical performances often commemorated anarchist martyrs who lost their lives during the Paris Commune or during anarchist holidays such as Primo Maggio.[92] The plays were framed in a way that conveyed anarchist principles—often including strong critiques of religion and capitalism—or addressed issues facing Italian migrants.

Judging from the available evidence, anarchist filodrammatiche did not collaborate with other drama groups on the Left. However, anarchists were aware of the performances of the drama groups of the wider Italian Left, which suggests that anarchists may have attended these productions. As Attilio Bortolotti recalled, "We left the socialists and communists way behind when it came to plays and recitals—followed, naturally, by dancing—for twenty-five cents a person."[93] An admission fee was collected to offset costs as well as raise funds for anarchist causes.[94]

The most popular plays among anarchist *filodrammatiche* were those written by the poet and playwright Pietro Gori. Gori was born in Messina, Sicily, in 1865 and became involved in the anarchist movement in his early twenties while studying the classics and then law at the University of Pisa. He was arrested on numerous occasions for his anarchist-themed writing and activism. Gori's involvement in organizing a May Day celebration in that city in 1890 led to a six-month stay in jail. After his release, Gori travelled to Milan and began to practise law. As a lawyer, he was an important asset to an Italian anarchist movement constantly facing state repression.[95] Gori was considered such a threat to social order by the Italian government that he was often arrested in the days leading up to May First. During his incarceration in May 1892, Gori wrote the one-act play "Primo Maggio." Two books of poetry, *Alla conquista dell'Avvenire* (Conquering the Future) and *Prigioni e Battaglie* (Prisons and Battles) were also published that year and quickly sold out, with 9,000 copies in print.[96]

Following anarchist Sante Caserio Geronimo's assassination of French President Sadi Carnot on 25 June 1894, the Italian press, inadvertently touting the playwright's widespread renown, blamed Gori for inciting the attack. The next month, three anti-anarchist laws were passed by the Italian government that curbed civil rights. Gori was now facing a possible five-year prison sentence and fled Italy. He made his way across Europe to London and set sail for the United States. Once Gori arrived in America in 1895, he quickly resumed his anarchist activities. He travelled extensively throughout the United States, visiting Italian communities wherever they existed. Gori is said to have held as many as 400 meetings in the short time he lived in North America. His appearances combined the singing of radical songs with speeches about anarchist philosophy.[97] Based in Paterson, New Jersey, Gori was also responsible for forming Il Gruppo 'Diritto all'Esistenza' (The Right to Exist Group) in that city as well as co-creating the group's weekly newspaper La Questione Sociale with the Spanish anarchist Pedro Esteve that same year. During that period, the organizationalist anarchist communist La Questione Sociale was the most popular Italian-language publication in the United States.[98] Due in large part to Gori's transnational activism, he was able to help lay the groundwork for anarchist networks in the United States between 1895 and 1896. Gori's activities did not end there. After he was allowed to return to Italy, he resumed his anarchist activities. Gori was again forced to leave the country in 1898, following the repression of the Left and labour unions, sparked by a series of bread riots. This time, Gori made his way to Buenos Aires, where he organized unions and taught criminology at the city's university.[99]

Gori's cultural legacy should not be minimized. His plays were the favourites of anarchist filodrammatiche throughout North America. The most popular play was "Primo Maggio." It focuses on a young peasant woman named Ida who, aware of her exploitation by the local landowners, dreams of a better world where people are free, women and men are comrades, and all work is for the common good and not for a few wealthy padroni. As the play is set on May First, the workers' holiday, Ida implores a worker, a sailor, and her father to heed the day's significance. The second main character of the play is a young gentleman who is Ida's love interest. It is his family that owns the land that Ida works; but the young gentleman, out of guilt due to his awareness that his wealth comes at the expense of poorly paid and overworked peasants, becomes mentally and physically ill. When Ida meets a stranger from a distant land— the land that she had seen in her dreams—the play becomes a discussion on who will travel with Ida and the stranger to this "promised land," an allegory for revolution. As the stranger explains, the path to the "promised land" will be difficult: "I have crossed mountains and hills; I have crossed rivers and seas. The thorns of the forests have lacerated my clothes and my flesh, the mid-day sun has burned my blood, the wintry rain has bruised my face."[100] Through a series of debates, Ida attempts to convince others to join her on the path to revolution. She is successful in persuading both the worker and the sailor, who begin to realize the power they wield by withholding their labour. Her father, however, thinks Ida is crazy and accepts his lot as an exploited labourer. And, though the young gentleman realizes his role in the exploitation of others, in the end he is unwilling to join Ida and her comrades.[101]

The play ends with the music of "Va pensiero, sull'ali dorate," adapted from Verdi's famous opera Nabucco, a song that was well-known among Italians. Gori, however, transformed it and retitled it "Inno del Primo Maggio" and changed Verdi's lyrics. Where the original featured the Jews grieving for the loss of their homeland following their expulsion by the Babylonian King Nebuchadnezzar (Nabucco in Italian), Gori's version was about the celebration of May First, which the anarchist likened to the "Sweet Easter of those who work."[102] The "Inno del Primo Maggio," like the play, was a call to workers to engage in revolutionary action and, according to historian Marcella Bencivenni, it was "an instant classic, both in Italy and the United States, which contributed significantly to the popularization of May Day among Italian workers."[103] "Primo Maggio" was first performed in Paterson, New Jersey, during Gori's time in America—he was even part of the cast—as part of a May Day celebration.[104]

Another popular play written by Pietro Gori was "Senza Patria" (Without a Country), which deals with migration. The protagonist is a peasant farmer who has fought to unify Italy during the Risorgimento. But the social reforms promised by the republicans prior to unification do not materialize and the *contadino*, disgusted with the Italian state, decides to emigrate. Exploring themes such as patriotism and the pain of leaving one's home, "Senza Patria," in anarchist fashion, demonstrated the limits of state-fostered national identities and argued, instead, for internationalism.[105]

Productions of Gori's plays could have a powerful influence. Joseph Moro was a deeply religious young man and would preach the gospel every Sunday to Italian immigrants. While working at a shoe factory in Stoneham, Massachusetts, Moro met an anarchist co-worker, Giovanni Eramo. Moro would try to talk about his religious beliefs to Eramo but the anarchist argued persuasively against religion. In 1912, Moro attended a picnic put on by Lynn anarchists near Wakefield, where he saw the Pietro Gori play "Calendimaggio." As he reminisced, "I was deeply moved. It inspired me so much that in twenty-four hours I gave up all my religion, all my former beliefs, and started to read anarchist literature, including *Cronaca Sovversiva*."[106]

As important as Gori's radical plays were within the Italian anarchist movement, it is important to keep in mind that he was not the only one who authored such works. Writing a play was open to anyone, regardless of whether they were involved in a *filodrammatica* or not. Even Carlo Tresca penned a one-act play titled "L'Attentato a Mussolini ovvero Il segreto di Pulcinella" (The Attempt on Mussolini's Life, or Pulcinella's Secret). The plot centres on two followers of Mussolini who infiltrated the antifascist movement in order to organize an attempt on Il Duce's life. The assassination would be thwarted and provide an excuse for further repression against the Italian Left. "L'Attentato a Mussolini," which opened on 19 December 1925 at the Central Opera House in New York City, may have lacked the sophistication of works like Gori's, but the play still provided a satirical and critical look at fascism.[107] Plays were also written, produced, and performed by the movement's women. These works depicted women as political and outspoken, and dealt with issues central to women's lives. For instance, "Il Ribelle" (The Rebel) revolved around a discussion on arranged marriage versus free love between a mother and a daughter.[108]

It must be noted, however, that not all plays performed by anarchist *filo-drammatiche* were written by anarchists. In 1930, Michele Schirru, an Italian fruit vendor and anarchist living in New York City, returned to Europe to assassinate Italy's Fascist dictator Benito Mussolini. Schirru hoped that the killing of Il Duce would lead to the end of fascism in Italy and spark a mass revolt against the far Right. In January 1931, Schirru was living in a hotel in Rome, working on his plans. Unfortunately, his activities were discovered by local police, and they attempted to arrest the anarchist in his hotel room. During the arrest and before he was physically searched, Schirru pulled out his gun, fired, and wounded all three police officers. He then pointed the gun at his own head and fired. The shot did not kill Schirru, but he was gravely injured. The anarchist was rushed to hospital and underwent an operation that saved his life. When he was well enough to talk, Schirru admitted to Italian authorities that he had come to Rome to assassinate Mussolini. In May of that year, the anarchist appeared before a special tribunal that found him guilty and sentenced him to death by firing squad. Schirru was shot eight and a half hours after the delivery of the verdict.[109]

Schirru left behind a wife and two children living in New York City. In order to help ease their financial burden, sympathizers organized a fundraiser on 22 February 1932 at the Castle Hall in the Bronx. The event featured a speech by Constantino Zonchello of *L'Adunata dei Refrattari,* who spoke on Schirru's martyrdom, and a play, Paolo Giacometti's *La Morte Civile* (Civil Death), organized by three of Schirru's comrades: Salvatore Dettori, Joe Melloni, and Amadeo Fulvi.[110] Giacometti (1816-882) was an Italian lawyer turned dramatist who penned a number of plays and does not appear to have been a radical.

His *La Morte Civile* is a tragedy that tells the story of a father who cannot provide for his daughter and wife after he is imprisoned for murder. Soon after, the wife and daughter are taken in by a local doctor. When the father escapes from prison he is torn between his desire to look after his daughter, as impossible as that would be, and the option of leaving her in the care of the doctor.[111] The play mirrors the experiences of the Schirru family up to a point. Michele Schirru may have wanted to look after his family, but his political convictions and the repercussions of carrying them out made this impossible. The performance was attended by 300 people and $174 was raised and given to Schirru's widow.[112]

In addition to writing plays, anarchists also wrote politically oriented fiction. In 1916, Osvaldo Maraviglia, who later became the treasurer of *L'Adunata dei Refrattari*, produced a book-length manuscript about life during the First World War. It is not clear whether this novel was ever published, either in book form or as a series of installments in an anarchist newspaper, and it is quite possible that no manuscript of this work exists today. Italian authorities caught wind of the manuscript after it was intercepted in the mail on its way to Maraviglia. A military censor stationed in Genoa had been reading Maraviglia's incoming and outgoing mail because the anarchist's letters were of a subversive and anti-militarist nature.[113] The anarchist had sent the manuscript to his sister Isolina Maraviglia, a teacher who lived in Caldarola, located in the Marche region of Italy, to be proofread. The story centred on two estranged stepbrothers who shared a German father but had grown up in two different countries: France and Germany. Both had enlisted in the armies of their respective nations and, due to unexplained circumstances, came face-to-face on the battlefield. The lieutenant colonel, who wrote the report from which this information is drawn, had this to say about Maraviglia's manuscript: "While the first part of the novel does not contain anything to censor, towards the end, and in the commentary, there are phrases of marked subversive character."[114] The report contained two excerpts from the manuscript, though the passages are not attributed to either of the stepbrothers or any other character in the novel. The first passage seems to be spoken by someone, possibly one of the brothers, who comes to the realization that war pits workers from one country against those of another: "'... such is the horror of war, it really is true what the anarchists and the socialists say, that war must not be made between workers. The war is fratricide ... it is disgraceful.'" In the second excerpt, it is not clear whether Maraviglia is directing his contempt towards the military's rank-and-file or its generals: "It is also true they are of the assassins, of the cowardly, of the seducers of our sisters these men ... that have their petty medals and crosses; they are more than delinquents, and every one of these [medals and crosses] represents who knows how many crimes they have committed. But this goes unnoticed by the people [who] as the old heroes pass by, bow, take off their hats, [and] erect monuments, because these vile achievements have their reward ... and we repeat the words of our rebel poets: no countries, no borders ... [and] the people united."[115] As his repressed manuscript reveals, Maraviglia, like many anarchists, saw novel-writing as a political mission.

Speaking tours provided another way to reach potential radicals, maintain established networks, and create new ones. The speaking tour was yet another form of anarchist education. It became a staple of the anarchist movement in the pre-radio days of the late nineteenth and early twentieth centuries. Public speaking events were invaluable for disseminating anarchist philosophy and critiques of capitalist society, discussing political events in Italy and North America, and raising money for comrades in legal trouble. They were also important social events. The lecture and question-and-answer period were typically followed by a dinner and dancing.[116] At public speaking events, speaker and audience could interact in a dynamic way that print media could not rival.

While in his late teens, Bartolomeo Provo worked in a skate shop in Torrington, Connecticut, and subscribed to the Federazione Socialista Italiana (FSI) weekly *Il Proletario*. However, after reading a few issues, he felt that the newspaper did not adequately reflect his political views. After being laid off in 1915, Provo moved to Springfield, Massachusetts, where he saw a leaflet advertising a lecture by the Galleanisti Constantino Zonchello. Impressed with the speaker's talk on "The Italians in America," Provo approached Zonchello afterwards and began to subscribe to *Cronaca Sovversiva*.[117] A public lecture also brought Catina D'Amico into the anarchist movement. She had heard Galleani speak at an open-air meeting as a teenager and was impressed by what he said and the way in which he delivered his speech. Recalling that event, D'Amico stated, "[Galleani] spoke directly to my heart." She then became an active anarchist in Brooklyn and took part in picnics, *filodrammatiche*, and other activities.[118]

For the majority of those who travelled the anarchist lecture circuit, tours were a demonstration of their commitment to anarchism and not a path to financial security. Emma Goldman, whose notoriety assured her large and attentive audiences, was one of the few anarchists to try to make a living by public speaking. Notwithstanding her reputation, Goldman was barely able to make ends meet and constantly relied on financial assistance from friends and comrades.[119] Various anarchist circles could organize a date for a speaker, book a venue, and advertise the event, but there was no guarantee that all expenses would be recouped. If it was difficult for someone like Goldman to make money from lecturing, could it have been any easier for less-renowned Italian anarchists to supplement their incomes in this way? Following a series of lectures in Sault Ste. Marie, Ontario, in December 1919, Carlo Tresca returned to the United States with a mere eight dollars in Canadian funds in his pocket.[120]

Tresca, who was not a naturalized American citizen, was taking a great risk by leaving the United States. It was possible that his re-entry would be barred by American border authorities. In order to get into Canada, he posed as a sportsman under an assumed name and had no difficulties. On his way home, when he crossed from Sault Ste. Marie to its sister city in Michigan, Tresca was interviewed at length about his identity and plans in America. He explained that he was on his way to visit relatives in Detroit for Christmas and had plans to open a school. Tresca also added that he wished to become an American citizen. His calm demeanour and ability to answer satisfactorily the questions posed to him, not to mention Tresca's respectable appearance—the suit, hat, spectacles, and Van Dyke—led to his shaking hands with immigration officers and being offered a cigar.[121] Evaded in this instance, the border often worked more effectively to hamper transnational activism. It was rare for those based in the United States to make public appearances in Canada. For someone like Tresca, unable to claim American citizenship, the personal danger of crossing the Canada–United States border was too great: he did not pay Canada a return visit.

The numerous *circoli*, newspapers, social and cultural events, and public speaking tours among the Italian anarchists attest to the vibrancy of their movement. Anarchist groups throughout North America (and beyond) created a transnational network that allowed for the circulation of anarchist ideas, publications, and plays. The newspapers and plays created by the Italian anarchists were, not surprisingly, written in the Italian language and aimed specifically at Italian audiences. This is mainly because Italian anarchist activism occurred most often within Italian communities in Canada and the United States. Like other migrant populations, Italians settled in the same areas as family, friends, and *paesani*. In these zones of *italianità*, traditional cultural practices, support networks, and a shared language were maintained. It made sense that the activism of radicals would occur in their own localities and among other Italian migrants. But to what extent did Italian anarchists intermingle with other migrant populations or the host societies of Canada and the United States? Was there much cooperation among anarchists of various ethnic backgrounds or did Italian an-archists remain insular in their radical work?

Cooperation did exist between Italian and non-Italian anarchists. This was probably most apparent during the Sacco-Vanzetti case, when anarchists of all ethnicities banded together to raise awareness of the two anarchists sen-tenced to death and campaign for their release. During this period, Sault Ste. Marie's Il Gruppo Libero Pensiero was joined in marches by the Finnish anar-chists living in the city. However, the relationship between these two anar-chist communities went beyond Sacco and Vanzetti activism and extended into the social and cultural spheres more generally. This meant that Finns would attend the activities of the Italians and vice versa.[122] The circle around *L'Adunata dei Refrattari* collaborated with the New York City–based group Road to Freedom, which was comprised of Jewish, French, and American members.[123] Both groups held a meeting in New York to coordinate efforts to pressure the Soviet government to release Francesco Ghezzi, an Italian anarchist who had been clandestinely agitating among Russian anarchists.[124] Ghezzi was arrested in May 1929 and charged with counter-revolutionary activities. He was sentenced to three years in a labour camp located 250 kilo-metres northeast of Moscow.[125] A report from the Italian consul general noted that "the meeting was attended by about 300 anarchists comprised of Polish, Spanish, Jewish, and Italians." Those in attendance were addressed by speak-ers in Italian, Spanish, Yiddish, and English.[126]

It is difficult to know how often Italian anarchists interacted with their counterparts of other ethnicities. The example mentioned above of the Gaetano Bresci commemoration in Detroit featured a speech in Spanish by Pedro Esteve, and there were Spaniards in attendance even if they were not as numerous as the Italians. In Toronto, Il Gruppo Libertario did not have a space of its own where members could stage their plays. But, because of the relationships established with the city's other ethnic anarchists, the group was able to make use of the Jewish Left's Labour Lyceum and an old church where Russian anarchists held meetings.[127] What is not known is whether Jewish and Russian anarchists attended the performances of Il Gruppo Libertario's *filodrammatica* or, if so, whether someone was able to act as a translator for the non-Italians. Some Italian radical plays were translated into English and performed, though it is not clear how often this may have occurred. A notice published in the New York City–based *The Road to Freedom* advertised an English production of Pietro Gori's "Without a Country" that was scheduled for 5 March 1927. The play was a benefit for *L'Adunata dei Refrattari* and pre-sented by the International Literature Group.[128]

Typically, Italian anarchist newspapers were written in standard Italian, which meant that their readership was largely, if not almost exclusively, Italian. It is not clear to what extent the editors of publications such as *L'Adunata dei Refrattari*, for example, felt it necessary to reach anarchists outside of the Italian milieu. Perhaps the existence of Spanish, Yiddish, and Russian-language newspapers meant that each ethnically specific anarchist group was perceived to be responsible for reaching its own demographic. Yet, there were exceptions to this pattern. Though outside this study's regional parameters, the example of the San Francisco–based *Man!* is worth mentioning. Between 1927 and 1932, Italian anarchists living in the city published the Italian-language newspaper *L'Emancipazione*. But, possibly due to their increasing contact with Jewish, Chinese, and English anarchists, the Italians decided that it would make more sense to create an English-language newspaper to reach more people. The first issue of *Man!* appeared in January 1933 and ran for seven years. Its publication was overseen by a mixed group of Italian and non-Italian anarchists.

It was far more common for Italians to belong to specifically Italian anarchist circles than to those comprised of multiple ethnicities. This is not to suggest that there was something about Italian anarchists in particular that made them avoid interaction with other migrant radicals—far from it—but the names of subscribers and contributors that appear in publications like *Il Martello* and *L'Adunata dei Refrattari* are almost completely Italian. Still, Italians did join mixed groups like those that formed around *Man!* During a visit to Toronto in 1934, Emma Goldman helped establish the Libertarian Group that was comprised of Italian, Jewish, Russian, Dutch, and English members. These anarchists, also trying to reach a wider audience, mounted campaigns among the city's wider Anglo-Celtic population and published their pamphlets in English.[130] Those Italians who were involved in the Libertarian Group, such as Attilio Bortolotti, Ruggero Benvenuti, and Ernesto Gava, continued to focus on antifascist work.[131]

The Italian anarchists in Canada and the United States created a vibrant cultural network that sustained their radical politics. Their various newspapers were a source of anarchist philosophy and critical commentary on current events in North America, Italy, and elsewhere. Publications such as *Il Martello* and *L'Adunata dei Refrattari* also publicized the myriad social gatherings organized by anarchist *circoli* around North America. Anarchist groups were an essential component of the movement. They planned political actions and organized various social and cultural events—dinners, dances, picnics, and plays. These

Figure 15. Ernesto Gava. Busta 2317, CPC, ACS.

gatherings acted not only as a way for anarchists to socialize and attract new members, but also as a means to raise money for the anarchist press, political prisoners, or legal defences. Typically, each anarchist *circolo* also had a *filodrammatica* that would perform plays, most often those written by Italian anarchist playwright Pietro Gori, which espoused anarchist principles and spoke of the

Italian migrant experience. Anarchists also observed their own "holidays" as a counter to religious and nationalist celebrations.

It was through their press, anarchist circles, social events, and public speaking that anarchists were able to maintain, reinforce, and expand their transnational movement. It also enabled them to reach a wider Italian migrant population, to challenge the liberal democratic capitalist order and organize resistance to it, and instill a sense of historical continuity via "invented traditions" as a means of sustaining anarchist culture.[132] Although Italian anarchist culture was aimed specifically at Italians, there were examples of ethnic crossover between Italian anarchists and anarchists from other migrant populations. However, it is difficult to determine exactly how widespread or frequent this intermingling may have been. With the exception of a few cases, Italian anarchists apparently did not invest themselves heavily in changing the Anglo-Celtic societies surrounding them. Their inability or unwillingness to do so would prove disastrous in later years when "black diaper babies" became more assimilated into Canadian or American culture than into the radical political culture of their parents, leading to a decline in Italian anarchist numbers in North America. The lived experience of migrant Italian anarchists could be quite different from that of their children.

CHAPTER FOUR

ANARCHIST IDENTITY FORMATION

There is a common misconception among scholars who study social movements that "old movements," that is, those that existed prior to the 1960s, "were largely motivated by economic and class interests." According to sociologists Hank Johnston, Enrique Laraña, and Joseph R. Gusfield, it was not until the sixties that activists moved beyond economics and class and began to organize around race, gender, and sexuality.[1] Similarly, even scholars who recognized the existence of ethnic/racial tensions within the working class in the pre–Second World War period still asserted that class overrode other forms of identity during strikes.[2] But, as historian Michael Miller Topp has shown in his study of the Federazione Socialista Italiana (FSI), for Italian syndicalists, "class politics were always informed by their ethnic identity [and] their gender identity."[3]

Much like other leftwing political philosophies, the world view of anarchists was informed by their everyday lived experience. For those Italian radicals who migrated to North America in search of employment or to escape political persecution at home, the reality of the "New World" was that conditions there were not necessarily better than those they had left behind. There was very little chance for upward mobility; so, the overwhelming majority of Italian anarchists remained working class. Those who persisted in their political activism still experienced state repression in its various forms. As migrants in the dominant Anglo-Celtic host societies of Canada and the United States, Italians found themselves to be targets of racism in a way they had seldom previously experienced. Even though most migrants identified with a particular region of Italy rather than a nation-state, they were now being collectively denigrated as Italians. Gender was similarly important—whether an anarchist was male or female could determine the extent of their inclusion within the wider society and the movement to which they belonged.

Of course, not every Italian who lived and worked in North America became an anarchist because of their migrant experiences. The formation of an anarchist identity was also based on shared feelings of resistance to capitalism, the state, and religion, among others.[4] As political scientist Martha Ackelsberg has argued, it is through "collective confrontation [that] radicalization seems to require—or at least be enhanced by—the existence of a community of others with whom one shares the experience and which then continues to validate the new sense of self."[5] But radical identities are not only informed by what a collectivity stands against, they are also bound by a shared vision of the future and by attempts to realize that future.[6] By examining the processes that led Italian migrants to anarchism, we can better understand how that identity and its political philosophy led to the activism in which these men and women engaged.

Italian migrants were generally employed as labourers and were drawn from the most proletarianized of all the European nationalities in North America. Between the years 1901 and 1910, for instance, 75 to 90 percent of Italian migrants to the United States were categorized as labourers by the Italian government. Another survey, this time conducted in New York City to determine the occupations of Italian men in 1916, found that more than 50 percent were employed as labourers while 15.7 percent worked in particular trades as tailors, barbers, shoemakers, and carpenters. Less than 2 percent held professional or clerical jobs.[7]

The majority of the roughly seventy Italian anarchists in this study who arrived in Canada and the United States were trained in some kind of trade, though this did not necessarily mean they found jobs in these areas. Even those anarchists who were able to find steady employment for decent pay rarely escaped their working-class origins. Nicola Sacco, who was later tried and executed for his supposed role in a payroll robbery in 1920, was employed as a skilled operator in a shoe factory in Milford, Massachusetts. During the late 1910s, he was earning almost fifty dollars a week, which was far more than his co-workers. A portion of Sacco's wages were sent as remittances to his family in Italy, which may help explain his modest lifestyle.[8] Still, Sacco's decent-paying job was an exception. Within the wider North American anarchist movement, the straitened circumstances of the Italians were well known. Writing to a comrade in 1939, Emma Goldman described Italian anarchists as "the poorest of the poor."[9] As historians Philip Cannistraro and Gerald Meyer have shown, upward mobility among Italians was a difficult process that could take many generations, especially for those concentrated in areas of low-waged work considered to be unskilled.[10]

Many anarchists who migrated to Canada and the United States already identified themselves as anarchists prior to their arrival. However, roughly one-third of the study group became radicalized post-migration, which suggests that the experiences of a migrant labourer could also lead to politicization.[11] Italian migrants may have hoped that Canada and the United States would be lands of promise, but this ideal quickly gave way to the realities of rapidly industrializing capitalist economies, dangerous and/or back-breaking working conditions, low wages, and job insecurity. Due to the racism directed against Italians, employment opportunities were limited, forcing some to work for local elites known as *prominenti*, who took advantage of the situation by paying migrants less than their non-Italian counterparts.[12] For some, including Bartolomeo Vanzetti, a comrade of Sacco's who shared the same fate, radicalization was a direct result of their experiences in North America.[13] In an oral history, Dominick Sallitto explained that the injustice Italian migrants felt and the brutal reality of life in a new country resulted in an interest in reading anarchist literature and attending meetings.[14]

An earlier chapter explored the ways in which Italians were racialized in both Canada and the United States. Race played a similarly complicated role in the shaping of anarchist identity because of the relationship between Italian migrants in North America and the Italian state. The creation of a unified Italy in 1861 meant that most migrants tended to identify with a hometown or region, as opposed to a unified nation-state. Indeed, they often did not consider themselves Italian. The Italian state's taxation policies and conscription of males in the military did nothing to endear "Italy" to the country's peasants. For most, Italy was irrelevant and migration was a means to avoid governmental policies.[15] Moreover, many spoke a regional dialect, not the newly official and consolidating "national language."[16] At the same time, anarchists did identify themselves as Italians on occasion, while those who truly embraced a transnational anarchist identity did not identify themselves with a particular nation-state at all. Significantly, such newspapers as *Il Martello* and *L'Adunata dei Refrattari* were written in standard Italian in place of the various dialects Italian anarchists spoke. Though an anarchist's relationship to Italy might be tenuous, he or she often participated in a community of activism and correspondence centred on newspapers written in standard Italian, might well have lived in a "Little Italy," and confronted forms of "anti-Italian" prejudice that paid little heed to the peninsula's regional complexity. The Galleanisti militant Vincenzo Farulla, for instance, recalled non-Italians calling him "guinea," "wop," and "macaroni strangler." He also believed that non-Italian children threw snowballs at him while living in Boston because he was Italian.[17] In his and other cases, it seems plausible to suggest that it took a voyage from Italy to North America for many activists to discover their "Italianicity."

Luigi Galleani wrote on the discrimination Italian migrants faced abroad in an article from *Cronaca Sovversiva* provocatively titled "Dagoes." Here, Galleani discussed the various kinds of manual labour in which Italians were employed building infrastructure projects or working in hazardous mines—contributing substantially to the countries where they had settled. But for all their hard work, Italian migrants were disparaged by the host societies, not least because of the "ambiguity" surrounding their whiteness. As Galleani asserted, "Americans and English, Polish and Slavs, Germans and French are *whites*; the blacks—there is no possible doubt—are *negroes*. The Italians? ... [T]he Italians are not more black, but they are still not white, they are *Italians*, something between the white and the black." Galleani argued further that Italians were not viewed as completely human: "The *dago* is not only the foreigner or the barbarian, he is ... in the anthropological classification, the bottom rung; something of a hybrid between a man and a gorilla."[18] The racism and discrimination experienced by Italian migrants within Canada and the United States could lead to their involvement in political activity. As historian Ruth Frager has demonstrated in her study of Jewish needle trades workers in interwar Toronto, experiences of racism informed their "political awareness and often sharpened their commitment to activism." This was especially the case for Jewish socialists whose "class consciousness and ethnic identity reinforced each other, deepening their commitment to radical social change."[19] Similarly, Annelise Orleck's historical study of working-class Jewish women in the New York labour movement shows that anti-Semitism influenced the activism of these radicals. Yet, she also found that issues of race and racism were rarely addressed by Jewish labour militants. Orleck suggests that this silence was the result of a particular focus; for these activists, it was class and gender and not race that were seen as the main reasons for their oppression as working-class women.[20] Galleani's article on the treatment of Italian migrants and their place in the racial hierarchies of Canada and the United States likely aided in the politicization of Italian anarchists. However, the extent to which Italian anarchists grappled with race and racism as part of a larger anarchist struggle needs more scholarly attention.

But how did anarchists see themselves? This is not to say that the old regional patterns quickly died. Consider, for example, the complex biography of Pietro Allegra. Allegra was born in Palermo in 1877 and later enrolled in a technical school. His radical politicization occurred during the 1894 state of siege declared by then Prime Minister Francesco Crispi and the resulting occupation of 40,000 Italian soldiers to quell two years of revolts among Sicilian peasants. Organized by the workers' and peasants' Fasci Siciliani, peasants mobilized and demonstrated for higher wages, improved sharecropping contracts, and an end to high taxation. Many peasants were arrested and more than a few were killed in clashes with local police and military.[21] Allegra joined a local anarchist circle and spent time in jail for his activism. In 1910, he migrated to the United States, first settling in Paterson, New Jersey, and then later in Long Island, New York, where he worked as a clerk at a cigar factory. During this time, Allegra was active in organizing cigar workers and began contributing to Carlo Tresca's newspapers *L'Avvenire* and later *Il Martello*. Now living in New York City, he became a member of the Bresci Group, named after the famed anarchist Gaetano Bresci. During the First World War, Allegra was involved in propaganda directed towards Italian men living in America to prevent their return to enlist in the Italian army. Under threat of deportation, Allegra returned to Palermo and carried on his anarchist activism until his return to the United States in 1920. Upon his return, Allegra resumed his involvement in *Il Martello* and in the 1920s was active in antifascist work. His support of and involvement in an antifascist united front not only strained his relationship with Tresca, who could not stomach working with the communists following the events of the Spanish Civil War, but also brought Allegra closer to the communist position until he broke with the anarchist movement. Allegra died in New York City shortly after the Second World War.[22]

In an article that appeared in *Il Martello* in 1924, Allegra discussed fascism in his home region of Sicily, briefly outlining the area's subjugation by foreign invaders throughout history. He then drew a correlation between past oppressors and the present fascist regime. As a result of this history, Allegra did not believe fascism would be able to take root in Sicily. Though he does not refer to himself directly as a Sicilian, he does demonstrate his ties to the region, not only through the article's topic but also in the way he refers to the region as his "dear Sicily."[23]

But to what extent did regionalism affect the ability of Italian anarchists to interact with one another? The evidence shows that regionalism did not greatly hinder the ability of Italian anarchists to engage in activism together. For the most part, factionalism was the result of diverging anarchist ideologies and not one's region of origin. The nature of Italian settlement in North America was such that migrants tended to settle and then work in the same areas as their co-regionalists. Thus, anarchist groups tended to replicate regional affinities. However, regionalism was not completely absent either. Frank Brand, an Italian anarchist active in New York City, stated in an interview that he, being from a small town near Milan, did not "mix very well" with the southern Italians who comprised the Circolo Volontà in Brooklyn where he lived. Instead, Brand preferred to work with Spanish anarchists.[24]

For other anarchists, internationalism played a greater role than regionalism. Alberico Pirani, another Galleanisti, did not identify with any nation states. As he declared in an interview, "I'm international. I ain't got no country.

When you mention country and religion, wash your mouth. That's the way you kill millions of people, for God and country and flag."[25] The anarchist poet and lecturer Virgilia D'Andrea also embraced an anti-state identity and during her lectures would urge audiences to view themselves as "citizen[s] of the world ... child[ren] of father Sun and mother Earth."[26] Attilio Bortolotti made a literal break with his Italian citizenship following the murder of Giacomo Matteotti, a socialist member of the Italian Parliament, by fascists in 1924 for his outspoken criticisms of the far Right. Disgusted, Bortolotti destroyed his Italian passport by burning it in a stove.[27]

However, anarchists also sometimes laid claim to a pan-Italian identity. This pattern was most visible during the years of antifascist struggle. Little Italies had always been contested terrain between radicals and reactionaries. Prior to the rise of fascism, Italian radicals went on the offensive against the *prominenti* and the Roman Catholic Church in an attempt to assert their vision of society within Italian communities.[28] After Mussolini assumed power, the conflicts between the Left and the Right became even more pronounced. Within Italian communities abroad, and often working through consular offices, the fascists hoped to create a strong lobby that would pressure foreign governments, like those of Canada and the United States, to support the political interests of Italy. They also sought to disseminate a specifically fascist reading of Italian culture. But the fascists first had to overcome the localism of Italians who often did not identify with a unified nation-state. This would be accomplished in two ways: first, by developing a sense of pride among Italians and encouraging them to become more involved in Canadian and American politics; and, second, through the diffusion of cultural programs, such as language courses.[29] To this end, the fascists exported the Opera Nazionale Dopolavoro (OND; National Afterwork Organization) to communities throughout North America. The aim of the Dopolavoro was to unify and oversee the operation of Italian social clubs and provide members and their families with popular forms of entertainment, such as sporting events and movies. In addition, the fascists created a separate organization—Gioventù Italiana del Littorio all'Estero (Italian Youths of the Lictor Abroad)—aimed specifically at children.[30] Fascists also sought to influence Italian communities in Canada and the United States by taking control of the benevolent society known as the Ordine Figli d'Italia (OFI; Order Sons of Italy) and through Italian language programs that would instill fascist values.[31]

The fascists' emphasis on nation and their perception of migrant settlements abroad as Italian colonies in some ways set the tone for antifascist responses to Italian identity.[32] Leftists may not have identified as Italians in the past, but with the fascists claiming to speak in the interests of Italians regardless of where they lived, antifascists, anarchists among them, also at times couched their alternative vision in nationalist terms. For example, on 20 March 1923, anarchists in New Haven, Connecticut, prevented Carlo Cattapane, a local fascist, from speaking at the Town Hall. Forced to leave the stage due to the hostility of the mostly antifascist crowd, Cattapane was afterwards asked why he held the meeting. In response, the fascist stated that he was Italian and only wanted to propagate *italianità* or Italianness. One of the anarchists then remarked, "We are, it is true, all Italians, we love Italy immensely, but we spit on the face of the assassins of the Italians."[33]

Italian neighbourhoods were important sites of struggle and radicalization for anarchists. It was here that Italians could communicate with *paesani* in their regional dialects, shop in various Italian-owned stores, socialize in saloons, purchase meals from *trattorie* or restaurants, join social clubs, find both classic and popular Italian literature, and read a politically diverse range of Italian-language newspapers.[34] Commentators have also discussed the ways in which Italian migrant communities allowed for the continuation of cultural traditions, such as religious practices, and the reliance on the extended family as a means of support in times of hardship. In addition, Italian migrants founded mutual aid societies to help ease financial burdens by providing small loans or other assistance to members in times of illness or death.[35]

In much the same way that Little Italies could replicate cultural and social traditions practised in Italy, they had the potential to sustain the radical thought and practise of leftist migrants and provide a site for its further development. These communities were generally able to shield themselves from assimilation into North American society. The majority of residents tended to be poor and working class, which increased the possibility for collective struggles against employers and capitalism. They were simultaneously Italians and exploited workers and this could act as the basis for solidarity.[36]

As Topp has shown with the FSI, the emphasis these syndicalists placed on activism within their own communities demonstrates both the continued significance of their Italian identity and the relationship between it and their class position. Influence on their neighbourhoods was paramount. The syndicalists challenged not only the fascists and the *prominenti* who supported them, but also others on the Italian Left, including anarchists, with the aim of establishing their specific political vision.[37] The same can be said of the anarchists who—with their press, public speakers, and demonstrations—put forward their own alternatives to a nationalist, capitalist, and religious leadership within the Little Italies. Italy and the "Little Italies" shaped the outlook and the struggles of these leftists more powerfully than "Canada" or the "United States."

Gender

During the late nineteenth and early twentieth centuries, the role of women within the Left became an important issue. Male radicals, often products of their time, tended to see women in their socially prescribed roles as wives and mothers tied to the domestic sphere instead of seeing them as equals or comrades. In addition, many leftist men felt that women, members of a supposed weaker sex, were inherently conservative in their thought and actions due to the "natural" aspects of motherhood, child-centred and risk-averse as it was thought to be.[38] Though leftist political philosophies such as socialism, communism, and anarchism called for equality between the sexes, when and how this equality was to be achieved was up for debate. Male socialists and communists may have believed they had no part to play in the oppression of women, pointing instead to an exploitative economic system; but for male anarchists, their relation with female comrades was far more complex.[39] Some male anarchists knowingly excluded women from the movement while others truly attempted to treat women as equals.

Based on the pages of publications like *Il Martello* and *L'Adunata dei Refrattari* as well as the CPC security files, men were far more visible within this movement than women. It also suggests that men may have outnumbered women adherents. To some extent this can be explained by the very male-dominated character of transatlantic Italian migration. Women of various ages also migrated, often as wives with children in tow or as children in the company of mothers, although some women who migrated from Italy were wage workers.[40] Another important reason for the lack of participation by women in the Italian anarchist movement was the treatment they experienced at the hands of male comrades. As Jennifer Guglielmo has shown, women were often ignored and marginalized, which led to the creation of anarchist *circoli* comprised solely of women. These women-only anarchist circles rarely attained the prominence of those of the men.[41]

Within Italian anarchist communities it was generally the men who edited and contributed to movement newspapers or became prominent lecturers. Women wrote articles for publications such as *Il Martello* and *L'Adunata dei Refrattari* but not to the extent that men did. During the 1930s, for example, *L'Adunata dei Refrattari* reprinted articles written by Luce Fabbri, the Italian anarchist writer and publisher then living in Uruguay, on the Spanish Civil War and anarchism, more generally. Roughly two or three articles by Fabbri appeared in the pages of *L'Adunata* each month during this period. The only semi-regular female contributor to this publication in North America was Philadelphia-based Aurora Alleva, but by the mid-1930s, she appears to have ceased writing for the newspaper. The writing on women did not feature prominently in the pages of *Il Martello* either. Again, articles written by women on the Left, such as Angelica Balabanoff,[42] might appear on occasion, but this was hardly usual.

The lack of women's voices within the pages of Italian anarchist newspapers was not particular to *L'Adunata dei Refrattari* or *Il Martello*. In her study on the radicalism of Italian women in New York City, Jennifer Guglielmo states that the same issue existed in similar publications in the late nineteenth and early twentieth centuries. Taking Paterson, New Jersey's *La Questione Sociale* (1895–1908) as an example, it too was dominated by male commentators, though women still authored articles. It was not until Spanish anarchist Pedro Esteve began editing the newspaper in 1899, however, that women's presence in the pages of *La Questione Sociale* increased dramatically. His partner Maria Roda, well-known for her writing and speaking abilities, contributed a number of articles on feminism, anarchism, and class struggle. According to Guglielmo, it was the collaboration between Roda and Esteve that led to the increased publication of women's writing during this time.[43]

The lack of women's involvement in the movement was an issue for male anarchists. In a 1923 article in *L'Adunata dei Refrattari*, Osvaldo Maraviglia, then the paper's editor, asked readers, "How many times have we observed with bitterness that at our meetings, conferences and recreational events, women are absent?"[44] By posing this question, Maraviglia demonstrated that women were present in Italian neighbourhoods but, for whatever reasons, were not part of the anarchist movement. But what was preventing Italian women from being active anarchists? Attempts were made by various circles to attract women to events by offering them free admission as well as requesting them to attend group meetings.[45] Yet, women were still not participating to the degree that men wanted.

Ideas surrounding women and their role within anarchist movements in the late nineteenth to early twentieth centuries ranged from very progressive to extremely unenlightened. Among the more open-minded anarchists was Mikhail Bakunin, who stated, "I am truly free only when all human beings, men and women, are equally free."[46] Emma Goldman, the most prominent woman of the first-wave anarchist movement, was another important writer and lecturer on themes of women's liberation. Born in the Jewish quarter of Kovno, Lithuania, in 1869, Goldman's experiences as a Jew living under the repressive anti-Semitism of tsarist Russia, and a strict and abusive father, had a great impact on her later political identity.[47] She migrated to the United States in 1885 and became an anarchist following the hanging of the Haymarket martyrs in November 1887. Active in New York City, Goldman was arrested numerous times for her activism. On one such occasion, she gave a speech in which she counselled her listeners to "demonstrate before the palaces of the rich [and] demand work." She then went on to say, "If they do not give you work, demand bread. If they deny you both, take bread. It is your sacred right."[48] Goldman was sentenced to one year at Blackwell's Island Penitentiary, where she learned the basics of nursing. After her release, Goldman travelled throughout Canada and the United States, lecturing on workers' issues, birth control, education, and women's rights.[49] In 1917, she was arrested for her anti-war work and imprisoned for two years. Quickly following her release from prison, Goldman, along with many other anarchists active in the United States, was rearrested and ordered deported to Russia at the height of the American Red Scare. Her time in Communist Russia opened her eyes to the reality of the revolution—any genuine and radical attempts at direct democracy or workers' control were stifled by the Bolsheviks, who wanted to consolidate their power and centralize the administration of the Russian state. Disgusted by the behaviour of the communists in violently suppressing radicals who challenged communist rule, Goldman left Russia and spent the rest of her life living in France, London, Spain, and Canada, where she continued her anarchist activism.[50] Her position in a male-dominated movement created a space where she was able to bring forward her criticism of marriage as a coercive institution and advocate such measures as birth-control education.[51]

In contrast, anarchist Pierre-Joseph Proudhon held less progressive views on women. He believed that the main social unit of a stateless society would be the patriarchal family. Proudhon was also an opponent of divorce and viewed the place of women in any society, anarchist or not, as tied to the domestic sphere. Peter Kropotkin had some problematic views of women as well. He felt that it was logical for women to be involved in anarchist activism but should not put their feminist politics before the interests of the largely male working class.[52] Kropotkin also appears to have believed that men were more intelligent than women. According to Emma Goldman, Kropotkin once told her that "when she [woman] is his equal intellectually and shares his social ideals, she will be as free as he."[53]

This appears to have been a sentiment shared by Osvaldo Maraviglia in 1923. In his article, he blamed men for women's absence from the movement. Women were not showing up because anarchist men were failing to promote the cause at home. Maraviglia, echoing the paternalism of many of his radical contemporaries, felt it was the role of male comrades to educate women on the topic of anarchism and thereby facilitate women's liberation.[54] In some ways, there seems to have been a gender hierarchy in this model of anarchist theory and practice. The males of the movement were the keepers of this knowledge, who would then pass it down to wives, sisters, and lovers, who would then in turn pass it on to their children.

These contrasting views on women among movement theorists were, not surprisingly, replicated among the rank and file. Writing on women in the Spanish anarchist movement during the Civil War, Martha Ackelsberg found that male comrades either saw women in a position of lower status or, alternately, as men's equals who should be treated accordingly.[55] The same situation developed among Italian anarchists. For example, in Spring Valley, Illinois, the women of Il Gruppo Femminile Luisa Michel were not allowed to enter the Prosperity Club, an important regional centre for the movement, wherein male anarchists held their meetings. In the winter of 1900, anarchist women and their male allies converged to protest the club's exclusionary practices. Since women were not allowed inside the Prosperity Club, they sent in their male comrades with a proposal to end the club's discrimination against women and open the venue to all anarchists. The proposal was not well received and an intense debate between both sides ensued. When the supporters of Il Gruppo Femminile Luisa Michel asked for a vote on the proposal, they were stymied by the moderator.[56] The existence of women-only groups within left-wing movements "provided women with a separate space to build their confidence and explore socialist issues from a woman's perspective."[57] Yet, for Il Gruppo Femminile Luisa Michel, such a path was the only way to engage in anarchist activities. In some cases, even those male comrades who paid lip service to women's equality in public did not practise anarchism in their homes. In private, with their families, some male comrades were domineering patriarchs whose authority was not to be questioned. John Vattuone, for example, was known to order his partner Elvira Ciminieri around the house by demanding she bring him whatever he wanted.[58]

The Prosperity Club may have represented an unusual case within North American anarchism—it is difficult to know. Yet, more subtle patterns of gender discrimination are well documented. However rare it may have been for women to be physically barred from meetings and venues, they could be excluded in different ways. Il Gruppo Libero Pensiero of Sault Ste. Marie, Ontario, which flourished in the 1920s, was comprised of both sexes. Women were left out of decision-making processes when events were held at their local hall. Their roles were those traditionally assigned to women—food preparation, for instance.[59] The gendered division of labour within the anarchist movement meant that both women and men travelled within their own social networks. For the movement's women, this could often mean the behind-the-scenes organizing of social events, such as lectures, dances, dinners, and plays, or canvassing for the movement's newspapers. The public meetings tended to be the preserve of males. Women would usually only attend meetings when there were critical issues to be discussed.[60] Women's contribution to the anarchist movement was important, yet their work tended to "[keep them] in a sex-stereotyped domestic role that isolated them from power and perpetuated [their] secondary status."[61] Still, women could take on roles that would usually be assigned to male comrades in times of crisis. For instance, during the Red Scare in the United States, the anarchist community of Paterson, New Jersey, was raided and many male comrades were taken into custody or forced underground. As a result, it was the women who began to distribute anarchist pamphlets and newspapers.[62]

Anarchist women were also expected to fill traditional roles as mothers. Those anarchists, whether theorists like Kropotkin or the less celebrated rank and file, who held conventional views of gender roles, argued that women were naturally suited for this function. They believed that women were biologically predisposed to want children and raise them, leading to the conclusion that it was not an imposition upon a woman's freedom to become a mother, a destiny aligned with her natural instincts.[63] Though Proudhon, Kropotkin, and others may not have viewed mothers as potential revolutionaries, women and men within the Italian anarchist movement in North America certainly did.[64] As mothers, anarchist women shared the important duty of raising the next generation of anarchist militants, a concept which Caroline Merithew has termed "anarchist motherhood." Anarchist women, as did their socialist and communist counterparts, redefined motherhood as a revolutionary act to challenge the patriarchy they experienced under a capitalist economic system as well as within the anarchist movement. As educators, they were instilling anarchist principles in their children to ensure that the social revolution continued. And in this role, women were laying equal claim to that of male comrades regarding their importance and contribution to the anarchist movement.[65]

In addition, it was through education that women could subvert patriarchy. In a *L'Adunata* article titled "To the Women," the author, one Delie, argued that "old moral religionist[s] ... antediluvian man, [and] the priest" had made proletarian women the slaves of men by reducing women to domestic beasts. It was these beneficiaries and promulgators of patriarchy whom the author charged with keeping women in a servile state by reinforcing dominant beliefs that relegated women to roles as servants and objects of sexual pleasure. These opponents of women's equality, according to Delie, also objected to women reading philosophy and becoming better educated. Addressing young and future mothers specifically, the author asserted that they had to resist the oppression of women. Mothers had to educate and raise their daughters to take their place in society as equals to men. If mothers were successful in this, they would be farther along the path to anarchism. But, if they did not, woman would "remain a beautiful plaything to satisfy the capricious lust of man."[66] Interestingly, this article does not address how important it would be also to educate sons regarding patriarchy and how to help combat it as males.

Some male comrades were also proponents of "anarchist motherhood." However, the way in which some men wrote on the subject could be quite patronizing. In "To Proletarian Mothers," which was published in the 2 November 1929 issue of *L'Adunata dei Refrattari*, Celestino Lalli told women directly that it was their responsibility to educate their sons to be "future champions" of anarchist ideals, and not be slaves to the greedy *padrone* or the priest, or fighters of wars for the wealthy. For Lalli, it was the "mission" of mothers to understand their role as "educators and liberators." No mention was made by the author of the education of daughters, nor did he bring up the ability of mothers/women to engage in social struggle or revolution beyond these circumscribed roles. Instead, mothers/women were seen additionally as the comforters and supporters of men whose activism was difficult and emotionally trying.[67]

"Anarchist motherhood" may have had its supporters among Italian anarchists of both genders, but not all anarchists believed it was the role of radical mothers to educate their children. A week after "To Proletarian Mothers" was published in *L'Adunata dei Refrattari*, the newspaper ran an excerpt, translated into Italian, from Benzion Liber's book *The Child and the Home*, titled "Fathers and Sons."[68] In contrast to Lalli's article, the Liber excerpt focuses on the role of fathers in teaching their sons about leftwing radicalism, capitalism, and the proletariat. Liber is critical of the way in which male comrades trained their sons to memorize revolutionary poems and songs but without providing sufficient context with respect to their meaning and import. Instead, the sons were simply acting as parrots, repeating what their fathers had taught them to say. He also felt that those male comrades who were considered leaders of radical movements were so busy in their activism that they had ignored their sons, thus breeding indifference or hatred within them. For Liber, it was the father, and not the mother, who was responsible for a son's radical education. However, such paternal pedagogy required proper preparation. As Liber suggested, "If our social ideas are true, we can reasonably presume that a child brought up rationally will be induced to embrace them. We must not prove to be absolutely secure in being right; rather we must add a degree of skepticism to those ideas for which we are most enthusiastic."[69] It is hard to discern if Liber's article on raising radical children in *L'Adunata* was published as a deliberate counter-thrust to Lalli's article of the previous week or whether the timing was purely coincidental.

While some anarchists felt the role of educator belonged to either the father or the mother, others felt that this task was the responsibility of both parents. Philadelphia's Aurora Alleva, who was well known for speaking publicly at anarchist events in her hometown as well as New York City, writing on the lack of children involved in the anarchist movement, blamed both parents for their inability to stimulate interest in anarchism in their sons. Believing that sons were too enamoured of baseball, movies, and comics, Alleva argued that parents were not spending enough time with their children and failing to instill anarchist principles. She suggested parents meet their children halfway. For example, if a son showed an interest in reading, parents should give him some anarchist literature to read. And if a child was not interested in reading, parents were told to accustom him to reading some anarchist publications every day. In addition, Alleva felt it was important for parents to bring their children to anarchist meetings and lectures in the hope that the latter would develop an interest in the movement as well as in the social question.[70]

With the exception of the article written by Delie, the above examples omit any mention of the education of daughters, focussing instead on the importance of ensuring that sons are properly radicalized to carry on anarchist struggles. What does this tell us about the Italian anarchist movement? It appears that a form of patriarchy existed within the movement whereby the education of sons was given primacy over that of daughters. But it was not only men who subscribed to this idea. Women themselves also wrote on the importance of educating sons. Even Aurora Alleva, who stated that the anarchist ideas instilled in her by "my mother and father are infinitely more beautiful and better than the school could ever have taught me," failed to mention girls in her article.[71] In the movement's key newspapers, one hears a fair bit about the women missing from anarchist meetings, but, ironically, little acknowledgement of the biased treatment of girls in the family that likely sustained this pattern.

"Anarchist motherhood" was not the only option open to women within the Italian anarchist movement. For those who combined feminism with their anarchism, the family structure was seen as a main factor in women's inequality and dependence on men. If women were to be truly equal, anarchist feminists believed, then women had to be economically, psychologically, and sexually independent of men and of such patriarchal institutions as marriage. Anarchist feminists did not accept claims that motherhood was a natural instinct and, though they agreed there were differences between women and men, challenged assumptions that intellect and psychology were based on gender.[72] Still, for Italian anarchist feminists, motherhood in addition to their roles as workers and migrants helped inform their anarchist politics.

Their experiences as some or all of these identifiers were in stark contrast to Catholic feminism's emphasis on women's spiritual superiority as well as liberal feminism and its insistence on political and legal equality between the sexes. Instead, Italian anarchist feminists were actively engaged in a revolutionary struggle to overthrow all oppressive and hierarchical forms of authority, regardless of whether it was the capitalist economic system, the Catholic Church, the so-called democratic political system, or that of Italian men at home, in the anarchist movement, or in the wider Italian community.[73]

As Guglielmo has shown in her work on the Italian anarchist newspaper *La Questione Sociale*, anarchist feminists like Maria Roda wrote extensively about women's treatment in the Italian anarchist movement. Increasingly frustrated with the way women were marginalized and ignored by male comrades, Roda wrote in in *La Questione Sociale* in September 1897 that women were insulted by men who considered women incapable of fighting against capitalist society and unable to understand anarchist philosophy. Her appeal to fellow female comrades was that women should organize their own women-only anarchist *circoli* so that they could educate themselves.[74]

This kind of criticism of women's place in the Italian anarchist movement, however, is lacking in the pages of both *L'Adunata dei Refrattari* and *Il Martello*, at least during the 1930s.[75] Though more research is needed on these newspapers during the 1920s, the fact that women were not writing on anarchist feminist issues during the 1930s suggests a few things. Both *L'Adunata dei Refrattari* and *Il Martello* were largely run and edited by men and they may not have provided women the opportunity to write on these themes. These newspapers did print articles written by women but, in the majority of cases, these articles were tied directly to anarchist philosophy or political events in North America or abroad. Whether women approached the editors of *L'Adunata dei Refrattari* and *Il Martello* with articles on women's marginalization in the movement and the decision was made not to publish is difficult to know. The lack of such subject matter in these publications could demonstrate a lack of interest on the part of editors or their belief that such criticism acted as a distraction from much larger issues, such as the struggle against fascism. It is quite telling that Maria Roda's relationship with Pedro Esteve, editor of *La Questione Sociale*, resulted in her articles and those of other female comrades being published within its pages.[76]

It was uncommon for women within the Italian anarchist movement in North America to attain the same prominence as men. One exception to this was Virgilia D'Andrea, who became the most prominent woman within this movement during the interwar period. She was renowned for her poetry, writings on anarchism, and her oratorical skills, which she demonstrated on lecture tours across the United States. Though D'Andrea garnered a great deal of respect from male and female comrades alike, being a woman meant she was scrutinized in a way that men within the movement were not.

D'Andrea was born in Sulmona on 12 February 1888 to parents Stefano and Sambascia. Her father worked as a civil servant while her mother was a homemaker. D'Andrea had a painful childhood; her mother died early and her father was later murdered by the lover of his second wife. She spent the rest of her youth in a convent and later enrolled in the University of Naples, where she received her teaching certificate. Afterwards, she returned to the Abruzzi region and began to teach elementary school at Avezzano. There, D'Andrea witnessed, first-hand, the poverty in which her students lived. Indeed, D'Andrea herself was barely able to meet her own needs as a self-supporting teacher. This experience, coupled with the region's 1915 earthquake, are thought to be two major events that politicized D'Andrea. Avezzano was at the quake's epicentre, and the disaster left most inhabitants dead and the city in ruins. The slow and inadequate response of the Italian state added to D'Andrea's sense of injustice.[77]

D'Andrea eventually left the teaching profession to dedicate herself to anti-militarist activism against Italy's involvement in the First World War, and this may have been around the time when she joined the Partito Socialista Italiano (PSI). As a member of the PSI, D'Andrea organized a women's section of the party in Sulmona. In 1917, while attending a meeting of the Unione Sindicale Italiana (USI), she met Armando Borghi, who was the leader of the union. When exactly D'Andrea moved from socialism to anarchism is not known, but it is possible that her contact and, later, romance with Borghi may have had some influence. She embraced anarcho-syndicalism as her political philosophy, taking her cue from Errico Malatesta, who had argued, "The task of anarchists is to work to strengthen the revolutionary conscience of organized workers and to remain in the Unions [sic] as anarchists."[78] And, like Malatesta by way of Bakunin, D'Andrea also conceptualized an anarchist society as a series of freely associated federations.[79]

D'Andrea was heavily active during *il biennio rosso*, the two years of radical leftist factory and land occupations that followed the First World War. She was arrested and charged with plotting the overthrow of the government and inciting others to revolt. Found guilty, D'Andrea's prison time was confined to a few weeks, in view of her womanly status.[80] Life became increasingly more dangerous for D'Andrea in Italy. In March 1921, three anarchists bombed Milan's Diana Theatre in an attempt to kill the city's fascist chief of police in retaliation for his severe treatment of their comrades. The fascists in turn used the incident as a pretext to attack the Left and its various institutions.

Figure 16. Armando Borghi. Busta 755, CPC, ACS.

Figure 17. Virgilia D'Andrea. Busta 1607, CPC, ACS.

D'Andrea was one of the few who defended the anarchists. She argued that the men were also victims who had acted out of desperation and in retaliation against the bourgeois state for the imprisonment of Malatesta and Borghi for their roles in *il biennio rosso*. With the fascists' growing power and growing attack on anarchists, D'Andrea and the recently emancipated Borghi left Italy near the end of 1922.[81]

The couple lived in Germany and France, and continued their anarchist activism, especially against fascism. In May 1927, Borghi was invited to tour the northeastern United States in support of Sacco and Vanzetti, who were set to be executed later that summer. A year later, D'Andrea arrived in New York City and in the fall of 1929 began a speaking tour of the country that continued into early 1930.[82] Both she and Borghi aligned themselves with the anti-organizationalist anarchist communists of *L'Adunata dei Refrattari*—a strange choice for two militant anarcho-syndicalists.

D'Andrea's topic for the fall lectures was titled "Our Violence and the Violence of Others," which explained the difference between state violence and anarchist rebellion. D'Andrea argued that state violence was carried out by the military during times of social unrest and labour strikes in order to protect private property and an exploitative capitalist economic system. Violence, according to D'Andrea, was not the preserve of anarchism. Instead, "it is sister of the slavery of man, therefore it is the negation of anarchy, it is the foundation and the base of the edifice of authority, of the State, of the Church." D'Andrea argued that anarchist violence was a form of rebellion—a legitimate form of self-defence against the violence of the state and the institutions that it protects.[83]

As a woman orator within the Italian anarchist movement in North America, D'Andrea was an anomaly. Most public speakers tended to be the males involved in the major Italian-language anarchist newspapers of the time. As a result, her lectures received a great deal of coverage and commentary in the pages of *L'Adunata dei Refrattari*. Those who reported on D'Andrea appear to have been exclusively male contributors to the newspaper. She was often described as a strong and confident speaker who was able to convince skeptics because of her well-argued presentations.[84] One letter described D'Andrea as "more than ... an incomparable orator ... [she] profoundly shakes the spirit of the listener with her dazzling ... words, [giving] to him ... true intellectual enjoyment."[85] Her west coast lectures in the winter of 1930 were such a success that one correspondent rejoiced that "Immense and profitable is the work that could be done on this coast if [we could] continually have our comrade [D'Andrea] among us."[86]

D'Andrea's experiences within the Italian anarchist movement paralleled those of other women orators involved in the radical Left. Mother Jones, the Irish-born community organizer and labour activist who was involved in a number of strikes while living in the United States, especially among miners, was described in similar terms. Her adeptness at public speaking was recalled by one striker: "No matter what impossible ideas she brought up, she made the miners think she and they could do anything."[87] Wobbly organizer Elizabeth Gurley Flynn's ability to rouse the workers was characterized thus: "She stirred them, lifted them up in her appeal for solidarity. Then at the end of the meeting, they sang. It was as though a spurt of flame had gone through the audience, something stirring and powerful, a feeling which has made the liberation of people possible, something beautiful and strong had swept through the people and welded them together, singing."[88] Like these more famous left-wing women orators, D'Andrea was something of an anarchist celebrity. Some, perhaps too enamoured with D'Andrea's physical appearance, impressed by the rarity of a woman lecturing among the Italian anarchist movement, and perhaps simply sexist, described her in ways that differed from male lecturers. One writer in *L'Adunata dei Refrattari*, Il Cronista (The Reporter), called D'Andrea's October lecture "beautiful" and described her delivery as a "woman's heart impassioned by liberation."[89] The San Francisco commentator's description of D'Andrea is worth quoting at length: "Only the resonant voice of [the] sweetest rhythm like a mountain waterfall, of the strong and kind orator, broke the silence … [the] melody of the most pure and most beautiful Italian that we rarely get to hear. Yes, the gentle language is truly gentle when spoken from the heart and blossoms on the lips of an ardent femininity … [such] as the femininity of Virgilia D'Andrea."[90]

Gurley Flynn was also sexualized by male commentators: "Her lithe figure, her flaming red tie, her beautiful oval face with the broad clear brow and mischievous eyes: these were seen on a make shift rostrum, and wherever she went she drew people, held them as ponderous philosophers and thumping haranguers of the labor movement were unable to."[91] These examples demonstrate some of the challenges that women like D'Andrea and Gurley Flynn faced within the radical movements to which they belonged. Each was taken seriously as a lecturer but that respect was tempered with their sexualization by male commentators. In this way, those who wrote of D'Andrea's passion and femininity or Gurley Flynn's "beautiful oval face" belittled both women, whether cognizant of the fact or not, by refusing to focus solely on their oratorical abilities and well-argued points.

The coverage given to men involved in public lectures were, not surprisingly, devoid of such gendered language. The reportage in *L'Adunata* of a series of lectures given by Constantino Zonchello in Detroit in June 1924, for instance, expressed the happiness of local comrades that Zonchello had returned to the city and commented on the anarchist's speaking abilities.[92] Pietro Allegra's speech at an antifascist rally in New Haven, Connecticut, was similarly straightforward. The writer discussed Allegra's fiery words against Mussolini and his supporters and the cries of support he received from the audience.[93] No comment was made of the speaker's facility with Italian or how the words blossomed from his lips.

Much like women of the wider Left, Italian women faced a number of challenges within the anarchist movement. But even given the various issues with which they had to contend, anarchism, like socialism and communism, provided women space for progressive organizing and activism that was generally unavailable in the mainstream feminist movement.[94] Male anarchists, as did their male counterparts on the Left, viewed women as equals to men, at least in theory. However, among socialists and communists the "woman question" never outranked arguments respecting the revolutionary seizure of state power.[95]

Feminist anarchists connected issues that their comrades kept separate. Bakunin, for instance, stated that "we demand, along with freedom, equal rights and duties for men and women—that is, equalization of the rights of women, political as well as social and economic rights, with those of men."[96] He was also opposed to compulsory marriage and felt that marriage as an institution would go the way of the state in an anarchist society to be replaced by free unions.[97] Bakunin may have written about the role of women in a postrevolutionary sense, but anarchists such as Voltairine de Cleyre and Emma Goldman addressed their contemporaries in the present. Both criticized marriage, seeing it as a form of slavery. De Cleyre even advised women not to move in with men they loved if it meant becoming the man's housekeeper and discussed marital rape in her essay entitled "Sex Slavery."[98] Goldman and De Cleyre also argued that women should have the right to be childless or to limit the number of children they had, and both supported the idea of free love.[99] It appears that women in the anarchist movement were more likely than their male counterparts to address issues that affected female comrades and non-anarchist women in general. In this, they resembled their sisters in competing Left movements. However, as historian Joan Sangster has shown, for Canadian communists in particular, the inclusion of birth control and free love in the party program was the result of these issues being addressed in the Soviet Union as well as by women party members in Canada.[100] For anarchists, on the other hand, the introduction of women's issues was due to their own initiatives and not because of a party line. Goldman and De Cleyre may also have had more influence among male comrades than most women in the movement, which in turn allowed them to speak on issues not normally broached by males. This is not to suggest that debates surrounding women's involvement did not occur—the incident at the Prosperity Club is an important example—but "the less authoritarian nature of anarchism and its loosely constructed ideological tenets ... attracted women of various cultural and economic backgrounds." The anarchist movement did provide women a contingent and vulnerable space for resistance against misogyny and sexism.[101]

The paths individuals travelled to their anarchism varied. Some were politicized before leaving Italy or may have been born into a family that identified itself as anarchist. For others, it was their experiences as transnational migrants and the exploitation they faced, first at home and then abroad, that radicalized them. If an Italian's experience as a transnational migrant did not lead to politicization, having a partner who identified as an anarchist or exposure to anarchist cultural events could prove influential.

The existence of an anarchist movement in Italy can be traced to the late nineteenth century, so it was not uncommon for families to be deeply rooted in anarchism and pass their politics along to future generations. Such was the case with Gabriella "Ella" Antolini, whose father and brothers were all anarchists. Antolini was imprisoned in 1918 after being caught transporting dynamite from Youngstown, Ohio, to Milwaukee, Wisconsin, to be used in retaliation against prosecutors who had recently sentenced eleven Italian anarchists to lengthy prison terms for a bombing they did not commit.[102] William Gallo was also born into a family of anarchists. While living in Paterson, New Jersey, at the age of ten, he worked for the Paterson-based anarchist newspaper *La Questione Sociale*, where he folded the paper, addressed it, and delivered it to the post office.[103]

Another avenue to anarchism, the one apparently followed more often by Italian women than men, was marriage. Irma Cassolino became an anarchist after marrying her husband Giobbe Sanchini. Both were deported from the United States in 1919 for their anarchist activities.[104] Concetta Silvestri, who lived in Massachusetts, was drawn to anarchism after meeting Silverio De Chellis, whom she later married.[105] Maria Vecile of Sault Ste. Marie, Ontario, turned to anarchism under the influence of her husband, Umberto Martignago.[106] In most of these cases, it is difficult to determine under what circumstances the acceptance of anarchism occurred. Did men put pressure on their spouses to become anarchists? Was the adoption of this political philosophy something that women who married anarchists gradually came into on their own? In the case of Vecile and Martignago, at least, the couple's daughter, Libera Martignago Bortolotti, explained that her father's role in developing her mother's anarchism arose not out of coercion but from mutual respect.[107]

Other Italian migrants already identified themselves as anarchists before they migrated from Italy, as was the case with the above-mentioned Giobbe Sanchini.[108] Some, such as Oreste Fabrizi, Alberico Pirani, and Bartolomeo Provo, were involved with the socialist movement in their native Italy but did not see themselves as anarchists until after their migration.

The plight of Nicola Sacco and Bartolomeo Vanzetti was another important way in which many Italian migrants were introduced to anarchism and led to the formation of anarchist identities. The arrest of the two anarchists for murders, stemming from a bankroll heist in Massachusetts in 1920, led to a trial the following year. Even though the evidence against them was circumstantial at best, both were found guilty and sentenced to death. Many believed that Sacco and Vanzetti had been tried not so much for their involvement in the robbery as for their political beliefs and immigrant status during the period of anti-foreign radical hysteria known as the Red Scare. In early 1922, Attilio Bortolotti, who was living and working in Windsor, Ontario, was given a pamphlet explaining why Sacco and Vanzetti were innocent and had not been given a fair trial. He wanted to know more about the men and what anarchism meant so he visited the library. Eventually, Bortolotti was able to gather some papers, including Malatesta's *Fra Contadini* (Between Peasants) and a pamphlet by Sébastien Faure, a prominent French anarchist who had written *Autorité ou liberté* (1891), *La question sociale* (1906), and *Douze preuves de l'inexistence de Dieu* (1914). It is possible that the pamphlet Bortolotti read was one of these three. It took Bortolotti half a year to understand the material, but it had a great influence on him, and led to his self-identification as an anarchist.[109] In addition, Valerio Isca and his partner Ida Pilat, both of New York City, became anarchists because of the Sacco and Vanzetti case.[110]

Previous scholarship on Italian leftists has demonstrated the roles that class, ethnicity, and gender all played with regards to the formation of radical identities. Italians were one of the most proletarianized migrant groups in North America, often working as poorly paid labourers in precarious job settings. In many cases, their post-migration experiences were little less repressive than those they had known before they left Italy. As exploited workers, their radicalization could occur before or after their arrival in Canada or the United States. This was certainly the case for the anarchists in this study. Many of them were skilled workers but this did not necessarily mean that they enjoyed a middle-class lifestyle as did their Canadian- or America-born counterparts. Some anarchists who already had a trade were forced to take whatever work they could find to support themselves and their families.

Most Italian migrants identified not with a unified nation-state but with a particular hometown or region. Yet, among the host Anglo-Celtic societies of Canada and the United States, these migrants were labelled as "Italians" and often referred to in explicitly racist ways. The discrimination Italian migrants faced in these host societies could be brutal at times. The relationship between anarchists and an Italian state was complicated. Many chose to either maintain regional identities or embrace a non-statist internationalism. Still, appeals to "Italianness" were made by anarchists most prominently during battles with fascists in Little Italies during the 1920s and 1930s, as they sought to demonstrate that there was a radical alternative to the fascist world view.

The Italian anarchist movement in North America was dominated by men to a large extent. They were the ones who edited anarchist newspapers and authored its articles. In addition, it tended to be men who gained prominence through their involvement with these newspapers or as public speakers. Women were active in the movement but they had to face a number of challenges from male comrades who questioned their ability to be anarchists or relegated them to domestic roles as meal providers for social events, or as mothers and educators for the next generation of anarchist militants. But even with its problems, the anarchist movement tended to be more progressive than the mainstream feminist movement and, in some cases, the wider Left.

Issues of identity were further complicated for anarchists due to the strong influence wielded by certain key figures within the movement. Men like Luigi Galleani and Carlo Tresca, for instance, identified with specific forms of anarchism that informed their theories and practices. And it was often with these "leaders" that the rank-and-file of the movement aligned themselves. Thus, it was not only class, ethnicity, and gender that informed transnational anarchist identities, but also the adoption of a particular anarchist philosophy. An anarchist might find his or her choices in life tightly circumscribed by belonging to a particular group led by a particular leader.[111] It could matter profoundly, for example, if one declared for Galleani or, conversely, aligned oneself with Tresca. This militancy could at times work against anarchists, especially when fascists began to assert their presence in Italian communities in North America. As the next chapter will show, the conflict between Galleani and Tresca—based both on personality and differing anarchist philosophies—had a significant effect on the movement.

CHAPTER FIVE

FACTIONAL DISPUTES

The two most influential personalities within the transnational Italian anarchist movement in North America were the anti-organizationalist anarchist communist Luigi Galleani and the anarcho-syndicalist Carlo Tresca.[1] Both of these men were able to garner loyal followers through the anarchist newspapers they edited, their speaking tours, and their involvement in labour struggles. Their differing views on anarchist theory and practice, as well as the rivalry between them for supporters, led to a deep schism within the Italian anarchist movement. And, after Galleani was deported to Italy in 1919, his adherents in the United States, who launched their own newspaper, *L'Adunata dei Refrattari*, maintained their attacks on Tresca. In fact, during the interwar period, the interactions between both factions became increasingly combative and irreconcilable. The pages of *L'Adunata dei Refrattari* and *Il Martello* often became the battleground for accusations and rebuttals.

Much has been made of the rift between Tresca and Galleani. Both Nunzio Pernicone and Dorothy Gallagher have described the adherents of Galleani, known as Galleanisti, as waging a personal war against the anarcho-syndicalist Tresca for a series of "crimes" that sullied his anarchist credentials. They have also demonstrated how this antagonistic relationship affected the ability of Italian anarchists to work together, even in the face of fascism—proving how divisive activist identities based on particular figures could be.[2] But how far-reaching was this feud? Since the editorship of *L'Adunata* was overseen from New York City and Newark, New Jersey, and Tresca was active in New York City, this rift was largely contained to these locales. The reality of anarchist activity in other sites—southern Ontario and the northeastern United States—was quite different. In fact, when it came to struggles against fascism, for example in such cities as Detroit and Toronto, the contrast was remarkable. These outlying Italian anarchists were not as divided amongst themselves as their comrades in New York City; they were also far more willing to work with the wider Italian radical community. The transnational perspective—with a heightened awareness of both the global and local contexts—thus gives us a different understanding of the Galleani/Tresca split, rather than one that just focuses on ideologies, personalities, and localities.

Luigi Galleani was instrumental in helping build an Italian anarchist movement in the United States during the time he lived there. He was a proponent of anti-organizationalist anarchist communism, a school that shunned organization in its furtherance of a philosophy that adhered to the anarchist communist premise "from each according to ability, to each according to need." Anarchists of this tendency believed that revolutionary activity should emerge spontaneously and that permanent organizations, whether labour unions or anarchist federations, would only lead to bureaucracy and dogma. Galleani's anarchism was also marked by a strong advocacy of violence as a revolutionary tool. The proletariat and the bourgeoisie were engaged in a class war and workers had to defend themselves in the same way as the ruling class.

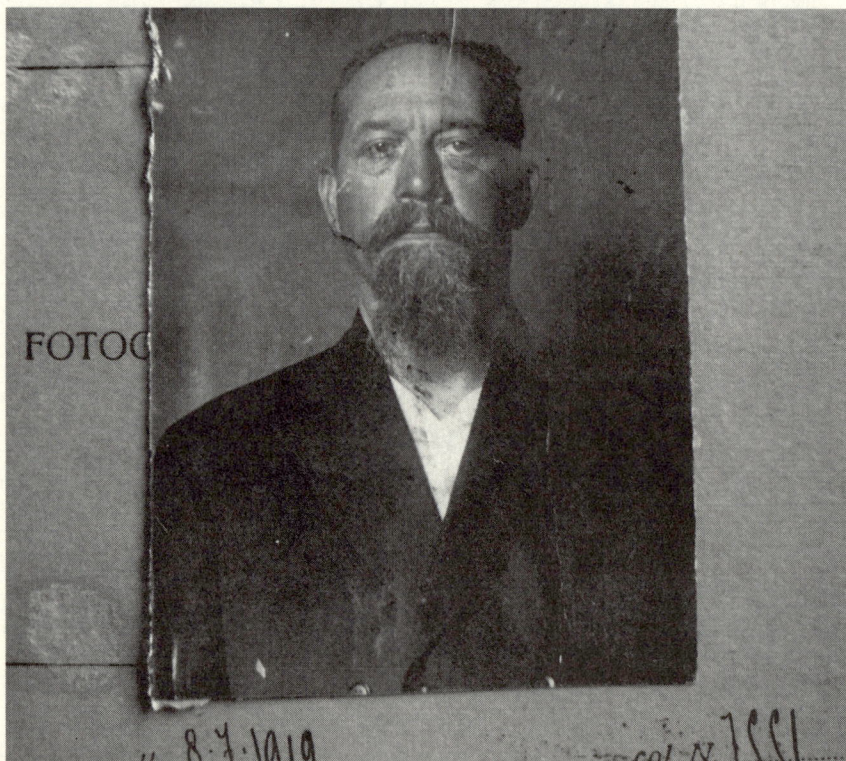

Figure 18. Luigi Galleani. Busta 2241, CPC, ACS.

Galleani has been described by comrades as an honest and humorous person who had many friends. He was renowned for his excellent oratorical abilities and debating skills. Galleani was university educated and very intelligent. He spoke so well during his speeches that "the ordinary guy in the street didn't understand him."[3] Galleani must have been a very charismatic personality because, even though it was hard for many anarchists to follow his words, people "loved him anyway."[4]

Galleani was born on 12 August 1861 in the town of Vercelli, not far from Turin. His father was a schoolteacher and the Galleani family enjoyed a middle-class existence. Galleani became interested in anarchism in his late teens, but it was not until he started a law degree at the University of Turin that he began to speak publicly against the government and capitalism. Galleani completed his degree but never practised this profession.[5] Instead, he focussed his energies full-time on Italian anarchism and the wider labour movement.[6] Galleani, along with others of his generation, became an important leader and militant within the Italian anarchist milieu.[7]

By the late 1880s, Galleani was contributing articles to the Italian anarchist press and establishing newspapers of his own, such as the Turin-based *Gazetta Operaia* (Workers' Gazette), which was oriented towards Malatesta's organizational anarchist-communism with a strong support of syndicalism. He went on speaking tours and became an important organizer for the Italian labour movement, especially during the textile workers' strikes in and around Turin. Galleani's efforts also led to important inroads for anarchism among Italian labourers. With all this activity, it did not take long for local authorities to become interested in the anarchist. The threat of arrest forced Galleani to flee Italy in 1889, but he was absent from the country for only a short while, returning that same year.[8] Upon his return, the anarchist's renewed activism and more visible profile made police more determined to put an end to his political work.

That chance finally came in early 1894, when Galleani and other anarchists were arrested by Genovese police and charged with conspiracy to commit a criminal act. Though evidence against the anarchists was lacking, they were found guilty. Galleani was sentenced to five years *domicilio coatto*, or forced domicile, on the island of Pantelleria.[9] While there, Galleani met his future companion Maria Rallo[10] and continued to write on anarchism. However, he did not serve his entire sentence on the island. Near the end of 1899, a plan was developed among some of Galleani's anarchist comrades who lived abroad to rescue him from the island. Given a false passport under the name of Antonio Valenza, Galleani, along with Rallo, sailed to Tunisia, Malta, and then to Cairo where he lived for almost one year. After Gaetano Bresci assassinated

King Umberto I on 29 July 1900, Galleani was arrested in Cairo but was not extradited to Italy. Instead, he was granted shelter by the British and moved to London. Unable to find adequate employment in the city, Galleani and Rallo relocated to the United States, arriving on 1 October 1901. Galleani was now forty years old.[11] The couple settled in Paterson, New Jersey, and Galleani began to edit the anarchist publication *La Questione Sociale*.[12]

During this time, Galleani's anarchist beliefs underwent a slight transformation. He was still an anarchist communist, but he came to believe that organization of any kind was the antithesis of anarchism. In the late nineteenth century, the Italian anarchist movement was experiencing a crisis over its future. The harsh repression unleashed by the Italian state and the anarchists' insurrectionary failures led to two different solutions: an organizationalist one that argued anarchists should form a semi-legal national party that would seek mass public support while spurning parliamentary action; and the other, anti-organizationalist, that would see the anarchist movement become invisible, allowing for continued class war against the state but providing no easy target for the Italian authorities. In addition to an emphasis on security culture among anti-organizationalists, they also nurtured a deeply held mistrust of institutions of any kind because of their potential authoritarian and bureaucratic behaviour. In their view, workers and peasants would organize spontaneously around specific grievances, struggle for change, and, once their demands were met, disband until other issues arose. This school of thought came out strongly against the formation of permanent organizations, such as labour unions, in which power would often be held by a minority acting in its own best interests and not those of its members.[13]

But Galleani's turn to anti-organizationalist anarchist communism did not mean his involvement in labour struggles came to an end. On the contrary, between April and June 1902, Galleani was involved in the dye workers' strike at Paterson's silk mills. The mostly Italian dye workers were attempting to form a union to improve their working conditions. On 18 June, Galleani led more than 6,000 workers to the mills where they seized control of operations. Six hours later, the state militia arrived to "restore order." While trying to free some strikers held by police, Galleani was wounded when a bullet grazed the left side of his face. Eight strikers died that day as did one police officer.[14] Because of his involvement in the violence, Galleani was indicted for incitement to riot. As previous experience had taught him, when trying to avoid legal prosecution, it was a good idea to cross an international border. This demonstrates the significance of the border among anarchists. Not only did it act as a confining barrier, but it could also be used to frustrate state repression.

Galleani entered Canada and lived in Montreal, staying with José Gonzalez,[15] a successful manufacturer of Cuban cigars, for at least five months while continuing to contribute to *La Questione Sociale*.[16] He did not enjoy his stay in the city. His separation from his wife Maria and the children, and the stress that came with not knowing whether he could return to the United States, had a great effect on him. He was also disappointed that the only reading material he could find in the city was religious in nature and he had to rely on comrades in Europe to send him anarchist literature.[17] Though Galleani wanted to leave Montreal, his delicate legal situation in the United States meant he had nowhere else to go.[18]

Around the time Galleani was living in Montreal, there were interesting developments among Jewish anarchists who had migrated from Eastern Europe, London, and New York to work in Montreal's burgeoning textile trade. One of the first activities was the establishment of a radical Yiddish library at the home of Hirsch "Harry" Hershman, originally from the region of Bukovina, which is now divided between Romania and Ukraine. Hershman migrated first to New York City where he was employed as a tailor, working anywhere from fifteen to eighteen hours a day. Under these conditions, it did not take long for him to join the local union movement. In 1901, he moved to Montreal and again worked in the garment industry. The radical library was originally situated in the home that Hershman shared with his wife Jenny, and it was she who oversaw its operation. Eventually, the library moved to a rented storefront located at 392 Saint-Laurent Boulevard. All the Yiddish-language books and pamphlets that the library carried had to be ordered from Berlin and New York City. Hershman was instrumental in organizing Mutual Aid, a discussion group that comprised many left-wing tendencies but with the majority identifying as anarchists.[19] Based on the few letters I have obtained written by Galleani during his time in Montreal, it does not appear as though he had any contact with the local Jewish anarchists and he makes no mention of an Italian anarchist presence in the city at this time. In 1905, the Italian consul general in Montreal wrote to then Canadian Prime Minister Wilfrid Laurier to ask if Canadian authorities could investigate whether Galleani was still living in Montreal. The Dominion Police looked into the matter and determined that, after a few months in the city, Galleani had returned to the United States.[20]

In fact, Galleani had resumed living in the United States in early 1903 after re-entering the country, using the false name of Luigi Pimpino, a pseudonym under which he wrote articles in anarchist publications. He settled at Barre, Vermont. Barre was home to a group of Italian anarchists who were mostly stone and marble cutters from Carrara and other northern Italian towns. In

June 1903, Galleani, with the help of local anarchists, began to publish *Cronaca Sovversiva*, which Paul Avrich described as "one of the most important and ably edited periodicals in the history of the anarchist movement." Most of the writing was done by Galleani under various assumed names.[21] The newspaper's circulation ranged from 4,000 to 5,000 copies per issue. It travelled along transnational Italian anarchist networks in North and South America, Europe, Northern Africa, and Australia. In 1912, Galleani moved to Lynn, Massachusetts, where he continued to publish *Cronaca Sovversiva*.[22]

While living in the United States, Galleani went on numerous speaking tours, travelling to Italian communities and lecturing at mining camps, meeting halls, and social events. Not only did Galleani's efforts increase the number of Italian anarchists by a few thousand, but the speaking tours also led to the creation of a network of Italian anarchist groups. They shared a subculture characterized by "passionate loyalty to the anarchist cause, indomitable courage in the face of adversity, sectarian inflexibility and intolerance in matters of ideology and tactics, and general endorsement of popular violence."[23] Galleani was not a pacifist and he believed that violence was necessary to avenge those who had felt the force of state repression, whether they be fellow anarchists, labour activists, or anti-war socialists. The state, regardless of whether it pertained to Italy, the United States, or elsewhere, was more than willing to conduct war against those who struggled to better their lot in life. Thus, the same means employed by government, often at the behest of capital, had to be used by anarchists in a violent class war. To this end, Galleani published *La Salute è in voi* (Health is Within You) in 1905. This was a forty-six-page pamphlet that called for retaliation against "tyrants and oppressors" and listed instructions for the manufacture of bombs. But it was not until the 1910s that the Galleanisti put the manual into practice. In 1914, anarchist Frank Tannenbaum led a procession of homeless and unemployed men to New York City's various churches to draw attention to the hardships faced by the jobless. Tannenbaum was eventually arrested for his activism after he and those he was leading were evicted from the Church of St. Alphonsus. He was sentenced to one year in prison and fined $500. In retaliation, a bomb detonated in the rectory of St. Alphonsus, causing minor damage. A relatively short time later, another bomb was planted beneath the court seat of Magistrate John A.L. Campbell, who had sentenced Tannenbaum. The bomb, however, was discovered and disarmed before it could detonate.[24] This was the first in a series of bombings that were carried out by anarchists and that targeted the anarchists' and workers' enemies—the police, robber barons, judges, senators, attorney generals, and postmasters.[25]

These multiple attacks did not lead to any legal action against Galleani because he was never directly involved. But American authorities were well aware of his standing within the Italian anarchist movement and closely watched his actions in order to bring charges forward. Their chance came in May 1917. After an anti-conscription article entitled "Matricolati!" (Registrants!) appeared in *Cronaca Sovversiva*, the newspaper's offices were raided and Galleani was arrested.[26] Shortly thereafter, *Cronaca Sovversiva* lost its mailing privileges, making it difficult to deliver issues to subscribers. In the fall of 1917, a law was passed that required all non-English newspapers to translate all articles on the war into English. Instead of complying with the new law, *Cronaca Sovversiva* suspended publication and went underground, producing issues intermittently.[27] The newspaper was finally banned outright in July 1918. In order to effectively deport those the United States government considered enemies of the state, it was necessary to make amendments to the existing Immigration Act, which targeted anyone who "advocate[d] or [taught] the duty, necessity, or propriety of the unlawful assaulting or killing of any officer or officers, either of specific individuals or of officers generally, of the Government of the United States or of any other organized government, because of his or their official character, or who advocate[d] or [taught] the unlawful destruction of property."[28] The revamped act of 1918 now named anarchists directly and made it possible for the United States government to deport anyone who identified as an anarchist or was involved in carrying out acts of political violence. Anyone in possession of anarchist literature could also be expelled from the country.[29] Thus, the American government was now legally empowered to rid itself of Galleani and his supporters.

Galleani and eight of his adherents were deported to Italy aboard the *Duca degli Abruzzi* on 24 June 1919. Galleani, a fifty-seven-year-old diabetic who had lived in the United States for eighteen years, had to leave behind his wife and five children, three of whom were born in America.[30] Galleani arrived in Genoa in July 1919 and settled in Turin, where he was closely watched by Italian police. In January 1920, Galleani began to publish *Cronaca Sovversiva* once more. After Mussolini came to power in October 1922, the anarchist was arrested, found guilty of sedition, and sentenced to fourteen months in prison. This was the first in a series of imprisonments for Galleani, who refused to abide by fascist rule.[31] In February 1930, because of his failing health, Galleani was released from prison and allowed to move to the Tuscan village of Caprigliola where he was under constant police surveillance. It was here, while on one of his daily walks, that Galleani suffered a heart attack and died on 4 November 1931.[32]

Galleani's nemesis, Carlo Tresca, was born on 9 March 1879 in Sulmona, located in the Abruzzi region. He came from a large and successful upper-class family who lived on an estate that produced wine and olive oil. His family also owned a stationery store. The Trescas experienced economic hardship during the 1890s, in part because of a tariff war between France and Italy, whereby French imports of Italian wine were cut by half. As a result, there was not enough money to pay for Tresca's university education; so, he was enrolled in an Istituto Tecnico (Technical Institute), where he was trained to become a bureaucrat. It was while taking courses at the institute that Tresca began to attend Partito Socialista Italiana (PSI) lectures. By 1898, he had joined the party.[33] As a member of the PSI, Tresca carried out propaganda amongst artisans and peasants living in Sulmona. His first arrest occurred in June 1902, after helping organize the disruption of a patriotism demonstration held by local monarchists. Tresca was charged with shouting subversive epithets and sentenced to a few months in jail.[34] After his release, and as editor of the Sulmona-based socialist paper *Il Germe*, Tresca used this platform to personally attack the *carabinieri* captain who had arrested him. In response, the captain sued Tresca for libel and the socialist returned to jail in the spring of 1903 to serve a brief sentence. His repeated attacks through the newspaper against Sulmona's elites meant more charges of libel, which in Italy during that time could mean imprisonment for up to five years. In April 1904, a penal tribunal sentenced Tresca to nineteen months and one day in jail, in addition to a 2,041-lire fine and court costs. Instead of serving the sentence and paying the fine, Tresca decided to immigrate to the United States.[35]

Tresca arrived in America in 1904 and settled in Philadelphia, where he joined the Federazione Socialista Italiana (FSI), the socialist, and later syndicalist, organization created the previous year by Italian migrants living in the United States. The purpose of the FSI was to provide an alternative voice in Italian communities controlled by colonial elites, as well as to build a movement that could mobilize supporters in times of strikes and the defence campaigns that often resulted.[36] That same year, Tresca became the director of the FSI newspaper *Il Proletario* and, as with *Il Germe* in Sulmona, he used this paper to attack the migrants' exploiters, the *padroni* and bankers and the Italian consuls who protected them. When the Industrial Workers of the World (IWW) was formed during a Chicago meeting in 1905, Tresca, who had always believed in the potential of direct action, began to advocate revolutionary syndicalism. This created conflict with the FSI, which during that period endorsed socialism by the ballot box and was affiliated to the Socialist Party of America (SPA) and the Socialist Labor Party (SLP) at different times. The following year, Tresca left *Il Proletario* and began writing for *La Voce del Popolo* and later *La Plebe,* where he again declared war on the enemies of Italian workers living in the United States. As in Italy, these personal attacks resulted in Tresca being charged with libel and he served a couple of short jail terms.[37] Upon his release from imprisonment in 1910, he launched the newspaper *L'Avvenire* (The Future).[38]

Figure 19. Carlo Tresca. Busta 5208, CPC, ACS.

But Tresca's activism was not limited to the printed word; his work with the IWW, though he never officially joined the organization, put him on the front lines of numerous strikes in the Midwest and northeastern United States. The first strike involving Tresca occurred in Lawrence, Massachusetts. It began in January 1912, when mill owners reduced wages after a state-wide law was introduced that limited the hours that women and children were allowed to work. In response, Italian, Lithuanian, and Polish mill workers, most of them women, stopped working, sabotaged looms, and left the mills. The Italian workers were represented by an IWW local and the union sent Joseph Ettor and Arturo Giovannitti to Lawrence to lead the strike. During the course of the labour struggle, both men were framed for the murder of Anna Lo Pizzo, an Italian striker, and John Rami, a Syrian boy, even though it was the police and militia, respectively, who were responsible for the deaths. As a result of the incarceration of Ettor and Giovannitti, a handful of IWW organizers were called to Lawrence, including "Big Bill" Haywood and Elizabeth Gurley Flynn, to lead the strike. This infusion of leadership led to a workers' victory. However, at the end of the strike Ettor and Giovannitti were still in prison, awaiting trial, and this was unacceptable to the IWW and the Lawrence mill workers. The resources mobilized for the strike were quickly transferred to the struggle to free the two incarcerated Wobblies. There was a dire need for a well-respected organizer to carry out this work among the Italian workers, and this led to Tresca's presence in Lawrence. Due to the efforts of Tresca and others, Ettor and Giovannitti were eventually acquitted of the murder charges. For Tresca, the Lawrence strike had two important personal outcomes: it was his position on the struggle's tactics that sparked the rift between him and Galleani, on which more will be written below; and in the course of the strike, he met the Wobbly speaker and organizer Elizabeth Gurley Flynn, with whom he was to have a thirteen-year relationship.[39]

After Tresca's successes in Lawrence, the IWW began to call on him to assist in strikes in which Italian workers were involved. In 1913, he took part in the Paterson silk workers' strike. The root causes of this conflict stemmed from the refusal of factory owners to implement an eight-hour day. At the same time, employers doubled the workload and lowered wages. Unfortunately, the factory owners refused to negotiate with the IWW and the strikers were forced to return to work under the same conditions that they were fighting against. Though the twenty-two-week strike ended in failure, Nunzio Pernicone attributes the militancy of the strikers to the efforts of Tresca and Flynn. The silk workers experienced police violence and mass arrests, and resisted attempts by employers to use patriotism to divide foreign and

American-born strikers. The employers also called upon the anti-IWW American Federation of Labor (AFL) in the hopes of derailing the strike. Through all of this, the strikers remained committed to a victory, until the economic burden on them and their families could no longer be tolerated.[40]

The Mesabi Range strike was sparked in 1916 when the Oliver Mining Company introduced a work speed-up to correspond with the new eight-hour day. This meant that there was no real increase in wages once hours had been reduced. Again, the IWW requested that Tresca travel to Minnesota and help lead the strike. The Oliver Mining Company refused to meet any of the strikers' demands and instead hired 1,000 "special guards" who meted out corporate "justice" through the beating and murder of striking employees. Clearly, this was no place for a union organizer. During the strike, Tresca, along with others, was indicted as an accessory "after the fact" for the murder of a deputized mine guard who had been killed by Phillip and Militza Masonovitch and three boarders, all strikers, in self-defence after the mine guard had forcibly entered their home and assaulted them. Tresca and the IWW organizers charged under the indictment, as well as Militza Masonovitch and one of the boarders, were allowed to go free while the rest were given prison terms. Haywood was outraged when he heard that a deal had been reached whereby workers were jailed and the organizers were freed. This event and its aftermath signalled the end of Tresca's involvement with the IWW.[41]

Tresca embraced anarcho-syndicalism only gradually. He did not begin to identify himself as an anarcho-syndicalist until his mid-thirties. His grassroots PSI connections in Italy and his IWW links in the United States foreshadowed his more explicit post-1914 advocacy of revolutionary syndicalism. During this period, Tresca began to question whether the IWW was still syndicalist. He believed in direct action as a tactic and, so, was no stranger to anarchists; Tresca had worked with them during strikes and he deeply respected Emma Goldman and Alexander Berkman. It may have been the influence of these two well-known anarchists during the unemployed actions in New York City in 1914 that led Tresca to identify himself as an anarcho-syndicalist.[42]

Prior to America's involvement in the First World War, Tresca had written articles and spoken publicly against the war. Once the United States declared war on Germany in April 1917, the anarcho-syndicalist began arguing that in order for workers to resist the war effort, they should engage in general strikes and revolution. It was these opinions that led to Tresca's close surveillance by federal authorities at a time when anything radical was considered un-American. During this time of heightened xenophobia and fear of the radical foreigner, Italian-language anarchist newspapers, such as *Cronaca Sovversiva* and

L'Era Nuovo, were having their offices raided and editors arrested. Tresca and his newspaper *L'Avvenire* had not been targeted in the same manner because of an impending indictment against him and many others who were involved with the IWW. Federal authorities charged almost 200 Wobblies with conspiracy to impede the war effort and Tresca was taken into custody. However, at the time of the indictment, Tresca had not been active with the IWW; so, charges against him were eventually dropped. He was one of the fortunate few since the overwhelming majority of Wobbly defendants were found guilty and given long prison terms and large fines.[43] That same year the state repression against *L'Avvenire* intensified as issues were continually being labelled "non-mailable," which increased the cost of producing the newspaper. Tresca had no choice but to cease its publication. However, this did not mean the end of his involvement in the radical press. In order to circumvent the problems he was having with the postal authorities, Tresca bought *Il Martello: Giornale politico, letterario ed artistico* (The Hammer: A Political, Literary, and Artistic Newspaper), an anti-religious publication, for less than $300 from Luigi Preziosi, who had started the newspaper in 1916. Because *Il Martello* was still under the name of Preziosi and published articles on non-political themes, such as astronomy and poetry, it was able to maintain its second-class mail privileges.[44] Following the First World War, Tresca's anarchist views began to resurface and he denounced the 1919 deportation of anarchists like Goldman, Berkman, and Galleani. After the arrest of Sacco and Vanzetti in May 1920, the newspaper made their plight a focus and, when Mussolini came to power in Italy, *Il Martello* went on the offensive against fascism.

During the interwar period, Tresca continued to report on labour struggles in the United States and Italy, and maintained his attacks against wealthy, often fascist-leaning Italian elites living in New York City. *Il Martello* was not Tresca's only venue. He often spoke against the far Right at rallies and was involved in more than a few altercations with local blackshirts. After the outbreak of the Spanish Civil War, Tresca provided coverage of the conflict and helped raise money for the Republican and anarchist cause. After the conflict's tragic conclusion, which the anarcho-syndicalist felt was due to the communist betrayal of the social revolution, Tresca severed his ties with American-based communists with whom he had willingly worked in the past.[45]

Tresca had garnered a great many enemies during his life because of his political activities. So when he was assassinated on 11 January 1943 after leaving the *Il Martello* office at Fifth Avenue and 15th Street, there was no shortage of possible suspects. The communists were angry with Tresca because he had testified under oath in front of a grand jury and accused Schachno Epstein,

Soviet spy and editor of the communist newspaper *Freiheit*, of involvement in the disappearance of former Communist Party member Julia Stuart Poyntz.[46] Some, such as Hugo Rolland (real name Erasmo Abate), believed members of the L'Adunata group were responsible for Tresca's death.[47] Generoso Pope, the wealthy construction contractor, supporter of Mussolini, and editor of *Il Progresso Italo-Americano*, had been attacked by Tresca in the pages of *Il Martello* on numerous occasions. Tresca's murder may also have been ordered by Frank Garofalo, a mobster who was Pope's enforcer. Tresca had publicly insulted Garofalo at a war bond banquet in Manhattan in the fall of 1942 and the strongman was overheard expressing his determination to get back at him.[48] The anarcho-syndicalist's murder has never been solved; only his killer, Carmine Galante, a convicted criminal with ties to organized crime, has been identified. His motives and connections remain obscure.[49]

Tresca may have had enemies, but he had even more friends and comrades. He has been described as outgoing, friendly, and the kind of person who "talked to everybody."[50] Sam Dolgoff, an anarchist comrade of Tresca's, recalled the time he travelled with Tresca to New Haven, Connecticut, for a meeting. Following Tresca's speech, men would bring their children to him and explain that Tresca was a great man. As Dolgoff reminisced, "These were not the sort of people to fall down on their knees, but they loved him."[51] Tresca was also known as a man of action and courage, a fighter who "more than any other man was responsible for checking the Blackshirt groups from treading the streets of New York."[52] A generous spirit, Tresca was willing to help comrades in need. In the 1930s, for instance, he let the Jewish, Russian, Chinese, and African-American anarchists of the Vanguard Group use the *Il Martello* office to hold meetings and also gave them a page in his publication for their English-language articles.[53]

Tresca and Galleani had different approaches to anarchism. Galleani was considered a leading theorist within the movement in North America. His views on anti-organizationalist anarchist communism were set down in *La Fine dell'anarchismo?* (The End of Anarchism?), a response to Francesco Saverio Merlino's assertion in 1907 that anarchism's importance as a political ideology had ended. Merlino had been an anarchist from 1877 to 1897, and as a lawyer had defended Gaetano Bresci. But it was the anti-organizationalist turn to political violence that caused Merlino to leave the movement and join the socialists.[54] His thoughts on anarchism were expressed during an interview he had with a reporter from the Turin-based newspaper *La Stampa* in June 1907 on the occasion of a regional anarchist congress taking place in Rome later that month.[55] During the interview, Merlino was asked to share his thoughts on the state of anarchism. He stated that the anarchist movement was no longer of any consequence because its most valuable aspects, on which he does not elaborate, had been adopted and put into practice by the socialists, while anarchism's less useful utopianism had been dispensed with altogether. He explained that the two existing tendencies in Italy, which he divided into organizationalists and anti-organizationalists,[56] were ineffectual because of their own political positions. The organizationalists, according to Merlino, could not "find a form of organization compatible with their anarchist principles," while the anti-organizationalists were unable to "find a clear way to action." When asked to share his thoughts on the future of anarchism, Merlino answered that anarchism did not have one. He pointed to a lack of "men of high calibre" and claimed that Elisée Reclus and Peter Kropotkin were the last intellectuals of the movement. Merlino also believed that anarchist thought and practice were stagnant and the movement's ability to recruit new members was non-existent. He did not feel that the congress in Rome would do anything to re-inspire the anarchist movement and predicted it would be plagued by tired debates between organizationalists and anti-organizationalists over which strain was true anarchism.[57]

Galleani's rejoinder appeared in the pages of *Cronaca Sovversiva* in ten instalments between 17 August 1907 and 25 January 1908 (all twenty-four parts of *La Fine dell'anarchismo?* were not published until the mid-1920s in *L'Adunata dei Refrattari*).[58] Within these articles, Galleani argued against Merlino's claim that anarchism had played itself out. Galleani denied Merlino's statement that socialism had co-opted the best aspects of anarchist philosophy. Had this been the case, socialists would have been opposed to government, elections, police, and courts, which, according to Galleani, was not the case.[59] He also denied that utopianism had ever been a central aspect of anarchist thought. As for the lack of promising new anarchist intellectuals, Galleani conceded the difficult-to-repress excellence of Reclus, Kropotkin, and Bakunin; but he pointed out that these three giants had been succeeded by others—such as Errico Malatesta, Max Nettlau, and the London-born historian of the First International James Guillaume.[60] Nor did Galleani deny that the anarchist movement had experienced internal conflict. However, he viewed this not as a crisis but as an important aspect of the movement's development and proof of its vitality.[61]

In *La Fine dell'anarchismo?*, Galleani also outlined his position on anarchism, revolution, and organization. Galleani's conception of an anarchist communist society meant that "everything must belong to everybody and must present the hypothesis of a world without god, without king, without government, without masters."[62] And like other anarchist communist theorists, such as Kropotkin and Malatesta, Galleani also believed that the means of production and exchange had to be owned by everyone and that each person was entitled to whatever he or she needed from what was collectively produced.[63] Anarchists rejected the ballot box and instead opted for direct action, rebellion, insurrection, and social revolution. Electoral abstentionism by anarchists did not mean apathy on their part but simply expressed their opposition to representation as well as a strong distrust of the state because of its protection of the ruling classes.[64]

Galleani believed in the general strike as a vehicle of revolution. A strike of this nature was to be openly revolutionary and demand more than better wages and shorter hours. A general strike would have to include all trades and use force and violence in order to secure the "unconditional surrender of the ruling classes."[65] However, Galleani was also a strong proponent of individual acts of violence committed in revenge against political leaders and monarchs who had dealt with anarchists in a harsh manner. This was what led to his writing *La Salute è in voi*. These acts, he believed, were the sparks that ignited the flames of insurrection and led to successful revolution. According to Galleani, violence was inevitable because the bourgeoisie was not going to allow its power to be challenged. Galleani believed that the existing order had to be destroyed to achieve a society of equal and free individuals.[66]

As an anti-organizationalist, Galleani opposed those anarchists who wanted to create an anarchist political party. For him, a project of this sort was anathema to anarchist principles because such an organization would need a constitution, a program, and various levels of bureaucracy in order to function; in short, it would come to have its own government. Party members would be forced to submit to party discipline for the greater good, even if in opposition to their own personal opinions or interests. Galleani felt that, whenever possible, anarchists had to resist compromise. With an anarchist political party, this would not be possible.[67] Labour unions were another form of organization that Galleani did not support because of their reformist character. Whether led by conservatives or syndicalists, unions recognized and consented to the capitalist economic system. Their demands did not challenge this system but only offered palliatives, such as pensions and old age security. Galleani supported anarchists who joined unions, but those who did so should always be the opposition to union leadership and never assume leadership roles themselves.[68]

Tresca and Galleani had different approaches to anarchism. Galleani was conTresca was not an anarchist theorist in the same way as Galleani. He never wrote at length about his views on anarcho-syndicalism or what a society based on these concepts would look like. In the pages of *Il Martello*, a reader could find the writings of a variety of anarchist and non-anarchist thinkers, meaning that the newspaper had no single theoretical focus. Instead, *Il Martello* gave greater attention to the struggles of the working class, attacked local fascists, and sought support for comrades who were in danger of imprisonment or deportation.[69] However, this did not mean that the newspaper was devoid of Tresca's opinions on anarcho-syndicalism, organization, and revolution, but, rather, that his views were implicit in numerous articles and never clearly articulated in a single work.

Tresca did not spend time theorizing anarcho-syndicalism but his views on the subject were similar to those of like-minded contemporaries. He believed that syndicalist unions, such as the IWW, demonstrated the best methods and forms of organizing to radicalize workers, while on the other hand, he viewed the AFL as a "bourgeois bulwark against the revolutionary aspirations of the masses."[70] In general, Tresca supported the idea of unions because he felt that only through the collective strength they offered could workers effectively struggle for their class interests. However, it was not enough for unions simply to demand better wages. They also had to organize for the abolition of wages and complete liberty for all workers.[71] Tresca was certain that workers united in syndicalist unions were capable of overthrowing the capitalist system.[72]

For Tresca, the general strike was the best means to bring about social revolution.[73] During the *biennio rosso*, he wrote with great enthusiasm on the orderly expropriation carried out by Italian workers: "They requisitioned. And it was a requisition made with method, with order, with firmness. The expropriations were granted by an improvised action committee. In all the acts of the masses was seen an expression of a conscious will not of an individual or a group of individuals, but of a class that asserted the proper authority."[74] Tresca viewed revolution as a process of social transformation begun and finished by a class or group of individuals that resulted in a conscious restructuring of society, both economically and politically.[75] He was also a proponent of insurrection and, though he did not call for acts of anarchist violence in the same way as Galleani, he did believe that workers murdered by the police and/or strike-breakers had to be avenged—as was the case when Valentino Modestino was murdered by private detectives at Paterson, New Jersey in 1913.[76] He also defended anarchists who carried out *attentats*. On 21 March

1921, anarchists Ettore Aguggini, Giuseppe Mariani, and Giuseppe Boldrini bombed Milan's Diana Theatre in an attempt to kill the city's chief of police, a fascist, for his treatment of arrested anarchists. Sadly, the attack killed twenty-one and wounded eighty, with Police Chief Gasti escaping harm.[77] In an article entitled *"Il Fascismo,"* Tresca argued against the anarchists' detractors by pointing out that less outrage had been expressed for the daily murders committed by fascists than over this one incident. Aguggini, Mariani, and Boldrini were not mercenaries, Tresca argued, but anarchist idealists motivated by the suffering that surrounded them and had been inflicted on their comrades. The anarcho-syndicalist even went so far as to call the three men "forerunners" who would be judged differently by future generations that appreciated the "humanitarian motive[s] that drove them to act."[78]

Galleani and Tresca had quite different personalities. The former has been described as a severe man too strict in his beliefs and whose word on matters he considered final.[79] However, he was also known for his honesty, humour, and oratorical skills. A few of Galleani's comrades recalled his abilities as a public speaker though one, Joseph Moro, did not always understand what was being said because Galleani's speaking style was hard to follow for those anarchists with little formal education.[80] Though it is not addressed specifically in the oral histories conducted by Paul Avrich, one has to wonder what role the language barrier played between Galleani and the rank-and-file of the movement. During this period, very few Italians spoke standardized Italian and most continued to communicate in their regional dialects. It is quite possible that Galleani, who may have spoken in his native Piedmontese, was not as easily understood by speakers of Sicilian, for instance. Tresca was a skilled orator in his own right. While on a speaking tour of California in 1915, the anarcho-syndicalist was described by a comrade as a "propagandist who knows how to communicate to the masses the virile throbbing of revolutionary sentiment." Tresca also left the crowd in a "state of emotional frenzy." [81] In contrast to those of Galleani, Tresca's speeches were never said to have been hard for his audiences to follow.

Other points of divergence between Galleani and Tresca were their differing strategies for working with others. Whereas Galleani was generally only willing to work with other anarchists, especially those who identified as anti-organizationalist anarchist communists, Tresca was far more open to collaborating with those outside the movement. The anarcho-syndicalist was on friendly terms with non-syndicalist labour leaders from the International Ladies Garment Workers' Union (ILGWU) and the Amalgamated

Clothing Workers Union (ACWU), and, before turning his back on the Communist Party following the Spanish Civil War/Revolution, joined forces with New York City communists in antifascist struggle. According to Sam Dolgoff, Tresca's willingness to work with and befriend those outside of the anarchist movement was a deliberate tactic; having such contacts with potentially helpful people meant that the anarcho-syndicalist could call upon them in time of need.[82] But another comrade of Tresca's, Jack Frager, thought the anarcho-syndicalist probably mixed too much with non-anarchists, to the detriment of his reputation.[83] And, as will be shown below, it was Tresca's willingness to work with those outside the movement that broadened the rift between him and Galleani's adherents from *L'Adunata dei Refrattari*.

Both Tresca and Galleani believed that violence was a necessary means in fighting the class war and they did not shy away from getting into physical confrontations. As mentioned above, Galleani was wounded during the 1902 Paterson strike when fired upon by a police officer. Then, in early December 1916, while Galleanisti were engaged in a confrontation with Boston police during an anti-war demonstration, Galleani stabbed a police officer in the hand with a knife.[84] Tresca was also involved in physical confrontations. For the anarcho-syndicalist, fascism could only be stopped "with out and out war."[85] During the 1920s when Italian antifascists were fighting their fascist compatriots in the streets of New York City, Tresca was in the thick of it. In fact, on more than one occasion, he and his comrades would walk into fascist-controlled neighbourhoods looking for fights.[86]

———

The antagonistic relationship between Tresca and Galleani can be traced to the former's involvement in the Ettor and Giovannitti defence campaign that followed the 1912 Lawrence, Massachusetts textile workers' strike. As strike resources were now redirected towards the defence of the jailed Wobblies, Tresca was called upon to act as a bridge between the defence committee and Lawrence's Italian workers. Speaking at a May Day rally in Lawrence, Tresca told the crowd that a general strike was the most effective way to free Ettor and Giovannitti, since American judges and courts could not be trusted to grant the two men their freedom. Plans were made to have the strike coincide with the beginning of the trial in late September. However, at a meeting to discuss preparations just days before the general strike was to be called, letters written by Ettor and Giovannitti asking that the strike be postponed were read aloud to those present. The two incarcerated Wobblies were afraid that a strike of such a political nature would end in failure, leading to serious repercussions against Italian workers.[87]

When the letters were read, everyone was in a state a shock. Tresca was not sure whether to go ahead with the strike and act against the IWW leaders or to heed the request of Ettor and Giovannitti; in the end, he chose the latter course.[88]

Tresca's decision to abide by the wishes of the jailed strike leaders and postpone the general strike angered Luigi Galleani and his adherents, who wanted the original plan to proceed. During the course of the Lawrence strike, the anti-organizationalist anarchists had worked hard to mobilize support for the workers and to raise badly needed funds. Their activism around this strike and others, as well as the popularity of Galleani and *Cronaca Sovversiva*, meant that they had influence among the workers. After the general strike plans had changed, the anti-organizationalists decided to organize workers for an industry-wide walkout. On the morning of 26 September, Umberto Postiglione, a regular contributor to *Cronaca Sovversiva*, and other anarchists showed up at various mills to tell workers to leave work at 3:00 pm, and by 3:15 the process had already begun. That night, a meeting was held in Lexington Hall with Wobblies and anarchists arguing their respective positions on a general strike. In the end, Italian workers overwhelmingly supported the labour action and as many as 12,000 went on strike the next day. The IWW wanted to reassert its control in Lawrence by curbing the duration of the strike. Their solution was a twenty-four-hour protest to occur on 30 September. The protest was well attended and it provided an opportunity for Tresca and Flynn to convince the strikers to return to work and wait for the conclusion of the Ettor and Giovannitti trial. Not everyone was willing to abandon the strike, however; Italians in particular argued for its continuation. But the majority of workers, exhausted by both the initial strike and the defence struggle for the arrested Wobblies, would not lend their support.[89] Ettor and Giovannitti were eventually acquitted of the murder charges and the strike, at least in the short term, had been successful, with all the workers' demands being met by the Lawrence mill owners. But partly because of the IWW's unwillingness to use contracts, within three years the gains achieved by the workers had all but disappeared.[90]

This disagreement over tactics at Lawrence caused the first cracks to appear in the relationship between Tresca and Galleani. Pernicone suggests that Galleani's singling out of Tresca when blame could also have been put on the IWW was based on Galleani's belief that Tresca was a rival for the leadership of Italian anarchists.[91] However, even after this event, Tresca and Galleani still continued to collaborate on occasion. Though both men differed in their anarchism, they did agree on the core anti-state, anti-capitalist, and anti-religion principles of anarchist philosophy. Thus, there were moments where concern for the other was put before their respective disagreements. In 1916, Galleani and his adherents demonstrated on behalf of Tresca after the latter's arrest during the Mesabi Range strike in Minnesota. The following year, Tresca invited Galleani to visit him in New York City, though the meeting never took place. He also denounced Galleani's deportation in 1919.[92]

Following Galleani's expulsion from the United States, some of his adherents became more hostile towards Tresca, possibly due to the fact that Tresca himself had not been deported.[93] Still, the relationship between the Galleanisti and Tresca, at least during the early 1920s, was more complicated than one based simply on mutual animosity. In April 1922, the first issue of the New York City–based *L'Adunata dei Refrattari* appeared.[94] This Italian-language anarchist newspaper was the philosophical successor to Galleani's *Cronaca Sovversiva*. It emphasized such themes as the inherent authoritarianism of organizations (whether syndicalist or communist), the complicity of the Italian monarchy and the Catholic Church in Mussolini's rise to power, and the legitimate use of political violence in response to violent state repression.[95] The day-to-day operation of the newspaper was in the hands of a few individuals, such as Efisio Constantino Zonchello, Raffaele Schiavina (using the alias Max Sartin), Osvaldo Maraviglia, Nicola "Nick" Di Domenico, and Michele "Mike" Magliocca. Zonchello was *L'Adunata's* first editor and he also wrote a number of articles under the pseudonyms Ilario di Castlered and Red. In 1928, Schiavina assumed the role of editor, but this did not mean an end to Zonchello's relationship with the newspaper. He continued to go on speaking tours and engaged in propaganda on behalf of *L'Adunata*.[96]

Schiavina's position as editor coincided with his illegal return to the United States after his deportation in 1919. It was a position he was to hold until the newspaper ceased publication in 1971. He had experience in the radical press because of his previous role as manager for *Cronaca Sovversiva*.[97] To avoid detection by American authorities and the Italian Opera Volontari Repressione Antifascista (OVRA) agents, he used the alias Max Sartin. Under Schiavina's direction, *L'Adunata dei Refrattari* maintained the high editorial standards attained while the newspaper was edited by Zonchello. But, according to Paul Avrich, Schiavina was more than just the editor; he was the newspaper's soul. He wrote most of the articles under various pseudonyms, looked after all the editorial work, and ensured the paper was sent to the printer.[98] Osvaldo Maraviglia held the position of treasurer and, in this capacity, he was responsible for sending money to various penurious anarchists or to assorted movement-related projects.[99] Nick Di Domenico acted as *L'Adunata's* manager, a position he held until at least 1926, before becoming the paper's publisher. He received and responded to correspondence sent to the newspaper.[100] And, finally, Michele Magliocca was secretary of *L'Adunata* from 1922 to 1971.[101] All of these men were also active, along with others, in Il Gruppo L'Adunata dei Refrattari, which was based in Newark, New Jersey.

Considering who was involved in publishing *L'Adunata*, it is surprising that Tresca helped with early issues of the newspaper by editing proofs and giving technical advice. During this time, both *L'Adunata dei Refrattari* and *Il Martello* posted advertisements for each other's social and fundraising events.[102] A May 1922 issue of *Il Martello*, for instance, featured a notice sent by Osvaldo Maraviglia regarding a benefit for political prisoners in Italy.[103] But this cooperation between Tresca and *L'Adunata* did not last long and the anarcho-syndicalist's actions were closely and critically scrutinized by Galleani's successors.

In the 1920s, the Galleanisti launched attacks against Tresca, prompted by a number of specific incidents. The first occurred in 1924, when the anarcho-syndicalist was charged and found guilty of sending birth-control literature through the mail. The issue for the anti-organizationalists was not the materials in question but Tresca's court-room denial that he was an anarchist. Following his release from a prison in Atlanta the next year, the anarcho-syndicalist stopped in Washington, D.C., and, in typical tourist fashion, visited the White House. His arrival coincided with that of a group of students who had travelled from Philadelphia just to meet President Coolidge. While Tresca was standing with the children, the president appeared and shook the hands of all those who were present, including the anarcho-syndicalist. Tresca then published an account of this chance meeting in *Il Martello*. The Galleanisti could not believe Tresca had stooped so low as to shake the hand of an American president.[104] Some of the anti-organizationalists believed that Tresca was an informer for the New York police. Emile Coda, for instance, had accused Tresca of supplying authorities with a picture of an anarchist wanted for questioning in New London, Connecticut.[105] It is hard to judge the veracity of this accusation, since it comes from an Italian security report; yet, if Coda and others believed this to be true, the charge does further explain the hostility of the Galleanisti towards Tresca. The other differences the anti-organizationalists had with the publisher of *Il Martello* stemmed from his willingness to work with communists in the antifascist struggle and his criticisms of Galleani.

These supposed transgressions culminated in the Galleanisti Emile Coda calling for a "Jury of Honour" to determine whether Tresca was guilty of acting in contravention of anarchist principles. The recourse to this unusual propaganda tactic demonstrated, more than anything, how thoroughly the Galleanisti, especially Coda, had come to despise Tresca. Coda himself selected the jury, comprised of six Galleanisti and Felice Guadagni, an anarcho-syndicalist who had been on the Sacco-Vanzetti Defence Committee (Tresca was not involved in any way). The jury met in Hartford, Connecticut, on 13 May 1928 and, not surprisingly, found Tresca guilty. However, the final decision was not unanimous because Guadagni refused to add his name to the published verdict that appeared in *L'Adunata*.[106]

The outcome of the "Jury of Honour" did not resolve anything between the anti-organizationalists and Tresca, and the attacks continued. In February 1938, Tresca testified in front of a federal grand jury regarding the disappearance of former communist Julia Stuart Poyntz the previous year. Poyntz was a prominent party member who was recruited by the Ob'edinennoe Gosudarstvennoe Politicheskoe Upravlenie (OGPU) and was recalled to Moscow, where she remained until returning to New York City in 1936. By this point, Poyntz had become disillusioned with the Soviet Union and the Communist Party of the United States of America (CPUSA). She had conveyed these opinions along with other information to her friend of twenty years, Carlo Tresca. The ex-OGPU agent had also told others that she was planning on exposing the communist movement based on her experiences in Russia. Poyntz's meeting with Tresca was the last time he ever saw her. She disappeared soon afterwards. He suspected that Schachno Epstein, also an OGPU agent and Poyntz's ex-lover, was involved in the disappearance. The anarcho-syndicalist met with the acting chief of the United States attorney's office and explained what he knew. A subpoena for Tresca to appear before a grand jury soon followed. Not only did Tresca's testimony lead to animosity from the communists, it also gave *L'Adunata* fresh ammunition to use in their quarrel with him: communists were bad but cooperating with the state was even worse. Max Sartin, in the pages of *L'Adunata*, described Tresca as a police collaborator who was engaged in the "act of informing and spying." Sartin's message was clear: cooperation with the state was antithetical to anarchist principles. This led to instances of accusations and counter-accusations between Sartin and Tresca in the pages of their respective newspapers. In response to his detractors, Tresca explained that his actions were motivated by the danger he felt the OGPU posed to the wider Left. He held the Soviet secret police responsible for the murder of Italian anarchist Luigi Camillo Berneri and other antifascists in Spain during the Civil War. Tresca described the OGPU as a "bestial and ferocious [organization] that from Moscow spread its tentacles across the globe and tries to stifle the voice of reason, truth, and theoretical opposition ... in the field of the class-conscious proletariat."[107]

The continued attacks from *L'Adunata* led Tresca to challenge Sartin to a public debate that never materialized. But it was not only the anti-organizationalists who censured the anarcho-syndicalist's actions. Many of Tresca's adherents could not believe he would cooperate with the state and never forgave him for it. Pernicone even suggests that Tresca's involvement in the Poyntz case ruined his reputation among anarchists and led to a decline in his once considerable influence.[108]

The fight between Tresca and the Galleanisti was replicated among each side's rank-and-file elements. Yet, such conflicting varieties of anarchism did not automatically conduce to factionalism. Many anarchists sympathized with multiple strains.[109] Ruggero Benvenuti, for example, subscribed to both the anti-organizationalist newspaper *L'Adunata dei Refrattari* and the anarcho-syndicalist *Il Martello*.[110] Some anarchists' political identities also shifted from one form of anarchism to another over time. When John Vattuone first came to New York City, he joined a group aligned with the anarcho-syndicalist Carlo Tresca. However, he increasingly felt himself drawn more to the ideas of *L'Adunata dei Refrattari* and joined the anti-organizationalist Circolo Volontà group.[111]

While the Galleanisti and Tresca were involved in their war of words during the 1920s and 1930s, fascists were organizing and becoming a strong presence in Italian communities throughout North America. Benito Mussolini promoted the establishment of fascist groups and the recruitment of members in Little Italies throughout the world. He hoped that the formation of *fasci* would provide both a financial and political base for his dictatorship.[112] Italian officials in embassies and consulates helped to facilitate this process. These institutions also used resources to keep track of the migrant Left wherever it was active. Naturally, the feud among the anarchists in New York City did not go unnoticed. As one report to Rome gleefully reported, "[*L'Adunata*] are going to produce a ferocious attack ... against Carlo Tresca that absolutely accuses him of being a spy for the Italian consulate."[113] Another piece of inter-governmental correspondence maintained that the anarchist infighting "would administer a mortal blow to anti-Fascism."[114] Not many Italian anarchists stepped forward to defend the anarcho-syndicalist, which Pernicone attributes to "an aura of infallibility with which Galleani had enveloped himself and his disciples [that] dissuaded many anarchists from dissenting with ... *L'Adunata*." Emma Goldman and Alexander

Berkman, who thought the infighting of the Italians ludicrous, spoke out against the accusations made by the Galleanisti, while Malatesta condemned any such infighting during a time when unity was needed to fight against fascism.[115]

The fascists were no doubt hoping that the schism would seriously damage the anarchist movement's ability to organize meaningful resistance against far right encroachment in Italian neighbourhoods. In their respective biographies on Carlo Tresca, Gallagher and Pernicone have both argued that the fractious relationship between Tresca and the Galleanisti actually did harm efforts to combat fascism.[116] But to what extent was this the case? Did those anarchists aligned with *L'Adunata* refrain from antifascist activity? Was there no cooperation between the two factions? Did the feud expand beyond New York City or was it localized?

During the 1920s, attempts were made at forming a united front among Italian radicals to fight the fascists in Little Italies throughout North America. The group that came out of this initiative was called the Alleanza Antifascista del Nord America (AAFNA), established in 1923. AAFNA strove to mount a continent-wide movement against fascism in North America and to aid left-wing institutions in Italy suffering state repression. The Alleanza Antifascista was largely social democratic in character, with leaders from Italian locals of the ILGWU and the ACWU directing the organization. The Alleanza Antifascista, however, was unable to mount a serious challenge to fascism. The unions concerned themselves more with union affairs and, in the case of the ILGWU, were consumed with a power struggle with the communists. Another reason why the AAFNA failed was the lack of involvement of anarchists and other far leftists who rejected common fronts with reformist social democrats. In less than a year, the Alleanza Antifascista had ceased its activities.[117]

The unwillingness of anarchists, communists, and syndicalists to join together in the AAFNA was no doubt also related to the creation of the Comitato Generale di Difesa Contro il Fascismo (CGDCF; General Defence Committee against Fascism) in February 1923, an initiative spearheaded by Tresca that sought to draw all radicals into the antifascist struggle. The committee's leadership included Tresca and a number of his well-known allies, including Elizabeth Gurley Flynn, Pietro Allegra, and Luigi Quintiliano. Surprisingly, it also featured (albeit for a short time) the first editor of *L'Adunata dei Refrattari*, Constantino Zonchello.[118] Due to the large concentration of anarchists in the CGDCF and the problems within the Alleanza Antifascista, it has been suggested that CGDCF was responsible for most of the antifascist activism during the 1923–1924 period.[119]

Tresca did not have much faith in the AAFNA when it existed and was not surprised when it finally became defunct, but he did think it was important that all Italian antifascists work together in a united front. After the socialist Giacomo Matteotti was murdered on 30 May 1924 by fascists for speaking out against them in the Italian Chamber of Deputies, antifascist activity in North America began to hit a new peak. With fascism's influence growing within Italian communities, Tresca felt it was now important for the Italian Left, broadly defined, to put aside sectarian squabbles and focus on destroying fascism. As a result, the anarcho-syndicalist helped resurrect the Alleanza Antifascista in the fall of 1925.[120]

The new AAFNA's first meeting was attended by representatives of all the radical tendencies among the Italians in New York City, with the exception of the Galleanisti.[121] It is unclear whether the anti-organizationalists chose not to be present of their own accord or because no invitation was offered. By May 1925, Tresca had been criticized in the pages of *L'Adunata dei Refrattari* for admitting he had shaken hands with President Calvin Coolidge. Perhaps this new round of attacks could not be forgiven by Tresca; so an invitation to the Galleanisti was withheld. On the other hand, the anti-organizationalists may have refused to involve themselves in a united front based on their anarchist principles. *L'Adunata dei Refrattari* made clear their position on antifascism and united fronts. The newspaper had been criticized for its perceived inaction against fascism by members of the Italian radical community. In a letter to the newspaper, Alfredo Gonello, from New York City, referred to *L'Adunata*'s antifascist propaganda as a "great colossal bluff." He also asserted that the newspaper's "propaganda against fascism is made exclusively among you, that is to say among the four lambs that wear the hat of editor and management of *L'Adunata*."[122] Gonello suggested that those involved in the publication of *L'Adunata dei Refrattari* join the Ordine Figli d'Italia (OFI; Order Sons of Italy), the fraternal organization founded in 1905 to help migrants assimilate into North American societies, in order to have direct contact with Italian workers. In a response to Gonello's letter published in the same issue, Costanzo—likely the paper's then editor Constantino Zonchello—scoffed at the idea of working within the OFI because the organization was composed of and run by the *prominenti* among the Italian community. For Costanzo, to work within this organization was simply reformism. As he stated, "It can be [the] work of those socialists [who] want to reform an organism born evil, those that intend to seize the state to bend it to their pleasure and to their benefit. It is not work for us."[123] Four months later, an article appeared in *L'Adunata dei Refrattari* titled "Il Fascismo e Noi" (Fascism and Us) that explained the newspaper's position on antifascism and united fronts. Earlier on in the piece, the author Tino—likely another pseudonym for Zonchello—openly admitted that "We acknowledge not being occupied in **L'ADUNATA exclusively** with fascism" (emphasis in original). For them, "Fascism is the new name of an old fact ... a universal attitude of the ruling class."[124] The newspaper would continue to keep its readers informed of events in Italy but not at the expense of the other important issues—such as anarchist philosophy, labour struggles, and the repression of anarchists around the world, to name but a few. *L'Adunata* recognized fascism for what it was but also believed it was equally important not to "lose sight of the causes that have determined it."[125] It was just as necessary to combat capitalism and its resulting class system, as well as the state and government.

The publishers of *L'Adunata dei Refrattari* did not view united fronts in a favourable light. In the Italian context, the article argued, socialists and communists wanted to replace fascism with their own dictatorships. Tino pointed to Russia and Germany as two examples demonstrating how communist and socialist rule was really no better than that of the fascists. With respect to Germany, Tino alluded to the repression against workers' revolt in 1919 by President Friedrich Ebert and Chancellor Philipp Scheidmann, both members of the Social Democratic Party. Tino proclaimed himself in favour of "struggle against fascism, but struggle also, no less fierce, against communism and state socialism."[126] With such a position, one would assume that the Galleanisti would refrain from cooperation with communists. Yet, the anti-organizationalists were involved in the CGDCF. It may have been the case that the communist component of the Comitato was small enough to be insignificant or perhaps the idea of a united front against fascism was important enough to warrant working together. Regardless, by the late 1920s, the Galleanisti were criticizing the role of communists in the AAFNA.

By early 1927, the Alleanza Antifascista had experienced a significant rupture. The continuing struggle between social democrats and communists for control of the ILGWU caused the AAFNA to split. Those social democrats involved in various unions formed a breakaway antifascist organization while the communists took over the Alleanza Antifascista.[127] The anti-organizationalists had always been wary of the AAFNA's claim to political neutrality and did not think it possible for the various tendencies of the Italian Left to put aside political positions to fight fascism. It was even harder for them to believe this would be the case, now that the communists had begun to lead the Alleanza Antifascista. In an article that appeared in a March 1929 issue of *L'Adunata dei Refrattari*, Armando Borghi noted the irony in the communists calling for a united front when they now led the AAFNA. By invoking the united front, Borghi asserted, the communists were actually asking other left-ist tendencies to suspend their politics while the communists were unwilling to do the same.[128] Thus, there would be no more cooperation between the Galleanisti and the communists.

The anti-organizationalists of *L'Adunata dei Refrattari* may not have cooperated with Tresca or the communists on the antifascist front but this did not mean that fascism went unchallenged in New York City. Numerous large demonstrations against the Italian Right took place there. Fascists and antifascists fought numerous times in the streets of Italian neighbourhoods. *L'Adunata*'s strong position on the antifascist struggle did not prevent those aligned with the newspaper from being involved in a united front or working with anarchists who were adherents of Tresca. The latter appears to have been the case during the Greco-Carrillo case. In the early morning of 30 May 1927, two Italian fascists, Giuseppe Carisi and Nicola Amoroso, were murdered in the Bronx on their way to a Memorial Day parade. Arrested and charged for the murders were Calogero Greco, a thirty-three-year-old tailor, who was a member of the *L'Adunata dei Refrattari*–aligned group Circolo Volontà, and Donato Carrillo, aged thirty-seven and also a tailor, who was both part of a mixed group of *L'Adunata* and *Il Martello* anarchists in the Bronx and a sup-porter of Tresca.[129] Both Greco and Carrillo wanted their defence committee to be comprised of various radical groups—suggesting that, at least for Greco, those whom *L'Adunata* deemed appropriate collaborators did not necessarily reflect the priorities of other anarchists affiliated with the newspaper. In the end, the Greco-Carrillo defence committee included Italian antifascists, lib-erals, socialists, communists, and even Trotskyists. The two anarchists were acquitted after it was determined in court that fascists had attempted to bribe a witness to place Greco and Carrillo at the scene of the murders.[130] The two anarchists were given their liberty and escaped the fate of Sacco and Vanzetti, who were executed in Massachusetts that same year. It was an on-the-ground victory for an unusual united front and one that contradicts any exaggerated account of the anarchist movement's paralyzing factiousness.

It also does not appear that *L'Adunata dei Refrattari*'s unwillingness to collabo-rate with a wider antifascist alliance in New York had much impact outside the city. On Columbus Day in Detroit, 12 October 1928, around sixty to seventy fascists dressed in black shirts with full regalia marched through the city to Ca-dillac Square. When they arrived, they were met by a small group of antifascists comprised of nine anarchists—one of whom was Attilio Bortolotti of Windsor—two socialists, and one communist. When the band started to play the fascist hymn "Giovenezza," the assembled antifascists began yelling "*Abasso il fascismo!*" and "*Assassini!*" One of the fascists put down the flag he was holding, drew a revolver, and shot the anarchists Antonio Barra and Angelo Lentricchia. Fighting then broke out between the antifascists and the fascists until the police arrived and both groups began to scatter. Barra died of his injuries two days later; Lentricchia survived.[131]

Toronto was another site of cooperation between anarchists and other Italian antifascists. A report written by G.B. Ambrosi, the Italian vice consul general, to superiors in Rome on antifascist activity in Toronto begins with a description of the local anarchist circle of Il Gruppo Libertario. The "leaders" of this group, according to the document, were Attilio Bortolotti and fellow Friulian Augusto Ongaro, but the exact number of members was hard to determine because they "move continually between the US and Toronto." The American cities mentioned in the report included Chicago and Detroit. The anarchists did not have a regular meeting place, so they would take turns meeting in their homes. When they did gather, the anarchists would discuss anarchism, drink, and dance.[132]

Toronto's antifascist group was led by Nicola Giancotti, a socialist and iron presser employed by Tip Top Tailors, who also published the antifascist organ *La Voce Operaia*. The antifascists had formed a cultural circle named after the Italian Republican Giuseppe Mazzini and held meetings at the Labour Lyceum. *L'Adunata dei Refrattari* supporters Attilio Bortolotti and Augusto Ongaro were not, evidently, directly involved in the Giuseppe Mazzini group. However, they, along with other anarchists, did unite with the antifascists in order to disrupt fascist events. It is unclear exactly how the anarchists and socialists became involved in joint antifascist activity. And, according to Ambrosi's report, the relationship between the anarchists and other antifascists was not necessarily harmonious: both "were struggling for control—one wanted to dominate the other," possibly due to differing ideas on the direction of antifascist activities.[133]

The fact that cooperation existed between anarchists and other antifascists in Detroit and Toronto seems to indicate that the *L'Adunata* stance, with regards to a wider antifascist movement incorporating non-anarchist elements, was most strictly adhered to by those involved in the publishing of the newspaper and its immediate circle of followers in the New York City–Newark area. Those *L'Adunata* adherents who lived outside of this metropolitan area had a different approach to antifascist struggle, which, possibly due to small numbers or a different understanding of the threat of fascism, meant a willingness to work with those who did not share their particular anarchist philosophy. The above examples also demonstrate the complexity of anarchist activist identities. For some, the decision to support a particular newspaper or key figure meant there were limits to their cooperation with other anarchists and the wider Left, while for others the exact opposite was true.

Luigi Galleani and Carlo Tresca were two of the most important figures among Italian anarchists in North America. Each subscribed to his own vision of anarchism while they both shared common ground on some topics, such as revolution and the necessity of violence in that process. Pernicone has tended to portray the Galleanisti as zealous in their attacks against Tresca, suggesting a strict adherence to a dogmatic approach to their relationship with the anarcho-syndicalist. This characterization does not accurately reflect how supporters of both *L'Adunata dei Refrattari* and *Il Martello* interacted with one another. Those who published the former definitely had strong feelings against Tresca and they made these views well known. But it does not appear that these views were shared by all readers of *L'Adunata* when it came to antifascist activism. Even within New York City, there existed anarchist groups comprised of both *L'Adunata* and *Il Martello* supporters. Beyond New York, Italian anarchists joined forces with non-anarchists to confront fascists. Though these alliances themselves may not have been devoid of conflict, they do demonstrate that, whether due to small numbers or because the threat of fascism was considered of greater importance than factional disputes among anarchists, supporters of *L'Adunata* did not behave in the same manner as those who published the newspaper. Thus, to paint all the Galleanisti with the same brush is to commit a disservice to the memories and activism of these transnational radicals. A transnational focus allows us to detect nuances and even contradictions within the conventional interpretation of anarchist factionalism.

DEPORTATION STRUGGLES

The activism that anarchists engaged in often led to state repression of various forms. In cases where comrades were threatened by imprisonment, deportation, or execution, they could look to the wider anarchist movement to agitate on their behalf. Anarchists were inspired not only by the movement's ethos of mutual aid but also by their individual identification as anarchists. After all, any anarchist could end up in trouble with authorities. Support was also given because many incarcerated comrades were friends, neighbours, and co-workers.

In the fall of 1939, two Italian anarchists, Attilio Bortolotti and Agostino Confalonieri, were arrested in Canada and under threat of deportation to Fascist Italy. The resulting mobilization and legal battle to help these men escape such a fate demonstrates how Italian anarchists responded to the victimization of their comrades. The coverage of Bortolotti's and Confalonieri's situations in Italian anarchist newspapers was constructed to facilitate outrage and sympathy among readers. This led to fundraising initiatives to cover legal expenses. However, the factional disputes among certain members of this larger network show the limits of solidarity among Italian anarchists. The Bortolotti-Confalonieri story was not reported on in all movement newspapers, nor was aid forthcoming from all quarters. In spite of the inter-movement challenges, the transnational character of the Italian anarchist movement was central in preventing the deportation of Bortolotti and Confalonieri. Regardless of where Italian anarchists were located, whether in large urban centres or smaller resource extraction towns, their ability to tap into a much larger movement was an important means for dealing with various crises and reflected the anarchist principle of mutual aid. This example also demonstrates the importance of self-sufficiency among politically marginalized groups, such as anarchists, that are unwilling or unable to draw upon state resources.

In the early morning of 4 October 1939, a combined force of the Toronto city police Red Squad and the Royal Canadian Mounted Police (RCMP) raided a shared residence at 847 Gladstone Avenue. Living at this address were five Italian anarchists, Attilio Bortolotti, Ruggero Benvenuti, Ernesto Gava, Vittorio Valopi, and Agostino Confalonieri. Benvenuti was a bricklayer who had come to Canada from the Marche region in 1931, while Gava hailed from Friuli and had been living in Toronto since 1927.[1] Valopi's origins remain a mystery. All of the men were taken into police custody and all literature found in the home was seized. Two revolvers were also discovered. Valopi was released uncharged by police after questioning because no subversive literature was found in his room,[2] but Bortolotti, Benvenuti, and Gava were charged under Sub-section (c) of Section 39a of the Defence of Canada Regulations, a part of the War Measures Act. This legislation had recently been invoked because of Canada's entry into the Second World War. It allowed for the prosecution of any person or persons who had "printed, circulated or distributed literature which might be prejudicial to the safety of the state or the efficient prosecution of the war."[3] Bortolotti was also charged under the Criminal Code for the illegal possession of the two firearms. He, along with Benvenuti and Gava, were confined in the Don Jail to await their court appearance. Confalonieri, who had entered Canada with a fake Cuban passport under the name of José Marcos Joaquin, was also detained at the jail in order to be questioned by immigration authorities at a later date.

Immediately following the arrests, Emma Goldman, who was living in Toronto during this time, became involved in Bortolotti's and Confalonieri's legal troubles. She and Bortolotti had become close friends during her time in the city and he was one of the original members of the Libertarian Group formed by Goldman in 1934. That same year, Goldman, who had been deported from the United States in 1919, was granted permission to enter the country on a three-month visa, with the condition that she would not speak on anarchism or political issues. According to Bortolotti, Goldman discussed her acceptance of the offer with him. He expressed his thoughts on the matter to Goldman: "'You're prostituting yourself, Emma.'" And in response, "She looked at me— you should have seen it—this fiery, deadly look. She resented [what I said] very much. But when she came back, she said, 'Art[,] you were right.' We became really close friends after that."[4] Bortolotti acted as Goldman's driver, taking her around the city and to lectures he organized for her in Windsor.[5]

Goldman's first act for the defence was to contact J.L. Cohen to represent the anarchists. Cohen was a local lawyer who had gained notoriety for defending members of the Communist Party of Canada (CPC) in the early 1930s.[6] He was able to get the case against Bortolotti, Benvenuti, and Gava for printing and distributing anti-war literature thrown out of court because the Crown prosecutor had been unable to demonstrate that the anarchists had carried out either activity. Cohen likewise had the gun charges against Bortolotti dismissed after it was revealed that the anarchist's statement to police on 4 October had been given involuntarily and under intimidation. It should also be mentioned that neither of the two revolvers was in working condition.[7]

Figure 20. Armando Del Moro. Busta 1698, CPC, ACS.

However, Bortolotti was still not granted his freedom, as Canadian authorities discovered that the anarchist had lived in the United States for an unknown period of time, thus forfeiting his Canadian domicile. He had also returned to Canada illegally. Canadian immigration law at the time stipulated that in order for a foreign-born individual to become naturalized, they first had to have lived in Canada for five years without any interruption and then formally apply to become naturalized.[8] Bortolotti had arrived in Canada in early July 1920 and had meant to fill out his naturalization application form. However, he had misplaced the paperwork and never submitted it. In 1926, Bortolotti had begun working for his brother Guglielmo, a masonry contractor in Detroit, while commuting from Windsor, Ontario. Then, from 1928 to 1929, Bortolotti lived in Detroit and worked at a Ford plant. That same year, he was arrested by Detroit police for distributing handbills commemorating the execution of Sacco and Vanzetti, and charged in contravention of a city by-law. During his court appearance, Bortolotti admitted to being an anarchist and the judge ordered his deportation to Italy. Bortolotti's lawyer was able to get him released on a $3,000 bail, a sum which was raised by Italian comrades from Detroit's Il Gruppo 'I Refrattari.' As mentioned earlier, Bortolotti was counselled by Raffaele Schiavina, then editor of *L'Adunata dei Refrattari*, to avoid deportation to Italy by forfeiting the bail and returning to Canada. This he did. His re-entry was technically illegal by the immigration standards of the time because he did not present himself to authorities at the Canadian border.[9] These were the circumstances that were used to deny Bortolotti any claim to Canadian citizenship, and resulted in the order for him to be deported to Italy.

Confalonieri, who was finally interviewed by immigration officer J.L. Malcolm on 5 December 1939, maintained that his true identity was the Cuban José Marcos Joaquin. During the course of this interview, Malcolm produced a number of letters written by Confalonieri to his comrades in Europe, explaining his difficulties with Canadian Immigration, his use of false documents, and suggestions for those anarchists who were planning to travel from Europe to the United States via Canada. Police records obtained from France not only revealed the anarchist's true identity, but also showed that Confalonieri had fought on the Republican side in the Spanish Civil War. Since Confalonieri had entered Canada with a false passport, he, too, was ordered deported to Italy.[10]

The Canadian government's use of deportation as a way to deal with radicals was nothing new. Deportation was an important means by which to rid Canada of those deemed undesirable. As Barbara Roberts has shown, it was government policy to eject from the country, often in contravention of existing laws, migrants considered unhealthy, indigent, immoral, radical, or unemployed.[11] For radicals in particular, according to Roberts, there were two periods when specific leftist organizations were targeted en masse: 1918–1922, when the Industrial Workers of the World (IWW) was the focus, and the 1930s, when the CPC was singled out. The crackdown against the IWW was facilitated by an order-in-council passed in 1918 as part of the already existing War Measures Act. The act was legislated in August 1914 and gave the federal government sweeping powers to police and intern so-called "enemy aliens"—those populations who had migrated from the German, Ottoman, and Austria-Hungary empires against whom Canada was at war—and who were considered a threat to the nation's security at that time. It was not until after the Bolshevik revolution of 1917 and the resulting Red Scare in Canada that the order-in-council was introduced, making radical left-wing organizations illegal and their foreign-born members deportable.[12] According to Roberts, the Canadian government and the new security apparatus saw the IWW organizers as the sparkplugs of the wartime and postwar labour revolt. They championed drastic measures to end the organization's influence.[13] The repression against the CPC began in earnest once the party was declared illegal in 1931. Those foreign-born individuals—even those who had become naturalized—who were found to be members of this organization could then be deported to their countries of birth. This last was possible due to a 1919 amendment to citizenship law that allowed for naturalization certificates to be revoked as a precursor to a convicted individual's removal from the country.[14]

In light of such anti-radical practices and conventions, it should come as no surprise that the Bortolotti-Confalonieri case was not the first time that Italian anarchists had mobilized to prevent the deportation of a comrade from Canada. On 24 June 1915, Armando Del Moro was arrested by police in Hamilton, Ontario, for anti-war and anti-religious propaganda.[15] Del Moro was born in the *comune* of Mondolfo located in the Marche region on 1 April 1890. Before migrating to North America, he worked as a farm labourer. Del Moro's involvement in the anarchist movement began while he was living in Italy where he belonged to a group active in Mondolfo. It is not clear when Del Moro migrated but his reasons for doing so appear to have been to avoid service in the Italian military.[16] He lived and worked in the United States before moving to Hamilton to find employment.[17] Del Moro was well-regarded among the Italian anarchists in North America. In the first article to appear on his arrest in the pages of *Cronaca Sovversiva*, Luigi Galleani described Del Moro as "a brave, ardent, [and] active comrade" who worked tirelessly to spread anarchist ideals: "[A]t home, on the street, with co-workers or at the boarding house, with the first that he happens to come across, he speaks, reasons, discusses, challenges prejudices, provokes reaction, awakens conscience and ... never leaves his interlocutor without leaving in his pocket [or] in his hands [anarchist pamphlets such as] *The God Pestilence, Between Peasants,* [and] *Evolution and Revolution.*"[18] At some point, following Del Moro's arrest, he was ordered deported to Italy. While incarcerated, he was unable to see or communicate with any of his friends. Somehow a co-worker, possibly the socialist Umberto Fiocca, learned of his arrest and persuaded local lawyer Thomas Somerset to act on Del Moro's behalf.[19] His anti-war propaganda came at a time when Canada, as part of the British Empire, was actively involved in the First World War and pro-war patriotism within the host society was rampant. Anti-war activism was also illegal under the War Measures Act of 1914, which had been passed in August of that year. Migrants who engaged in such activities could be deported. As Roberts has demonstrated, the Canadian Department of Immigration used the War Measures Act as a means to rid the country of foreign-born radicals and labour agitators.[20] If deported to Italy, Del Moro would be forced to fulfill his military obligation.

More than three weeks had passed since Del Moro's arrest and Galleani's 17 July article, which meant that the Italian anarchists had to move quickly. Galleani implored readers to send money to *Cronaca Sovversiva* within the next two weeks to help cover legal costs. He even tried to guilt readers into donating money, stating that Del Moro's deportation would "weigh severely, perhaps for a long time on the shoulders of the ones that have responded to the appeal with the slump of the shoulders of the beggars, of the lazy and of the indolent."[21] The following week, Rizieri Fantini's article in *Cronaca Sovversiva* again called for people to give. Fantini was more than aware that appeals to Italian comrades were numerous: "yesterday, today, tomorrow, it is the sick comrade or the journal at the point of death, the raffle for the group, for the injured .... We are small: it takes so little to clean our pockets!"[22] But he also believed anarchists could contribute more if they made some personal changes in spending. Referring to comrades, he asked, "How many glasses of beer have they drunk, how many cigars have they smoked, in front of how many stupid movies have they [wasted their time], in the course of a week! A partial reduction ... on the expenses of these kinds of distractions ... would be 25 dollars for every comrade, would be suddenly, in five days ... $125 to fund the agitation and legal assistance for Armando Del Moro. Are there five hundred comrades prepared to do ... as we do?"[23] The Italian anarchists responded to the appeals of Galleani and Fantini and were able to raise $165.45—a considerable sum in 1915.[24] In the end, Del Moro was not deported. By early August, he had been released with a forty-five-dollar fine and one year of probation.[25]

Unlike Del Moro, Agostino Confalonieri had not entered Canada legally to find work. But how exactly did he get to Canada from Europe? In early March 1939, a transnational network was established by Italian anarchists to aid comrades who needed to leave Europe for North America. These anarchists tended to be veterans of the Spanish Civil War who faced persecution for their involvement in aiding the Republican government or for their anarchist activities generally.[26]

It is difficult to determine how many anarchists this network managed to send to Canada and the United States, or whether more than one of them existed. However, this particular network was able to send an unknown number of Italian anarchists from Europe to Canada, with the United States as their final destination. One of those anarchists was Agostino Confalonieri.

Confalonieri was born in Monza, Italy, and had left home, like many other Italian migrants, to find work. He arrived at Bellinzona, Switzerland, in the early 1930s and began sending money home to his family in Italy.[27] In 1936, Confalonieri was working in a luggage factory owned and operated by Luigi Mainetti, a known communist.[28] Based on his Casellario Politico Centrale file, it is hard to determine to what extent Confalonieri was politicized before he arrived in Switzerland, since he was not known to have expressed any opinions contrary to the Fascist regime and had no previous criminal record while living in Italy.[29] Under these circumstances, it is possible that Mainetti may have had some influence on Confalonieri's political development.

The Spanish Civil War began on 17 July 1936, after General Francisco Franco's attempted nationalist coup against the Popular Front government met fierce opposition. In November of that same year, Confalonieri travelled to Spain and enlisted in the Rosselli Column, named after the Paris-based antifascist. He spent almost four months fighting on the Huesca front in the province of Aragon before leaving Spain. His reasons for this departure are unclear.[30] Confalonieri then made his way to Geneva, where he presented himself to the Spanish consul and received a Spanish passport so he could return to fight in Spain. Confalonieri travelled to Bourg Madame, France, carrying the passport issued under the name of Agostino Gonzalo Neri. Just inside the border with Spain on 3 April 1937, he was arrested with fellow Italians Domenico Girelli, Valentino/Martino Segata, and Francesco Luigi Prevosto by French authorities for possession of false documents and for attempting to enlist in the Spanish militia. Confalonieri was sentenced to a three-month imprisonment.[31] After his release, Confalonieri, using the alias Neri, settled at Suresnes, a suburb of Paris, where he became active in anarchist and antifascist circles. One of his activities included membership in a Paris-based antifascist committee—most likely Giustizia e Libertà—in support of Republican Spain. In May 1938, Confalonieri was expelled from France because of his political activities and went to Belgium. While in Brussels, he was arrested at the home of Renzo Carro, an Italian Trotskyist and antifascist, and jailed. After his release, Confalonieri demanded to be taken to the French border. He was arrested as soon as he reached Tourcoing, possibly because Belgian authorities had sent word that the anarchist had re-entered France. After being jailed for three days, Confalonieri left Tourcoing and secretly re-entered Belgium, where he stayed with anarchist Mario Angel and his partner. It was this constant harassment by the police in Belgium and France that led to Confalonieri's decision to leave Europe.[32]

Another anarchist who wanted to leave Europe for North America was Ernesto Bonomini. He had left Italy in 1922, following the Fascists' rise to power and their subsequent repression of radicals. He arrived in France, where he became an anarchist. In February 1924, Bonomini assassinated Nicola Bonservizi, the editor of the Paris-based fascist newspaper *L'Italie Nouvelle*, because he was providing information on exiled Italian radicals to the Italian secret police in France. Bonomini was sentenced to eight years in prison and, after his release in 1932, was expelled from the country and went to Belgium. Eventually, he travelled to Spain to help in the struggle against fascism. In April 1938, he attended a meeting in Paris but, even under an alias, was discovered and arrested for his illegal return to France. He was interned in the Rieucros camp in the Lozère department,[33] but was able to escape a year later and again went to Belgium.[34]

Brussels was an important destination for anarchists who sought to leave Europe because it was the location of a group coordinating departures to North America. This group of twenty to twenty-five members was organized by the Belgian anarchist Hem Day[35] and was made up almost entirely of Italian anarchists, including Milan's Mario Mantovani, a typographer and contributor to Italian-language newspapers, such as *L'Adunata dei Refrattari,* among others.[36] The formation of this group, evidently focussed on assisting Italian anarchists who had fought in the conflict, was likely a result of the impending defeat of Republican forces in Spain. The first meeting was held on 4 March 1939, a month before the end of the Spanish Civil War. The group had a total of 22,000 Belgian francs at its disposal. The money had come from anarchist Luigi Bertoni, the Milan-born typographer and syndicalist, who lived in Geneva, and from comrades in Paris.[37] Mantovani's role in the group was to provide anarchists with false Cuban passports for their travels. It is unclear whether he forged the passports himself, was able to obtain these kinds of documents from someone else, or if they were actually supplied by someone at the Cuban consulate. Confalonieri's passport, for instance, was issued by the Cuban consul in Paris on 1 July 1939.[38]

While in Brussels, most Italian anarchist refugees would stay at Day's Mont des Arts bookstore, and it is possible that both Confalonieri and Bonomini did so.[39] After leaving the city, anarchists would travel to Antwerp and depart, two or three at a time, on steamships for North America. With the help of Mantovani, Confalonieri and Bonomini had their passage booked through Canadian Pacific, which, according to Mantovani's testimony to Italian authorities, accepted travellers to Canada without much legal formality.[40] The plan was that these men, who travelled with Cuban passports under false names, could travel from Europe, land in Canada, and then make their way into the United States, claiming that they were returning to Cuba. New York appears to have been the destination of choice for Italian anarchists departing from Europe because it was a centre of anarchist activity and home to *L'Adunata dei Refrattari*. The Cuban passports were issued from Paris and were only valid for a single journey.[41]

Figure 21. Mario Mantovani. Busta 3002, CPC, ACS.

Bonomini arrived in Canada sometime before Confalonieri and did not have any problems with Canadian Immigration. Allowed to continue his journey, Bonomini arrived in New York City and had already made contact with *L'Adunata* by 3 September. An Italian security report from New York around that time stated that Bonomini was known as Diego Semper, which may have been the name from his Cuban passport.[42] Things did not go quite as smoothly for Confalonieri, who arrived at Quebec City on 2 September 1939 on the SS *Montrose*. Upon his arrival, the anarchist was questioned by a Canadian Immigration official about his identity, profession, and the amount of money that he carried. His luggage was also searched. Confalonieri's responses and the fact that he did not have the required visa to enter the United States caused the immigration officer to detain him for further questioning. He spent three nights in an immigration detention centre before finally being interviewed.[43] After four hours of interrogation, immigration officers were not convinced by Confalonieri's story that he was a Cuban businessman returning to his country of birth after a twenty-year absence. The anarchist spent a total of ten days in detention, during which time he was waiting for a visa that would allow him to enter the United States. After the visa was issued by the American consulate in Montreal, Canadian immigration officials were unable to prove Confalonieri's actual identity and released him under the condition that he would book passage to New York and leave Canada within twenty-four hours. With his ticket to the United States purchased, the anarchist travelled to Montreal. Once in Montreal, he decided not to continue on to the United States, for fear that he would experience trouble with American Immigration and actually be sent to Cuba.[44]

In Montreal, Confalonieri contacted a comrade named Martini, most likely a contact involved in this transnational network, and stayed in the city for a few days. Even though the anarchist was offered work as a painter by a comrade, he wanted to put some distance between himself and Quebec-based immigration officials. In addition, Confalonieri had in his possession a letter from a Paris-based anarchist named Giuseppe Benvenuti addressed to his brother Ruggero, who lived in Toronto. Martini sent a telegram to Attilio Bortolotti in Toronto to notify him that Confalonieri was in Montreal and wanted to leave the city.[45] Bortolotti's involvement in the network reflected his earlier attachment to the cause of aiding Italian anarchists fleeing Europe. He had been in previous contact with Mantovani, who had been instrumental in channelling monies raised for the CNT-FAI in Spain, and with Luigi Mancini, who was also a Friulian. In a letter to Mancini, Bortolotti had expressed his willingness to help anarchist comrades who arrived in Canada, as long as the resources were available.[46] Bortolotti made the proper arrangements and drove to Montreal with some of his Toronto comrades to meet Confalonieri and bring him back to the city.[47] On 18 September, Confalonieri arrived in Toronto and was brought to the 847 Gladstone Avenue residence that would be the site of the 4 October raid. In letters to comrades in Europe, Confalonieri stated that he was not sure whether to stay in Canada, which depended upon his ability to find work, or make his way to New York to meet with the *L'Adunata* anarchists.[48]

Upon Confalonieri's arrival in Toronto, several centres were notified about his troubles with Canadian Immigration so that anarchists coming to Canada from Europe would not experience the same problems.[49] In a letter to Mantovani, Confalonieri also passed along suggestions that would help each prospective anarchist travelling to Canada, posing as a Cuban. His recommendations included having a Cuban address stated in the passport; procuring a certificate of employment; having a visa for entry into the United States; maintaining a Cuban identity no matter what happened; explaining that the trip from Europe to Cuba via Canada and the United States was faster and cheaper than a direct trip; having a working knowledge of the history of Cuba; and being in possession of at least $150 or more if one were posing as a tourist. Confalonieri was curious about how Bonomini was able to pass by Canadian Immigration without any problems and surmised that his favourable treatment was related to the larger sum of money Bonomini carried.[50]

It is difficult to discern how many Italian anarchists came to North America with the help of Day, Mantovani, and the other anarchists in Belgium, France, and Switzerland. In a written statement to Italian agents in Brussels, Mantovani admitted to helping Confalonieri and Bonomini in this way. These two were, evidently, neither the first nor the last that the network assisted.[51] Confalonieri stated in a letter that "I am not the first who has passed the Immigration control with those documents, nor am I the second or the third." In addition, an immigration officer had mentioned to Confalonieri that a Cuban had passed through Canada two weeks prior and was detained for one day before being granted permission to continue on his travels. However, Confalonieri was not certain whether this person was an anarchist or an actual Cuban citizen. He did not appear to believe that the immigration officer was referring to Bonomini.[52] In December 1939, Nicola "Nick" Di Domenico, publisher of *L'Adunata dei Refrattari*, wrote Goldman to inform her that another anarchist, using a Cuban passport under the name Pedro Mateo y Hernandez, was in trouble with United States Immigration. Hernandez had successfully entered Canada but American authorities declared his passport invalid and returned him to Montreal for deportation back to Europe. Di Domenico hoped that Goldman would be able to have Cohen look into the case and see how Hernandez could be helped. However, because of the tense legal situation of Bortolotti and Confalonieri at that time, as well as the lack of resources necessary to maintain this network, it was not possible for anyone to act on Hernandez's behalf before he was sent back to France. Goldman apologized to Di Domenico for not being able to help Hernandez but blamed "Ham" for not notifying the Toronto comrades about this particular anarchist in time. Is Ham actually Hem Day? It could be the same person but it is difficult to establish a definite link. In a letter to Di Domenico dated 9 January 1940, Goldman wrote, "One thing is certain[,] dear comrade[,] you must write HAM again that we in Canada can handle no more cases of the nature of J[oaquin] or the one already deported [Hernandez]. Please impress that on [h]is mind." Goldman reiterated her position again in a letter three days later.[53]

Indeed, it was Goldman who, living in Toronto at the time of the raid and subsequent arrests, spearheaded the struggle to prevent the deportation of Bortolotti and Confalonieri. Her involvement in the case was motivated by her close friendship with Bortolotti. She did not want Bortolotti and Confalonieri to suffer the same fate as Nicola Sacco and Bartolomeo Vanzetti.[54] In addition to hiring J.L. Cohen as the defence lawyer for the anarchists charged under the War Measures Act and retaining him as counsel for the deportation hearings, Goldman reached out to all her contacts among the transnational anarchist movement, but with a specific focus on North America, to ask for financial support and/or coordinate events to raise funds to cover legal and other fees related to these cases. She contacted the *Freie Arbeiter Stimme*, the Yiddish-language anarchist newspaper from New York, to ask for their assistance, and received the newspaper's subscription list.[55] Appeals were also made to Toronto's Jewish anarchists, the Spanish anarchists of the Solidaridad Internacional Antifascista (SIA) based in New York, and most importantly, the Italian anarchists of *L'Adunata dei Refrattari*, who Goldman had initially hoped would be able to cover Cohen's $1,500 legal fee.[56]

After Bortolotti and Confalonieri had been ordered deported to Italy, defence committees were struck for both of the men, though emphasis was placed on Bortolotti because he had a stronger case to remain in Canada. These committees appear to have been comprised of the same people, since both struggles were so closely related. However, it is difficult to know exactly who was involved. Emma Goldman and Dorothy Giesecke Rogers were the only two who can easily be identified, since both were responsible for sending and receiving correspondence.[57] Rogers was born in England and later immigrated to Canada. Initially, she was a supporter of the Co-operative Commonwealth Federation (CCF), the socialist-labour party founded in 1932 that was the precursor to Canada's present New Democratic Party (NDP). She and her Dutch husband lived in Scarborough Bluffs near Toronto. Rogers had heard of anarchism but did not know much about the political philosophy. She attended two lectures that Emma Goldman gave in Toronto in 1934 that sparked Rogers's interest to read more on anarchism. According to Attilio Bortolotti, within a few months of attending Goldman's lectures, Rogers had declared herself an anarchist and become involved in the Libertarian Group that Goldman established that same year. Rogers acted as Goldman's secretary when the well-known lecturer was living in Toronto and the two became close friends. Following Goldman's death in 1940, Rogers moved to New York City and, with anarchists from that city, founded the Why? Group and its publication of the same name.[58]

It is also possible that Ruggero Benvenuti and Ernesto Gava were part of these defence committees because they travelled to Detroit to deliver letters that could be sent around the United States. Rogers travelled to both Detroit and Buffalo in the same capacity as the two Italians.[59] This tactic ensured that correspondence containing sensitive information was not seized by Canadian authorities. How these anarchists were able to cross the Canada–United States border without any difficulty remains a mystery. It seems likely that Benvenuti, Gava, and Rogers were being surveilled during this critical time but, perhaps, Canadian security resources had already been redirected towards the war effort.

When it came to aid for Bortolotti and Confalonieri, Goldman focussed on the anarchist movement. However, she did reach out to others on the Left even if in a limited way. James Heney, a friend of Goldman's involved in the IWW of Port Arthur, Ontario, was one such contact. Goldman explained the case and its repercussions to the Left: "Needless to say we intend to make a big fight and to do everything in our power to prevent the railroading of our people. In point of fact, it is not only a question of the liberties of the arrested Italians.... It is also a question of civil liberties which the War Ruling [War Measures Act] abrogates. Once the authorities will succeed in making a precedent of the indicted people no one will be safe from being raided and rounded up."[60] In the end, Heney forwarded $17.25 to the defence fund.[61] Goldman also contacted the prominent social gospeller Protestant Reverend Salem Bland, with whom she had shared a stage at a Sacco and Vanzetti memorial meeting at Toronto's Standard Theatre in September 1927. At that meeting, to roaring applause, Bland had declared the two anarchists innocent. Now, with regard to the Bortolotti deportation, the reverend met with Thomas A. Crerar, then Minister of Mines and Resources, and in charge of immigration. He pleaded on behalf of the Italian anarchist.[62] Another person Goldman attempted to interest in the case was the CCF's federal leader J.S. Woodsworth. It might seem strange that an anarchist would seek the aid of a political party—even one that was socialist—but Goldman had already appealed to the wider anarchist movement and the situation with Bortolotti and Confalonieri was becoming increasingly dire. Goldman and Woodsworth met in person in Winnipeg during the anarchist's lecture tour in December 1939. After he heard the facts of the case, Woodsworth suggested that J.L Cohen contact David Lewis, the secretary of the CCF, and the party's national chair M.J. Coldwell, who were both in Ottawa. He added that Cohen should also meet with top immigration officials. Other members of the CCF played a more direct role in the case. John Walter, for instance, wrote an article about Bortolotti and his impending deportation for the New York City–based *Nation*. He also contacted a fellow CCFer and member of Parliament, W.D. Euler. Walter placed particular emphasis on the role the fascists played in Bortolotti's current predicament. Euler immediately appealed to Immigration to allow Bortolotti to be released on bail. However, by that time (8 January 1940), bail had already been granted.[63] In order to interest a broader range of people in the case, Goldman also wrote letters that were published in *Nation*, *New Republic*, and *Canadian Forum*.[64]

Goldman apparently made no attempts to contact the Communist parties of either Canada or the United States. Like many anarchists, Goldman had been at first supportive of the Bolshevik seizure of power in Russia, seeing in that revolution many opportunities for a society truly organized by peasants and workers. She longed to be involved in building this new society.[65] After her deportation to Russia in 1919, she was able to see the realities of Bolshevik rule first-hand: mandatory identification permits, the murder of those critical of Bolshevik policies by the secret police, the imprisonment of anarchists, and the crushing of the Kronstadt Rebellion.[66] All were objectionable indications of the realities of Bolshevik rule. After leaving Russia in December 1921, Goldman criticized the Bolsheviks in her lectures. Indeed, Goldman was accused by communists who attended her speaking engagements of being in the employ of the "capitalist press," as was the case during a lecture she delivered in Regina, Saskatchewan, in 1926. Jewish communists in Winnipeg also boycotted a meeting she held in the city in February the following year, ostensibly because of her stance on the Soviet Union.[67] In addition, Goldman did not trust the communists to be involved in the Bortolotti-Confalonieri case, based on their handling of the earlier Sacco and Vanzetti affair. As she explained to the Wobbly James Heney,

> I am very glad to know that you have followed the terrible crime the Communists have committed against Sacco and Vanzetti. It would be outrageous enough if it would be merely a question of having appropriated the huge sums collected for the defence of Sacco and Vanzetti. But in addition to this the damnable Communists also used the propaganda for our two men to enhance their own [image] thereby sacrificing their lives. I have always felt that if the fellow-workers in America would have procured competent and earnest legal help, and if the Communists had been eliminated from the campaign Sacco and Vanzetti would still be alive and free.[68]

In short, Goldman, in the late 1930s, was unlikely to appeal to the communists for help.

During the mobilization to prevent the deportation of Bortolotti and Confalonieri, a very considerable correspondence passed between Goldman/Rogers and Nick Di Domenico of *L'Adunata dei Refrattari*. The newspaper published articles on the impending deportation of the two men and its supporters raised the largest sum of money.[69] The majority of the letters sent to Di Domenico provided updates on the two cases and asked him to continue his appeals to the readers of *L'Adunata* to provide badly needed funds. For the most part, this back-and-forth between Goldman/Rogers and Di Domenico was cordial, but there were serious disagreements that erupted, based upon who the defence committees should approach for help. One of those people was Carlo Tresca.

Activist identities—based on a specific anarchist philosophy or support for a certain personality or newspaper—could determine whether or not anarchists of different tendencies would work together. The anarchists of *L'Adunata dei Refrattari*, for instance, had very strong feelings with respect to their political collaborators. They were unwilling to associate themselves with individuals or groups they believed to be working against the interests of workers, whether as informants, pro-fascists, or corruptionists. Some have suggested that *L'Adunata* anarchists were far too critical of certain individuals, such as Tresca, or were unwilling to compromise or work with those who did not share their anti-organizationalist anarchist communist philosophy. Some, like Sidney Solomon, a former member of New York City's anarchist Vanguard Group, considered those involved with *L'Adunata dei Refrattari* to be puritan anarchists.[70] It was important for *L'Adunata* to maintain its political integrity and the publication reacted strongly when this integrity was challenged or undercut by others.

The antagonism that existed between *L'Adunata dei Refrattari* and Tresca continued to be in evidence during the Bortolotti-Confalonieri deportation case. The situation was so delicate that Goldman was reluctant to approach Tresca for help. However, M. Eleanor "Fitzi" Fitzgerald, a close friend of Goldman's and former assistant editor of Goldman's *Mother Earth* newspaper, who was the unofficial representative of the United States branch of Bortolotti's and Confalonieri's defence funds, had met with a number of New York–based labour leaders and all of them suggested that she should get in touch with the anarcho-syndicalist.[71] For Goldman, the struggle over Bortolotti and Confalonieri was too important for it to be sacrificed to the rift between the two factions of Italian anarchists.[72] She did not want the readers of *L'Adunata* to stop giving money, which they were doing at an impressive level. Because of the strong dislike the anti-organizationalists had for Tresca, Goldman felt it prudent to first broach the subject with Di Domenico. Quoting directly from the letter Fitzgerald had written on the need to contact Tresca, Goldman argued that the two anarchists' looming fate far outweighed the risks of approaching the anarcho-syndicalist. Still, Goldman would contact Tresca only if Di Domenico was in agreement.[73]

Not surprisingly, Di Domenico was against enlisting Tresca's aid. Having never met Tresca, the publisher of *L'Adunata dei Refrattari* still had strong feelings against the man. In a 29 November 1939 letter to Goldman, he stated: "I strongly believe [Tresca] to be dishonest, both morally and politically, and ... a dangerous [and] insidious enemy of our movement and comrades. [I'm not saying] he is a paid spy, but I am sure he acts like an 'agent provocateur' and a spy.... [It] is ... my belief that within himself he wishes [Bortolotti] to be jailed or deported, and underhandedly will do his best to neutralize whatever agitation might be undertaken on his favour. This is my candid opinion."[74]

Di Domenico deferred to Goldman's judgment on whether to involve Tresca and promised Goldman that *L'Adunata* would continue to raise money for the defence fund. But any cooperation between them and Tresca was strictly out of the question.[75] Goldman lamented the fact that these divisions existed among her Italian comrades and suggested to Di Domenico that the anarchist movement had made some members "fanatical and unrelenting" because of their inability to transcend personal quarrels when greater issues were at stake.[76] This statement sparked an exchange between Goldman and Di Domenico, which forced the latter to restate the position of *L'Adunata dei Refrattari*, as well as respond to Goldman's slight: "I have shown your preceding letter and my answer to a number of friends who are completely in accord with what I wrote to you. I am sorry to see that you consider as fanatics such comrades as have a different opinion of that man, whom they certainly know better than you do. But there is nothing to be done about it. No amount of abuse can change my opinion, or theirs, on this matter."[77] Perhaps fearing a withdrawal of aid from *L'Adunata dei Refrattari*, Goldman was quick to apologize for her observations of Italian comrades. In her response to Di Domenico's letter, she apologized for her unintentional insult. She wanted to contact Tresca, she explained, because she was so intensely worried about Bortolotti.[78]

Goldman was not the only one wrestling with the factional dilemma. When Bortolotti declared himself an anarchist in 1921, he was enamoured of Luigi Galleani and was a supporter and contributor to *L'Adunata*. While living in Windsor during the early 1920s, Bortolotti had spent Sundays in Detroit with Il Gruppo 'I Refrattari,' which was aligned with the newspaper. He was also friends with *L'Adunata dei Refrattari*'s editor, Raffaele Schiavina.[79] When J.L. Cohen asked Bortolotti whether to involve Tresca in the deportation case, Bortolotti did not think it would be useful.[80] Goldman attributed Bortolotti's unwillingness to seek Tresca's help to the feud between the anti-organization-alists and the anarcho-syndicalist.[81]

Goldman, however, did eventually write to Tresca on 14 January 1940, asking for his help.[82] The seriousness of Bortolotti's and Confalonieri's situation must have superseded any worries she had regarding the possible fallout with *L'Adunata*; and it appears as though her outreach to Tresca was conducted without the knowledge of Di Domenico or the rest of the *L'Adunata dei Refrattari* group, since none of the continuing letters between Goldman/Rogers and the newspaper discuss the issue. However, there would be no help forthcoming from Tresca. In his reply, he refused to get involved with Bortolotti's defence, stating, "Very sorry for Bortolotti: I think that [he] is a swell fellow and comrade. But in the past I have experienced very bad ingratitude from the bunch he is associated [*L'Adunata*]. You must know the sordid story. Of course! You don't believe that I am a spy." The only support that Tresca gave was an undisclosed amount of money to the defence fund.[83] Tresca did, however, approach Luigi Antonini to help with the Confalonieri case. Antonini was the second individual with whom *L'Adunata* refused to work.[84]

Luigi Antonini was the president of Local 89 of the International Ladies Garment Workers' Union (ILGWU). He immigrated to the United States in 1910 at the age of twenty-seven and quickly became involved with the union. He rose through the ranks of the ILGWU, becoming president of Italian Dressmakers' Local 89 in 1939, which, at that time, had a membership of 40,000.[85] Antonini identified as a socialist and was involved in anti-fascist activities. However, he is known to have stopped his public attacks against a wealthy New York City–based fascist sympathizer, Generoso Pope, in exchange for favourable press coverage of Local 89 in Pope's newspaper *Il Progresso Italo-Americano*. This in turn led antifascists to harshly condemn the union leader.[86] One of the issues that led to the conflict between *L'Adunata* and Antonini was his involvement in the Vincenzo Ferrero and Domenico Sallitto deportation case. These two Italian anarchists, who owned a restaurant in California, were arrested in April 1934 and ordered deported to Italy by United States authorities because of their political identities. The ILGWU had put up the $2,000 required for the men's collective bail. Sallitto eventually had the charges against him dropped, but Ferrero did not. He went into hiding in order to be spared a return to Italy, which meant the forfeit of his bail.[87] Antonini was angered that the $1,000 bail for Ferrero had been lost and felt that the *L'Adunata* anarchists were laughing at him as a result. According to Max Sartin (Raffaele Schiavina), Antonini also believed himself to be above personal criticism because he had given money to help an anarchist.[88]

Antonini was approached by the Joaquin Defence Committee in Toronto to ask for his assistance in obtaining a passport for Confalonieri[89] (perhaps to avoid confusion, the Joaquin Defence Committee continued to use Confalonieri's assumed name in its title even though his real identity had been discovered by Canadian Immigration on 26 January 1940).[90] At this point, the committee was trying to secure the anarchist's deportation to a country less hostile than Italy. Dorothy Rogers, who was now chiefly responsible for correspondence after Goldman's stroke on 17 February 1940, stated in a letter to Di Domenico that Antonini had been contacted. Di Domenico was outraged that the union leader would be asked to help an anarchist, since Antonini had been involved in the purges of anarchists and other radicals from the ILGWU during the 1920s and 1930s.[91] In addition, Di Domenico accused the union leader of being the dictator of Local 89 and of having personal and political relations with known Italian fascists. He felt that the defence committee had brought a great deal of shame upon Confalonieri for soliciting Antonini's help. They should have explained the situation in order for the anarchist to decide whether the union leader's help should be requested. Di Domenico stated that he would print *L'Adunata dei Refrattari*'s position on the matter so that those who had contributed to Confalonieri's defence would "know what was being done in his name."[92]

In response, Rogers, who was not surprised by Di Domenico's criticism, stated that the Joaquin Defence Committee's decision to approach Antonini had not been arrived at lightly and only because Confalonieri's situation was so dire. As she explained, "The question finally came down to this—deportation to Italy for Marco [sic] or an appeal to Local 89 to obtain a passport to some other country."[93] To inflame the situation further, Di Domenico claimed that Antonini was spreading the word around New York that *L'Adunata dei Refrattari* had begged for his help. As a result, he wrote:

It will take us years to try to persuade people that we had nothing to do with what you have done. And there will always be some at least who will not believe that we have since the beginning been against it. This is certainly one of the things which would not have happened if Emma [Goldman] had been able to continue her work. At any rate she would not have done it without letting us know before the thing happened. Of what will happen when the comrades are informed about this thing, you—I mean those who suggested it—will be the only ones responsible.[94]

This quote demonstrates the fragility of transnational networks that relied heavily on personal contacts and relations. Without Goldman and her knowledge of the intricacies of the *L'Adunata* anarchists, Rogers and the rest of the defence committee were running the risk of alienating their most important allies. To aggravate the situation further, only a few days after Di Domenico sent his reply, a New York City–based Italian-language radio program broadcast news that Antonini was planning to help Confalonieri.[95] When word of this reached Rogers, she drafted a letter, to be published in *L'Adunata dei Refrattari*, that pointed out that Antonini had not been in contact with the Joaquin Defence Committee even after two letters had been sent to the Local 89 leader, requesting his aid. She wanted it made clear to the newspaper's readers that the committee had received neither reply nor help, financial or otherwise, with regards to Confalonieri from Antonini.[96]

The disagreement between *L'Adunata* and the Joaquin Defence Committee over the involvement of Antonini appears to have stemmed from a misunderstanding after a February 1940 meeting between representatives of the newspaper and J.L. Cohen. After the meeting, Cohen reported to the committee that *L'Adunata* would still support efforts to prevent Confalonieri's deportation, even if Tresca and Antonini were approached. However, according to Di Domenico, during the meeting it was made clear to the lawyer that *L'Adunata* was against enlisting the aid of both men because they were viewed, not as personal enemies, but as dishonest people whose actions were contrary to the anarchist movement, working people, and *L'Adunata*'s principles. For the Committee or Cohen to ask for the help of Tresca and Antonini would be against the advice and without the consent of Di Domenico and the other representatives of the newspaper at the meeting. He stressed that the choice to involve the two men should have been left to Confalonieri and no one else. As he put it, "We told [Cohen] that, personally, we would rather die than ask them [Tresca and Antonini] the slightest favor, and that we would not do for any friend, relative or comrade a thing we would not do for ourselves."[97]

Still, even given the conflicts between *L'Adunata* and the Toronto defence committee, the newspaper's commitment to helping both anarchists escape deportation was beyond reproach. From 28 October 1939 until 9 March 1940, a total of twelve articles on the arrests of the Toronto anarchists and the subsequent Bortolotti-Confalonieri deportation case appeared in the pages of *L'Adunata dei Refrattari*. During this period, articles appeared almost weekly and kept readers updated on the various developments of the case. The size of the articles ranged from a few paragraphs to multiple columns.

The information regarding the plight of the Toronto anarchists was supplied to the newspaper, first by Emma Goldman and subsequently by Dorothy Rogers. After the initial raid, Goldman did not want to associate herself
directly with defending the arrested anarchists because she felt her name
could potentially jeopardize the case's outcome. In addition, Goldman was
concerned that her public involvement could lead to her deportation from
Canada. However, given her precarious position and the heightened sense
of security following the legislation of the War Measures Act, Goldman felt
it prudent to have her letters to *L'Adunata dei Refrattari* delivered by Rogers to Detroit or Buffalo, and from there be sent on to New York City.[98] Later,
Ernesto Gava and Ruggero Benvenuti were involved in delivering letters and
picking up money raised by *L'Adunata*, forwarded to Detroit comrades from
Il Gruppo "I Refrattari."[99] The information that Goldman provided *L'Adunata*
was used to draft the articles.[100]

But the articles on Toronto's arrested anarchists did not only provide sum-
maries of events and update readers with the progression of the cases. They
also "framed" these events for a transnational network of activists. Theorist
David Snow has defined framing as "the conscious strategic efforts by groups
of people to fashion shared understandings of the world and of themselves
that legitimate and motivate collective action."[101] *L'Adunata dei Refrattari's*
analysis of the deportation cases was couched in terms of anarchist persecution, the hypocrisy of the Canadian state, collusion between the Italian consul
and the Toronto police, and the serious threat posed to Bortolotti and Confalonieri if their deportations to Italy were carried out.

L'Adunata described the arrest of the Toronto anarchists as an act of political persecution. The facts spoke for themselves. Canada had invoked the War
Measures Act on 3 September 1939, after Britain declared war on Germany,[102]
and legislated new regulations under the War Measures Act on 28 September.
Known as Section 39a of the Defence of Canada Regulations, this legislation
gave Canadian security forces sweeping powers to arrest anyone involved in
the printing or distribution of literature that interfered with Canada's war
effort, the nation's safety, and the morale of its military.[103] And it was under
these new regulations that the three anarchists had been charged. The author
of the *L'Adunata dei Refrattari* article argued that in the six days that had
passed since the introduction of the new regulations on 28 September and the
arrest of the anarchists on 4 October, "it would be materially impossible for the
accused to publish and circulate the material confiscated with the intention of
violating these laws." The author claimed that the Toronto Crown attorney was
using the pretext of the War Measures Act to further the "work of persecution

in hatred of the arrested comrades." Noting how quickly the arrests occurred following the introduction of the new laws, the newspaper asserted that this was a "case of political persecution, devoid of any relation with the war, of which the state of war simply offers the pretext."[104] Continuing with this line of reasoning, in a 2 December 1939 article, *L'Adunata* asked how it was possible that Canadian police had been able to uncover the "dangerous plot" of Bortolotti and the others in less than a week in a city of over half a million inhabitants: "That would mean that in the brief space of six days the Canadian police ... carried out a general investigation on the anti-war activities in the city of Toronto, that has around 631,000 inhabitants, discovered the dangerous plot around the person of comrade Bortolotti and reached the certainty that the conspirators did criminal work."[105] The article's author did not believe the arrests of 4 October to be a demonstration of skilled policing. Instead, it was charged that: "The reality is more modest. The Italian consular authorities in Toronto followed the antifascist activities of the comrades and as soon as they knew of the draconian laws of war, hurried to denounce them to the Canadian police—in which certainly there is no lack of fascists and pseudo-fascists—with the hope that they definitely be taken from circulation."[106]

This alleged cooperation between Toronto police and the Italian vice consul could hardly have been surprising to the readers of *L'Adunata dei Refrattari*. The police were part of the state's repressive structure and anarchists were no strangers to persecution by various security forces in different countries. And, because anarchists believed all states to behave in the same oppressive ways, perhaps with the exception of Britain, which had become a haven for persecuted anarchists from other countries, the cooperation between the Italian state and Canadian police seemed natural.[107] The *L'Adunata* article of 2 December stated that Canadian police had no qualms about working with Italy, even though Mussolini was allied with Nazi Germany, with whom Canada was at war. As the author suggested, with regards to Bortolotti's impending deportation: "The fact that Mussolini still sustains the alliance with Hitler's Germany, against which the British Empire and Canada find themselves in a state of war, does not disturb the Toronto police. They searched for pretexts on which to base the delivery of Arturo [sic] Bortolotti to the black shirts of the fascist monarchy, and went to ransack the archives of Canadian Immigration and those of the US, where it found diligent collaboration."[108]

At the same time, in another article, the author was amazed that any kind of cooperation would exist between Canada, a member of the British Commonwealth, and Italy, since the latter had begun a propaganda campaign aimed at Italians, which argued for the forceful end of England's control of the

Mediterranean: "It seems incredible that one of the component governments of the British Commonwealth of Nations is about to [cooperate with] the fascist dictatorship ... right at the moment in which Italy revived an Anglophobic campaign and the loudspeakers of Mussolini claim the necessity of removing—naturally with the army and war—the English domination of access to the Mediterranean, that is Gibraltar, Suez and the Bosphorus."[109]

The articles in *L'Adunata* made much of the contradictions demonstrated by the Canadian state's persecution of antifascists when it was at war with Germany, a war supposedly "for the defence of democracy and of civilization."[110] And though Canada was part of the British Empire, fighting on the side of Britain against Nazi aggression, it was more than willing to "trampl[e] down the best traditions of liberalism of the mother country, [and] ... sacrific[e] human life to the iniquitous letter of her inquisitorial and barbaric laws."[111]

Of course, when it came to dealing with leftist radicals, the Canadian government willingly colluded with fascist or reactionary regimes.[112] For example, in 1933, Tomo Čačić, a Croat from Yugoslavia, was arrested by Canadian authorities for being a member of the CPC. Found guilty of these charges, Čačić was ordered deported to his country of birth. In a recent study on the Čačić deportation, historian Dennis Molinaro has shown that the RCMP was in contact with the Yugoslav consulate in Canada regarding the case. The consulate was forthcoming in telling the RCMP that Čačić was going to be arrested upon his return to Yugoslavia, leaving Canadian authorities under no illusion as to the fate that awaited the communist.[113]

Once the original charges against Bortolotti, Benvenuti, and Gava under the War Measures Act and Bortolotti's possession of illegal firearms were successfully defeated in court, *L'Adunata dei Refrattari* shifted its focus to the impending deportation of Bortolotti and Confalonieri to Italy. The seriousness of this possibility could not be understated; the return of the two anarchist antifascists would mean either prison or death in the hands of the Italian state.[114] In fact, imprisonment was the least punishment that Bortolotti and Confalonieri could hope to receive upon their return to Italy.[115] The deportation cases of the two anarchists were put in a larger historical context of Italian anarchists who had faced similar deportations. In a *L'Adunata* article from 9 December 1939, the author mentioned Ugo Fedeli's deportation from Uruguay and Nicola Recchi's expulsion from Argentina.[116] The paper also reprinted part of an article written by Luigi Galleani that appeared in *Cronaca Sovversiva* discussing the arrest of Hamilton's Armando Del Moro in 1915.[117]

Bortolotti was also "framed" by *L'Adunata dei Refrattari* as someone being slowly martyred for his convictions. The three months in the cold and damp Don Jail were causing the anarchist health problems. He had lost twelve pounds during his incarceration and suffered from a fever of 103°F.[118] As a result of such squalid conditions, Bortolotti was moved to the jail's hospital to receive medical attention.[119] As *L'Adunata* reported, "The condition of [Bortolotti's] health was undermined by the long detention in the infected prisons of Canada."[120] This issue became another means by which the paper stressed the dire situation faced by Bortolotti in particular.

L'Adunata also commented on the lack of press coverage on the Bortolotti-Confalonieri case in the Canadian mainstream press, as well as the general silence among left-wing publications. Prior to January 1940, the only non-anarchist publication to cover the story was an IWW publication from Chicago called *Industrial Worker*.[121] The apparent lack of interest on the part of the Canadian media, with regard to the impending deportations of the two anarchists, was constructed by *L'Adunata* as part of a conspiracy to hand the anarchists over to the Italian government: "[I]n Canada, the press has plotted the most airtight conspiracy of silence on [Bortolotti's and Confalonieri's] fate and on the [fact] that the Canadian government plan to return [the men] to the *squadristi* of the fascist dictatorship."[122] According to Emma Goldman, in her letter to *L'Adunata dei Refrattari* published on 18 November 1939, the lack of media coverage was compounded by the absence of any initiative on the part of Canadian defenders of civil liberties to take a public stand against the treatment of the arrested anarchists. As Goldman stated, "we need the help of all comrades and of all the lovers of liberty that exist in the US. And this is certainly not because we have not attempted to arouse the interest of the Canadian masses. Unfortunately there exists a conspiracy of silence among the daily journals, and no public [way] by which to reach the people of this city [or] of this country. More sad still is the complete absence of individual animation of civic sense, disposed to defend civil rights from the invasion of authority."[123] As Goldman insisted, if not for anarchist publications such as *L'Adunata*, there would have been no coverage on this deportation case: "there are … Canadian Socialists, which [sic] boast that only they remain to guard the constitutional rights of the people of Canada. But it remains a fact that no journal, no magazine, socialist, liberal, unionist or other, in the US or Canada, said one word in defence of the arrested of Toronto."[124] *L'Adunata* expressed the importance of the anarchist press in the deportation struggle: "[I]n the US, the anarchist papers are the only ones that interest themselves in [Bortolotti and Confalonieri], the others make themselves busy and, in every way, are completely indifferent to the persecution to which anarchists are subject as a result of their convictions."[125]

A final important aspect of the framing process for the Bortolotti-Confalonieri case—one tied directly to the mobilization of resources—was the necessity of U.S.-based comrades to provide financial assistance for legal costs because the anarchist movement in Canada, whether Italian or non-Italian, was not large enough to raise the money on their own. In fact, Toronto-based anarchists who involved themselves in the legal struggle, on behalf of the 4 October arrestees, counted on the solidarity of comrades living in the United States.[126] As Emma Goldman explained to Nick Di Domenico, two weeks after the initial arrests: "I wish I could hold out hope that part of the amount can be raised here from the Jewish Comrades. The trouble is we have no more than half a dozen and so far they have contributed only around forty dollars. There is no English movement or comrades.... The Italians, also very few comrades, but antifascists have collected $133. They may raise a little more. I do not know."[127]

J.L. Cohen's lawyer fee of $1,500 was the largest expense to be covered. Goldman felt he charged a fair price, considering all the work it would take to free the arrested anarchists from jail.[128] The appeals for financial assistance appeared in the first article *L'Adunata* published regarding the original raid and arrests in Toronto. Readers were invited to send financial contributions to the paper directly to help "fight for the liberty ... of the hostages of Canadian reaction."[129] Goldman had requested that *L'Adunata dei Refrattari* collect funds from its readers and then forward them on to her because it would be less work on her part to keep track of all monies coming in.[130] It was imperative that the paper's readership raise the necessary funds to cover legal costs in Toronto because the Canadian media ignored the plight of the arrested and no one, apart from local anarchists, was coming to their aid.[131] Goldman had wanted the information on the arrests to appear in *L'Adunata* as soon as possible and, though not explicit in this, wanted the paper to publish news on the Toronto anarchists weekly.[132] When she received an advance copy of the 25 November 1939 issue of the newspaper, which had no information on Bortolotti's deportation, save totals of money raised, Goldman wrote to Di Domenico to express her disappointment and stressed the need of "keeping this struggle in the public eye due to the short term memory of most."[133] In his response, Di Domenico explained that the reason for the omission had to do with sending the issue to presses a day earlier because of the Thanksgiving holiday, and reiterated that Bortolotti would not be forgotten.[134]

Raising enough money to cover legal costs stemming from the initial arrest of the Italian anarchists and for the Bortolotti-Confalonieri deportation case was always a pressing issue for the anarchists in Toronto involved in this struggle. Within the two and a half weeks following the 4 October arrests, only $400—not even one-third of Cohen's $1,500 fee—had been raised to off-set expenses. Even before the first appeal appeared in the pages of *L'Adunata dei Refrattari*, Goldman had asked Di Domenico if it was possible for the Italian comrades in the United States to raise $1,000. She realized that the Italian anarchists were "the poorest of the poor," but her desperation was evident.[135] In his reply, Di Domenico wrote that he understood the need for raising the money quickly but stated it was materially impossible for this to happen in a short time. The newspaper's readership had not forgotten the arrested comrades and were doing everything they could to find the means to raise the funds.[136] Goldman was to continually press Di Domenico on issues of money. Between early December 1939 and mid-February 1940, she wrote six letters to the publisher of *L'Adunata*, asking if more money could be sent and expressing her concern over whether Cohen's fee would be paid.[137] After Cohen was able to negotiate Bortolotti's release on $4,000 bail with J.S. Fraser of the Department of Mines and Resources, Immigration Branch, Goldman's concern was expanded to include worries over raising the bail money.[138] However, it must be stated that Goldman did not single out *L'Adunata dei Refrattari* in this regard; she was constantly writing comrades, whether Italian or not, to find out what they were doing to raise money and when she could expect it. In fairness to Goldman, her persistence was more the result of her great concern for the arrested anarchists, which was exacerbated once Bortolotti and Confalonieri were ordered deported, than an overbearing personality. She began to loathe her constant reminding of comrades for contributions and began to fear that they were beginning to think that all she cared about was money.[139]

To demonstrate the continued need for contributors, *L'Adunata* printed an article that featured part of a letter Goldman had sent to the publishers of the Spanish-language anarchist newspaper *Cultura Proletaria*. Goldman had recently returned from a lecture trip in Winnipeg to find that no new contributions had come in. The letter expressed Goldman's exasperation and indignation at the anarchist movement's apparent indifference to the fate of Bortolotti and Confalonieri. As she stated: "I must say that the enthusiasm and generosity demonstrated by the comrades at the beginning of this struggle has now almost completely disappeared. During my trip to Winnipeg and after my return I have received little correspondence and no contributions for this endeavour. You understand, comrades, that because of this indifference it becomes extremely difficult to continue ... with the deliberate intention of getting the hostages from the hands of the jailers. Frankly and sincerely I don't ... understand the reason of this change of attitude."[140] Letters of a similar tone had also been received by *L'Adunata dei Refrattari*. The article reiterated

Goldman's concerns and invited readers to continue their urgent work in saving the anarchists from deportation.[141]

Creating a framing process that receives mass support is important in determining the success of a particular social issue. It would be ideal for a social movement to draw in as many different actors from as wide a segment of the population as possible. However, as an anarchist Italian-language publication, *L'Adunata dei Refrattari*'s focus appears to have been directed solely at its readership and not to the wider Italian population, nor the larger non-Italian society in Canada or the United States. More wide-ranging campaigns to solicit aid from outside of the Italian anarchist milieu were conducted by the Bortolotti and Confalonieri defence committees based in Toronto. The articles *L'Adunata* printed on these events stressed the urgency of raising the required funds to successfully mount the struggle to save the two anarchists. Within less than five months, the paper and its readership were able to raise more than $700, the largest single sum of all the contributors, almost one-fifth of the total amount spent by the Bortolotti-Confalonieri defence committees.[142] This was quite an accomplishment, considering the modest means of most Italian anarchists in North America.

The Italian anarchist movement did not have a stable source of funding outside of the movement. Its survival and ability to support various causes was only possible through the contributions of its supporters. As mentioned above, *L'Adunata dei Refrattari* played an important role in mobilizing its readers to financially support the Bortolotti-Confalonieri deportation struggle. The different Italian anarchist circles that were allied to the newspaper raised funds in a variety of ways. Il Gruppo I Liberi of Chicago held a spaghetti dinner on 2 December 1939 and raised fifty-six dollars, while Il Gruppo Libertà of Needham Heights, Massachusetts, organized an event that earned twenty-four dollars for the defence funds. On 25 February 1940, Circolo Volontà coordinated a three-act drama and a dance at the Galilei Club in Brooklyn. The play was written by F. Cavalotti and presented by the Filodrammatica Volontà. All money raised was sent to *L'Adunata* on behalf of Bortolotti and Confalonieri.[143]

During the Bortolotti-Confalonieri case, the Italian anarchists used education to raise awareness of the two anarchists' plight and the need for direct aid to cover legal expenses. As mentioned above, *L'Adunata dei Refrattari* published updates on the case as events unfolded, keeping its readership informed. Though it does not appear as if *L'Adunata* itself was involved in disseminating information on the deportation case amongst the larger non-anarchist Italian communities of Canada and the United States, it is possible that groups like Il Gruppo Liberi and Circolo Volontà may have reached non-anarchist Italians in their respective cities through the events they held to raise money for the two anarchists. It was typical for Italian workers to attend radical theatre productions, not only as a means of social interaction with others but also as a diversion from lives of hardship.[144] Again, it is difficult to make the claim with certainty, but the plays presented by Filodrammatica Volontà, for instance, may very well have attracted members of the Brooklyn Italian community who did not identify as anarchist or even considered themselves sympathizers. These events also could have drawn community members, whether on the Left or not, who wanted to help two Italians seen as facing discrimination in Canada.[145] *L'Adunata dei Refrattari* also became the vehicle for direct aid by collecting the money raised by different Italian groups and individuals, and then forwarding the funds to the Bortolotti-Confalonieri defence committees in Toronto.

In the end, the struggle to prevent the deportation of Attilio Bortolotti and Agostino Confalonieri to Italy was successful. Bortolotti was allowed to remain in Canada as long as he maintained a clean record.[146] Confalonieri, on the other hand, could not challenge his deportation order because of his illegal entrance into Canada, but he was also spared a return trip to Italy thanks to the efforts of Augusto Bellanca of the Amalgamated Clothing Workers' Union (ACWU) and Frank Tannenbaum, a former anarchist and Wobbly who had served as an advisor to the Mexican government during the 1930s.[147] These men, both from New York City, were able to persuade the Mexican government to allow Confalonieri to reside there. However, complications arose for Confalonieri when the American consul in Toronto refused to grant the anarchist a transit visa to allow him to travel to New York City to board a ship sailing for Mexico.[148] Bortolotti contacted some smugglers who could help Confalonieri get into the United States via Niagara Falls, so he could make his way to New York City.[149] Confalonieri arrived in Mexico on 8 April 1940 with $150 supplied by Cohen and the contact information for a Jewish anarchist who had fought in Spain, given to him by Emma Goldman before his departure from Toronto.[150]

As part of their decades-long struggles of resistance, Italian anarchists established networks to aid Italian veterans of the Spanish Civil War who wanted to leave an increasingly repressive Europe. This network involved anarchists from France, Switzerland, Belgium, Canada, and the United States, and was funded by Italian anarchists in Europe and, most likely, North America. The money raised for this endeavour was used to help cover travel costs and pay for transit visas. Both Attilio Bortolotti and Agostino Confalonieri were involved in this network, though in different capacities. After the arrest of the two men, along with their anarchist comrades, in Toronto in October 1939, the Italian anarchist movement was quickly mobilized to prevent Bortolotti's and Confalonieri's deportation to Italy. Though this campaign was spearheaded by Emma Goldman, the Italian anarchists played an instrumental role in this struggle. They, through appeals in the Italian-language publication *L'Adunata dei Refrattari* and autonomous fundraising activities, were able to supply the defence funds of Bortolotti and Confalonieri with the largest single financial contribution: $1,437.37 of the $3,540.76 total, just over 40 percent of all expenses.[151] If not for the involvement of the Italian anarchists, the ability of Goldman and others to mount their campaign would have been jeopardized. Nevertheless, the conflicts among the Italian anarchists in North America had consequences for the wider deportation struggle. Had the conflict between *L'Adunata* and Carlo Tresca not existed, it is possible that the Italian anarchists could have raised even more money more quickly for the two anarchists; or, perhaps, Tresca would have been more involved in approaching non-anarchist contacts within the labour movement and media, thus expediting the process. Tresca refused to involve himself in aiding anarchists aligned with *L'Adunata*, and those responsible for publishing the newspaper were unwilling to tarnish their integrity by cooperating with the anarcho-syndicalist. Still, even with a part of the Italian anarchist movement involved in this case, their contribution was sizable.

The transnational character of the Italian anarchist movement was such that, in a time of crisis, a smaller number of anarchists based in Canada could call upon the aid of other anarchists in the United States. If these networks and relationships had not existed, those anarchists in Canada who were involved in the Bortolotti-Confalonieri case would have been hard pressed to cover legal fees and other expenses associated with preventing the deportations to Italy, since the greater share of the expenses were paid by United States–based comrades.[152]

In much the same way as contemporary websites for Anarchist Black Cross[153] and the Earth Liberation Prisoners Support Network[154] keep anarchists abreast of the movement's political prisoners and ways to support them, the Italian anarchist press was an important means by which information on issues, such as the deportation of comrades, could be disseminated. In this particular instance, *L'Adunata dei Refrattari* acted as the main source of news on the development of the Bortolotti-Confalonieri case as well as a destination point for all monies being raised by Italian anarchists throughout the United States. The Italian anarchist press played a central and indispensable role in linking the autonomous groups that comprised this transnational movement. It acted as a unifying presence that was able to organize Italian anarchists to come to the aid of comrades in crisis.

CONCLUSION

As the 1940s wore on, the Italian anarchists in North America grew older and their children, who had assimilated into Canadian and American culture, did not replenish the movement's ranks. Anarchist militants who had been in their twenties and thirties during the interwar period were now in their forties and fifties and did not necessarily have the same energy, as in their younger years, for political activism. In 1943, Carlo Tresca was murdered and *Il Martello* ceased publication shortly afterwards. Of the two major Italian-language anarchist newspapers of this period, only *L'Adunata dei Refrattari* continued to appear weekly into the 1960s, and then bi-weekly before ceasing operations in 1971, due to a lack of subscribers.[1] Following the Second World War, the transnational Italian anarchist movement was on the decline.

The Italian anarchist movement in North America had its roots in Italy. There, following the Risorgimento, Bakunin, Cafiero, Costa, Galleani, Gori, Malatesta, and others began to organize and put anarchist principles into action. Their activism among Italian workers, attempts at insurrection, congresses, debates over theory and practice, and the vicious repression they experienced at the hands of the Italian state, created a distinct political and social culture. As these anarchists began to leave Italy in the late nineteenth century, either in search of work abroad or to escape persecution, their anarchist philosophies and culture migrated with them. And it was through anarchist and non-anarchist migration networks that Italian anarchist *circoli* in other parts of Europe, northern and southern Africa, Australia, the Middle East, and South and North America were established. In the Italian communities of these regions, Italian anarchists recreated the political and cultural milieux they had left in Italy. They began to organize unions, lead strikes, publish newspapers, and sponsor a myriad of social events that included dinners, dances, and theatrical performances. These activities were central to maintaining and building local anarchist movements. Italian anarchists also replicated the antagonisms over organization that fuelled so much debate in Italy.

In the North American context, this enmity existed between the anarcho-syndicalists and the anti-organizationalist anarchist communists. Though this rift was largely limited to Luigi Galleani and Carlo Tresca, as well as their adherents in New York City, it also, to some extent, affected cooperation between both factions in times of crisis, such as during the Bortolotti-Confalonieri deportation case.

Another aspect of Italian anarchism transplanted to Canada and the United States, among other countries, was the gender roles between men and women. A central tenet of anarchist political philosophy is that no one has the right to oppress another. Yet, not all of the Italian movement's men saw female comrades as equals. In fact, at least a few felt women had no place at all in the anarchist movement. In many cases, women were relegated to the domestic sphere; they were involved in food preparation during social events and expected to raise and educate the next generation of anarchist militants while the men edited newspapers, lectured, and led. As repressive as the Italian movement may have been for women, it did provide a space for them to resist gender oppression, address specific issues of concern, and, in a few cases, become well-known for their abilities.

At this point in studies about left-wing movements in the early twentieth century, it is common for the scholar to lament that particular movement's passing or attribute the movement's death to a particular point in time.[2] While it is true that the Italian anarchists in North America were on the decline following the Second World War, the Italian anarchist movement itself did not die. Instead, the centre of anarchist activity shifted back to Italy. In 1949 and 1950, anarchist congresses were organized by the Federazione Anarchici Italiana (FAI) and took place in Livorno and Ancona, respectively. Further research would need to be conducted to find out whether Italian anarchists from North America were present at these conferences. At the very least, anarchists in North America were kept informed of developments in Italy. A 1949 letter from Pio Turroni, a Cesena-based anarchist who had fought in Spain during the Civil War, to Armando Borghi in New York City, explained what happened at the first convergence in Livorno: the Italians were still split over the issue of organization.[3] At Livorno, Pier Carlo Masini, a former communist who was then the editor of *Umanità Nova*, and a contingent of Italian youths argued for the formation of a libertarian party based on anarchist principles that were to be adapted to the economic, social, and political realities of postwar Italy. It is unclear whether Masini and his adherents wanted to build a political party to run in elections, but they did want to establish a strong presence among Italian workers.[4] Turroni, an anti-organizationalist, was disappointed in the direction the anarchist movement was taking. As he lamented to Borghi, "the ... youth ... don't understand anarchism or how we understand it. And the 'old-timers' don't exist any more."[5] By 1954, Masini and his group had broken away from the FAI over the issue and Borghi had returned to Italy to take over the editorship of *Umanità Nova*.[6]

And what of the other Italian anarchists? Ernesto Bonomini, who served a prison sentence in France for the murder of an Italian fascist and had entered the United States illegally in 1939, became an upholsterer and was employed by Twentieth Century Fox in Hollywood. He wrote for various anarchist publications under the pseudonym Dick Perry and eventually retired to Florida.[7] John Vattuone stayed active with the anarchist movement in New York City. He aided the anarchists involved in the fledgling English-language publication *Why?* by helping deliver issues with his truck. Some of the young Italians who were part of the *Why?* group were on good terms with Raffaele Schiavina, the editor of *L'Adunata dei Refrattari*. This relationship led to financial support from the older generation of Italian anarchists and access to the print shop that produced *L'Adunata*.[8]

Relations between Italian anarchists and the New Left of the 1960s were less harmonious. In his memoirs, Sam Dolgoff, the Russian-born writer and anarchist activist, recalls a meeting between the secretary of an unidentified Brooklyn-based anarchist circle and members of New York City's Up Against the Wall Motherfuckers (UAWMF). The Motherfuckers identified as anarchists and wanted to conduct a guerrilla war against the police, fire department, and all state institutions. In need of money to help with legal costs, members of the Motherfuckers approached Dolgoff who, hesitantly, put them in contact with the Brooklyn group's secretary. The meeting did not go well. The Italian anarchist understood the UAWMF's hatred of the police but could not understand why they wanted to destroy the fire department, considering the useful role it played in putting out fires and saving lives. The secretary also had a problem with the group's name. As Dolgoff explains, "The Italians respect and revere motherhood. They violently object to the term 'Motherfuckers' and would indignantly refuse to help anyone using such language." The meeting ended with UAWMF receiving no aid from the Italian anarchists.[9]

As for the transnational anarchist networks, they were still operational in the late 1940s, if not later. Near the end of the Second World War, Armando Borghi had originally been deported from the United States, having resided illegally in that country since 1927. Once he arrived in postwar Italy, Borghi, now sixty-three, found conditions too difficult and wanted to return to the United States. He, along with John and Elvira Vattuone, and Attilio and Libera

Bortolotti, collectively worked out a plan to get Borghi back to New York City. It is unclear how someone like Borghi, who was deported from the United States, could be allowed into Canada, but this is what happened. He arrived in Montreal at some point during 1948 and was met there by the Bortolottis, who then brought him to Toronto. The plan was for Borghi and Libera Bortolotti to cross the Canada–United States border on a bus that travelled between the Canadian and American sides of Niagara Falls. In order to get past United States border security, Borghi would have the passport of Umberto Martignago, Libera Bortolotti's father. At the crossing, Borghi, possibly as a result of his age and being well-dressed, was lucky enough not to be asked for his papers. Once he and Libera Bortolotti were safely through customs, the Vattuones drove Borghi back to Brooklyn.[10]

If one is to judge the success of the transnational Italian anarchist movement, based on its ability to rid the world of capitalist exploitation, governments, states, and religion, then the only possible conclusion is that the movement was a failure. Of course, such a judgment would be selling the activism of these radicals short. Within Italian migrant communities in many parts of the world, anarchists attempted to build a movement to challenge the oppressive institutions that prevented people from living lives free of oppression, misery, and want. This movement was susceptible to internal strife and gender divisions, its tactics did not always prove successful, and opportunities were, doubtless, missed. Nonetheless, the Italian anarchists built an impressive movement that spanned continents and the Atlantic Ocean. Its adherents were militants of the first order who gave their lives to making the world a more bearable place.

An identifiable Italian anarchist movement in North America no longer exists. Anarchism has long since moved beyond the Little Italies and other ethnic communities of Canada and the United States. Though it is beyond the scope of this book to explore anarchism in North America from the 1940s to the 1960s, it does appear, even in a limited way, that the disconnection between first- and second-wave anarchism was not as great as is generally believed. The Italian anarchists did not just pass into history after Sacco and Vanzetti were executed, nor did the anarchist movement end after the victory of the fascists in Spain in 1939; instead, anarchist militants stayed involved to the best of their ability and helped pass along their knowledge and experience to a new generation.

Unfortunately, a great deal of the history of these first-wave militants has never been recorded and the historical legacy of these anarchists is generally not well-known. Many contemporary anarchists are not aware of the past

150 years of anarchist history that preceded their involvement in the movement. Though there are aspects of life in the twenty-first century that differ dramatically from that of the earlier (twentieth) century, there are still many important lessons we can learn from the first wave—especially about movement building and the articulation and celebration of a specifically anarchist culture.

The Italian anarchists demonstrate the importance of culture in movement maintenance and expansion. Their newspapers sought to educate readers about anarchist theory, practice, and history, report local and international news important to anarchists, and record the activities of anarchist *circoli* in North America. The numerous plays anarchists wrote and performed explored themes of liberty, free love, revolution, and militancy. In addition, there were innumerable dances, dinners, and picnics, almost always accompanied by a speaker, to celebrate anarchist "holidays" or raise money for an anarchist cause. These social events were vitally important in sustaining the movement and attracting new members while a predominantly Italian-speaking potential membership existed. However, as the first wave of Italian anarchists began to get older and their children assimilated into the larger host societies, a strictly Italian anarchist movement was unable to survive. Unfortunately, the movement's retention of the Italian language in its newspapers, the inability to move beyond the boundaries of Italian communities, and distance from the wider non-Italian society of which they were part led to the gradual decline of Italian anarchism in North America.

Today, however, anarchist groups and movements in Canada and the United States are not tied to a specific ethnicity and have a better chance to avoid the insularity of the Italian anarchists. In the here and now, radical/resistance cultures can be created and celebrated as a means of building and uniting a larger movement. This is an important way to challenge and provide alternatives to the hegemony of the current right-wing/pro-capitalist culture pervasive among North America's corporate media and national governments; a right-wing culture that implements austerity programs, cuts social programs, and further criminalizes dissent.

It is my hope that this book, in addition to demonstrating what a transnational radical history might look like, will help contemporary anarchists to understand the role that culture can play in creating vibrant and militant movements. We need to be less disconnected from the anarchist past and have a better sense of those who came before us, their tactics, and their debates. And we need to do this, not only to avoid repeating some of the same mistakes, but also to understand how such activists created an anarchist culture and were able to build upon it. How contemporary anarchists attempt to create a culture or cultures is up to them. Perhaps there could be a return to commemorating important events in anarchist history with a social gathering of some kind. Or different kinds of social events—plays, dances, concerts—might target those outside of the anarchist movement. However this is done, two things are obvious: we will need a culture of resistance to challenge and act as an alternative to that of the far Right, and we must reach out to larger numbers to pose a serious challenge to capitalism.

ACKNOWLEDGEMENTS

All projects are collective efforts and there are many people I'd like to thank for their contributions to this book. The volume you are holding in your hands began as a dissertation in the History Department at Queen's University. I would like to thank my supervisor Ian Mckay for his guidance, enthusiasm, immense knowledge, patience, and dedication. I would also like to thank my defence committee—Karen Dubinsky, Ariel Salzmann, Richard Day, and my external reviewer, Kirk Shaffer—for a stimulating and enjoyable defence. My ability to work with the Italian language was made possible by Donato Santeramo of the Department of Spanish and Italian at Queen's University who let me participate in his Italian lectures for three semesters. I would also like to express my gratitude to Yvonne Place, Cathy Dickison, and Deborah Stirton-Massey in the Department of History at Queen's University. Their administrative expertise is unsurpassed and of great benefit to history grad students.

While conducting research at archives in Canada and abroad I met many helpful people. I would like to thank the fine folks at Library and Archives Canada in Ottawa, the Archivio Centrale dello Stato in Rome, the Immigration History Research Centre at the University of Minnesota, and the Boston Public Library Special Collections. Special thanks to Julie Herrada, Curator of the Labadie Collection at the University of Michigan in Ann Arbor, for her help navigating the archives, and to Mieke Ijzermans, formerly of the International Institute of Social History in Amsterdam, for showing me around and for the accommodations. In Toronto, Angelo Principe was kind enough to share his collection of *Il Martello* with me. I would like to thank Federico Arcos for welcoming me into his home and showing me his collection of anarchist materials. He was also kind enough to speak to me about the anarchists he knew in southern Ontario and Detroit, some of whom are featured in this book. I am equally indebted to Libera Martignago Bortolotti, who spent an afternoon telling me of the Italian anarchist movement that existed during her youth in Sault Ste. Marie, Ontario.

During the course of my research, I was fortunate to come into contact with fellow "anarcho-nerds" Kirk Shaffer, Kenyon Zimmer, Davide Turcato, and Allan Antliff. All four have been a tremendous help whether it was sharing research, organizing panel presentations, providing feedback, or just hanging out and talking anarchist history. Friends in different places were a massive help when I was travelling for research purposes. I would like to thank Mel Mongeon and Topon Das for putting me up when conducting research in Ottawa and Steve Saranga for letting me crash when in Boston. A big thanks to Stijn, Séverine, Norah, and Mats for letting me stay at their Belgian home during research trips to Europe. When Eyjafjallajökull erupted in April 2010 and my flight home was cancelled, they let me extend my stay and gave me the chance to cut their lawn. A massive thanks to all the rad folks engaged in social activism on and off Queen's campus. Your dedication to all progressive issues made life in a small conservative town very rich and rewarding. It's easy to get buried under mountains of primary documents and sometimes lose your way. I'd like to thank Sean Haberle for reminding why I had started this project. And thanks to Nolan Reilly, my MA supervisor and friend, who told me before embarking on a PhD: "Do the project because you believe in it, not because you expect a job at the end of it." Sage advice.

At the University of Manitoba Press, I would like to thank Glenn Bergen, David Carr, David Larsen, Ariel Gordon, and the rest of the team. These folks have been stellar and their interest in and support of this book has been amazing. Not only did they provide me with books and microfilm via Interlibrary Loan, they also rounded up a microfilm reader so I could read Italian-language anarchist newspapers in the comfort of my own home! I would also like to thank my manuscript readers Mark Leier and Jennifer Guglielmo for their enthusiasm for the topic as well as their comments and advice.

Thanks also to the Tomchuk and Gallant families and, in particular, my parents Ernie and Trudy Tomchuk for their moral and financial support while I was a grad student. They have also put up with my warped sense of humour for many years and should be congratulated for their perseverance. Massive amounts of love and gratitude to my partner Meghan Gallant for her support, love, encouragement, and general awesomeness. And to our son Darius who arrived while I was working on this book.

NOTES

INTRODUCTION

1.   Tim Buck, *Yours in the Struggle: Reminiscences of Tim Buck*, eds., William Beeching and Dr. Phyllis Clarke (Toronto: NC Press, 1977).

2   Paul Avrich, *Anarchist Voices: An Oral History of Anarchism in America* (Oakland: AK Press, 2005) 178.

3   Ibid., 179.

4   Ibid.; G.B. Ambrosi, Vice Console, Toronto, to Consolato Generale d'Italia, Ottawa, 7 July 1933, Fortunato Marriotti, busta 3075, Casellario Politico Centrale (CPC), Archivio Centrale dello Stato (ACS), Rome.

5   Avrich, *Anarchist Voices*, 179; Attilio Bortolotti and Rossella Di Leo, "Between Canada and the US: A Tale of Immigrants and Anarchists," Kate Sharpley Library, http//:www.katesharpleylibrary.net/8pk1h4 (accessed 18 July 2010); Attilio Bortolotti, "Guardian of the Dream: A [sic] Oral History with Art Berthelet," *Kick It Over* 17 (Winter 1986/1987): 1.

6   Avrich, *Anarchist Voices*, 179–80; Prefetto di Messina, Messina, to Ministero dell'Interno, Rome, 5 Dec. 1912, Fortunato Cernuto, busta 1257, CPC, ACS, Rome.

7   Avrich, *Anarchist Voices*, 179–180; Bortolotti and Di Leo, "Between Canada and the US: A Tale of Immigrants and Anarchists."

8   Bortolotti, "Guardian of the Dream," 1.

9   The chairman of this meeting was actually a former boss of Bortolotti's by the name of Luigi Merlo, a prominent member of Windsor's Italian community. Merlo came to Canada in his teens and later established companies in construction and land development among others. He was involved in the Separate School Board, was a member of Knights of Columbus, in addition to two golf and country clubs, and "a loyal Liberal Party supporter," ostensibly after his involvement chairing fascist meetings. Susan Petkovic, "Italians in Windsor: The Development of the Erie Street Community from Ghetto to Via Italia," MA Thesis, Queen's University, 1992, 64–65.

10   Avrich, *Anarchist Voices*, 181.

11   Ibid., 182; Bortolotti and Di Leo, "Between Canada and the US."

12   Avrich, *Anarchist Voices*, 183–184; Bortolotti and Di Leo, "Between Canada and the US."

13   Avrich, *Anarchist Voices*, 184; Bortolotti and Di Leo, "Between Canada and the US."

14   Paul Avrich, *Sacco and Vanzetti: The Anarchist Background* (Princeton: Princeton University Press, 1991), 54.

15   Linda Basch, Nina Glick Schiller, and Cristina Szanton Blanc, *Nations Unbound: Transnational Projects, Postcolonial Predicaments, and Deterritorialized Nation-States* (Amsterdam: Gordon and Breach Science Publishers, 2000), 7.

16   A network is a social structure that includes actors and relations. An actor can be a person or a group while a relation refers to the specific type of bond between actors. According to sociologists David Knoke and Song Yang, "Structural relations are crucial to sustaining cohesion and solidarity within a group." Networks also help "to create interests and shared identities and to promote shared norms and values." David Knoke and Song Yang, *Social Network Analysis*, 2nd ed. (Los Angeles: Sage Publications, 2008), 5–7.

17   Theresa Moritz and Albert Moritz, *The World's Most Dangerous Woman: A New Biography of Emma Goldman* (Vancouver: Subway Books, 2001), 25–26.

18   Michael Mann in Marcel van der Linden, *Workers of the World: Essays toward a Global Labour History* (Leiden: Brill, 2008), 7–8.

19   David Berry, *A History of the French Anarchist Movement, 1917–1945* (Westport: Greenwood Press, 2002), 181, 188.

20   See Matthew Thomas, *Anarchist Ideas and Counter-Cultures in Britain, 1880–1914: Revolutions in Everyday Life* (Aldershot: Ashgate Publishing, 2005).

21   Mathieu Houle-Courcelles, *Sur les traces de l'anarchisme au Québec* (Montreal: Lux Éditeur, 2008).

22   Pernicone lists the periods of apparent anarchist resurgence in Italy as follows: 1884–1885, 1889–1891, 1892–1894, and 1897–1898. Nunzio Pernicone, *Italian Anarchism, 1864–1892* (Princeton: Princeton University Press, 1993), 7.

23   Davide Turcato, "Italian Anarchism as a Transnational Movement, 1885–1915," *International Review of Social History* 52 (2007): 410–411, 444.

24   See Avrich, *Sacco and Vanzetti*; Dorothy Gallagher, *All the Right Enemies: The Life and Murder of Carlo Tresca* (New Brunswick: Rutgers University Press, 1988); Jennifer Guglielmo, *Living the Revolution: Italian Women's Resistance and Radicalism in New York City, 1880–1945* (Charlotte: University of North Carolina Press, 2010); Caroline Waldron Merithew, "Anarchist Motherhood: Toward the Making of a Revolutionary Proletariat in Illinois Coal Towns," *Women, Gender, and Transnational Lives: Italian Workers of the World*, ed. Donna Gabaccia and Franca Iacovetta (Toronto: University of Toronto Press, 2002), 217–246; Nunzio Pernicone, *Carlo Tresca: Portrait of a Rebel* (New York: Palgrave Macmillan, 2005); Nunzio Pernicone, "War among the Italian Anarchists: The Galleanisti's Campaign against Carlo Tresca," *The Lost World of Italian-American Radicalism: Politics, Labor, and Culture*, ed. Phillip V. Cannistraro and Gerald Meyer (Westport: Praeger Publishers, 2003), 78–97; Nunzio Pernicone, "Luigi Galleani and Italian Anarchist Terrorism in the United States," *Studi emigrazione* 30, 111 (1993): 469–488; and Robert Ventresca and Franca Iacovetta, "Virgilia D'Andrea: The Politics of Protest and the Poetry of Exile," *Women, Gender, and Transnational Lives: Italian Workers of the World*, ed. Donna Gabaccia and Franca Iacovetta (Toronto: University of Toronto Press, 2002), 299–326.

25   A translation that appears on the masthead of *L'Adunata dei Refrattari* reads "Call of the Refractaires," which is a mix of English and French. The choice of the French *refractaire* may have been a result of the difficulty in translating *refrattari* into English.

26   Salvatore Salerno, *Red November, Black November: Culture and Community in the Industrial Workers of the World* (Albany: State University of New York Press, 1989), 13.

27   Paul Avrich's invaluable books on first-wave anarchism in the United States include *Anarchist Voices: An Oral History of Anarchism in America* (Edinburgh: AK Press, 2005); *The Modern School Movement: Anarchism and Education in the United States*

(Oakland: AK Press, 2005); *Sacco and Vanzetti: The Anarchist Background* (Princeton: Princeton University Press, 1991); *Anarchist Portraits* (Princeton: Princeton University Press, 1988); *The Haymarket Tragedy* (Princeton: Princeton University Press, 1984); and *An American Anarchist: The Life of Voltairine de Cleyre* (Princeton: Princeton University Press, 1978).

28 "L'Archivio," Archivio Centrale dello Stato, http://www.archivi.beniculturali.it/ACS/cpcarchivio.html (accessed 21 May 2010).

29 Michael Schmidt and Lucien van der Walt, *Black Flame: The Revolutionary Class Politics of Anarchism and Syndicalism* (Oakland: AK Press, 2009), 71–72.

30 Jason Adams, *Non-Western Anarchisms: Rethinking the Global Context* (Johannesburg: Zabalaza Books, n.d.), 6.

31 Ibid.

32 See Gustav Landauer, *For Socialism*, trans. David J. Parent (St. Louis: Telos Press, 1978).

33 See Richard J.F. Day, *Gramsci is Dead: Anarchist Currents in the Newest Social Movements* (Toronto: Between the Lines, 2005). It may seem a contradiction to problematize the term "classical anarchism" because of its inherent link to European thinkers and use Gustav Landauer as an example of the styles of anarchist thought which are, in a sense, being rediscovered. However, I must stress that the classical anarchist canon refers specifically to the handful of thinkers mentioned above. Landauer, despite his European origins, is not considered a part of this special club, and, thus, I see no contradiction in acknowledging him to make my point.

34 Adams, *Non-Western Anarchisms*, 4.

35 Ibid., 4–5; Arif Dirlik, *Anarchism in the Chinese Revolution* (Berkeley: University of California Press, 1991), 2.

36 George Woodcock, *Anarchism: A History of Libertarian Ideas and Movements* (Peterborough: Broadview Press, 2004), 7, 404.

37 Adams, *Non-Western Anarchisms*, 3.

38 Antonio Gramsci, *The Southern Question*, trans. Pasquale Verdicchio (Toronto: Guernica, 2005), 33.

39 For a discussion of the factional war between the adherents of Luigi Galleani and Carlo Tresca, see Pernicone, "War among the Italian Anarchists," 78–97.

CHAPTER ONE
ANARCHISM AND THE ITALIAN TRADITION

1 Allan Antliff, *Anarchist Modernism: Art, Politics, and the First American Avant-Garde* (Chicago: University of Chicago Press, 2001), 3.

2 On stateless federation see Pierre-Joseph Proudhon, *The Principle of Federation*, trans. Richard Vernon (Toronto: University of Toronto Press, 1979). For Proudhon's views on property and government see Pierre-Joseph Proudhon, *What is Property? An Inquiry into the Principle of Right and of Government* (New York: Dover Publications, 1970).

3 Peter Marshall, *Demanding the Impossible: A History of Anarchism* (London: Harper Perennial, 2008), 8.

4 Michael Schmidt and Lucien van der Walt, *Black Flame: The Revolutionary Class Politics of Anarchism and Syndicalism* (Oakland: AK Press, 2009), 153–155.

5   Mikhail Bakunin, *Bakunin on Anarchism*, trans. and ed. by Sam Dolgoff (Montreal: Black Rose Books, 1980), 255.

6   Rudolf Rocker, *Anarcho-Syndicalism: Theory and Practice* (Oakland: AK Press, 2004), 59.

7   G.D.H. Cole, *History of Socialist Thought: Marxism and Anarchism, 1850–1890*, vol. 2 (London: MacMillan, 1957), 358.

8   Rocker, *Anarcho-Syndicalism*, 78. The meaning of direct action has changed during the last thirty years. At present, direct action is a form of protest that identifies a particular problem and offers either an alternative or a solution. Often these types of action employ an element of theatre to get a point across. Some forms of direct action include sit-ins, blockades, occupations of land or buildings, or disruption of hunts. Aidan Ricketts, *The Activists' Handbook: A Step-by-Step Guide to Participatory Democracy* (London: Zed Books, 2012), 167–168.

9   Rocker, *Anarcho-Syndicalism*, 60. For a wider discussion of anarcho-syndicalism see V.V. Damier, *Anarcho-Syndicalism in the 20th Century* (Edmonton: Black Cat Press, 2009); Sam Dolgoff, *The Anarchist Collectives: Workers' Self-Management in the Spanish Revolution, 1936–1939* (Montreal: Black Rose Books, 1974); Murray Bookchin, *The Spanish Anarchists: The Heroic Years, 1868–1936* (San Francisco: AK Press, 1998); Graham Kelsey, *Anarchosyndicalism, Libertarian Communism and the State: The CNT in Zaragoza and Aragon, 1930–1937* (Dordrecht: Kluwer Academic Publishers, 1989); Karl Marx and Friedrich Engels, *Anarchism and Anarcho-Syndicalism* (Moscow: Progress, 1972); G.P. Maximoff, *The Programme of Anarcho-Syndicalism* (Sydney: Monty Miller, 1985); Rocker, *Anarcho-Syndicalism*; and Schmidt and van der Walt, *Black Flame*.

10   For a discussion of the IWW's significance in the Lakehead during the 1920s, see Michel S. Beaulieu, *Labour at the Lakehead: Ethnicity, Socialism, and Politics, 1900–35* (Vancouver: University of British Columbia Press, 2011), 101–140. For a study of the IWW in Grays Harbor, Washington, see Aaron Goings, "Red Harbor: Class, Violence, and Community in Grays Harbor, Washington" (PhD diss., Simon Fraser University, 2011).

11   Rocker, *Anarcho-Syndicalism*, 93; Melvyn Dubofsky, *We Shall Be All: A History of the Industrial Workers of the World*, ed. Joseph McCartin, abridged ed. (Chicago: University of Illinois Press, 2000), 86.

12   Schmidt and van der Walt, *Black Flame*, 171.

13   Salvatore Salerno, *Red November, Black November: Culture and Community in the Industrial Workers of the World* (Albany: State University of New York Press, 1989), 90.

14   Goings, "Red Harbor," 23.

15   Salerno, *Red November*, 89.

16   Pernicone, *Carlo Tresca*, 30.

17   Pernicone, *Italian Anarchism*, 112–113; Pier Carlo Masini, "Carlo Cafiero," *Dizionario Biografico degli Anarchici Italiani*, eds. Maurizio Antonioli et al., vol. 1 (Pisa: Biblioteca Franco Serantini, 2003), 281–286.

18   Pernicone, *Italian Anarchism*, 112–113.

19   Max Stirner, *The Ego and Its Own*, ed. David Leopold (Cambridge: Cambridge University Press, 1995), 111, 276.

20   Errico Malatesta, *Errico Malatesta: His Life and Ideas*, ed. Vernon Richards (London: Freedom Press, 1965), 48–49.

21   Ibid., 48–49.

22   Ibid., 27.

23   Peter Kropotkin, *Kropotkin's Revolutionary Pamphlets*, ed. Roger N. Baldwin (New York: Benjamin Blom, 1968), 210.

24   Bakunin, *Bakunin on Anarchism*, 133–134.

25   Emma Goldman, *Red Emma Speaks: An Emma Goldman Reader*, ed. Alix Kates Shulman (New York: Schocken Books, 1983), 113. See also Benedict Anderson, *Imagined Communities: Reflections on the Origin and Spread of Nationalism* (London: Verso, 2006).

26   Bakunin, *Bakunin on Anarchism*, 235.

27   Goldman, *Red Emma Speaks*, 119.

28   Mikhail Bakunin, *The Political Philosophy of Bakunin: Scientific Anarchism*, ed. G.P. Maximoff (Glencoe: The Free Press, 1953), 212.

29   Bakunin, *Bakunin on Anarchism*, 81–88; Pierre-Joseph Proudhon, *The Principle of Federation*, 70.

30   Alexander Berkman, *What is Anarchism?* (Oakland: AK Press, 2003), 8.

31   Ibid., 7. For changes to labour processes under industrial capitalism in the North American context see Michael Burowoy, *Manufacturing Consent: Changes in the Labor Process under Monopoly Capitalism* (Chicago: The University of Chicago Press, 1979); Richard Edwards, *Contested Terrain: The Transformation of the Workplace in the Twentieth Century* (New York: Basic Books, 1979); Craig Heron and Robert Storey, eds., *On the Job: Confronting the Labour Process in Canada* (Kingston and Montreal: McGill-Queen's University Press, 1986); and David Montgomery, *The Fall of the House of Labor: The Workplace, the State, and American Labor Activism, 1865–1925* (Cambridge: Cambridge University Press, 1987).

32   Pierre-Joseph Proudhon, *Selected Writings of Pierre-Joseph Proudhon*, ed. Stewart Edwards (Garden City: Anchor Books, 1969), 36-37; Edward S. Krebs, *Shifu: Souls of Chinese Anarchism* (Lanham: Rowman and Littlefield Publishers, 1998), 128.

33   Goldman, *Red Emma Speaks*, 73.

34   Berkman, *What is Anarchism?*, 60.

35   Goldman, *Red Emma Speaks*, 232–248; Berkman, *What is Anarchism?*, 39–41, 60–63.

36   Victor Garcia, *Three Japanese Anarchists: Kotoku, Osugi and Yamaga* (Berkeley: Kate Sharpley Library, 2000), 3.

37   Bakunin, *Bakunin on Anarchism*, 238; Bakunin, *The Political Philosophy of Bakunin*, 117.

38   Malatesta, *His Life and Ideas*, 183.

39   Goldman, *Red Emma Speaks*, 56, 245; Berkman, *What is Anarchism?*, 62.

40   Bird and Forster did not identify as anarchists but did see themselves as sex radicals. They were regular contributors to *Lucifer: The Light Bearer*, an anarchist publication that focussed on issues of free love and sexuality that was edited by the American individualist anarchist Moses Harman. Angus McLaren, "Sex Radicalism in the Canadian Pacific Northwest, 1890–1920," *Journal of the History of Sexuality* 2, 4 (1992): 529, 541.

41   Martha Ackelsberg, *Free Women of Spain: Anarchism and the Struggle for the Emancipation of Women* (Oakland: AK Press, 2005), 167; Margaret S. Marsh, *Anarchist Women, 1870–1920* (Philadelphia: Temple University Press, 1981), 69–70; McLaren, "Sex Radicalism," 533; Martin Henry Blatt, *Free Love and Anarchism: The Biography of Ezra Heywood* (Chicago: University of Illinois Press, 1989), 106–108; Bonnie Haaland, *Emma Goldman: Sexuality and the Impurity of the State* (Montreal: Black Rose Books, 1993), 155.

42   Pernicone, *Carlo Tresca*, 152–155.

43   McLaren, "Sex Radicalism," 546.

44   Blatt, *Free Love and Anarchism*, 108.

45   Pernicone, *Carlo Tresca*, 74, 239, 244–245; Maurizio Antonioli and S. Cicolani, *Dizionario Biografico degli Anarchici Italiani*, vol. 2, 624.

46   Haaland, *Emma Goldman*, 1, 140.

47   Max Nettlau, *A Short History of Anarchism* (London: Freedom Press, 1996), 288–289.

48   Ackelsberg, *Free Women of Spain*, 172.

49   Guglielmo, *Living the Revolution*, 171–172.

50   For an engaging study on first-wave anarchism and homosexuality, see Terrance Kissack, *Free Comrades: Anarchism and Homosexuality in the United States, 1895–1917* (Oakland: AK Press, 2008).

51   Haaland, *Emma Goldman*, 164.

52   Emma Goldman, *Living My Life*, vol. 2 (London: Pluto Press, 1987), 556.

53   Haaland, *Emma Goldman*, 163.

54   Alexander Berkman was imprisoned in 1892 for his attempted assassination of Henry Clay Frick of Carnegie Steel during a bitter strike in Homestead, Pennsylvania.

55   Berkman's fellow inmate's name was really Johnny but he wanted Berkman to call him Felipe, just as the anarchist wanted Johnny to call him Sasha. Alexander Berkman, *Prison Memoirs of an Anarchist* (New York: Schocken Books, 1970), 322.

56   Berkman, *Prison Memoirs of an Anarchist*, 318–324.

57   Ibid., 433–440.

58   Moritz and Moritz, *The World's Most Dangerous Woman*, 103.

59   Goldman, *Living My Life*, 555.

60   "For Jihadist, Read Anarchist," *Economist*, 20 Aug. 2005, 17–20. My thanks to Andrew Stevens for bringing this article to my attention. For an even more recent work linking first-wave anarchists to "terrorism," see John Merriman, *The Dynamite Club: How a Bombing in Fin-de-Siècle Paris Ignited the Age of Modern Terror* (Boston: Houghton Mifflin Harcourt, 2009). Merriman's treatment of the subject is far more nuanced than the *Economist* article.

61   On 4 May 1886, during an anarchist rally to condemn the murder by police of a striker at the McCormick Reaper Works the previous day, a bomb was thrown into a crowd of nearby police, killing one instantly. Another six died later of injuries from the blast or from firing in panic by fellow officers. Eight anarchists were held responsible for the bombing though there was no direct evidence to support these charges. However, whether the eight were guilty of direct or indirect involvement with the bomb-throwing incident was beside the fact. They were to be made examples of by the state in order to send a message to present and future radicals that violent resistance to the present system would not be tolerated. Four of the eight anarchists, Albert Parsons, August Spies, Adolf Fischer, and George Engel were sentenced to hang and were executed on 11 November 1887. Louis Lingg was also sentenced to death but took his own life the night before he was to be hanged. Oscar Neebe was given fifteen years in prison while Sam Fielding and Michael Schwab were sentenced to life. These three men would be pardoned by Illinois Governor John P. Altgeld in 1893. See Avrich, *The Haymarket Tragedy*.

62   See Carl Smith, *Urban Disorder and the Shape of Belief: The Great Chicago Fire, the Haymarket Bomb, and the Model Town of Pullman* (Chicago: University of Chicago Press, 1995).

63   Smith, *Urban Disorder*, 136.

64   Most had been born illegitimately in Augsburg, Germany, in 1846 to a governess and an office clerk. At the age of seventeen he began travelling throughout central Europe perfecting his bookbinding skills and learning about politics. It was not long before Most was involved in radical political organizations and speaking publicly, overcoming such obstacles as a facial disfigurement which was the result of a bone infection during his youth. The bone infection led to an operation to stop the inflammation of Most's left jawbone. Two inches of the jawbone were removed causing the disfigurement. After innumerable arrests for speaking publicly to workers, Most left Germany for England and began publishing the newspaper *Freiheit* (Liberty), which became the international organ of German-speaking anarchists. In the early 1880s, Most was invited by the Social Revolutionary Club of New York to conduct a speaking tour of the United States. His tour gained him notoriety among Germans living in America and was instrumental in unifying non-German radical organizations. Most stayed in New York City and resumed publication of *Freiheit* there. Following the Haymarket bombing in May 1886, he was arrested for having previously published the *Science of Revolutionary Warfare*, a pamphlet that promoted the seizure of explosives by any means necessary. It also contained instructions on the manufacture of bombs and advice with regards to their efficacious placement. As a result, Most was sentenced to one year at New York's Blackwell's Island. Most was well-known for his violent editorials and public lectures in which he advocated the murder of politicians and capitalists because they were enemies of the working class. Martha Solomon, *Emma Goldman* (Boston: Twayne Publishers, 1987), 9–10; A. Wesley Johns, *The Man Who Shot McKinley* (South Brunswick: A.S. Barnes, 1970), 34; Max Nomad, *Apostles of Revolution* (New York: Collier Books, 1961), 257, 280, 285–288.

65   Smith, *Urban Disorder*, 136.

66   For sympathetic treatments of Haymarket see Avrich, *The Haymarket Tragedy* and James Green, *Death in the Haymarket: A Story of Chicago, the First Labor Movement and the Bombing that Divided Golden Age America* (New York: Pantheon Books, 2006). For inconclusive revisionist histories that suggests the Haymarket anarchists may have been involved in the construction of bombs, see Timothy Messer-Kruse et al., "The Haymarket Bomb: Reassessing the Evidence," *Labor: Studies in Working-Class History of the Americas* 2, 2 (2005): 39–51; Timothy Messer-Kruse, *The Trial of the Haymarket Anarchists: Terrorism and Justice in the Gilded Age* (New York: Palgrave Macmillan, 2011); and Timothy Messer-Kruse, *The Haymarket Conspiracy: Transatlantic Anarchist Networks* (Champaign-Urbana: University of Illinois Press, 2012).

67   Avrich, *Sacco and Vanzetti*, 48.

68   Vernon L. Briggs, *The Manner of Man That Kills* (New York: Da Capo Press, 1983), 243.

69   "Sermon by Dr Herridge," *The Globe* (Toronto), 17 Sept. 1901, 5.

70   "Uncle Sam is Thinking," *Toronto Star*, 16 Sept. 1901, 4.

71   "Czolgosz a Human Misfit," *Manitoba Free Press*, 10 Sept. 1901, 4.

72   Voltairine de Cleyre, *Exquisite Rebel: The Essays of Voltairine de Cleyre – Anarchist, Feminist, Genius*, eds. Sharon Presley and Crispin Sartwell (Albany: State University of New York Press, 2005), 302–303.

73   Ibid., 302.

74 Martin Clark, *The Italian Risorgimento* (London: Longman, 1998), 36–40; Lucy Riall, *Risorgimento: The History of Italy from Napoleon to Nation-State* (New York: Palgrave Macmillan, 2009), 6, 14–19.

75 Riall, *Risorgimento*, 22–25, 31–33.

76 Clark, *Italian Risorgimento*, 80–85; Riall, *Risorgimento* 33; Lucy Riall, *Sicily and the Unification of Italy: Liberal Policy and Local Power 1859–1866* (Oxford: Clarendon Press, 1998), 73.

77 Donna Gabaccia, *Italy's Many Diasporas* (Seattle: University of Washington Press, 2000), 109–110; Antonio Gramsci, *The Southern Question*, trans. Pasquale Verdicchio (Toronto: Guernica, 2005), 44.

78 Gabaccia, *Italy's Many Diasporas*, 109. It has further been suggested that the creation of the Partito Socialista Italiana (PSI) in the 1890s was in "sharp reaction to the Bakuninist tradition of populist and 'anarchoid' revolt" and the party "defined itself in total rejection of anarchism and its communal tradition." Gwyn A. Williams, foreword, *The Occupation of the Factories: Italy 1920*, by Paolo Spriano, trans. Gwyn A. Williams (London: Pluto Press, 1975), 12.

79 Gabaccia, *Italy's Many Diasporas*, 8–9, 109–110; Carl Levy, *Gramsci and the Anarchists* (Oxford: Berg, 1999), 5; Pernicone, *Italian Anarchism*, 53.

80 Pernicone, *Italian Anarchism*, 3; Michael Miller Topp, *Those without a Country: The Political Culture of Italian American Syndicalists* (Minneapolis: University of Minnesota Press, 2001), 30.

81 Clark, *Italian Risorgimento*, 57; Riall, *Risorgimento*, 90–91.

82 Clark, *Italian Risorgimento*, 58; George Woodcock, *Anarchism: A History of Libertarian Ideas and Movements* (Peterborough: Broadview Press, 2004), 275.

83 Nettlau, *Short History of Anarchism*, 91–92; Pernicone, *Italian Anarchism*, 11–13; Woodcock, *Anarchism*, 275–276.

84 The Decembrist uprising or revolt occurred following the death of Tsar Alexander I in December 1825. Alexander's brother Constantine, who was next in line for the throne, publicly renounced his claim which led to another brother, Nicholas to step forward to accept rule. Some military officers felt that Constantine was the rightful tsar and refused to swear allegiance to Nicholas I. They assembled in Senate Square in St. Petersburg on the morning of 14 December with 3000 soldiers under their command and hoped to spark a larger uprising with the rest of the city's military. However, this result did not actually materialize and the soldiers in Senate Square were in a stand-off with 9000 soldiers loyal to Nicholas. The rebels were eventually fired upon, causing them to scramble and regroup on the frozen Neva River, but this location also came under fire, causing the ice to break apart, killing many. In the aftermath of the uprising, military officers were executed for their role while others were jailed or deported to Siberia. Marshall, *Demanding the Impossible*, 266; Anatole G. Mazour, *The First Russian Revolution, 1825: The Decembrist Movement: Its Origins, Development, and Significance* (Stanford: Stanford University Press, 1961), 154–180; Marc Raeff, *The Decembrist Movement* (Englewood Cliffs: Prentice-Hall, 1966), 1–2.

85 For biographical studies of Mikhail Bakunin see Edward Hallett Carr, *Michael Bakunin* (London: Macmillan and Company, 1937); Mark Leier, *Bakunin: The Creative Passion* (New York: St. Martin's Press, 2006); and Brian Morris, *Bakunin: The Philosophy of Freedom* (Montreal: Black Rose Books, 1993).

86 Bakunin, *Bakunin on Anarchism*, 332–333.

87 For instance, see Peter Singer, *A Darwinian Left: Politics, Evolution and Cooperation* (London: Weidenfeld and Nicolson, 1999), 3–5.

88   However, he did not explain how the amount of labour contributed to the creation of social wealth would be determined or by whom. Bakunin, *Bakunin on Anarchism*, 133–134; Bakunin, *The Political Philosophy of Bakunin*, 118, 209, 213, 409.

89   Bakunin, *The Political Philosophy of Bakunin*, 374–375, 410.

90   T.R. Ravindranathan, *Bakunin and the Italians* (Kingston and Montreal: McGill-Queen's University Press, 1988), 71.

91   Nettlau, *Short History of Anarchism*, 92.

92   Woodcock, *Anarchism*, 276.

93   Carl Levy, "Italian Anarchism, 1870–1926," *For Anarchism: History, Theory, and Practice*, ed. David Goodway (London: Routledge, 1989), 26.

94   Pernicone, *Italian Anarchism*, 15.

95   Ravindranathan, *Bakunin and the Italians*, 13.

96   Pernicone, *Italian Anarchism*, 23–25; Ravindranathan, *Bakunin and the Italians*, 85.

97   Pernicone, *Italian Anarchism*, 19–20; Ravindranathan, *Bakunin and the Italians*, 39–40.

98   Ravindranathan, *Bakunin and the Italians*, 47–48.

99   According to Bakunin, religious worship would not be banned outright: "Neither society, nor any part of society ... has the right to prevent free individuals from associating freely for any purpose whatsoever: political, religious, scientific, artistic.... But society is obliged to refuse to guarantee civic rights to any association or collective body whose aims or rules violate the fundamental principles of human justice. Individuals shall not be penalized or deprived of their full political or social rights solely for belonging to such unrecognized societies. The difference between the recognized and unrecognized associations will be the following: the juridically [sic] recognized associations will have the right to the protection of the community against individuals or recognized groups who refuse to fulfill their voluntary obligations. The juridically unrecognized associations will not be entitled to such protection by the community and none of their agreements will be regarded as binding." Bakunin, *Bakunin on Anarchism*, 82.

100   Bakunin, *Bakunin on Anarchism*, 76–97.

101   Pernicone, *Italian Anarchism*, 22; Ravindranathan, *Bakunin and the Italians*, 52–60.

102   Pernicone, *Italian Anarchism*, 25–26; Ravindranathan, *Bakunin and the Italians*, 64.

103   Cole, *History of Socialist Thought*, 88, 120; Marshall, *Demanding the Impossible*, 282–283, 302.

104   Woodcock, *Anarchism*, 210–223.

105   Levy, "Italian Anarchism," 27; Pernicone, *Italian Anarchism*, 31–32, 79.

106   Levy, "Italian Anarchism," 27–28.

107   Pernicone, *Italian Anarchism*, 82.

108   Ibid., 82–94.

109   Ibid., 119–121, 124–126.

110   Levy, "Italian Anarchism," 28; Pernicone, *Italian Anarchism*, 127.

111   Levy, "Italian Anarchism," 29–30; Pernicone, *Italian Anarchism*, 283–285.

112   Luigi Galleani, *The End of Anarchism?*, trans. Max Sartin and Robert D'Attilio. Orkney: Cienfuegos Press, 1982), ii–iii; P. Iuso, "Francesco Saverio Merlino," *Dizionario Biografico degli Anarchici Italiani*, 162–168.

113 G. Berti, "Errico Malatesta," *Dizionario Biografico degli Anarchici Italiani*, eds. Maurizio Antonioli et al., vol. 2 (Pisa: Biblioteca Franco Serantini, 2003), 57–66; Marshall, *Demanding the Impossible*, 345–361; Malatesta, *Errico Malatesta*, 201–240. See also, Davide Turcato, *Making Sense of Anarchism: Errico Malatesta's Experiments with Revolution, 1889–1900* (Basingstoke: Palgrave Macmillan, 2012), 14–16.

114 An irredentist movement existed in Italy during the late nineteenth and early twentieth centuries. Irredentists believed that the Italian state should encompass all ethnically Italian peoples. Since ethnic Italians lived in Switzerland, Corsica, and other regions near Italy, the irredentists were militarist and nationalist—two positions anathema to anarchism.

115 Pernicone, *Italian Anarchism,* 170, 255–256, 264, 269.

116 Martin Blinkhorn, *Mussolini and Fascist Italy* (London: Routledge, 2006), 5; Levy, *Italian Anarchism,* 30.

117 Emilio Covelli has received little scholarly attention though he was considered "one of the most important and original thinkers in the Italian anarchist movement" during the late 1870s and the early 1880s. Covelli studied law at Naples before attending universities in Germany, where he became a socialist. He is considered the first Italian to have written on Marx's *Das Kapital* and wrote the first Italian work that conceptualized socialism as a science. Upon his return to Italy in 1874, he joined the Naples section of the IWA. Carlo Cafiero, as mentioned above, was a friend and ally of Bakunin. He, like Covelli, was trained as a lawyer though he did not work as such. The Paris Commune had a strong influence on Cafiero and he became a revolutionary as a result. While living in London, he met Marx and Engels and joined the International. They were impressed with the Italian and made him the General Council's special agent in Italy. When Cafiero returned to Italy in 1871, and began his work on behalf of the General Council at Naples, he was viewed with distrust by Bakunin's adherents. However, Cafiero effectively demonstrated his commitment and played an important role in the Naples section of the International. Cafiero would later join the legalitarian socialists in 1882. Pernicone, *Italian Anarchism*, 64–65, 112, 185–186, 197.

118 Pernicone, *Italian Anarchism*, 187.

119 Ibid., 186–188, 190–193.

120 Auguste Vaillant was a French anarchist who threw a bomb into the Chamber of Deputies in Paris in December 1893. Though no one was killed during the attack, Vaillant was sentenced to death. Vaillant carried out this bombing because he was outraged at the social inequities suffered by the lower classes who went without food when the wealthy spent thousands of francs on trivial enjoyments. Émile Henry, another French anarchist, tossed a bomb into a crowded café which he believed to be frequented by members of the bourgeoisie though some workers were present at the time of the attack. Henry was motivated by Vaillant's execution the previous week. Goldman, *Red Emma Speaks*, 268–271; James Joll, *The Anarchists* (London: Eyre and Spottiswoode, 1964), 132, 137–139; Merriman, *The Dynamite Club*, 1–3.

121 Levy, *Gramsci*, 8–9.

122 Donna Gabaccia, *Militants and Migrants: Rural Sicilians Become American Workers* (New Brunswick: Rutgers University Press, 1988), 55; Levy, "Italian Anarchism," 48–49; Pernicone, *Italian Anarchism*, 283–284; Topp, *Those without a Country*, 234–238.

123 Levy, *Gramsci*, 9; Levy, "Italian Anarchism," 46, 54; Robert Ventresca and Franca Iacovetta, "Virgilia D'Andrea: The Politics of Protest and the Poetry of Exile," *Women, Gender, and Transnational Lives: Italian Workers of the World*, eds. Donna Gabaccia and Franca Iacovetta (Toronto: University of Toronto Press, 2002), 303.

124 Levy, *Gramsci*, 51; Levy, "Italian Anarchism," 56–60.

125 Levy, *Gramsci*, 119–120; Topp, *Those without a Country*, 231–232; Ventresca and Iacovetta, "Virgilia D'Andrea," 305.

126 Alexander De Grand, *Italian Fascism: Its Origins and Development* (Lincoln: University of Nebraska Press, 2000), 24; Levy, *Gramsci*, 119–120; Topp, *Those without a Country*, 231–232; Ventresca and Iacovetta, "Virgilia D'Andrea," 305.

127 Spriano, *The Occupation of the Factories*; De Grand, *Italian Fascism*, 22–37; Levy, "Italian Anarchism," 61-68; Levy, *Gramsci*, 119–166; Philip Morgan, *Italian Fascism, 1915-1945* (Houndmills: Palgrave Macmillan, 2004), 37–49; Peter Neville, *Mussolini* (London: Routledge, 2004), 43–46; and Topp, *Those without a Country*, 233.

128 Levy, *Gramsci*, 122–123; Topp, *Those without a Country*, 244.

129 The UIL is an interesting example of a nationalist syndicalist union that spurned electoral politics. It was founded in June 1918 by Alceste De Ambris, Edmondo Rossoni, and Angelo Olivetti and acted as a direct challenge to the USI. The UIL supported national revolution and the masthead of their paper *L'Italia Nostra* (Our Italy) proclaimed: "The Fatherland should not be denied, it should be conquered!" It saw returning veterans of the First World War as the likely vanguard for a nationalist revolution. The UIL always maintained its independence from the fascists and, once the National Fascist Party was founded by Mussolini in November 1921, it was denounced by the UIL as simply another political party. Topp, *Those without a Country*, 223–234, 245.

130 De Grand, *Italian Fascism*, 34; Morgan, *Italian Fascism*, 56–59; Neville, *Mussolini*, 46–50.

131 Blinkhorn, *Mussolini and Fascist Italy*, 27; Topp, *Those without a Country*, 244–245.

132 Blinkhorn, *Mussolini and Fascist Italy*, 27; De Grand, *Italian Fascism*, 36–37.

133 Levy, *Gramsci*, 122–123, 223.

CHAPTER TWO
MIGRANT ANARCHISTS

1 Gabaccia, *Italy's Many Diasporas*, 3; Rudolph J. Vecoli and Suzanne M. Sinke, eds., *A Century of European Migrations, 1830–1930* (Urbana: University of Illinois Press, 1991), 8.

2 Samuel L. Baily, *Immigrants in the Lands of Promise: Italians in Buenos Aires and New York City, 1870–1914* (Ithaca: Cornell University Press, 1999), 24; Mark I. Choate, *Emigrant Nation: The Making of Italy Abroad* (Cambridge: Harvard University Press, 2008), 238.

3 For studies on Italian migration from particular regions of Italy to North and South America, see Baily, *Immigrants in the Lands of Promise*; Konrad Eisenbichler, *An Italian Region in Canada: The Case of Friuli-Venezia Giulia* (Toronto: Multicultural History Society of Ontario, 1998); Gabaccia, *Militants and Migrants*; Franc Sturino, *Forging the Chain: A Case Study of Italian Migration to North America, 1880–1930* (Toronto: Multicultural Historical Society of Ontario, 1990); and Virginia Yans-McLaughlin, *Family and Community: Italian Immigrants in Buffalo, 1880–1930* (Ithaca: Cornell University Press, 1977). For general histories on the subject consult Choate, *Emigrant Nation*; Gabaccia, *Italy's Many Diasporas*; John Potestio and Antonio Pucci, eds., *The Italian Migrant Experience* (Thunder Bay: Canadian Italian Historical Association, 1988); Bruno Ramirez, *Crossing the 49th Parallel: Migration from Canada to the United States, 1900–1930* (Ithaca: Cornell University Press, 2001); Bruno Ramirez, *On the*

Move: French-Canadian and Italian Migrants in the North Atlantic Economy, 1860–1914 (Toronto: McClelland and Stewart, 1991); Bruno Ramirez, *The Italians in Canada* (Ottawa: The Canadian Historical Association, 1989); Bruno Ramirez and Michael Del Balso, *The Italians of Montreal: From Sojourning to Settlement 1900–1921* (Montreal: Les Éditions du Courant, 1980); and John Zucchi, *Italians in Toronto: Development of a National Identity 1875–1935* (Kingston and Montreal: McGill-Queen's University Press, 1988).

4   Franco Ramella, "Emigration from an Area of Intense Industrial Development: The Case of Northwestern Italy," *A Century of European Migrations, 1930–1930*, eds. Rudolph J. Vecoli and Suzanne M. Sinke (Urbana: University of Illinois Press, 1991), 265, 269; Robert F. Harney, "Men Without Women: Italian Migrants in Canada, 1885–1930," *A Nation of Immigrants: Women, Workers, and Communities in Canadian History, 1840s–1960s*, eds. Franca Iacovetta with Paula Draper and Robert Ventresca (Toronto: University of Toronto Press, 1998), 207.

5   See Gabaccia, *Militants and Migrants* and Topp, *Those without a Country.*

6   Kenyon Zimmer, "'The Whole World is Our Country': Immigration and Anarchism in the United States, 1885–1940," PhD diss., University of Pittsburgh, 2010, 25.

7   My thanks to Davide Turcato for bringing this valuable online resource to my attention.

8   Egidio Artico, busta 202, CPC, ACS, Rome.

9   Donato Carrillo, busta 1116, CPC, ACS, Rome.

10   All translations are my own except where otherwise noted. Il Prefetto di Spezia, "Biografia di Vincenzo Capuana," 12 Dec. 1925, Vincenzo Capuana, busta 1055, CPC, ACS, Rome.

11   Prefetto di Pesaro, Pesaro, "Biografica di Dulio Giorgini," 20 July 1908 to 25 Feb 1931; and Prefetto di Pesaro, Pesaro, to Ministero dell'Interno, Rome, 29 May 1935, Dulio Giorgini, busta 2429, CPC, ACS, Rome.

12   Nick Di Domenico, Newark, to Giuseppe De Luisi, Pozzuoli, 13 Mar. 1936; De Luisi, Pozzuoli, to Di Domenico, Newark, 7 Sep. 1937; and De Luisi, Pozzuoli, to Di Domenico, Newark, Nov. 1937, Nicola Di Domenico, busta 1781, CPC, ACS, Rome.

13   See Raffaele Schiavina, busta 4690; and Domenico Moscardelli, busta 3435, CPC, ACS, Rome.

14   Avrich, *Anarchist Voices*, 166–167.

15   See Caroline Waldron Merithew, "Anarchist Motherhood: Toward the Making of Revolutionary Proletariat in Illinois Coal Towns," *Women, Gender, and Transnational Lives: Italian Workers of the World*, eds. Donna Gabaccia and Franca Iacovetta (Toronto: University of Toronto Press, 2002), 217–246; and Guglielmo, *Living the Revolution.*

16   Maria Vecile's CPC file was actually listed as "Mario" Vecile by Italian authorities. See Mario Vecile, busta 5399, CPC, ACS, Rome.

17   Guglielmo, *Living the Revolution*, 154–155.

18   Gabaccia, *Italy's Many Diasporas*, 69.

19   Ramirez, *The Italians in Canada*, 7; Rudolph J. Vecoli, "The Italian Immigrants in the United States Labour Movement from 1880 to 1929," *Gli italiani fuori d'italia: gli emigrati italiani nei movimenti operai dei paesi d'adozione 1880–1940* (Milan: Franco Angeli Editore, 1983), 259; and Baily, *Immigrants in the Lands of Promise*, 54.

20   Harney, "Men Without Women," 209–210; John Zucchi, *A History of Ethnic Enclaves in Canada* (Ottawa: The Canadian Historical Association, 2007), 6.

21   Harney, "Men Without Women," 209–210; Sturino, *Forging the Chain*, 76.

22 Harney, "Men Without Women," 209–210; Zucchi, *A History of Ethnic Enclaves in Canada*, 6.

23 Donald H. Avery, *Reluctant Host: Canada's Response to Immigrant Workers, 1896–1994* (Toronto: McClelland and Stewart, 1995), 20–21; Zucchi, *A History of Ethnic Enclaves in Canada*, 6; Harney, "Men Without Women," 209–210; Gabaccia, *Italy's Many Diasporas*, 74–75; Ramirez, *The Italians in Canada*, 6.

24 Harney, "Men Without Women," 209–210.

25 Ramirez, *The Italians in Canada*, 6, 11.

26 Gabaccia, *Italy's Many Diasporas*, 59. Ella Antolini, for example, worked on a plantation in Louisiana where she picked cotton alongside her family. Avrich, *Anarchist Voices*, 134.

27 Ramirez, *On the Move*, 108.

28 Guglielmo, *Living the Revolution*, 45, 59.

29 Gabaccia, *Italy's Many Diasporas*, 7, 75, 101.

30 Ibid., 91–92.

31 Sturino, *Forging the Chain*, 70, 72.

32 Bruno Ramirez, "Immigration, Ethnicity, and Political Militance: Patterns of Radicalism in the Italian-American Left, 1880–1930," *From 'Melting Pot' to Multiculturalism: The Evolution of Ethnic Relations in the United States and Canada*, ed. Valeria Gennaro Lerda (Rome: Bulzoni Editore, 1990), 122–123.

33 Robert F. Harney, "Montreal's King of Italian Labour: A Case Study of Padronism," *Labour/Le Travail* 4 (1979): 57–84; Gunther Peck, "Reinventing Free Labor: Immigrant Padrones and Contract Laborers in North America," *Journal of American History* 83, 3 (1996): 851, 858; Gabaccia, *Italy's Many Diasporas*, 65.

34 Gabaccia, *Italy's Many Diasporas*, 66. Chain migration is the "movement in which prospective migrants learn of opportunities, are provided with transportation, and have initial accommodation and employment arranged by means of primary social relationships with previous migrants." Franc Sturino, "Italian Immigration: Reconsidering the Links in Chain Migration," *Arrangiarsi: The Italian Immigration Experience in Canada*, eds. Roberto Perin and Franc Sturino (Montreal: Guernica, 1989), 64.

35 Joseph P. Cosco, *Imagining Italians: The Clash of Romance and Race in American Perceptions, 1880–1910* (Albany: State University of New York Press, 2003), 17.

36 For studies on whiteness see Toni Morrison, *Playing in the Dark: Whiteness and the Literary Imagination* (Cambridge: Harvard University Press, 1992); David R. Roediger, *The Wages of Whiteness: Race and the Making of the American Working Class* (London: Verso, 2007); David R. Roediger, *Colored White: Transcending the Racial Past* (Berkeley: University of California Press, 2002); Ruth Frankenberg, *White Women, Race Matters: The Social Construction of Whiteness* (Minneapolis: University of Minnesota Press, 1993); Maurice Berger, *White Lies: Race and the Myths of Whiteness* (New York: Farrar, Straus, and Giroux, 1999); Joe L. Kincheloe, Shirley R. Steinberg, Nelson M. Rodriguez, and Ronald E. Chennault, eds., *White Reign: Deploying Whiteness in America* (New York: St Martin's Press, 1998); Grace Elizabeth Hale, *Making Whiteness: The Culture of Segregation in the South, 1890–1940* (New York: Vintage Books, 1999); and George Lipsitz, *The Possessive Investment in Whiteness: How White People Profit from Identity Politics* (Philadelphia: Temple University Press, 1998).

37   I realize that "Social Darwinism" is a contested term among scholars, some of whom feel that the Left used Darwin's ideas in a far more creative and progressive manner than the Right, though it is for the Right that this term is generally reserved. For studies on the progressive applications of Darwinism see Robert C. Bannister, *Social Darwinism: Science and Myth in Anglo-American Social Thought* (Philadelphia: Temple University Press, 1979); Mike Hawkins, *Social Darwinism in European and American Thought 1860-1945: Nature as Model and Nature as Threat* (Cambridge: Cambridge University Press, 1997); Richard Hofstadter, *Social Darwinism in American Thought*, Revised Edition (Boston: The Beacon Press, 1955); Ian McKay, *Reasoning Otherwise: Leftists and the People's Enlightenment in Canada, 1890-1920* (Toronto: Between the Lines, 2008), 13–77; and Richard Weikart, *Socialist Darwinism: Evolution in German Socialist Thought from Marx to Bernstein* (San Francisco, London and Bethesda: International Scholars Publications, 1999).

38   Here Haeckel is using the term Caucasian as a stand-in for white European. Ernst Haeckel, *The History of Creation: Or the Development of Evolution in General and its Inhabitants by the Action of Natural Causes*, trans. E. Ray Lankster, vol. 2 (London: Henry S. King and Company, 1876), 321. For contemporary studies on Ernst Haeckel see Robert J. Richards, *The Tragic Sense of Life: Ernst Haeckel and the Struggle over Evolutionary Thought* (Chicago: The University of Chicago Press, 2008); and Nolan Heie, "Ernst Haeckel and the Redemption of Nature," PhD diss., Queen's University, 2008.

39   Michael Miller Topp, "'It's Providential that there are Foreigners Here': Whiteness and Masculinity in the Making of Italian American Syndicalist Identity," *Are Italians White?: How Race Is Made in America*, ed. Jennifer Guglielmo and Salvatore Salerno (New York: Routledge, 2003), 105.

40   Harney, *From the Shores of Hardship*, 51–52; Antonio Gramsci, *The Southern Question*, trans. Pasquale Verdicchio (Toronto: Guernica, 2005), 33.

41   The irony of Niceforo's research is that he was born in Sicily. Harney, *From the Shores of Hardship*, 51–52. See also Daniel Pick, "The Faces of Anarchy: Lombroso and the Politics of Criminal Science in Post-Unification Italy," *History Workshop* 2 (Spring 1986): 62–63; and Daniel Pick, *Faces of Degeneration: A European Disorder, 1848-1918* (Cambridge: Cambridge University Press, 1989), 114–115.

42   Harney, *From the Shores of Hardship*, 51.

43   Ibid., 50.

44   For the American context see Cosco, *Imagining Italians*, 16; Louise DeSalvo, "Colour: White/Complexion: Dark," *Are Italians White?: How Race Is Made in America*, eds. Jennifer Guglielmo and Salvatore Salerno (New York: Routledge, 2003), 22; and Jennifer Guglielmo, "Introduction: White Lies, Dark Truths," *Are Italians White?: How Race Is Made in America*, eds. Jennifer Guglielmo and Salvatore Salerno (New York: Routledge, 2003), 11. For the construction of Italians in Canada see J.S. Woodsworth, *Strangers Within Our Gates: Or, Coming Canadians* (Toronto: University of Toronto Press, 1972), 132–135; Zucchi, *Italians in Toronto*, 72–76; and Franca Iacovetta, *Such Hardworking People: Italian Immigrants in Postwar Toronto* (Montreal and Kingston: McGill-Queen's University Press, 1992), 103–123.

45   Cosco, *Imagining Italians*, 11; Topp, *Those without a Country*, 105.

46   Cosco, *Imagining Italians*, 16; Guglielmo, *Are Italians White?*, 11.

47   Cosco, *Imagining Italians*, 16; Vincenza Scarpaci, "Walking the Colour Line: Italian Immigrants in Rural Louisiana, 1880-1910," *Are Italians White?: How Race Is Made in America*, eds. Jennifer Guglielmo and Salvatore Salerno (New York: Routledge, 2003), 63.

48   Harney, *From the Shores of Hardship*, 55.

49   Thomas A. Guglielmo, *White on Arrival: Italians, Race, Color, and Power in Chicago, 1890–1945* (Oxford: Oxford University Press, 2004), 7, 9. See also Cybelle Fox and Thomas A. Guglielmo, "Defining America's Racial Boundaries: Blacks, Mexicans, and European Immigrants, 1890–1945," *American Journal of Sociology* 18, 2 (Sep. 2012): 327–379.

50 . Harney, *From the Shores of Hardship*, 50.

51   Cosco, *Imagining Italians*, 11; Harney, *From the Shores of Hardship*, 63.

52   Harney, *From the Shores of Hardship*, 57, 61, 63.

53   For studies on Italian labour radicalism in Canada and the United States see Phillip V. Cannistraro and Gerald Meyer, eds., *The Lost World of Italian-American Radicalism: Politics, Labor, and Culture* (Westport: Praeger Publishers, 2003); Gabaccia and Iacovetta, eds., *Women, Gender, and Transnational Lives*; Gallagher, *All the Right Enemies*; Pernicone, *Carlo Tresca*; Ramirez, "Immigration, Ethnicity, and Political Militance," 115–141; Topp, *Those without a Country*.

54   For a study on Canada's forced deportation of unwanted migrant labour, see Barbara Roberts, *Whence They Came: Deportation from Canada, 1900–1935* (Ottawa: University of Ottawa Press, 1988).

55   Sturino, *Forging the Chain*, 147–148.

56   McKay, *Reasoning Otherwise*, 422.

57   Sturino, *Forging the Chain*, 64–65.

58   Gabaccia, *Italy's Many Diasporas*, 135–136.

59   In 1928, 200,000 to 400,000 Italians left Italy, roughly the same number as during the 1880s and 1890s. It was not until the Great Depression that migration from Italy was curbed. Gabaccia, *Italy's Many Diasporas*, 133, 135.

60   Sturino, *Forging the Chain*, 142–143.

61   Ibid., 146–147; R.J.B. Bosworth, *Italy and the Wider World 1860–1960* (London: Routledge, 1996), 123. The continuous journey regulation was passed by the Canadian government in 1908 initially as a means to curb Indian migration. Due to the distance between India and the western coast of Canada, vessels would have to stop in Japan or Hawaii meaning that once passengers arrived in Canada they were not allowed to land.

62   Gabaccia, *Italy's Many Diasporas*, 3, 133, 181–182.

63   Ramirez, *The Italians in Canada*, 6–7.

64   Reg Whitaker, *Canadian Immigration Policy since Confederation* (Ottawa: Canadian Historical Association, 1991), 5, 12–13.

65   Sturino, *Forging the Chain*, 155.

66   Gabaccia, on the other hand, suggests that the First World War and the Second World War had the greater impact on preventing migration and not so much economic crisis, racist immigration laws, or Fascist regime curbing of migration. Gabaccia, *Italy's Many Diasporas*, 133.

67   Sturino, *Forging the Chain*, 154–155.

68   Gabaccia, *Italy's Many Diasporas*, 134.

69   Ramirez, *The Italians in Canada*, 6–7.

70 The CPC was created by the Italian government in 1894 as a means to surveil those it "considered dangerous to public order and security." This collection spans nearly fifty years and includes more than 150,000 files on republicans, socialists, communists, antifascists, and anarchists. "L'Archivio," Archivio Centrale dello Stato, http://www.archivi.beniculturali.it/ACS/cpcarchivio.html (accessed 21 May 2010).

71 Ramirez, *The Italians in Canada*, 8–9. The *Mezzogiorno* refers to southern Italy and includes the regions of Calabria, Campania, Abruzzi, Molise, Sardegna, and Sicily.

72 The breakdown of regions of origin is as follows: northwestern Italy: Friuli-Venezia Giulia: 7; Veneto: 2; and Emilia-Romagna: 1. The *Mezzogiorno*: Calabria: 4, Molise: 1, and Apulia: 1. The place of origin for four anarchists is unknown because this information was not included in their files.

73 Vecoli, "The Italian Immigrants in the United States Labour Movement from 1880 to 1929," 259. The actual breakdown is Abruzzi: 5; Apulia: 1; Calabria: 2; Campania: 3; Sardegna: 3; and Sicily: 6.

74 Of the twelve anarchists who came from regions in northern Italy five came from the Northwest (Liguria: 2 and Piedmont: 3) while seven came from the Northeast (Emilia-Romagna: 6 and Trentino-Alto Adige: 1). The eight anarchists who migrated from central Italy came from the following regions: Marche: 4; Tuscany: 3; and Umbria: 1. The region of origin for six of the anarchists is unknown.

75 Prefetto di Pesaro-Urbino, Pesaro-Urbino, to Ministero del'Interno, Rome, 27 Apr 1943, Ruggero Benvenuti, busta, 508, CPC, ACS, Rome; J.L. Cohen Papers (JLCP), MG30, A94, Vol. 14, File 2761A, Library and Archives Canada (LAC), Ottawa.

76 Pennetta, Ministero dell'Interno, Rome, to Ministero degli Affari Esteri, Rome, 3 Sep 1939, Ernesto Bonomini, busta 740, CPC, ACS, Rome. Of course, such conclusions are only suggestive, because of the size of the group and the lack of concrete details surrounding the year in which some anarchists arrived in North America. The number of anarchists whose date of arrival in Canada or the United States is unknown is seven and fourteen, respectively.

77 The elite migrants included artists, scholars, or trained professionals who may also have travelled for purposes of work. However, their reasons for migrating differed drastically from those of agricultural and factory workers in Italy. Gabaccia, *Italy's Many Diasporas*, 43, 68.

78 The percentages for Italian labour migrants who travelled to North America for both the 1876–1914 and 1915–1945 periods are 31 percent and 25 percent, respectively. Gabaccia, *Italy's Many Diasporas*, 68, 135.

79 Console Generale d'Italia, Ottawa, to Ministero dell'Interno, Rome, 29 July 1935, Vincenzo Gabbani, busta 2211, CPC, ACS, Rome.

80 Prefetto di Udine, Udine, to Ministero dell'Interno, Rome, 10 Nov. 1937; Carmine Senise, Ministero dell'Interno, Rome, to Prefetto di Udine, Udine, 17 Oct. 1937, Russiani, CPC, ACS, Rome. See also Craig Heron, *Working in Steel: The Early Years in Canada, 1883–1935* (Toronto: McClelland and Stewart, 1988), 135, 166.

81 Libera Bortolotti, personal interview, 6 June 2005.

82 Ministero dell'Interno, Rome, to Console Generale, NYC, 13 Dec. 1912, Giuseppe Rolle, busta 4377, CPC, ACS, Rome.

83 Avrich, *Anarchist Voices*, 177–178.

84 Prefetto of Spezia, "Biografia di Vincenzo Capuana," 27 Jan. 1931, Vincenzo Capuana, busta 1055, CPC, ACS, Rome.

85 David Koven Papers (hereafter DKP), File 131, "Giovanni 'John' Vattuone 1899–1994," unpublished manuscript, 1994, International Institute of Social History (IISH), Amsterdam, 4–5.

86 Prefetto di Nuora, "Biografia di Efisio Constantino Zonchello," 21 May 1938, Efisio Constantino Zonchello, busta 5592, CPC, ACS, Rome.

87 Avrich, *Anarchist Voices*, 179.

88 Ministero degli Affari Esteri, Rome, to Ministero dell'Interno, Rome, 20 Aug. 1929, Giulio Ghetti, busta 2355, CPC, ACS, Rome.

89 Agostino Confalonieri, Toronto, to Bipi, Brussels, 19 Sep. 1939, JLCP, MG30, A94, V14, File 2761A, LAC, Ottawa.

90 Bortolotti, personal interview. See also Giuseppe Coleffi, busta 1402; Dante Dezi, busta 1763; Domenico Moscardelli, busta 3435; Nazzareno Taus, busta 5049, CPC, ACS, Rome.

91 John E. Zucchi, "Cultural Constructs or Organic Evolution? Italian Immigrant Settlements in Ontario," *The Luminous Mosaic: Italian Cultural Organizations in Ontario*, eds. Julius Molinaro and Maddalena Kuitunen (Welland: Éditions Soleil Publishing, 1993), 24; Heron, *Working in Steel*, 78; Bortolotti, personal interview.

92 Bortolotti, personal interview; Carlo Tresca, *The Autobiography of Carlo Tresca*, ed. Nunzio Pernicone (New York: The John D. Calandra Italian American Institute, 2003), 191–193.

93 Zucchi, *A History of Ethnic Enclaves in Canada*, 6; Sturino, *Forging the Chain* 170.

94 Zucchi, *Italians in Toronto*, 41, 57–58.

95 Sturino, *Forging the Chain*, 169; Zucchi, *Italians in Toronto*, 41.

96 See Ruggero Benvenuti, busta 508; Attilio Bortolotti, busta 772; and Ernesto Gava, busta 2317, CPC, ACS, Rome.

97 Avrich, *Anarchist Voices*, 184–185.

98 Moritz and Moritz, *The World's Most Dangerous Woman*, 139–140.

99 Petkovic, "Italians in Windsor," 65, 69; Armando Delicato, *Italians in Detroit* (Charleston: Arcadia Publishing, 2005), 81.

100 Petkovic, "Italians in Windsor," 64, 67.

101 G.B. Ambrosi, Vice Console, Toronto, to Consolato Generale d'Italia, Ottawa, 7 July 1933, Fortunato Marriotti, busta 3075, CPC, ACS, Rome. Avrich, *Anarchist Voices*, 179.

102 Avrich, *Anarchist Voices*, 180.

103 Delicato, *Italians in Detroit*, 8.

104 Justin R. Cristaldi, "Little Italy Across the Hudson," *Primo* (Sep./Oct. 2001), http://www.sicilianculture. com/littleitaly/nj-newark.htm (accessed 9 July 2010).

105 Console Generale, NYC, to Ministero dell'Interno, Rome, 24 July 1931, Efisio Constantino Zonchello, busta 5592, CPC, ACS, Rome.

106 See George E. Pozzetta, "The Mulberry District of New York City: The Years before World War One," *Little Italies in North America*, ed. Robert F. Harney and J. Vincenza Scarpaci (Toronto: The Multicultural History Society of Ontario), 7–40.

107 Console Generale, NYC, to Ministero dell'Interno, Rome, 24 July 1931, Efisio Constantino Zonchello, busta 5592, CPC, ACS, Rome.

CHAPTER THREE
ANARCHIST CULTURE

1   Salerno, *Red November, Black November*, 149–150.

2   Rudolph J. Vecoli, "'*Primo Maggio*' in the United States: An Invented Tradition of the Italian Anarchists," *May Day Celebration*, ed. Andrea Panaccione (Venice: Marsilio Editori, 1988), 56.

3   Marcella Bencivenni, *Italian Immigrant Radical Culture: The Idealism of the Sovversivi in the United States, 1890–1940* (New York: New York University Press, 2011), 3.

4   Avrich, *Sacco and Vanzetti*, 54.

5   Ibid.

6   Topp, *Those without a Country*, 53.

7   For collections of Gori's writings see Pietro Gori, *Scritti Scelti* (Cesena: L'Antistato, 1968); Maurizio Antonioli, *Pietro Gori: Il cavaliere errante dell'anarchia* (Pisa: Biblioteca Franco Serantini, 1995).

8   Vecoli, "'*Primo Maggio*' in the United States," 58.

9   Salerno, *Red November, Black November*, 8.

10 Doug McAdam, John D. McCarthy, and Mayer N. Zald, "Introduction," *Comparative Perspectives on Social Movements: Political Opportunities, Mobilising Structures, and Cultural Framings*, ed. Doug McAdam, John D. McCarthy, and Mayer N. Zald (Cambridge: Cambridge University Press, 1996), 3.

11 Bencivenni, *Italian Immigrant Radical Culture*, 69–70.

12 *Il Martello* (*IM*), 19 Apr. 1919, 1.

13 *IM*, 9 July 1921, 1.

14 *IM*, 12 Jan. 1924, 1.

15 *L'Adunata dei Refrattari* (*AdR*), 15 Sep. 1923, 1.

16 *AdR*, 6 July 1929, 1.

17 *AdR*, 17 Jan. 1932, 1.

18 Pietro Allegra, "Fascismo e Klu Klux Klan [sic]," *IM*, 27 Jan. 1923, 3.

19 The inclusion of the Robert Minor illustration demonstrates *Il Martello*'s eclectic nature and Carlo Tresca's willingness to include art from the wider Left, including Communists.

20 *IM*, 26 Apr. 1924, 3.

21 "Revolutionary Radicalism: Its History, Purpose and Tactics with an Exposition and Discussion of the Steps Being Taken and Required to Curb It," *Report of the Joint Committee Investigating Seditious Activities*, vol. 1 (Albany: J.B. Lyon, 1920), 2; Pernicone, *Carlo Tresca*, 105.

22 Avrich, *Anarchist Voices*, 317.

23 Paul Berman, "The Torch and the Axe: The Unknown Aftermath of the Sacco-Vanzetti Affair," *The Village Voice*, 17 May 1988.

24 Robert D'Attilio, "L'Adunata dei Refrattari," *Encyclopedia of the American Left*, ed. Mari Jo Buhle et al. (Chicago: St. James Press, 1990), 4.

25 Avrich, *Anarchist Voices*, 186.

26 Guglielmo Boattini, Detroit, to Luigi Bertoni, Geneva, 1936, Guglielmo Boattini, busta 679, Casellario Politico Centrale (CPC), Archivio Centrale dello Stato (ACS), Rome; Marcella Bencivenni, "Italian American Radical Culture in New York City: The Politics and Arts of the *Sovversivi*, 1890–1940," PhD diss., City University of New York, 2003, 80.

27 Avrich, *Anarchist Voices*, 179–180; Prefetto di Messina, Messina, to Ministero dell'Interno, Rome, 5 Dec. 1912, Fortunato Cernuto, busta 1257, CPC, ACS, Rome.

28 Guglielmo, *Living the Revolution*, 51.

29 Vecoli, "'*Primo Maggio*' in the United States," 78.

30 Pernicone, *Carlo Tresca*, 212–213.

31 Ibid., 151.

32 Avrich, *Anarchist Voices*, 152.

33 Enrique Baldeuna et al., "Agli anarchici e simpatizzanti dell'Argentina," *AdR*, 17 Jan. 1932, 2.

34 "Vive pericolosamente," *AdR*, 17 Jan. 1932, 1.

35 "Al Tribunale Squadrista," *AdR*, 17 Jan. 1932, 3.

36 Gigi Damiani, "Per la nostra rivoluzione: Dall'esperienza spagnuola di oggi and quella possible, di domani, in Italia," *AdR*, 17 Jan. 1932, 4.

37 "Giornali-Riviste-Libri" (Journals-Magazines-Books), *AdR*, 17 Jan. 1932, 7.

38 "Le lotte dei minatory del bituminoso" (The Struggle of the Bituminous Miners), *IM*, 1 Aug. 1931, 2.

39 Carlo Tresca, "La Tragedia del Lavoro Organizzato" (The Tragedy of the Organised Worker), *IM*, 1 Aug. 1931, 1.

40 "Fatti e Commenti," *IM*, 1 Aug. 1931, 1.

41 Ibid.

42 Giusto Volcelo, "Sullo stesso argomento," *IM*, 1 Aug. 1932, 3.

43 Ibid.

44 Max Nettlau, "Luigi Galleani nei ricordi di Max Nettlau" (Memories of Luigi Galleani), *AdR*, 17 Jan. 1932, 3.

45 Max Nettlau, "I precedenti del movimento anarchic spagnolo: Rapporti colla Internazionale del 1864" (The Beginnings of the Spanish Anarchist Movement: With Reference to the International of 1864), *IM*, 1 Aug. 1931, 3.

46 Castelli, Alto Commisario per la Provincia di Napoli, Napoli, to Ministero dell'Interno, Rome, 2 Apr. 1926, Osvaldo Maraviglia, busta 3017, CPC, ACS, Rome.

47 Console Generale, NYC, to Ministero dell'Interno, Rome, 4 Apr. 1928, Maraviglia, busta 3017, CPC, ACS, Rome.

48 Maraviglia, busta 3017, CPC, ACS, Rome.

49 Osvaldo Maraviglia, NYC, to Elena Melli, Rome, 12/13 July 1933, Nicola Di Domenico, busta 1781; Divisione di Polizia Politica to unknown, 15 May 1936, Maraviglia, busta 3017, CPC, ACS, Rome.

50 The notice for this event does not state whether the orchestra was comprised of anarchists or non-anarchists. "Communicazioni," *AdR*, 6 Jan. 1940, 8.

51 "Communicazioni," *AdR*, 17 Feb. 1940, 8.

52 *IM*, 28 Jan. 1922, 4.

53 *AdR*, 15 Apr. 1939, 8.

54 Capo della Sezione Prima, Rome, to Direzione Generale della Pubblica Sicurezza, Rome, 26 Sep. 1931, Salvatore Dettori, busta 1758, CPC, ACS, Rome.

55 Attilio Bortolotti, "Guardian of the Dream: A [sic] Oral History with Art Berthelot," *Kick It Over* 17 (Winter 1986/1987): 1; Attilio Bortolotti and Rossella Di Leo, "Between Canada and the USA: A Tale of Immigrants and Anarchists," Kate Sharpley Library, http://www.katesharpleylibrary.net/8pk1h4 (accessed 18 July 2010).

56 Avrich, *Anarchist Voices*, 184–185; Bortolotti, "Guardian of the Dream," 1.

57 Avrich, *Anarchist Voices*, 184–185.

58 Guglielmo, *Living the Revolution*, 142–143.

59 Bencivenni, *Italian Immigrant Radical Culture*, 52–53.

60 Libera Bortolotti, personal interview, 6 June 2005.

61 Guglielmo Marconi was an Italian inventor who developed a wireless telegraph system. In 1909 he was the recipient of the Nobel Prize in Physics for his work. Ministero degli Affari Esteri, Rome, to Ministero dell'Interno, Rome, 2 Oct. 1934, Giuseppe Coleffi, busta 1402, CPC, ACS, Rome.

62 Avrich, *Anarchist Voices*, 129.

63 Julia Barnett, "The Life and Times of Marie Tiboldo," *New Socialist* 46 (April/May 2004), 20.

64 "Giovanni 'John' Vattuone, 1899–1994," David Koven Papers (DKP), File 131, IISH, unpublished manuscript, 1994, 10.

65 Guglielmo, *Living the Revolution*, 190, 247.

66 Ibid., 153.

67 Avrich *Anarchist Voices*, 179–180.

68 Barnett, "The Life and Times of Marie Tiboldo," 20. Tiboldo does not name her father's anarchist group in the interview from the *New Socialist* but I am inclined to believe it was not the same as Il Gruppo Libertario, also from Toronto.

69 Bortolotti, "Guardian of the Dream," 1. I have been unable to locate any copies of *Il Libertario*.

70 Salerno, *Red November, Black November*, 150.

71 Bencivenni, *Italian Immigrant Radical Culture*, 51–52.

72 "Communicazioni," *AdR*, 12 Jan. 1929, 7.

73 Libera Bortolotti, personal interview, 6 June 2005.

74 *IM*, 1 Aug. 1931, 3.

75 Topp, *Those without a Country*, 53.

76 *IM*, 1 Aug. 1931, 3.

77 Vecoli, "'Primo Maggio' in the United States," 58.

78 Here I am using the word "convergence" to mean a radical gathering in the same way that contemporary anarchists use this term to refer to political gatherings.

79 Vecoli, "'Primo Maggio' in the United States," 77.

80 The event was originally scheduled to take place on 29 July 1923, the exact day twenty-three years earlier that Bresci assassinated King Umberto I. However, for unknown reasons, the convergence was postponed to 2 September. *AdR*, 4 Aug. 1923, 4.

81 The figure of more than 2000 in attendance comes courtesy of Attilio Bortolotti. Avrich, *Anarchist Voices*, 180. Though the number seems quite high, reportage of the event in *L'Adunata dei Refrattari* indicates that an incredible $2600.00 was raised at the event. Anarchist social gatherings were generally inexpensive and if tickets were as high as $1.25 per person it would have meant 2,080 were in attendance. After $153.53 in expenses, $2,471.47 remained and was earmarked in the following manner: $1,853.56 was given to political victims in Rome, Turin, Milan, and Sicily while $642.91 was divided among the following anarchist newspapers: *L'Adunata dei Refrattari, Il Vespro Anarchico, Rivendicazione, Il Messaggero della Riscossa, Il Risveglio* (Geneva), and *Il Martello. AdR*, 15 Sep. 1923, 4.

82 Avrich, *Anarchist Voices*, 180.

83 Libera Bortolotti, personal interview, 6 June 2005.

84 Philip S. Foner, *May Day: A Short History of the International Workers' Holiday, 1886–1986* (New York: International Publishers, 1986), 39–40.

85 Vecoli, "'Primo Maggio' in the United States," 61.

86 Robert D'Attilio, "*Primo Maggio*: Haymarket as Seen by Italian Anarchists in America," *Haymarket Scrapbook*, eds. Dave Roediger and Franklin Rosemont (Chicago: Charles H. Kerr Publishing Company, 1986), 230.

87 Bencivenni, *Italian Immigrant Radical Culture*, 101, 104, 105.

88 Ugo Baldi was born in the city of Pistoia in Tuscany in 1876 to parents Joseph and Annunciata. The date of his emigration from Italy and arrival in the United States is unknown. In 1918, while in Chicago, Baldi was stabbed during a protest against the Italian Workers Mission's visit to that city. The Italian Workers Mission was comprised of former syndicalists and radicals who, during the First World War became supportive of Italy's involvement in the conflict. The mission was sponsored by then AFL president Samuel Gompers, in an attempt to curb the spread of radicalism among Italian workers in America. Baldi was known to make his living as an actor but in 1931 his CPC file mentions his operating a small candy store. Attilio Bortolotti also claims Baldi was a doctor. He died of pancreatic cancer in Detroit on 16 December 1934. Topp, *Those without a Country*, 220; Bortolotti and Di Leo, "Between Canada and the USA"; Consolato d'Italia, NYC, to Prefetto di Pistoia, Pistoia, 26 Nov. 1931; Certified Record of Death, State of Michigan, County of Wayne, 16 Dec. 1934, Ugo Baldi, busta 273, CPC, ACS, Rome.

89 Avrich, *Anarchist Voices*, 180; *AdR*, 22 Dec. 1934, in Ugo Baldi, busta 273, CPC, ACS, Rome.

90 Avrich, *Anarchist Voices*, 184.

91 Guglielmo, *Living the Revolution*, 172–173.

92 Vecoli, "The Italian Immigrants in the United States Labour Movement," 278.

93 Avrich, *Anarchist Voices*, 184.

94 Bencivenni, *Italian Immigrant Radical Culture*, 128.

95 Pernicone, *Italian Anarchism*, 258–259; M. Antonioli and F. Bertolucci, "Pietro Gori," *Dizionario Biografico degli Anarchici Italiani*, eds. Maurizio Antonioli et al., vol. 1 (Pisa: Biblioteca Franco Serantini, 2003), 745–746.

96 Antonioli and Bertolucci, "Pietro Gori," 746.

97 Topp, *Those without a Country*, 28.

98 *La Questione Sociale* (1895–1917) shifted from the organizationalist to the anti-organizationalist position following Giuseppe Ciancabilla's editorship of the paper in 1899. The next editor was Luigi Galleani who maintained the paper's anti-organizationalist line. Topp, *Those without a Country*, 28; Vecoli, "The Italian Immigrants in the United States Labour Movement," 271–272; Vecoli, "*Primo Maggio*' in the United States," 61, 65; Avrich, *Anarchist Voices*, 503; Antonioli and Bertolucci, "Pietro Gori," 747.

99 Antonioli and Bertolucci, "Pietro Gori," 747.

100 Maurizio Antonioli, *Pietro Gori: Il cavaliere errante dell'anarchia* (Pisa: Biblioteca Franco Serantini, 1995), 133.

101 Antonioli, *Pietro Gori*, 128–146.

102 Bencivenni, *Italian Immigrant Radical Culture*, 99–100; D'Attilio, "*Primo Maggio* 230; Vecoli, "*Primo Maggio*' in the United States" 59–60. It was a common practice for radical songwriters to draft lyrics to the tune of a well-known song. Jim Connell's "The Red Flag" is sung to the music of "O Tannenbaum," for instance. Salerno, *Red November, Black November*, 147.

103 Bencivenni, *Italian Immigrant Radical Culture*, 100.

104 Vecoli, "*Primo Maggio*' in the United States," 59–60.

105 Bencivenni, *Italian Immigrant Radical Culture*, 100.

106 Avrich, *Anarchist Voices*, 112–113.

107 Bencivenni, *Italian Immigrant Radical Culture*, 127.

108 Guglielmo, *Living the Revolution*, 173.

109 Maurizio Antonioli, "Michele Schirru," *Dizionario Biografico degli Anarchici Italiani*, eds. Maurizio Antonioli et al., vol. 2 (Pisa: Biblioteca Franco Serantini, 2003), 528–529; Melchior Steele [Raphaele Schiavina], "1931: Michele Schirru and the Attempted Assassination of Mussolini," *Man!* 1, 5–6 (May–June 1933), http://libcom.org/history/articles/murder-michael-schirru (accessed 28 July 2010).

110 Grossardi, Console Generale, NYC, to Ministero dell'Interno, Rome, 25 Feb. 1932, Salvatore Dettori, busta 1758, CPC, ACS, Rome.

111 Paolo Giacometti, *La Morte Civile* (New York: George F. Nesbitt and Company, 1873), 2.

112 Grossardi, Console Generale, NYC, to Ministero dell'Interno, Rome, 25 Feb. 1932, Salvatore Dettori, busta 1758, CPC, ACS, Rome.

113 F. Sora, "Osvaldo Maraviglia," *Dizionario Biografico degli Anarchici Italiani*, eds. Maurizio Antonioli et al., vol. 2 (Pisa: Biblioteca Franco Serantini, 2003) 84; Tenente Colonnello, Capo Reparto Censura Militare Posta Estera, Genoa, to Ministero dell'Interno, Rome, 10 Nov. 1916, Osvaldo Maraviglia, busta 3017, CPC, ACS, Rome.

114 Ten. Colonnello, Capo Reparto Censura Militare Posta Estera, Genoa, to Ministero dell'Interno, Rome, 10 Nov. 1916, Osvaldo Maraviglia, busta 3017, CPC, ACS, Rome.

115 Ten. Colonnello, Capo Reparto Censura Militare Posta Estera, Genoa, to Ministero dell'Interno, Rome, 10 Nov. 1916, Osvaldo Maraviglia, busta 3017, CPC, ACS, Rome.

116 Bencivenni, *Italian Immigrant Radical Culture*, 54.

117 Avrich, *Anarchist Voices*, 116–117.

118 Ibid., 111.

119 Goldman received a mere $50 for a 1927 lecture in London, Ontario—and after paying Goldman her fee and the hall rental, and owing to low attendance and the small amount of literature sold, her anarchist enthusiasts in London lost $35.00, according to police estimates. "Report re Lecture on Russia in London, Ontario by Emma Goldman—Anarchist," H.M. Newson, Superintendent, Commanding Western Ontario District, London ON, to H.D.X., Commissioner, RCMP, 11 January 1927, File: Emma Goldman, RG 18, Vol. 3317, LAC, Ottawa.

120 Tresca, *Autobiography*, 193, 197.

121 Ibid., 191–193.

122 Libera Bortolotti, personal interview, 6 June 2005.

123 Avrich, *Anarchist Voices*, 149, 420–421.

124 Barbara Ielasi and Mikhail Tsovma, "Francesco Ghezzi: Italian Anarchist in Vorkuta," Kate Sharpley Library, http://www.katesharpleylibrary.net/sj3w24 (accessed 27 July 2010); Consolato Generale d'Italia, NYC, to Casellario Politico Centrale, 7 Jan. 1931, Carlo Pagella, busta 3652, CPC, ACS, Rome.

125 Ghezzi was eventually released from the labour camp due to the lobbying efforts of an unknown number of supporters. However, he was not allowed to leave the Soviet Union. In 1937, Ghezzi was re-arrested, again for counter-revolutionary activities but also for accusations of being a Nazi sympathiser and pro-Trotskyist—both of which he denied. He was imprisoned for two years before being given an eight-year sentence in another labour camp. Ghezzi died there in 1942. Ielasi and Tsovma, "Francesco Ghezzi."

126 Consolato Generale d'Italia, NYC, to Casellario Politico Centrale, 7 Jan. 1931, Carlo Pagella, busta 3652, CPC, ACS, Rome.

127 Avrich, *Anarchist Voices*, 184–185.

128 *The Road to Freedom*, Mar. 1927.

129 Marcus Graham, ed., *Man! An Anthology of Anarchist Ideas, Essays, Poetry and Commentaries* (London: Cienfuegos Press, 1974), xviii; Avrich, *Anarchist Voices*, 163, 489.

130 Avrich, *Anarchist Voices* 79, 185.

131 Moritz and Moritz, *The World's Most Dangerous Woman*, 139–140; Emma Goldman, Toronto, to James Heney, Port Arthur, 17 Oct 1939, Federico Arcos: Emma Goldman Papers (FA:EGP), Labadie Collection (LC), Ann Arbor.

132 Vecoli, "'Primo Maggio' in the United States," 58. See also Eric J. Hobsbawm and Terence O. Ranger, eds., *The Invention of Tradition* (Cambridge: Cambridge University Press, 1992).

CHAPTER FOUR
ANARCHIST IDENTITY FORMATION

1 Hank Johnston et al., "Identities, Grievances, and New Social Movements," *New Social Movements: From Ideology to Identity*, eds. Enrique Laraña et al. (Philadelphia: Temple University Press, 1994), 21.

2 See, for example, Elizabeth Jameson's *All That Glitters: Class, Conflict, and Community in Cripple Creek* (Urbana and Chicago: University of Illinois Press, 1998). She states on page 235: "Class overshadowed all other sources of social identity during the [1904] strike."

3   Topp, *Those without a Country*, 8–9.

4   Gustav Landauer, *For Socialism*, trans. David J. Parent (St. Louis: Telos Press, 1978), 44.

5   Ackelsberg, *Free Women of Spain*, 203.

6   Joseph R. Gusfield, "The Reflexivity of Social Movements: Collective Behavior and Mass Society Theory Revisited," *New Social Movements: From Ideology to Identity*, ed. Enrique Laraña et al. (Philadelphia: Temple University Press, 1994), 63; Johnston et al., "Identities, Grievances, and New Social Movements," 12.

7   Cannistraro and Meyer, "Introduction: Italian American Radicalism," 8–9.

8   Avrich, *Sacco and Vanzetti*, 25–26.

9   Emma Goldman, Toronto, to Nick Di Domenico, NYC, 22 Oct 1939, Federico Arcos: Emma Goldman Papers (FA:EGP), Labadie Collection (LC), Ann Arbor.

10 Cannistraro and Meyer, "Introduction: Italian American Radicalism," 8–9.

11 Forty-eight Italians, twenty-one in Canada and nineteen in the United States, were identified as anarchists before migrating to North America while twenty-one, four in Canada and seventeen in the United States, became anarchists afterwards. For the remaining twenty identified anarchists, eleven in Canada and nine in the United States, it is unclear when they adopted this political identification.

12 Paola A. Sensi-Isolani, "Italian Radicals and Union Activists in San Francisco, 1900–1920," *The Lost World of Italian-American Radicalism: Politics, Labor, and Culture*, ed. Phillip V. Cannistraro and Gerald Meyer (Westport: Praeger Publishers, 2003), 191.

13 Avrich, *Sacco and Vanzetti*, 34–35; Cannistraro and Meyer, "Introduction," 8.

14 Avrich, *Anarchist Voices*, 166.

15 Gabaccia, *Italy's Many Diasporas*, 52–53.

16 Guglielmo, "Introduction: White Lies, Dark Truths," 10; Sturino, *Forging the Chain*, 3.

17 Avrich, *Anarchist Voices*, 120.

18 "Dagoes!" *Cronaca Sovversiva* (CS), 28 Aug 1916, 1.

19 Ruth A. Frager, *Sweatshop Strife: Class, Ethnicity, and Gender in the Jewish Labour Movement of Toronto 1900–1939* (Toronto: University of Toronto Press, 1992), 35.

20 Annelise Orleck, *Common Sense and a Little Fire: Women and Working-Class Politics in the United States, 1900–1965* (Chapel Hill: The University of North Carolina Press, 1995), 89–90.

21 *Fasci* is a Roman word meaning "bundle of sticks." Gabaccia, *Militants and Migrants*, 55–56; M. Minardi, "Pietro Allegra," *Dizionario Biografico degli Anarchici Italiani*, ed. Maurizio Antonioli et al., vol. 1 (Pisa: Biblioteca Franco Serantini, 2003), 25.

22 Minardi, "Pietro Allegra," 25–26; Gallagher, *All the Right Enemies*, 188; Pernicone, *Carlo Tresca*, 233–234.

23 Pietro Allegra, "Può un siciliano essere fascista?" (Can a Sicilian be Fascist?), *Il Martello* (*IM*), 5 Jan. 1924, 2.

24 Avrich, *Anarchist Voices*, 173.

25 Ibid., 141.

26 Jennifer Guglielmo, "Donne Ribelli: Recovering the History of Italian Women's Radicalism in the United States," *The Lost World of Italian-American Radicalism: Politics, Labour, and Culture*, ed. Philip V. Cannistraro and Gerald Meyer (Westport: Praeger, 2003), 125.

27 Avrich, *Anarchist Voices*, 184; Attilio Bortolotti and Rossella Di Leo, "Between Canada and the USA: A Tale of Immigrants and Anarchists," Kate Sharpley Library, http://www.katesharpleylibrary.net/8pk1h4 (accessed 18 July 2010).

28 Topp, *Those without a Country*, 48.

29 Robert F. Harney, "Toronto's Little Italy, 1885–1945," *Little Italies in North America*, ed. Robert F. Harney and J. Vincenza Scarpaci (Toronto: The Multicultural History Society of Ontario, 1981), 55.

30 Morgan, *Italian Fascism*, 135–136, 147; Luigi G. Pennacchio, "Exporting Fascism to Canada: Toronto's Little Italy," *Enemies Within: Italian and Other Internees in Canada and Abroad*, ed. Franca Iacovetta, Roberto Perin, and Angelo Principe (Toronto: University of Toronto Press, 2000), 56–57, 61.

31 Bortolotti, "Guardian of the Dream," 2; Avrich, *Anarchist Voices*, 186; Petkovic, "Italians in Windsor," 1992, 84.

32 Ramirez, *The Italians in Canada*, 16–18; Harney, *From the Shores of Hardship*, 116.

33 Bifolco, "Antifascismo pratico," *IM*, 31 Mar 1923, 4.

34 Baily, *Immigrants in the Lands of Promise*, 161, 195–197; Pozzetta, "Mulberry District," 24–25; Zucchi, *A History of Ethnic Enclaves in Canada*, 7.

35 Ramirez, *The Italians in Canada*, 12; Vincenza Scarpaci, "Observations on a Ethnic Community: Baltimore's Little Italy," *Little Italies in North America*, ed. Robert F. Harney and J. Vincenza Scarpaci (Toronto: The Multicultural History Society of Ontario, 1981), 117; Gary Mormino, "The Hill upon a City: The Evolution of an Italian-American Community in St. Louis, 1882–1950," *Little Italies in North America*, ed. Robert F. Harney and J. Vincenza Scarpaci (Toronto: The Multicultural History Society of Ontario, 1981), 148.

36 Cannistraro and Meyer, "Introduction," 12.

37 Topp, *Those without a Country*, 48.

38 Linda Kealey, *Enlisting Women for the Cause: Women, Labour, and the Left in Canada, 1890–1920* (Toronto: University of Toronto Press, 1998), 8.

39 Joan Sangster, *Dreams of Equality: Women on the Canadian Left, 1920–1950* (Toronto: McClelland and Stewart, 1989), 25.

40 Guglielmo, *Living the Revolution*, 45.

41 Ibid., 155–156.

42 It might seem strange that the writings of a Ukrainian-born communist would appear in an anarcho-syndicalist publication, but it demonstrates Carlo Tresca's openness to publishing leftist thought beyond his own political philosphy.

43 Guglielmo, *Living the Revolution*, 150, 159.

44 Osvaldo, "Ritorna a Te" (It Returns to You), *L'Adunata dei Refrattari* (AdR) 30 Jan. 1923, 3.

45 Guglielmo, *Living the Revolution*, 151.

46 Bakunin, *Bakunin on Anarchism*, 237.

47 Moritz and Moritz, *The World's Most Dangerous Woman*, 7.

48 Ibid., 123.

49 Ibid., 9.

50   For biographical treatments of Emma Goldman see Richard Drinnon, *Rebel in Paradise: A Biography of Emma Goldman* (Chicago: University of Chicago Press, 1961); Candace Falk, *Love, Anarchy, and Emma Goldman* (New York: Holt, Rinehart, and Winston, 1984); Emma Goldman, *Living My Life*, vols. 1 and 2; Moritz and Moritz, *The World's Most Dangerous Woman*; C. Brid. Nicholson, *Emma Goldman: Still Dangerous* (Montreal: Black Rose Books, 2010); Solomon, *Emma Goldman*; Alice Wexler, *Emma Goldman in Exile: From the Russian Revolution to the Spanish Civil War* (Boston: Beacon Press, 1989); Wexler, *Emma Goldman: An Intimate Life* (New York: Pantheon Books, 1984); and the documentaries *Emma Goldman*, dir. Mel Bucklin, 2004, and *Emma Goldman: The Anarchist Guest* dir. Coleman Romalis, 2000. For collections of Goldman's political writings see Peter Glassgold, ed., *Anarchy! An Anthology of Emma Goldman's Mother Earth* (Washington, DC: Counterpoint, 2001) and Emma Goldman, *My Disillusionment in Russia* (New York: Dover, 2004); Goldman, *Red Emma Speaks*; *Vision on Fire: Emma Goldman on the Spanish Revolution*, ed. David Porter (New Paltz: Commonground Press, 1983); and Emma Goldman, *Anarchism and Other Essays* (New York: Mother Earth Publishing, 1911).

51   Goldman, *Red Emma Speaks*, 204–213.

52   Marsh, *Anarchist Women*, 19.

53   Goldman, *Living My Life*, 253.

54   Osvaldo, "Ritorna a Te," *AdR* 30 Jan. 1923, 3.

55   Ackelsberg, *Free Women of Spain*, 117.

56   Merithew, "Anarchist Motherhood," 217–218.

57   Sangster, *Dreams of Equality*, 53.

58   Ackelsberg, *Free Women of Spain*, 117; David Koven Papers (DKP), File 131, "Giovanni "John" Vattuone 1899–1994," unpublished manuscript, 1994, International Institute of Social History (IISH), Amsterdam, 17.

59   Libera Bortolotti, personal interview, 6 June 2005.

60   Guglielmo, *Living the Revolution*, 151, 228.

61   Sangster, *Dreams of Equality*, 53.

62   Guglielmo, *Living the Revolution*, 202–203.

63   Marsh, *Anarchist Women*, 19–20.

64   José Moya's research on the Italian anarchist movement in Buenos Aires has argued that women in that city placed less importance on motherhood than did their counterparts in the United States. He attributes this difference to the greater involvement of women in the Buenos Aires labour movement which allowed for the possibility of choosing labour struggle over child rearing. José Moya, "Italians in Buenos Aires's Anarchist Movement: Gender Ideology and Women's Participation, 1890–1910," *Women, Gender, and Transnational Lives: Italian Workers of the World*, eds. Donna Gabaccia and Franca Iacovetta (Toronto: University of Toronto Press, 2002), 210.

65   Merithew, "Anarchist Motherhood," 218; Sangster, *Dreams of Equality*, 163.

66   Delie, "Alle Donne" (To the Women), *AdR*, 15 Jan. 1923, 3–4.

67   Celestino Lalli, "Alle Madri Proletarie" (To Proletarian Mothers), *AdR*, 2 Nov. 1929, 4.

68   Benzion Librescu (1875–1958) was born in Romania and changed his last name to Liber after his arrival in the United States in 1905. He was a physician and hygienist who wrote books on diet, health, and child rearing. Liber was also involved in the founding of the single tax colony at Free Acres, New Jersey, and a treasurer of the Anarchist Red Cross. Avrich, *Anarchist Voices*, 196–197.

69   B. Liber, "Padri e Figli" (Fathers and Sons), *AdR*, 9 Nov. 1929, 5–6.

70   Aurora Alleva, "Perchè" (Why), *AdR*, 27 July 1929, 5. Aurora Alleva came from an anarchist family from Ascoli Picena in the Marche region of Italy. Her partner, Dominick Sallitto, was also an active anarchist in New York City. Guglielmo, *Living the Revolution*, 150.

71   Aurora Alleva, "Una Breve Riposta a L.D.C." (A Brief Response to L.D.C.), *AdR*, 2 Nov. 1929, 4.

72   Marsh, *Anarchist Women*, 45–46.

73   Guglielmo, *Living the Revolution*, 164.

74   Ibid., 155–156.

75   I have consulted *L'Adunata dei Refrattari* from 1929 to 1940 and *Il Martello* from 1931 to 1940 and did not find any articles written by women in the Italian anarchist movement that criticized their treatment or role by male comrades. More research is needed for these newspapers' issues from the 1920s to uncover whether this theme was completely ignored during the interwar period.

76   Guglielmo, *Living the Revolution*, 159.

77   Crescenzo Pacelli, Prefetto di Bologna, "Biografia di Virgilia D'Andrea," 27 Mar. 1919, Virgilia D'Andrea, busta 1607, CPC, ACS, Rome; Ventresca and Iacovetta, "Virgilia D'Andrea," 301–302.

78   Malatesta, *Errico Malatesta*, 114; Crescenzo Pacelli, Prefetto di Bologna, "Biografia di Virgilia D'Andrea," 27 Mar. 1919, Virgilia D'Andrea, busta 1607, CPC, ACS, Rome; Ventresca and Iacovetta, "Virgilia D'Andrea," 302–3.

79   Ventresca and Iacovetta, "Virgilia D'Andrea," 304.

80   Prefetto di Milan, Milan, to Ministero dell'Interno, Rome, 27 Feb. 1921, Virgilia D'Andrea, busta 1607, CPC, ACS, Rome; Ventresca and Iacovetta, "Virgilia D'Andrea," 305.

81   Ventresca and Iacovetta, "Virgilia D'Andrea," 305.

82   Ibid., 306–307; Il Cronista, "Conferenze di V. D'Andrea: La Nostra e l'Altrui Violenza" (Virgilia D'Andrea Lecture: Our Violence and the Violence of Others), *AdR* 5 Oct. 1929: 5; "Corrispondenze," *AdR*, 7 Dec. 1929, 7; Il Veggente, "La Nostra Propaganda," *AdR*, 1 Feb. 1930, 7; "Corrispondenze," *AdR*, 22 Feb. 1930, 7–8.

83   Il Cronista, "Conferenze di V. D'Andrea: La Nostra e l'Altrui Violenza," *AdR*, 5 Oct. 1929, 5.

84   Il Cronista, "Conferenze di V. D'Andrea: La Nostra e l'Altrui Violenza," *AdR*, 5 Oct. 1929, 5; "Corrispondenze," *AdR*, 7 Dec. 1929, 7; Il Veggente, "La Nostra Propaganda," *AdR*, 1 Feb. 1930, 7; "Corrispondenze," *AdR*, 22 Feb. 1930, 7–8.

85   "Corrispondenze," *AdR*, 7 Dec. 1929, 7.

86   Il Veggente (The Clairvoyant), "La Nostra Propaganda," *AdR*, 1 Feb. 1930, 7.

87   Dale Fetherling, *Mother Jones: The Miners' Angel – A Portrait* (Carbondale: Southern Illinois University Press, 1974), 10.

88   Rosalyn Fraad Baxandal, introduction, *Words on Fire: The Life and Writing of Elizabeth Gurley Flynn*, by Elizabeth Gurley Flynn (New Brunswick: Rutgers University Press, 1987), 17.

89   Il Cronista, "Conferenze di V. D'Andrea: La Nostra e l'Altrui Violenza," *AdR*, 5 Oct. 1929, 5.

90   Il Veggente, "La Nostra Propaganda," *AdR*, 1 Feb. 1930, 7.

91   Baxandal, introduction, *Words on Fire*, 9.

92 Uno che c'era, "Tre conferenze del compagno C. Zonchello" (The Three Lectures of Comrade C. Zonchello), *AdR*, 7 June 1924, 4.

93 Il Corrispondente, "Imponente manifestazione antifascista a New Haven, Conn.," *IM*, 20 Jan. 1923, 4.

94 Moya, "Italians in Buenos Aires's Anarchist Movement," 195–196; Kealey, *Enlisting Women for the Cause*, 255; Sangster, *Dreams of Equality*, 25.

95 Kealey, *Enlisting Women for the Cause*, 112; Sangster, *Dreams of Equality*, 52.

96 Bakunin, *The Political Philosophy of Bakunin*, 326.

97 Ibid., 326.

98 de Cleyre, *Exquisite Rebel*, 223, 229.

99 Goldman, *Anarchism and Other Essays*, 211; De Cleyre, *Exquisite Rebel*, 224.

100 Sangster, *Dreams of Equality*, 25, 53.

101 Merithew, "Anarchist Motherhood," 219.

102 Avrich, *Anarchist Voices*, 134; Avrich, *Sacco and Vanzetti*, 104–113.

103 Avrich, *Anarchist Voices*, 155.

104 Ibid., 138.

105 Ibid., 107.

106 Libera Bortolotti, personal interview, 6 June 2005.

107 Ibid.

108 Avrich, *Anarchist Voices*, 138.

109 Ibid., 179.

110 Ibid., 145.

111 Johnston et al., "Identities, Grievances, and New Social Movements," 16.

CHAPTER FIVE

FACTIONAL DISPUTES

1 Errico Malatesta was a third influential Italian anarchist within North America though he lived in Italy following the First World War until his death in 1932. Both *L'Adunata dei Refrattari* and *Il Martello* printed many of Malatesta's writings and selected quotes in their respective publications and he garnered a great deal of respect among Italian anarchists wherever they settled. However, Malatesta never involved himself in the rift between Carlo Tresca and Luigi Galleani or his adherents.

2 Pernicone, *Carlo Tresca*; Pernicone, "War among the Italian Anarchists," 78–97; Gallagher, *All the Right Enemies*; and Avrich, *Anarchist Voices*.

3 Louis Tarabelli in Avrich, *Anarchist Voices*, 130.

4 Alberico Pirani in Avrich, *Anarchist Voices*, 142.

5 Pernicone, "Luigi Galleani and Italian Anarchist Terrorism in the United States," 472.

6 Avrich, *Sacco and Vanzetti*, 48.

7 Pernicone, *Italian Anarchism*, 238.

8   Ibid., 223, 233, 258–259; Pernicone, "Luigi Galleani and Italian Anarchist Terrorism in the United States," 473; Levy, *Gramsci and the Anarchists*, 19–20. The paper later changed its name to "La Nuova Gazzetta Operaia." M. Scavino, "Galleani, Luigi," *Dizionario Biographico degli Anarchici Italiani*, eds. Maurizio Antonioli et al., vol. 1 (Pisa: Biblioteca Franco Serantini, 2003), 654.

9   *Domicilio coatto* was the forced banishment by the Italian state of a political dissident to an isolated island in the Adriatic, Mediterranean, or Tyrrhenian Seas. In addition to Pantelleria, other island locations for forced exile included Favignana, Lampedusa, Lipari, Tremiti, and Ventotene. On these islands, dissidents were not always imprisoned and, depending on which island they were sent to, could be allowed free movement and the ability to intermingle with the local inhabitants; Pantelleria was such an island. In these instances, the idea behind *domicilio coatto* was that a dissident would be effectively isolated and not continue their activities against the Italian state. And, as Galleani demonstrated, it was possible for those sentenced to forced exile to escape. Pernicone, *Italian Anarchism*, 132.

10 Very little information exists on Maria Rallo. When she met Galleani she already had a son named Salvatore. Maria and Luigi would have four children together. Avrich, *Anarchist Voices*, 136.

11 Scavino, "Galleani, Luigi," 655.

12 Ibid., 655; Rudolph J. Vecoli, "The Italian Immigrants in the United States Labour Movement from 1880 to 1929," *Gli italiani fuori d'italia: gli emigrati italiani nei movimenti operai dei paesi d'adozione 1880–1940*, eds. O Bayer et al. (Milan: Franco Angeli Editore, 1983), 272; Vecoli, "'Primo Maggio' in the United States," 65.

13 Galleani, *The End of Anarchism?*, 49.

14 Luigi Galleani to Jacques Gross, July 1902 and Sep. 1902, Jacques Gross Papers (JGP), International Institute of Social History (IISH), Amsterdam; Pernicone, *Carlo Tresca*, 65.

15 Avrich, *Sacco and Vanzetti*, 48–49. I have been unable to find more information on who Gonzalez was or how he came to know Galleani. During his time living in Montreal, Galleani resided at two different addresses with Gonzalez. Those addresses were 38 St. Peter Street, most likely St. Pierre Street, and 203 Murray Street. Galleani to Gross, July 1902 and 2 Nov 1902, JGP, IISH, Amsterdam. My thanks to Meghan Gallant for translating these letters from French.

16 Avrich, *Sacco and Vanzetti*, 48–49; Scavino, "Galleani, Luigi," 656.

17 Galleani to Gross, Sep. 1902, JGP, IISH, Amsterdam.

18 Galleani to Gross, July 1902, Sep. 1902, Nov. 1902, JGP, IISH, Amsterdam.

19 Mathieu Houle-Courcelles, *Sur les Traces de l'Anarchisme au Québec* (Montréal: Lux Éditeur, 2008), 49–54.

20 Ibid., 95–96.

21 Some of Galleani's assumed names included Mentana, Tramp, Luigi Pimpino, and L'Eretico. Avrich, *Sacco and Vanzetti*, 221; Topp, *Those without a Country*, 293; Vecoli, "'Primo Maggio' in the United States: An Invented Tradition of the Italian Anarchists," 82.

22 Galleani, *The End of Anarchism?*, iv; Avrich, *Sacco and Vanzetti*, 49–51.

23 Pernicone, "Luigi Galleani and Italian Anarchist Terrorism in the United States," 475.

24 Avrich, *Sacco and Vanzetti*, 99–100.

25 Ibid., 98, 143.

26 Galleani, along with the paper's printer, Giovanni Eramo, were charged with conspiracy to obstruct the draft and arrested in June of that same year. Both were later fined $300 and $100 respectively and released. Avrich, *Sacco and Vanzetti*, 94–96.

27 Ugo Fedeli, *Luigi Galleani: Quarant'anni di lotte rivoluzionarie, 1891–1931* (Catania: Centrolibri, 1984), 102.

28 Avrich, *Sacco and Vanzetti*, 130.

29 Ibid., 127–128, 130–131, 133–134.

30 The other eight anarchists were Raffaele Schiavina, Giovanni Fruzzetti, Giuseppe Solari, Tugardo Montanari, Vincenzo De Lecce, Alfonso Fagotti, and Giobbe and Irma Sanchini, who were joined by their two young daughters. Avrich, *Sacco and Vanzetti*, 135–136; Scavino, "Galleani, Luigi," 657.

31 Scavino, "Galleani, Luigi," 657.

32 Avrich, *Sacco and Vanzetti* 209.

33 Pernicone, *Carlo Tresca*, 7–9, 11.

34 Pernicone states the sentence was 30 days while Antonioli states it was a three-month term. Ibid., 14; Maurizio Antonioli, "Tresca, Carlo," *Dizionario Biographico degli Anarchici Italiani*, eds. Maurizio Antonioli et al, vol. 2 (Pisa: Biblioteca Franco Serantini, 2003), 623.

35 Pernicone, *Carlo Tresca*, 14, 18; Antonioli, "Tresca, Carlo," 623.

36 Topp, *Those without a Country*, 27–28.

37 Pernicone, *Carlo Tresca*, 30; Antonioli, "Tresca, Carlo," 624.

38 Pernicone, *Carlo Tresca*, 39–40.

39 The relationship was actually an affair, since Tresca had been married to Helga Guerra since 1904. He abandoned Guerra and their daughter Beatrice in 1913 to live with Gurley Flynn. Guerra filed for divorce that year, though it was not granted until 1942. Pernicone, *Carlo Tresca*, 74, 239; Antonioli, "Tresca, Carlo," 624.

40 Pernicone, *Carlo Tresca*, 65–69.

41 Ibid., 88–93.

42 Ibid., 78, 80.

43 Ibid., 40, 96–98.

44 Although he bought the anti-religious paper from Luigi Preziosi in 1916, Tresca did not actually list himself as publisher until June 1918, which caused him immediate problems with American authorities (even though *Il Martello* at that time was still devoid of political content). The paper was constantly losing its mailing privileges during the 1920s. Pernicone, *Carlo Tresca*, 103–104.

45 Pernicone, *Carlo Tresca*, 229.

46 Ibid., 232–233; Gallagher, *All the Right Enemies*, 172–173.

47 Avrich, *Sacco and Vanzetti*, 160.

48 Pernicone, *Carlo Tresca*, 259–260, 271–273.

49 Ibid., 269–173; Gallagher, *All the Right Enemies*, 215–221.

50 Avrich, *Anarchist Voices*, 143.

51 Gallagher, *All the Right Enemies*, 178.

52 Pernicone, *Carlo Tresca*, 267.

53 Avrich, *Anarchist Voices*, 423–424, 445, 450, 458.

54 Merlino was a former anarchist who had left the movement and became a parliamentary socialist. Galleani, *The End of Anarchism?*, v, 1, 73.

55 Ibid., i.

56 Merlino actually refers to the anti-organizationalists as "individualists" but I have chosen to stick with the former term for the sake of coherence and because "anti-organizationalist" and "individualist" were used interchangeably during this period.

57 Galleani, *The End of Anarchism?*, 2–3.

58 Ibid., v.

59 Ibid., 68.

60 Ibid., 66–67.

61 Ibid., 5.

62 Ibid., 16.

63 Ibid., 21.

64 Ibid., 13–14.

65 Ibid., 11–12.

66 Ibid., 34–35.

67 Ibid., 44–46.

68 Ibid., 49–50.

69 Pernicone, *Carlo Tresca*, 106.

70 Carlo Tresca, "Bisogna sfondare L'A.F. of L." (We Must Break the A.F. of L.), *Il Martello* (*IM*) 15 Apr. 1922, 1.

71 Carlo Tresca, "Una sola grande unione" (One Big Union), *IM*, 19 Apr. 1919, 6.

72 Carlo Tresca, "Le elezioni in Italia," *IM*, 1 Dec. 1919, 2.

73 Ibid.

74 Carlo Tresca, "La Tendenza economica della rivoluzione Italiana" (The Economic Tendency of the Italian Revolution), *IM*, 15 Sep. 1920, 1.

75 Carlo Tresca, "La Tendenza economica della rivoluzione Italiana," *IM*, 15 Sep. 1920, 1.

76 Pernicone, *Carlo Tresca*, 80; Gallagher, *All the Right Enemies*, 79.

77 "Ettore Aguggini," Dictionaire international des militants anarchistes, http://militants-anarchistes.info/spip.php?article1171 (accessed 23 Feb. 2009).

78 Ego Sum, "Il Fascismo," *IM*, 17 June 1922, 1.

79 Concetta Silvestri and Joseph Moro in Paul Avrich, *Anarchist Voices*, 107, 113.

80 Joseph Moro, Bartolomeo Provo, and Harry Richal in Avrich, *Anarchist Voices*, 113, 117, 129.

81 Pernicone, *Carlo Tresca*, 43, 87.

82 Gallagher, *All the Right Enemies*, 89.

83 Ibid., 89.

84 Avrich, *Sacco and Vanzetti*, 101–102.

85 Gallagher, *All the Right Enemies*, 129.

86 Pernicone, *Carlo Tresca*, 171.

87   Pernicone attributes the postponement of the general strike, which was never called by the IWW but rather by Tresca and Italian workers, to Haywood, who felt that a direct confrontation with the state would end in disaster. The IWW leader believed that the acceptance of the change in strike plans would be better received if delivered by Ettor and Giovannitti. Ibid., 53.

88   Ibid., 53.

89   Ibid., 54–55.

90   Ibid., 50, 58.

91   Ibid., 58.

92   Pernicone, *Carlo Tresca*, 189; Gallagher, *All the Right Enemies*, 76–77.

93   Gallagher, *All the Right Enemies*, 76–77.

94   *Refrattari*, derived from the Italian word *refrattario*, was a term used to identify anarchists in late-nineteenth-century anti-anarchist legislation in Italy. Robert D'Attilio, "L'Adunata dei Refrattari," *Encyclopedia of the American Left*, eds. Mari Jo Buhle et al. (Chicago: St. James Press, 1990), 4.

95   F. Bucci and G. Piermaria, "Schiavina, Raffaele," *Dizionario Biographico degli Anarchici Italiani*, eds. Maurizio Antonioli et al., vol. 2 (Pisa: Biblioteca Franco Serantini, 2003), 518. *L'Adunata dei Refrattari*'s circulation between 1922 and 1945 was 5,000 copies per issue. According to Paul Berman, its circulation increased to 10,000 copies per issue following the Second World War, when it was distributed widely in Italy for a time. Paul Berman, "The Torch and the Axe: The Unknown Aftermath of the Sacco-Vanzetti Affair," *The Village Voice*, 17 May 1988. My thanks to Kenyon Zimmer for passing along this information. *L'Adunata dei Refrattari* continued to publish until 1971, when a declining subscription list no longer made the paper feasible. Avrich, *Anarchist Voices*, 317.

96   Prefetto di Nuora, "Biografia del Efisio Constantino Zonchello," 21 May 1938; and Consolato d'Italia, NYC, to unknown, 9 Jan. 1932, Efisio Constantino Zonchello, busta 5592, CPC, ACS, Rome.

97   Bucci and Piermaria, "Schiavina, Raffaele," 516.

98   Avrich, *Sacco and Vanzetti*, 214. In addition to Max Sartin, Schiavina also signed his articles in *L'Adunata dei Refrattari* as "Max," "Calibano," "Manhattanite," "L'osservatore," "Melchior Steele," "m.s.," "m.," "r.s.," and "X.Y." Bucci and Piermaria 517. Schiavina also used the name Bruno Rossi, Rossi being the surname of his wife Fiorina. Avrich, *Sacco and Vanzetti*, 215.

99   Prefetto di Macerata, Macerata, to Ministero dell'Interno, Rome, 12 Mar. 1927, Osvaldo Maraviglia, busta 3017, CPC, ACS, Rome; Avrich, *Anarchist Voices*, 503.

100 Tullio Tamburini, Prefetto di Avelino, "Biografia del Nicola Di Domenico," 16 July 1938, Nicola Di Domenico, busta 1781, CPC, ACS, Rome.

101 Avrich, *Anarchist Voices*, 121.

102 Pernicone, "War among the Italian Anarchists," 82.

103 *IM*, 13 May 1922, 4.

104 Pernicone, *Carlo Tresca*, 154, 159; *IM*, 23 May 1925.

105 Author unknown, Divisione Polizia Politica, to unknown, 14 May 1928, Nicola Di Domenico, busta 1781, CPC, ACS, Rome.

106 Pernicone, *Carlo Tresca*, 160, 199–210; Gallagher, *All the Right Enemies*, 108; *L'Adunata dei Refrattari* (AdR), 2 June 1928.

107 Carlo Tresca, "I sicari di Stalin incitano all'aggressione di Tresca," *IM*, 7 Mar. 1938, 3.

108 Pernicone, *Carlo Tresca*, 232–236; Pernicone, "War among the Italian Anarchists," 91; Gallagher, *All the Right Enemies*, 72.

109 Avrich, *Sacco and Vanzetti*, 52–53.

110 Norman Borins to J.L. Cohen, 26 Oct. 1939, Jacob Lawrence Cohen Fonds (JLCP), MG30, A94, Vol. 14, File 2761: Rex vs. Attilio Bortolotti et al, 1939–40, Library and Archives Canada (LAC), Ottawa.

111 "Giovanni 'John' Vattuone," 1899–1994," DKP, File 131, unpublished manuscript, Feb. 1994, IISH, Amsterdam, 6, 10.

112 Pernicone, *Carlo Tresca*, 128.

113 Author unknown, Divisione Polizia Politica, to unknown, 14 May 1928, Di Domenico, busta 1781, CPC, ACS, Rome.

114 Pernicone, *Carlo Tresca*, 135.

115 Ibid., 200–201; Gallagher, *All the Right Enemies*, 135.

116 Pernicone, *Carlo Tresca*, 200–201; Gallagher, *All the Right Enemies*, 135–136.

117 Pernicone, *Carlo Tresca*, 145.

118 Ibid., 145; Comitato Generale di Difesa Control il Fascismo, "L'Agitazione antifascista in New York e Brooklyn," *IM*, 9 June 1923, 3.

119 Pernicone, *Carlo Tresca*, 145.

120 Ibid., 175.

121 Ibid.

122 Alfredo Gonello with response by Costanzo, "Senza Connubii Ripugnanti!" (Without Repulsive Marriages!), *AdR*, 22 Dec. 1923, 3.

123 Ibid.

124 Tino, "Il Fascismo e Noi" (Fascism and Us), *AdR*, 8 Mar. 1924, 1.

125 Ibid.

126 Ibid.

127 Pernicone, *Carlo Tresca*, 180–181.

128 Biarmando (Armando Borghi), "'Fiere' Internazionali" ('Proud' International), *AdR*, 23 Mar. 1929, 6–7.

129 Console Generale, NYC, to Ministero dell'Interno, Rome, 24 July 1931, Calogero Greco, busta 2521, CPC, ACS, Rome.

130 Pernicone, *Carlo Tresca*, 189, 192.

131 Avrich, *Anarchist Voices*, 182–183; *Un trentennio di attività anarchica, 1914–1945* (Forli: del gruppo "L'Antistato," 1953), 163.

132 G.B. Ambrosi, Vice Console Generale, Toronto, to Sezione Della Divisione Affari Generali e Riservata, Rome, 5 Mar. 1934; and G.B. Ambrosi, Vice Console Generale, Toronto, to Console Generale, Ottawa, 16 Feb. 1934, Attilio Bortolotti, busta 772, CPC, ACS, Rome.

133 G.B. Ambrosi, Vice Console Generale, Toronto, to Sezione Della Divisione Affari Generali e Riservata, Rome, 5 Mar. 1934; and G.B. Ambrosi, Vice Console Generale, Toronto, to Console Generale, Ottawa, 16 Feb. 1934, Attilio Bortolotti, busta 772, CPC, ACS, Rome; Rizzo Babuscio, Ministero Affari Esteri, Rome, to Ministero dell'Interno, Rome, 13 July 1934, Nicola Giancotti, busta 2385, CPC, ACS, Rome.

CHAPTER SIX
DEPORTATION STRUGGLES

1 See Ruggero Benvenuti, busta 508, and Ernesto Gava, busta 2317, Casellario Politico Centrale (CPC), Archivio Centrale dello Stato (ACS), Rome.

2 "Gli arrestati di Toronto," *AdR*, 2 Dec. 1939, 3.

3 Copy of Evidence, Rex vs. Attilio Bortolotti et al., Jacob Lawrence Cohen Papers (JLCP), 18 Oct. 1939, MG30, A94, Volume 14, File 2761, Library and Archives Canada (LAC), Ottawa.

4 Bortolotti, "Guardian of the Dream," 1.

5 Avrich, *Anarchist Voices*, 185, 460.

6 For a lengthy biography on Cohen that, surprisingly, makes no mention of his involvement in this case, see Laurel Sefton MacDowell, *Renegade Lawyer: The Life of J.L. Cohen* (Toronto: The Osgoode Society for Canadian Legal History/University of Toronto Press, 2001).

7 Court Transcript, Rex vs. Attilio Bortolotti et al., 6 Nov. 1939, JLCP, MG30, A94, Volume 14, File 2761, LAC, Ottawa.

8 "Naturalisation in Canada," *The Quebec History Encyclopedia*, http://faculty.marianopolis.edu/c.belanger/quebechistory/encyclopedia/NaturalizationinCanada.htm (accessed 29 May 2010).

9 Moritz and Moritz, *The World's Most Dangerous Woman*, 192–193; Avrich, *Anarchist Voices*, 182–184.

10 Agostino Confalonieri Immigration Interview, 6 Dec. 1939, JLCP, MG30, A94, Volume 14, File 2761A, LAC, Ottawa.

11 See Roberts, *Whence They Came.*

12 Under the War Measures Act bans were placed on various radical and worker organizations, and any publications by these groups or foreign-language presses were either banned or singled out for investigation. The Act clearly stated that any current member of a banned organization or any person distributing its literature could face one to five years in jail, and that anyone found printing revolutionary literature or attending meetings in Russian, Ukrainian, or Finnish was susceptible to a $5,000 fine and at least five years in jail. Organizations banned under the 1914 War Measures Act included the Social Democratic Party of Canada, the Industrial Workers of the World, the Russian Socialist Democratic Party, the Russian Revolutionary Group, the Russian Socialist Revolutionaries, the Russian Workers' Farband, the Ukrainian Revolutionary Group, the Ukrainian Social Democrat Party, the Socialist Labor Party, the Social Democratic Bolshevik Group, the Social Democratic Anarchist Group, the Workers' International Industrial Union, the Chinese Nationalist League, and the Chinese Workers' Association. Roseline Usiskin, "Toward a Theoretical Reformulation of the Relationship Between Political Ideology, Social Class, and Ethnicity: A Case Study of the Winnipeg Jewish Community, 1905-1920," MA Thesis, University of Manitoba, 1978, 223. See also Dennis G. Molinaro, "'A Species of Treason?': Deportation and Nation-Building in the case of Tomo Čačić, 1931–1934," *Canadian Historical Review* 91, 1 (March 2010): 70–71.

13 Roberts, *Whence They Came*, 71–97.

14 Ibid., 126–129.

15 Mentana [Luigi Galleani], "Del Moro Arrestato in Canada," *Cronaca Sovversiva* (CS) 17 July 1915, 2; *Un trentennio di attività anarchica, 1914-1945* (Forli: del gruppo "L'Antistato," 1953), 126.

16 Prefetto di Pesaro-Urbino, Pesaro, to Ministero Interno, Rome, 24 Jan. 1916; Console Generale Reggente, NYC, to Ministero dell'Interno, Rome, 27 Apr. 1917, Armando Del Moro, busta 1698, CPC, ACS, Rome.

17 Mentana, "Del Moro Arrestato in Canada," *CS*, 17 July 1915, 2.

18 *The God Pestilence* was written by Johann Most, Errico Malatesta wrote *Between Peasants*, and *Evolution and Revolution* was authored by Elisée Reclus. Mentana, *CS*, 17 July 1915.

19 Mentana, *CS*, 17 July 1915, 2; "Del Moro in Libertà," *CS*, 7 Aug. 1915, 2.

20 Roberts, *Whence They Came*, 71.

21 Mentana, "Del Moro Arrestato in Canada," *CS*, 17 July 1915, 2.

22 Rizieri Fantini, "Per Armando Del Moro," *CS*, 24 July 1915, 3.

23 Fantini, "Per Armando Del Moro," *CS*, 24 July 1915, 3.

24 "Per A. Del Moro," *CS*, 28 Aug. 1915, 2; "Per A. Del Moro," *CS*, 11 Sep. 1915, 4.

25 "Del Moro in Libertà," *CS*, 7 Aug. 1915, 2; *Un trentennio di attività anarchica, 1914–1945* (Forli: del gruppo "L'Antistato," 1953), 126.

26 Direttore Leto, Capo Divisione Polizia Politica, Rome, to Divisione Affari Generali e Riservati, Rome, 17 Mar. 1939, Mario Mantovani, busta 3002, CPC, ACS, Rome.

27 In a letter dated 15 August 1934, Confalonieri enclosed 20 francs. Agostino Confalonieri, Bellinzona, to Confalonieri Family, Monza, 15 Aug. 1934, Agostino Confalonieri, busta 1438, CPC, ACS, Rome.

28 Console Generale, Canton Ticino, Lugano, to Ministero degli Affari Esteri, Rome, June 1937; Ministero degli Affari Esteri, Rome, to Ministero dell'Interno, Rome, 14 Feb. 1936, Confalonieri, CPC, ACS, Rome.

29 Prefetto di Milan, Milan, to Ministero dell'Interno, Rome, 31 Oct. 1934, Agostino Confalonieri, busta 1438, CPC, ACS, Rome.

30 Prefetto di Milano, "Biografico del Agonstino Confalonieri," nd, Confalonieri, CPC, ACS, Rome; Nick Heath, "Bifolchi, Giuseppe, 1895–1978," http://libcom.org/history/bifolchi-giuseppe-1895-1978 (accessed 3 Feb. 2008); J.L. Cohen to Louis Fitch, 14 Mar. 1940, JLCP, MG30, A94, Volume 14, File 2761, LAC, Ottawa.

31 Stefano, Divisione Polizia Politica, Rome, to Divisione Affari Generali e Riservati, Rome, 17 Apr. 1937; Divisione Polizia Politica to Ministero dell'Interno, Rome, 22 Apr. 1937; Stefano, Divisione Polizia Politica to Divisione Affari Generali e Riservati, Rome, 30 Apr. 1937; Alberto Brugnoli, Console, Montpellier, to Ministero degli Affari Esteri, Rome, 18 May 1937, Agostino Confalonieri, busta 1438, CPC, ACS, Rome.

32 Prefetto di Milano, Milan, to Ministero dell'Interno, Rome, 7 Mar. 1938; Divisione Polizia Politica to Ministero dell'Interno, Rome, 3 Nov. 1938; Ministero della Guerra, Rome, to Ministero dell'Interno, Rome, 23 May 1938; Prefetto di Milano, Milan, to Ministero dell'Interno, Rome, 9 June 1938; Direttore, Divisione Polizia Politica, Rome, to Divisione degli Generale e Riservati, Rome, 5 July 1939; Direttore, Divisione Polizia Politica, Rome, to Divisione degli Generale e Riservati, Rome, 27 July 1939; Divisione Polizia, Rome, to Ministero dell'Interno, Rome, 5 June 1939; Mario Mantovani, Brussels, to Ministero Dell'Interno, Rome, 15 July 1940, Agostino Confalonieri, busta 1438, CPC, ACS, Rome.

33 The Lozère department is located in the Languedoc-Roussillon region.

34 Maccotta, Consule Generale, Paris, to Ministero Esteri, Rome, 2 Aug. 1938; Direttore, Divisione Polizia Politica, Rome, 31 May 1939; Ambasciatore, Paris, to Ministero degli Affari Esteri, Rome, 24 Apr. 1939, Ernesto Bonomini, busta 740, CPC, ACS, Rome.

35 Day had been helping anarchist refugees since at least the late 1920s. The Spanish anarchists Buenaventura Durruti and Francisco Ascaso were expelled from France in July 1927 because of their political activities and taken to the Belgian border. However, the Belgian border guards were unwilling to allow the notorious anarchists into their country. As a result, French authorities had to wait until nightfall to sneak Durruti and Ascaso into Belgium. After crossing into Belgium in this way, the two anarchists made their way to Brussels where they contacted Hem Day. Day had hoped that the anarchists would be granted political asylum by the Belgian government but this was not to be. Durruti and Ascaso were eventually found by Belgian police and taken to the French border. Immediately after crossing into France they were arrested by French authorities who had most likely been given advance warning by the Belgians that the anarchists would be arriving. Abel Paz, *Durruti in the Spanish Revolution* (Oakland: AK Press, 2007), 127–128.

36 In addition to Day and Mantovani, this anarchist group included Antonio Moscardini, Paulo Catani, Azelio Bucchioni, Cafierio Meucci, Guido Schiaffonati, Marcello Bianconi, Ernesto Bruna, Pietro Montaresi, Celso Bendanti, Renato Riva and a few others. Leto, Direttore, Divisione Polizia Politica, Rome, to Divisione Affari Generali e Riservati, Rome, 17 Mar. 1939, Mario Mantovani, busta 3002, CPC, ACS, Rome; M. Granata, "Mario Mantovani," *Dizionario Biografico degli Anarchici Italiani*, Maurizio Antonioli et al., vol. 2 (Pisa: Biblioteca Franco Serantini, 2003), 80–82.

37 It is not clear how these funds were procured. Leto, Direttore, Divisione Polizia Politica, Rome, to Divisione Affari Generali e Riservati, Rome, 17 Mar. 1939, Mario Mantovani, busta 3002, CPC, ACS, Rome; G. Bottinelli, "Luigi Bertoni," *Dizionario Biografico degli Anarchici Italiani*, Maurizio Antonioli et al., vol. 1 (Pisa: Biblioteca Franco Serantini, 2003), 159–164.

38 Confalonieri Immigration Interview, JLCP, MG30, A94, Volume 14, File 2761A, LAC, Ottawa. At this point I have been unable to determine Cuba's role in the issuance of passports to Italian anarchists who fought in Spain. During the war, Fulgencio Batista was the military leader of Cuba and, though he promised support to the Republic, did not actually come through with any concrete aid. After the war ended, he quickly recognized Franco and was lukewarm to Mexico's pleas for Cuba to accept large numbers of Spanish refugees. Restrictions were placed on which refugees would be accepted with preference given to those willing to work as agricultural labourers or who had the financial means to invest in industry. T.G. Powell, *Mexico and the Spanish Civil War* (Albuquerque: University of New Mexico Press, 1981), 92, 153. However, according to Frank Fernandez, an unknown number of surviving Spanish anarchists left Spain and France with Cuban passports that were obtained through anarchist comrades with contacts within the Cuban Ministry of State. Some of the Spanish anarchists were detained by Cuban immigration authorities but later released after Cuban anarchists intervened. For Spanish anarchists, Cuba was also a gateway to North and South America. Frank Fernandez, *Cuban Anarchism: The History of a Movement* (Tucson: See Sharp Press, 2001), 63.

39 Paz, *Durruti in the Spanish Revolution*, 140.

40 Confalonieri, Toronto, to Mario Mantovani, Brussels, 18 Sep. 1939, JLCP, MG30, A94, Volume 14, File 2761A, LAC, Ottawa; Mario Mantovani, Brussels, to Ministero dell'Interno, Rome, 15 July 1940, Agostino Confalonieri, busta 1438, CPC, ACS, Rome; Leto, Direttore, Divisione Polizia Politica, Rome, to Divisione Affari Generali e Riservati, Rome, 17 Mar. 1939, Mario Mantovani, busta 3002, CPC, ACS, Rome.

41 Confalonieri Immigration Interview, JLCP, MG30, A94, Volume 14, File 2761A, LAC, Ottawa.

42 Ministero dell'Interno, Rome, to Ministero degli Affari Esteri, Rome, 3 Sep. 1939, Ernesto Bonomini, busta 740, CPC, ACS, Rome.

43　Confalonieri arrived on a Saturday and the centre was closed Sunday and for the Labour Day Monday. Confalonieri, Montreal, to Mantovani, Brussels, 13 Sep. 1939, JLCP, MG30, A94, Volume 14, File 2761A, LAC, Ottawa.

44　Confalonieri, Toronto, to Mantovani, Brussels, 18 Sep. 1939; Confalonieri Immigration Interview, JLCP, MG30, A94, Volume 14, File 2761A, LAC, Ottawa.

45　Confalonieri Immigration Interview; and Confalonieri, Toronto, to Jiosef Tavernari, Brussels, 19 Sep. 1939, JLCP, MG30, A94, Volume 14, File 2761A, LAC, Ottawa.

46　Attilio Bortolotti and Rossella Di Leo, "Between Canada and the USA: A Tale of Immigrants and Anarchists," Kate Sharpley Library, http://www.katesharpleylibrary.net/8pk1h4 (accessed 18 July 2010).

47　Confalonieri Immigration Interview; and Confalonieri, Toronto, to Jiosef Tavernari, Brussels, 19 Sep. 1939, JLCP, MG30, A94, Volume 14, File 2761A, LAC, Ottawa.

48　Confalonieri, Toronto, to Tavernari, Brussels, 19 Sep. 1939; and Confalonieri, Toronto, to Luigi Mainetti, Bellinzona, 23 Sep. 1939, JLCP, MG30, A94, Volume 14, File 2761A, LAC, Ottawa.

49　One of the cities was New York while another was most likely Brussels. The third centre may have been Paris, Geneva, or Antwerp. Confalonieri, Toronto, to Mainetti, Brussels, 23 Sep. 1939, JLCP, MG30, A94, Volume 14, File 2761A, LAC, Ottawa.

50　Bonomini was carrying more than $200. Confalonieri, Toronto, to Mantovani, Brussels, 18 Sep. 1939, JLCP, MG30, A94, Volume 14, File 2761A, LAC, Ottawa.

51　Mantovani, Brussels, to Ministero dell'Interno, Rome, 15 July 1940, Agostino Confalonieri, busta 1438, CPC, ACS, Rome. Spanish anarchists may also have used this network or one similar to it. During Goldman's seventieth-birthday celebration in Toronto in June 1939, she was greeted on behalf of the Confederación Nacional del Trabajo (CNT) by a Spanish anarchist who had recently fled from Spain. Ahrne Thorne also recalled a number of Spanish anarchists travelling from France to Canada. Avrich, *Anarchist Voices*, 81–82. However, it should be pointed out that Italian anarchists travelled under Spanish names and that Toronto anarchists did not realize Confalonieri was Italian until months after his arrest. Thus, it is possible that the Spanish anarchists that Thorne refers to could have been Italians.

52　Confalonieri, Toronto, to Mantovani, Brussels, 18 Sep. 1939, JLCP, MG30, A94, Volume 14, File 2761A, LAC, Ottawa.

53　Di Domenico, NYC, to Goldman, Toronto, 12 Dec. 1939; Goldman, Toronto, to Di Domenico, NYC, 14 Dec. 1939, 6 Jan. 1940, 9 Jan. 1940, and 12 Jan. 1940, FA:EGP, LC, Ann Arbor.

54　Goldman, Toronto, to James Heney, Port Arthur, 9 Nov. 1939, FA:EGP, LC, Ann Arbor.

55　James Prasow, Medicine Hat, to Goldman, Toronto, 10 Dec. 1939, FA:EGP, LC, Ann Arbor.

56　Goldman, Toronto, to Clara Solomon, NYC, 22 Oct. 1939, FA:EGP, LC, Ann Arbor.

57　Rogers became the central figure in the defence committees after Goldman suffered her stroke in February 1940.

58　Bortolotti, "Guardian of the Dream," 1; Avrich, *Anarchist Voices*, 187, 455, 496; Moritz and Moritz, *The World's Most Dangerous Woman*, 181.

59　Goldman, Toronto, to M. Eleanor Fitzgerald, NYC, 17 Nov. 1939; Goldman, Toronto, to Millie Rocker, Stelton, 17 Nov. 1939, FA:EGP, LC, Ann Arbor; Moritz and Moritz, *The World's Most Dangerous Woman*, 187.

60　Goldman, Toronto, to Heney, Port Arthur, 24 Oct. 1939, FA:EGP, LC, Ann Arbor.

61 Dorothy Rogers, "Bortolotti Defence Committee Financial Statement," FA:EGP, LC, Ann Arbor.

62 [Agent] No. 30 [Royal Canadian Mounted Police], "Report re Sacco-Vanzetti Memorial Meeting," Toronto, 2 Sep. 1927, to RCMP Commissioner, Emma Goldman Papers Project (EGPP), Berkeley; Moritz and Moritz, *The World's Most Dangerous Woman*, 93–94, 190–191.

63 Moritz and Moritz, *The World's Most Dangerous Woman*, 184, 188.

64 Ibid.

65 Goldman, *Living My Life*, 644–646, 726.

66 Ibid., 737, 740, 753–755, 809–811, 876–887. See also Goldman, *My Disillusionment in Russia*. Kronstadt was a naval base located on an island in the Gulf of Finland that was home to the Russian Baltic Fleet. The Kronstadt Rebellion of March 1921 was sparked by the suppression of labour strikes in nearby Petrograd. As a result, the Kronstadt sailors did not feel that the Bolsheviks properly represented the October Revolution. They held a meeting and passed a series of resolutions calling for new elections to the Soviets, freedom of speech, the right of assembly, and the liberation of all political prisoners, among others. Fearing a possible attack by the Bolsheviks, the Kronstadt sailors voted to form a Provisional Revolutionary Committee. When word reached Moscow of the rebellion, 60,000 Soviet soldiers were sent to the island. After ten days of fighting, the Kronstadt sailors had been defeated. See Paul Avrich, *Kronstadt, 1921* (Princeton: Princeton University Press, 1970).

67 "Report re Emma Goldman," 3 Feb. 1927, EGPP, Berkeley.

68 Goldman, Toronto, to Heney, Port Arthur, 9 Nov. 1939, FA:EGP, LC, Ann Arbor.

69 *L'Adunata* raised $733.54, with the SIA raising the second largest sum of $684.23. Detroit raised $436.00 while Toronto forwarded $310.00. However, in the case of Detroit and Toronto it is not clear who exactly contributed in these cities since the Bortolotti Defence Committee Financial Statement only states "Friends" as contributors. In other words, it was not necessarily the case that Italians were the sole contributors in these cities. Dorothy Rogers, "Bortolotti Defence Committee Financial Statement," n.d., FA:EGP, LC, Ann Arbor; "Comitato Difesa Bortolotti," *AdR*, 13 July 1940, 7.

70 Solomon was involved in the publication of Vanguard, an anarchist newspaper based in New York during the 1930s. Avrich, *Anarchist Voices*, 449–450.

71 Tresca's pragmatic approach to political activity meant that he had many advantageous connections among labour unions and the media, and could raise necessary funds to pay for legal costs. He was also experienced in preventing Italian comrades from being deported to Italy. Fitzgerald to Goldman, 25 Nov. 1939, FA:EGP, LC, Ann Arbor; Moritz and Moritz, *World's Most Dangerous Woman*, 22.

72 Goldman, Toronto, to Fitzgerald, NYC, 27 Nov. 1939, FA:EGP, LC, Ann Arbor.

73 Goldman, Toronto, to Di Domenico, NYC, 27 Nov. 1939, FA:EGP, LC, Ann Arbor.

74 Goldman, Toronto, to Di Domenico, NYC, 29 Nov. 1939, FA:EGP, LC, Ann Arbor.

75 Ibid.

76 Goldman, Winnipeg, to Di Domenico, NYC, 2 Dec. 1939, FA:EGP, LC, Ann Arbor.

77 Di Domenico, NYC, to Goldman, Winnipeg, 5 Dec. 1939, FA:EGP. LC, Ann Arbor.

78 Goldman, Winnipeg, to Di Domenico, NYC, 7 Dec. 1939, FA:EGP, LC, Ann Arbor.

79 Avrich, *Anarchist Voices* 180, 187–188.

80 Cohen, Toronto, to Goldman, Winnipeg, 1 Dec. 1939, JLCP, MG30, A94, Volume 14, File 2761A, LAC, Ottawa.

81 Goldman, Toronto, to Fitzgerald, NYC, 27 Nov. 1939, FA:EGP, LC, Ann Arbor. Confalonieri's relationship with *L'Adunata dei Refrattari* is less clear. It is difficult to pinpoint when he became an adherent of the paper's anarchist philosophy, but before his travels to New York were interrupted by Canadian Immigration he was on his way to contact the publishers of the paper. Confalonieri, Toronto, to Mainetti, Bellinzona, 23 Sep. 1939; Confalonieri, Toronto, to Mantovani, Brussels, 18 Sep. 1939, JLCP, MG30, A94, Volume 14, File 2761A, LAC, Ottawa. Confalonieri's opinion of Tresca is uncertain as well. It may be that he shared views similar to those of Bortolotti and the wider *L'Adunata* network but it is also possible that he may not have been aware of the feud.

82 Emma Goldman, "Emma a Carlo", *Il Martello*, 28 May 1940. Tresca most likely printed this letter in *Il Martello* as a tribute to Goldman, who passed away on 14 May.

83 Carlo Tresca, NYC, to Goldman, Toronto, Jan. 1940, FA:EGP, LC, Ann Arbor.

84 Luigi Antonini, NYC, to Dorothy Rogers, Toronto, 12 Apr. 1940, FA:EGP, LC, Ann Arbor.

85 Rudolph J. Vecoli, "The Italian Immigrants in the United States Labour Movement from 1880 to 1929," *Gli italiani fuori d'italia: gli emigrati italiani nei movimenti operai dei paesi d'adozione 1880-1940*, ed. O. Bayer et al. (Milan: Franco Angeli Editore, 1983), 295; Console Generale, NYC, to Ministero degli Affari Esteri, Rome, 31 May 1939, Luigi Rocco Antonini, busta 160, CPC, ACS, Rome.

86 Pernicone, *Carlo Tresca*, 255; Gallagher, *All the Right Enemies*, 195.

87 Avrich, *Anarchist Voices*, 147–148, 163.

88 The Editor, "Lettera spedita" (Quick Letter), *AdR*, 20 July 1940, 6.

89 Rogers, Toronto, to Di Domenico, NYC, 10 Mar. 1940, FA:EGP, LC, Ann Arbor.

90 Confalonieri Immigration Interview, JLCP, MG30, A94, Volume 14, File 2761A, LAC, Ottawa.

91 Di Domenico, NYC, to Rogers, Toronto, 6 Mar. 1940, FA:EGP, LC, Ann Arbor; Jennifer Guglielmo, "Italian Women's Proletarian Feminism in the New York City Garment Trades, 1890s–1940s," *Women, Gender, and Transnational Lives: Italian Workers of the World*, ed. Donna Gabaccia and Franca Iacovetta (Toronto: University of Toronto Press, 2002), 249.

92 Di Domenico, NYC, to Rogers, Toronto, 6 Mar. 1940, FA:EGP, LC, Ann Arbor.

93 Di Domenico, NYC, to Rogers, Toronto, 10 Mar. 1940, FA:EGP, LC, Ann Arbor.

94 Di Domenico, NYC, to Rogers, Toronto, 14 Mar. 1940, FA:EGP, LC, Ann Arbor.

95 Antonini, NYC, to Rogers, Toronto, 12 Apr. 1940, FA:EGP, LC, Ann Arbor.

96 Di Domenico, NYC, to Rogers, Toronto, 22 Mar. 1940, FA:EGP, LC, Ann Arbor.

97 Di Domenico, NYC, to Rogers, Toronto, 29 Mar. 1940, FA:EGP, LC, Ann Arbor.

98 Goldman, Toronto, to Fitzgerald, NYC, 17 Nov. 1939, FA:EGP, LC, Ann Arbor.

99 Goldman, Toronto, to Di Domenico, NYC, 19 Oct. 1939; 9 Jan. 1940; 15 Feb. 1940, FA:EGP, LC, Ann Arbor.

100 The authorship of the *L'Adunata* articles is unknown because they were left unsigned. It is possible that they were written by Max Sartin, i.e., Raffaele Schiavina, the paper's editor. Avrich, *Anarchist Voices*, 499.

101 John D. McCarthy, "The Globalisation of Social Movement Theory," *Transnational Social Movements and Global Politics: Solidarity Beyond the State*, ed. Jackie Smith et al. (Syracuse: Syracuse University Press, 1997), 244.

102 Canada did not formally declare war on Germany until 10 September 1939.

103 Rex vs. Attilio Bortolotti et al, JLCP, MG30, A94, Volume 14, File 2761, LAC, Ottawa.

104 "Gli arrestati di Toronto," *AdR*, 11 Nov. 1939, 6.

105 "Gli arrestati di Toronto," *AdR*, 2 Dec. 1939, 3.

106 Ibid.

107 "Gli arrestati di Toronto," AdR, 3 Feb. 1940, 2.

108 "Gli arrestati di Toronto," AdR, 2 Dec. 1939, 3.

109 "Gli arrestati di Toronto," AdR, 16 Dec. 1939, 5.

110 "Gli arrestati di Toronto," AdR, 18 Nov. 1939, 3; "Gli arrestati di Toronto," AdR, 2 Dec 1939, 3.

111 "Gli arrestati di Toronto," AdR, 3 Feb. 1940, 2.

112 Roberts, *Whence They Came,* 154–155; Molinaro, "'A Species of Treason?'" 83.

113 Molinaro, "'A Species of Treason?'" 83.

114 "Gli arrestati di Toronto," AdR, 9 Dec. 1939, 7; "Gli arrestati di Toronto," AdR, 23 Dec. 1939, 4.

115 "Gli arrestati di Toronto," AdR, 3 Feb. 1940, 2.

116 "Gli arrestati di Toronto," AdR, 9 Dec. 1939, 7. Fedeli was deported from Uruguay in 1933 by the Terra dictatorship because of his anarchist activities. Upon his return to Italy he was imprisoned until 1943. Recchi was part of an anarchist circle in Buenos Aires involved in expropriations and bombings. He had lost his left hand while making explosives. In spite of this injury, he worked as a bricklayer and supported his family. After the execution of Severino Di Giovanni, a prominent figure in the circle of which Recchi was part, Recchi was arrested, tortured, and deported to Italy. He, too, was immediately arrested and imprisoned when he arrived. Recchi was not released from prison until after the Fascist regime fell. Afterwards he returned to Buenos Aires where he reunited with his family. Paul Avrich, *Sacco and Vanzetti: The Anarchist Background* (Princeton: Princeton University Press, 1991), 210.

117 "Gli arrestati di Toronto," *AdR*, 23 Dec. 1939, 4.

118 Goldman, Toronto, to Di Domenico, NYC, 12 Jan. 1940; and 18 Jan. 1940, FA:EGP, LC, Ann Arbor.

119 "Gli arrestati di Toronto," *AdR*, 23 Dec. 1939, 4.

120 "Gli arrestati di Toronto," *AdR*, 20 Jan. 1939, 4.

121 It was not until early 1940 that letters regarding the case were printed in *Nation, New Republic, and Canadian Forum*. Moritz and Moritz, *World's Most Dangerous Woman,* 188–189.

122 "Gli arrestati di Toronto," *AdR*, 9 Dec. 1939, 7.

123 "Gli arrestati di Toronto," *AdR*, 18 Nov. 1939, 3.

124 "Gli arrestati di Toronto," *AdR*, 16 Dec. 1939, 5.

125 "Gli arrestati di Toronto," *AdR*, 9 Dec. 1939, 7.

126 "La reazione liberale in Canada," *AdR*, 28 Oct. 1939, 2; "Gli arrestati di Toronto," *AdR*, 2 Dec. 1939, 3.

127 Goldman, Toronto, to Di Domenico, NYC, 22 Oct. 1939, FA:EGP, LC, Ann Arbor.

128 Ibid.

129 "La reazione liberale in Canada," *AdR*, 28 Oct. 1939, 2.

130 Goldman, Toronto, to Di Domenico, NYC, 19 Oct. 1939, FA:EGP, LC, Ann Arbor.

131 "Gli arrestati di Toronto," *AdR*, 18 Nov. 1939, 3.

132 Goldman, Toronto, to Di Domenico, NYC, 19 Oct. 1939, FA:EGP, LC, Ann Arbor.

133 Goldman, Toronto, to Di Domenico, NYC, 22 Nov. 1939, FA:EGP, LC, Ann Arbor.

134 Di Domenico, NYC, to Goldman, Toronto, 22 Nov. 1939, FA:EGP, LC, Ann Arbor.

135 Goldman, Toronto, to Di Domenico, NYC, 22 Oct. 1939, FA:EGP, LC, Ann Arbor.

136 Goldman, Toronto, to Di Domenico, NYC, 4 Nov. 1939, FA:EGP, LC, Ann Arbor.

137 Goldman, Winnipeg, to Di Domenico, NYC, 7 Dec. 1939; Goldman, Toronto, to Di Domenico, NYC, 19 Dec. 1939; 12 Jan., 25 Jan., 6 Feb., 15 Feb. 1940, FA:EGP, LC, Ann Arbor.

138 Goldman, Toronto, to Di Domenico, NYC, 6 Jan. and 9 Jan. 1940, FA:EGP, LC, Ann Arbor.

139 Goldman, Toronto, to Di Domenico, NYC, 19 Dec. 1939, FA:EGP, LC, Ann Arbor.

140 "Gli arrestati di Toronto," *AdR*, 6 Jan. 1940, 3.

141 Ibid.

142 Dorothy Rogers, "Bortolotti Defence Committee Financial Statement," nd, FA:EGP, LC, Ann Arbor.

143 Goldman, Toronto, to Anna Olay, Chicago, 24 Nov. 1939, and Leo Becchetti, Needham, to Goldman, Toronto, 3 Feb. 1940, FA:EGP, LC, Ann Arbor; Il Circolo Volontà, "Pro Gli Arrestati del Canada," *AdR*, 24 Feb. 1940, 8.

144 Marcella Bencivenni, "Italian American Radical Culture in New York City: The Politics and Arts of the *Sovversivi*, 1890-1940," PhD diss., City University of New York, 2003, 204–205.

145 In a personal interview Libera Martignago Bortolotti stated that events held by the Italian anarchists in Sault Ste. Marie were attended by Italians who did not identify as anarchists. Libera Bortolotti, personal interview, 6 June 2005.

146 FC Blair, Ottawa, to Cohen, Toronto, 29 Apr. 1940, JLCP, MG30, A94, Volume 14, File 2761, LAC, Ottawa.

147 Avrich, *Anarchist Voices*, 507; Pernicone, *Carlo Tresca*, 76–7.

148 Cohen, Toronto, to Augusto Bellanca, NYC, 3 Apr. 1940, JLCP, MG30, A94, Volume 14, File 2761, LAC, Ottawa.

149 Bortolotti, "Guardian of the Dream," 2. In *Forging the Chain*, Franc Sturino mentions that channels existed whereby Italian migrants in Toronto could pay $300 to a "mafia" member to be smuggled into the United States. Sturino, *Forging the Chain*, 158.

150 Cohen, Toronto, to Louis Fitch, Ottawa, 25 Mar. 1940, JLCP, MG30, A94, Volume 14, File 2761, LAC, Ottawa. It is possible that the Jewish anarchist living in Mexico was Simon Radowitzky. In an article from *Kick It Over*, Bortolotti explains that the contact in Mexico given to Confalonieri was a Jewish anarchist who had assassinated a president of Argentina and fought in Spain. Bortolotti, "Guardian of the Dream," 2. I have been unable to find any reference to a Jewish anarchist killing an Argentine president, though an attempt was made on the life of Manuel Quintana, president of Argentina from 1904 to 1906, by a Catalan anarchist named Salvador Planas y Virella, which was unsuccessful. Radowitzky, on the other hand, did successfully assassinate Colonel Ramon Falcon, a police chief who ordered a cavalry charge against workers on 1 May 1909 in Buenos Aires that killed twelve and wounded 100. Radowitzky was disgusted by Falcon's actions and later threw a bomb into the colonel's coach. The anarchist was imprisoned for twenty years before being released and expelled from Argentina. He went to Uruguay, where his anarchist activities again caused his deportation. Radowitzky went to Spain in 1936 to fight in the revolution but fled to Mexico via France after Franco's victory. "Radowitzky, Simon, 1891–1956," libcom.org, http://libcom.org/history/simon-radowitzky-1891-1956 (accessed 23 Mar. 2008). Whether

Confalonieri contacted Radowitzky upon his arrival in Mexico City is unclear. But, in a letter to his cousin Stefano, Confalonieri mentions that he is living with a friend in a house in the city. Agostino Confalonieri, Mexico City, to Stefano Confalonieri, Monza, 17 June 1940, Agostino Confalonieri, busta 1438, CPC, ACS, Rome.

151 This figure is a total of the following amounts: *L'Adunata*/New York – $733.54, Chicago – $135.25, Detroit – $436.00, East Boston – $44.58, Rouyn, Quebec, – $47.00, and Windsor – $41.00. Anarchists from Toronto also contributed but their amount is unknown and lumped into a general Toronto total. The other cities listed may also include monies from non-Italian anarchist sources, but these localities were centres of Italian anarchist activity. Thus it seems likely that the majority of funds raised in these cities came mostly from Italian anarchist sources. Dorothy Rogers, "Bortolotti Defence Committee Financial Statement," nd, FA:EGP, LC, Ann Arbor.

152 Dorothy Rogers, "Bortolotti Defence Committee Financial Statement," n.d., FA:EGP, LC, Ann Arbor.

153 See http://www.abcf.net.

154 See http://www.spiritoffreedom.org.uk.

CONCLUSION

1 Avrich, *Anarchist Voices*, 317.

2 Michael Miller Topp, for instance, dates the death of the Italian syndicalist movement in the United States to the execution of Sacco and Vanzetti. Topp, *Those without a Country*, 264.

3 Pio Turroni, Cesena, to Armando Borghi, NYC, 6 Mar. 1949, Federico Arcos: Emma Goldman Papers (FA:EGP), Labadie Collection (LC), Ann Arbor; P. Sensini, "Pio Turroni," *Dizionario Biografico degli Anarchici Italiani*, eds. Maurizio Antonioli et al., vol. 2 (Pisa: Biblioteca Franco Serantini, 2003): 635–638.

4 "Obituaries: Two Historians of Anarchism—Roland Biard and Carlo Pier Masini, Anarchist Federation, http://www.afed.org.uk/org/issue50/obit.html (accessed 30 May 2010); F. Bertolucci, "Pier Carlo Masini," *Dizionario Biografico degli Anarchici Italiani*, ed. Maurizio Antonioli et al., vol. 2 (Pisa: Biblioteca Franco Serantini, 2003), 121–125.

5 Pio, Cesena, to Borghi, NYC, 6 Mar. 1949, FA:EGP, LC, Ann Arbor.

6 "Armando Borghi," *Dizionario Biografico degli Anarchici Italiani*, eds. Antonioli, Maurizio, et al., vol. 1 (Pisa: Biblioteca Franco Serantini, 2003), 234; "Obituaries: Two Historians of Anarchism – Roland Biard and Carlo Pier Masini," Anarchist Federation, http://www.afed.org.uk/org/issue50/obit.html (accessed 30 May 2010).

7 Avrich, *Anarchist Voices*, 131.

8 "Giovanni 'John' Vattuone, 1899–1994," David Koven Papers (DKP), File 131, International Institute of Social History (IISH), Amsterdam, 14–15.

9 Sam Dolgoff, *Fragments: A Memoir* (Cambridge: Refract Publications, 1986), 102.

10 "Giovanni 'John' Vattuone, 1899–1994," DKP, File 131, IISH, Amsterdam, 12–13.

BIBLIOGRAPHY

ARCHIVAL SOURCES

Archivio Centrale dello Stato, Rome
Casellario Politico Centrale Collection

Abate Erasmo, busta 1

Allegra Pietro, busta 69

Antonini Luigi Rocco, busta 160

Artico Egidio, busta 202

Baldi Ugo, busta 273

Beduz Pietro, busta 435

Bellanca Augusto, busta 444

Benvenuti Ettore, busta 507

Benvenuti Giuseppe, busta 507

Benvenuti Ruggero, busta 508

Bin Pietro, busta 651

Boatini Ermanno, busta 678

Boatini Guglielmo, busta 679

Bonomini Ernesto, busta 740

Borghi Armando, busta 755

Bortolotti Attilio, busta 772

Capuana Vincenzo, busta 1055

Carra Renzo, busta 1110

Carrillo Donato, busta 1116

Ciccotti Pacifico, busta 1334

Ciccotti Pilade, busta 1334

Ciofalo Andrea, busta 1354

Coleffi Giuseppe, busta 1402

Confalonieri Agostino, busta 1438

Crisi Vincenzo, busta 1535

Cristiano Giovanni, busta 1537

Crudo Vincenzo, busta 1549

D'Andrea, Virgilia, busta 1607

De Benedetti Angelo, busta 1639

Del Moro Armando, busta 1698

Dettori Salvatore, busta 1758

Dezi Dante, busta 1763

Di Domenico Nicola, busta 1781

Fabbri Amleto, busta 1902

Fabrizi Oreste, busta 1917

Falsini Luigi, busta 1940

Felicani Aldino, busta 1991

Fulvi Amedeo, busta 2196

Gabbani Vincenzo, busta 2211

Galleani Luigi, busta 2241

Gava Ernesto, busta 2317

Ghetti Giulio, busta 2355

Giancotti Nicola, busta 2385

Giorgini Dulio, busta 2429

Gioventu Enrico, busta 2441

Grandi Serafino, busta 2504

Greco Calogero, busta 2521

Greco Luigi, busta 2521

Lentricchia Angelo, busta 2761

Manarin Pietro, busta 2968

Mantovani Mario, busta 3002

Maraviglia Osvaldo, busta 3017

Mariotti Fortunato, busta 3075

Martignago Umberto, busta 3094

Mingarelli Angelo, busta 3299

Moscardelli Domenico, 3435

Ongaro Augusto, busta 3594

Pagella Carlo, busta 3652

Peronne Filippo, busta 3875

Postiglione Umberto, busta 4097

Procopio Saverio, busta 4136

Provo Bartolo, busta 4145

Regiani Sante, busta 4264

Rolle Giuseppe, busta 4377

Rosati Domenico, busta 4413

Russiani Giulio Cesare, busta 4496

Salerno Cosimo, busta 4534

Santarelli Turibbio, busta 4582
Schiavina Raffaele, busta 4690
Schirru Michele, busta 4697
Semprini Domenico, busta 4742
Talevi Giuseppe, busta 5010
Tarica Gioacchino, busta 5032
Tavani Rocco, busta 5049
Taus Nazzareno, busta 5049
Tecchi Adimero, busta 5054
Tresca Carlo, busta 5208
Valdinoci Carlo, busta 5287
Viccelli Mario, busta 5399
Viggiani Vincenzo, busta 5410
Vigna Pietro, busta 5412
Zonchello Efisio Constantino, busta 5592

International Institute for Social History, Amsterdam
David Koven Papers
Jacques Gross Papers

Labadie Collection, Ann Arbor
Federico Arcos: Emma Goldman Papers

Library and Archives Canada, Ottawa
Royal Canadian Mounted Police Subject Files, RG 18, Series F-3, Vol. 3317, "Emma Goldman (Mrs EG Colton)"
Jacob Lawrence Cohen Papers, MG 30, A94, Vol. 14, File 2761 and 2761A

University of California, Berkeley
Emma Goldman Papers Project

Newspapers and Periodicals
L'Adunata dei Refrattari (New York City)
Cronaca Sovversiva (Lynn, Massachusetts)
The Globe (Toronto)
The Manitoba Free Press (Winnipeg, Manitoba)
Il Martello (New York City)
The Road to Freedom (New York City)
Toronto Star
The Voice (Winnipeg, Manitoba)

Theses and Other Unpublished Works

Bencivenni, Marcella. "Italian American Radical Culture in New York City: The Politics and Arts of the *Sovversivi*, 1890–1940." PhD diss. City University of New York, 2003.

Goings, Aaron. "Red Harbor: Class, Violence, and Community in Grays Harbor, Washington." PhD diss. Simon Fraser University, 2011.

Heie, Nolan. "Ernst Haeckel and the Redemption of Nature." PhD diss. Queen's University, 2008.

Petkovic, Susan. "Italians in Windsor: The Development of the Erie Street Community from Ghetto to Via Italia." MA thesis. Queen's University, 1992.

Tomchuk, Travis. "There are Anarchists at Large in Winnipeg: Local Anarchists and Commentaries on Anarchism in the Winnipeg Labour Press, 1900–1919." Essay. Queen's University, 2005.

Turcato, Davide. "Making Sense of Anarchism: The Experiments with Revolution of Errico Malatesta, Italian Exile in London, 1889–1900." PhD diss. Simon Fraser University, 2009.

Usiskin, Roseline. "Toward a Theoretical Reformulation of the Relationship Between Political Ideology, Social Class, and Ethnicity: A Case Study of the Winnipeg Jewish Community, 1905–1920." MA thesis. University of Manitoba, 1978.

Zimmer, Kenyon. "'The Whole World is Our Country': Immigration and Anarchism in the United States, 1885–1940." PhD diss. University of Pittsburgh, 2010.

Articles, Books, and Pamphlets

Ackelsberg, Martha. *Free Women of Spain: Anarchism and the Struggle for the Emancipation of Women*. Oakland: AK Press, 2005.

Adams, Jason. *Non-Western Anarchisms: Rethinking the Global Context*. Johannesburg: Zabalaza Books, n.d.

Anderson, Benedict. *Imagined Communities: Reflections on the Origin and Spread of Nationalism*. London: Verso, 2006.

Antliff, Allan. *Anarchist Modernism: Art, Politics, and the First American Avant-Garde*. Chicago: University of Chicago Press, 2001.

Antonioli, Maurizio, et al. *Dizionario Biografico degli Anarchici Italiani*. 2 vols. Pisa: Biblioteca Franco Serantini, 2003.

Antonioli, Maurizio. *Pietro Gori: Il cavaliere errante dell'anarchia*. Pisa: Biblioteca Franco Serantini, 1995.

"L'Archivio." Archivio Centrale dello Stato. http://www.archivi.beniculturali.it/ACS/cpcarchivio.html.

Avery, Donald H. *Reluctant Host: Canada's Response to Immigrant Workers, 1896–1994*. Toronto: McClelland and Stewart, 1995.

———. *"Dangerous Foreigners": European Immigrant Workers and Labour Radicalism in Canada 1896–1932*. Toronto: McClelland and Stewart, 1979.

———. "The Radical Alien and the Winnipeg General Strike of 1919." *The West and the Nation: Essays in Honour of W.L. Morton*. Ed. Carl Berger and Ramsay Cook. Toronto: McClelland and Stewart, 1976. 209–231.

Avrich, Paul. *Anarchist Voices: An Oral History of Anarchism in America*. Oakland: AK Press, 2005.

———. *Sacco and Vanzetti: The Anarchist Background*. Princeton: Princeton University Press, 1991.

————. *The Haymarket Tragedy*. Princeton: Princeton University Press, 1984.

————. *An American Anarchist: The Life of Voltairine de Cleyre*. Princeton: Princeton University Press, 1978.

————. *Kronstadt, 1921*. Princeton: Princeton University Press, 1970.

Baily, Samuel L. *Immigrants in the Lands of Promise: Italians in Buenos Aires and New York City, 1870–1914*. Ithaca: Cornell University Press, 1999.

Bakunin, Mikhail. *Statism and Anarchy*. Trans. Marshall S. Shatz. Cambridge: Press Syndicate of the University of Cambridge, 1990.

————. *Bakunin on Anarchism*. Trans. and ed. Sam Dolgoff. Montreal: Black Rose Books, 1980.

————. *The Political Philosophy of Bakunin*. Ed. G.P. Maximoff. New York: Free Press, 1953.

Bannister, Robert C. *Social Darwinism: Science and Myth in Anglo-American Social Thought*. Philadelphia: Temple University Press, 1979.

Barbini, Guido. "The Friulian Community in Canada: Between Integration and Assimilation." *An Italian Region in Canada: The Case of Friuli-Venezia Giulia*. Ed. Konrad Eisenbichler. Toronto: Multicultural History Society of Ontario, 1998. 45–62.

Barnett, Julia. "The Life and Times of Marie Tiboldo." *New Socialist* 46 (April/May 2004): 20–21.

Basch, Linda, Nina Glick Schiller, and Cristina Szanton Blanc. *Nations Unbound: Transnational Projects, Postcolonial Predicaments, and Deterritorialized Nation-States*. Amsterdam: Gordon and Breach Science Publishers, 2000.

Baxandal, Rosalyn Fraad. Introduction. *Words on Fire: The Life and Writing of Elizabeth Gurley Flynn*. By Elizabeth Gurley Flynn. New Brunswick: Rutgers University Press, 1987.

Beaulieu, Michel S. *Labour and the Lakehead: Ethnicity, Socialism, and Politics, 1900–35*. Vancouver: University of British Columbia Press, 2011.

Bencivenni, Marcella. *Italian Immigrant Radical Culture: The Idealism of the Sovversivi in the United States, 1890–1940*. New York: New York University Press, 2011.

Berger, Maurice. *White Lies: Race and the Myths of Whiteness*. New York: Farrar, Straus, and Giroux, 1999.

Berkman, Alexander. *What Is Anarchism?* Oakland: AK Press, 2003.

————. *Prison Memoirs of an Anarchist*. New York: Schocken Books, 1970.

Berman, Paul. "The Torch and the Axe: The Unknown Aftermath of the Sacco-Vanzetti Affair." *The Village Voice*, 17 May 1988.

Berry, David. *A History of the French Anarchist Movement, 1917–1945*. Westport: Greenwood Press, 2002.

"Biography." Jacques Gross Papers. International Institute of Social History. http://www.iisg.nl/archives/pdf/10749476.pdf.

Blatt, Martin Henry. *Free Love and Anarchism: The Biography of Ezra Heywood*. Chicago: University of Illinois Press, 1989.

Blinkhorn, Martin. *Mussolini and Fascist Italy*. London: Routledge, 2006.

Bookchin, Murray. *The Spanish Anarchists: The Heroic Years, 1868–1936*. San Francisco: AK Press, 1998.

Bortolotti, Attilio. "Guardian of the Dream: A [sic] Oral History with Art Berthelot." *Kick It Over* 17 (Winter 1986/1987): 1–2.

Bortolotti, Attilio, and Rossella Di Leo. "Between Canada and the USA: A Tale of Immigrants and Anarchists." Kate Sharpley Library. http://www.katesharpleylibrary.net/8pk1h4.

Bosworth, R.J.B. *Italy and the Wider World 1860–1960*. London: Routledge, 1996.

Briggs, Vernon L. *The Manner of Man That Kills*. New York: Da Capo Press, 1983.

Buck, Tim. *Yours in the Struggle: Reminiscences of Tim Buck*. Ed. William Beeching and Dr. Phyllis Clarke. Toronto: NC Press, 1977.

Burgan, Michael. *Immigration to the United States: Italian Immigrants*. New York: Facts On File, Inc., 2005.

Burowoy, Michael. *Manufacturing Consent: Changes in the Labor Process under Monopoly Capitalism*. Chicago: The University of Chicago Press, 1979.

Cannistraro, Philip V., and Gerald Meyer. "Introduction: Italian American Radicalism – An Interpretive History." *The Lost World of Italian-American Radicalism: Politics, Labour, and Culture*. Ed. Philip V. Cannistraro and Gerald Meyer. Westport: Praeger, 2003. 1–48.

Casanova, Julian. *Anarchism, the Republic, and Civil War in Spain, 1931–1939*. London: Routledge, 2005.

Choate, Mark I. *Emigrant Nation: The Making of Italy Abroad*. Cambridge: Harvard University Press, 2008.

Clark, Martin. *The Italian Risorgimento*. London: Longman, 1998.

Cole, G.D.H. *History of Socialist Thought: Marxism and Anarchism, 1850–1890*. Vol. 2. London: MacMillan, 1957.

Cosco, Joseph P. *Imagining Italians: The Clash of Romance and Race in American Perceptions, 1880–1910*. Albany: State University of New York Press, 2003.

Cristaldi, Justin R. "Little Italy Across the Hudson." *Primo* (Sep./Oct. 2001). http://www. sicilianculture. com/littleitaly/nj-newark.htm.

Crump, John. *Hatta Shuzo and Pure Anarchism in Interwar Japan*. New York: St. Martin's Press, 1993.

Damier, V.V. *Anarcho-Syndicalism in the 20th Century*. Edmonton: Black Cat Press, 2009.

D'Attilio, Robert. "L'Adunata dei Refrattari." *Encyclopedia of the American Left*. Ed. Mari Jo Buhle et al. Chicago: St. James Press, 1990. 4–5.

———. "*Primo Maggio*: Haymarket as Seen by Italian Anarchists in America." *Haymarket Scrapbook*. Ed. Dave Roediger and Franklin Rosemont. Chicago: Charles H. Kerr Publishing Company, 1986. 229–231.

Davies, Thomas Richard. *The Possibilities of Transnational Activism: The Campaign for Disarmament between the Two World Wars*. Leiden: Martinus Nijhoff Publishers, 2007.

Davis, Minerva. *The Wretched of the Earth and Me*. Toronto: Lugus Publications, 1992.

Day, Richard J.F. *Gramsci is Dead: Anarchist Currents in the Newest Social Movements*. Toronto: Between the Lines, 2005.

De Cleyre, Voltairine. *Exquisite Rebel: The Essays of Voltairine de Cleyre – Anarchist, Feminist, Genius*. Ed. Sharon Presley and Crispin Sartwell. Albany: State University of New York Press, 2005.

De Grand, Alexander. *Italian Fascism: Its Origins and Development*. Lincoln: University of Nebraska Press, 2000.

Delicato, Armando. *Italians in Detroit*. Charleston: Arcadia Publishing, 2005.

DeSalvo, Louise. "Colour: White/Complexion: Dark." *Are Italians White?: How Race Is Made in America*. Ed. Jennifer Guglielmo and Salvatore Salerno. New York: Routledge, 2003. 17–28.

Dirlik, Arif. *Anarchism in the Chinese Revolution*. Berkeley: University of California Press, 1991.

Dolgoff, Sam. *Fragments: A Memoir.* Cambridge: Refract Publications, 1986.

———. *The Anarchist Collectives: Workers' Self-Management in the Spanish Revolution, 1936–1939.* Montréal: Black Rose Books, 1974.

Drinnon, Richard. *Rebel in Paradise: A Biography of Emma Goldman.* Chicago: University of Chicago Press, 1961.

Dubofsky, Melvyn. *We Shall Be All: A History of the Industrial Workers of the World.* Ed. Joseph McCartin. Abridged ed. Chicago: University of Illinois Press, 2000.

Edwards, Richard. *Contested Terrain: The Transformation of the Workplace in the Twentieth Century.* New York: Basic Books, 1979.

Eisenbichler, Konrad. *An Italian Region in Canada: The Case of Friuli-Venezia Giulia.* Toronto: Multicultural History Society of Ontario, 1998.

Engels, Friedrich, and Karl Marx, and Vladimir I. Lenin. *Anarchism and Anarcho-Syndicalism.* Moscow: Progress Publishers, 1972.

"Ettore Aguggini." Dictionaire international des militants anarchistes. http://militants-anarchistes.info/spip.php?article1171.

Falk, Candace. *Love, Anarchy, and Emma Goldman.* New York: Holt, Rinehart, and Winston, 1984.

Fedeli, Ugo. *Luigi Galleani: Quarant'anni di Lotte Rivoluzionarie, 1891–1931.* Catania: Centrolibri, 1984.

Federal Writers' Project. *The Italians of New York: A Survey.* New York: Arno Press, 1969.

Fernandez, Frank. *Cuban Anarchism: The History of a Movement.* Tucson: See Sharp Press, 2001.

Fetherling, Dale. *Mother Jones: The Miners' Angel – A Portrait.* Carbondale: Southern Illinois University Press, 1974.

Foner, Philip S. *May Day: A Short History of the International Workers' Holiday, 1886–1986.* New York: International Publishers, 1986.

"For Jihadist, Read Anarchist." *The Economist,* 20 Aug. 2005, 17–20.

Fox, Cybelle, and Thomas A. Guglielmo. "Defining America's Racial Boundaries: Blacks, Mexicans, and European Immigrants, 1890–1945." *American Journal of Sociology* 18, 2 (Sep. 2012): 327–379.

Frager, Ruth A. *Sweatshop Strife: Class, Ethnicity, and Gender in the Jewish Labour Movement of Toronto 1900–1939.* Toronto: University of Toronto Press, 1992.

Frankenberg, Ruth. *White Women, Race Matters: The Social Construction of Whiteness.* Minneapolis: University of Minnesota Press, 1993.

Gabaccia, Donna R., and Fraser M. Ottanelli, eds. *Italy's Workers of the World: Labor, Migration, and the Formation of Multiethnic States.* Urbana: University of Illinois Press, 2001.

Gabaccia, Donna R. *Italy's Many Diasporas.* Seattle: University of Washington Press, 2000.

———. *Militants and Migrants: Rural Sicilians Become American Workers.* New Brunswick: Rutgers University Press, 1988.

Gallagher, Dorothy. *All the Right Enemies: The Life and Murder of Carlo Tresca.* New Brunswick: Rutgers University Press, 1988.

Galleani, Luigi. *The End of Anarchism?* Trans. Max Sartin and Robert D'Attilio. Orkney: Cienfuegos Press, 1982.

Garcia, Victor. *Three Japanese Anarchists: Kotuku, Osugi and Yamaga.* Berkeley: Kate Sharpley Library, 2000.

Giacometti, Paolo. *La Morte Civile.* New York: George F. Nesbitt and Company, 1873.

Glassgold, Peter, ed. *Anarchy! An Anthology of Emma Goldman's Mother Earth.* Washington, DC: Counterpoint, 2001.

Goldberg, David Theo. *Racist Culture: Philosophy and the Politics of Meaning.* Oxford: Balckwell Publishers, 1993.

Goldman, Emma. *My Disillusionment in Russia.* New York: Dover, 2004.

———. *Living My Life.* 2 vols. London: Pluto Press, 1987.

———. *Red Emma Speaks: An Emma Goldman Reader.* Ed. Alix Kates Shulman. New York: Schocken Books, 1983.

———. *Anarchism and Other Essays.* New York: Mother Earth Publishing, 1911.

Gori, Pietro. *Scritti Scelti.* Cesena: L'Antistato, 1968.

Graham, Marcus, ed. *Man! An Anthology of Anarchist Ideas, Essays, Poetry and Commentaries.* London: Cienfuegos Press, 1974.

Gramsci, Antonio. *The Southern Question.* Trans. Pasquale Verdicchio. Toronto: Guernica, 2005.

Green, James. *Death in the Haymarket: A Story of Chicago, the First Labor Movement and the Bombing that Divided Golden Age America.* New York: Pantheon Books, 2006.

Guglielmo, Jennifer. *Living the Revolution: Italian Women's Resistance and Radicalism in New York City, 1880–1945.* Chapel Hill: The University of North Carolina Press, 2010.

———. "Introduction: White Lies, Dark Truths." *Are Italians White?: How Race is Made in America.* Ed. Jennifer Guglielmo and Salvatore Salerno. New York: Routledge, 2003. 1–14.

———. "Donne Ribelli: Recovering the History of Italian Women's Radicalism in the United States." *The Lost World of Italian-American Radicalism: Politics, Labour, and Culture.* Ed. Philip V. Cannistraro and Gerald Meyer. Westport: Praeger, 2003. 113–142.

———. "Italian Women's Proletarian Feminism in the New York City Garment Trades, 1890s–1940s." *Women, Gender, and Transnational Lives: Italian Workers of the World.* Ed. Donna Gabaccia and Franca Iacovetta. Toronto: University of Toronto Press, 2002. 247–298.

Guglielmo, Thomas A. *White on Arrival: Italians, Race, Color, and Power in Chicago, 1890–1945.* Oxford: Oxford University Press, 2004.

Gusfield, Joseph R. "The Reflexivity of Social Movements: Collective Behaviour and Mass Society Theory Revisited." *New Social Movements: From Ideology to Identity.* Ed. Enrique Larana et al. Philadelphia: Temple University Press, 1994. 58–78.

Haaland, Bonnie. *Emma Goldman: Sexuality and the Impurity of the State.* Montréal: Black Rose Books, 1993.

Haeckel, Ernst. *The History of Creation: Or the Development of Evolution in General and its Inhabitants by the Action of Natural Causes.* Trans. E. Ray Lankster. Vol. 2. London: Henry S. King and Company, 1876.

Hale, Grace Elizabeth. *Making Whiteness: The Culture of Segregation in the South, 1890–1940.* New York: Vintage Books, 1999.

Hanagan, Michael. "Irish Transnational Social Movements, Migrants, and the State System." *Globalization and Resistance: Transnational Dimensions of Social Movements.* Ed. Jackie Smith and Hank Johnston. Lanham: Rowman and Littlefield Publishers, 2002. 53–74.

Harney, Robert. F. "Men Without Women: Italian Migrants in Canada, 1885–1930." *A Nation of Immigrants: Women, Workers, and Communities in Canadian History, 1840s–1960s.*

Ed. Franca Iacovetta with Paula Draper and Robert Ventresca. Toronto: University of Toronto Press, 1998. 206–230.

———. *From the Shores of Hardship: Italians in Canada*. Welland: Éditions Soleil, 1993.

———. "Toronto's Little Italy, 1885–1945." *Little Italies in North America*. Ed. Robert F. Harney and J. Vincenza Scarpaci. Toronto: The Multicultural History Society of Ontario, 1981. 41–62.

———. "Montreal's King of Italian Labour: A Case Study of Padronism." *Labour/Le Travail* 4 (1979): 57–84.

Hawkins, Mike. *Social Darwinism in European and American Thought 1860–1945: Nature as Model and Nature as Threat*. Cambridge: Cambridge University Press, 1997.

Heath, Nick. "Bifolchi, Giuseppe, 1895–1978." http://libcom.org/history/bifolchi-giuseppe-1895-1978.

Heron, Craig. *Working in Steel: The Early Years in Canada, 1883–1935*. Toronto: McClelland and Stewart, 1988.

Heron, Craig, and Robert Storey, eds. *On the Job: Confronting the Labour Process in Canada*. Kingston and Montreal: McGill-Queen's University Press, 1986.

Hobsbawm, E.J., and Terence O. Ranger, eds. *The Invention of Tradition*. Cambridge: Cambridge University Press, 1992.

Hobsbawm, E.J. *Primitive Rebels: Studies in Archaic Forms of Social Movements in the 19th and 20th Centuries*. Manchester: Manchester University Press, 1971.

Hoerder, Dirk. "International Labour Markets and Community Building by Migrant Workers in the Atlantic Economies." *A Century of European Migrations, 1930–1930*. Ed. Rudolph J. Vecoli and Suzanne M. Sinke. Urbana: University of Illinois Press, 1991. 78–107.

Hofstadter, Richard. *Social Darwinism in American Thought*. Revised Edition. Boston: The Beacon Press, 1955.

Houle-Courcelles, Mathieu. *Sur les traces de l'anarchisme au Québec*. Montréal: Lux Éditeur, 2008.

Hyams, Edward. *Pierre-Joseph Proudhon: His Revolutionary Life, Mind, and Works*. London: J. Murray, 1979.

Iacovetta, Franca. *Such Hardworking People: Italian Immigrants in Postwar Toronto*. Montreal and Kingston: McGill-Queen's University Press, 1992.

Ielasi, Barbara, and Mikhail Tsovma. "Francesco Ghezzi: Italian Anarchist in Vorkuta." Kate Sharpley Library. http://www.katesharpleylibrary.net/sj3w24.

Jameson, Elizabeth. *All That Glitters: Class, Conflict, and Community in Cripple Creek*. Urbana and Chicago: University of Illinois Press, 1998.

Johns, A. Wesley. *The Man Who Shot McKinley*. South Brunswick: A.S. Barnes, 1970.

Johnston, Hank, Enrique Laraña, and Joseph R. Gusfield. "Identities, Grievances, and New Social Movements." *New Social Movements: From Ideology to Identity*. Ed. Enrique Laraña, Hank Johnston, and Joseph R. Gusfield. Philadelphia: Temple University Press, 1994. 3–35.

Joll, James. "Anarchism – A Living Tradition." *Anarchism Today*. Ed. David E. Apter and James Joll. Garden City: Doubleday and Company, 1971.

———. *The Anarchists*. London: Eyre and Spottiswoode, 1964.

Kealey, Linda. *Enlisting Women for the Cause: Women, Labour, and the Left in Canada, 1890–1920*. Toronto: University of Toronto Press, 1998.

Keil, Hartmut. "Socialist Immigrants from Germany and the Transfer of Socialist Ideology and Workers' Culture." In *A Century of European Migrations, 1930–1930*. Ed. Rudolph J. Vecoli and Suzanne M. Sinke. Urbana: University of Illinois Press, 1991. 315–338.

Kelsey, Graham. *Anarchosyndicalism, Libertarian Communism and the State: The CNT in Zaragoza and Aragon, 1930–1937*. Dordrecht: Kluwer Academic Publishers, 1989.

Kincheloe, Joe L., Shirley R. Steinberg, Nelson M. Rodriguez, and Ronald E. Chennault, eds. *White Reign: Deploying Whiteness in America*. New York: St Martin's Press, 1998.

Kissack, Terrance. *Free Comrades: Anarchism and Homosexuality in the United States, 1895–1917*. Oakland: AK Press, 2008.

Knoke, David, and Song Yang. *Social Network Analysis*. 2nd ed. Los Angeles: Sage Publications, 2008.

Krebs, Edward S. *Shifu: Soul of Chinese Anarchism*. Lanham: Rowman and Littlefield Publishers, 1998.

Kropotkin, Peter. *Mutual Aid: A Factor of Evolution*. Montréal: Black Rose Books, 1989.

———. *Anarchism and Anarchist Communism: Its Basis and Principles*. London: Freedom Press, 1987.

———. *The Conquest of Bread*. Ed. Paul Avrich. London: Penguin Books, 1972.

———. *Fields, Factories and Workshops of Tomorrow*. Introduction by Colin Ward. London: Freedom Press, 1974.

———. *Kropotkin's Revolutionary Pamphlets*. Ed. Richard N. Baldwin. New York: Dover Press, 1972.

Landauer, Gustav. *For Socialism*. Trans. David J. Parent. St. Louis: Telos Press, 1978.

Leier, Mark. *Bakunin: A Biography*. New York: St. Martin's Press, 2006.

Levy, Carl. *Gramsci and the Anarchists*. Oxford: Berg, 1999.

———. "Italian Anarchism, 1870–1926." *For Anarchism: History, Theory, and Practice*. Ed. David Goodway. London: Routledge, 1989.

Liber, Benzion. *The Child and the Home: Essays on the Rational Bringing-up of Children*. New York: Vanguard Press, 1927.

Linden, Marcel van der. *Workers of the World: Essays toward a Global Labour History*. Leiden: Brill, 2008.

Lipsitz, George. *The Possessive Investment in Whiteness: How White People Profit from Identity Politics*. Philadelphia: Temple University Press, 1998.

MacDowell, Laurel Sefton. *Renegade Lawyer: The Life of J.L. Cohen*. Toronto: The Osgoode Society for Canadian Legal History/University of Toronto Press, 2001.

Malatesta, Errico. *Errico Malatesta: His Life and Ideas*. Ed. Vernon Richards. London: Freedom Press, 1965.

———. *Anarchy*. London: Freedom Press, 1949.

Marsh, Margaret S. *Anarchist Women, 1870–1920*. Philadelphia: Temple University Press, 1981.

Marshall, Peter. *Demanding the Impossible: A History of Anarchism*. London: Harper Perennial, 2008.

Marx, Karl, and Friedrich Engels. *Anarchism and Anarcho-Syndicalism*. Moscow: Progess, 1972.

Maximoff, G.P. *The Programme of Anarcho-Syndicalism*. Sydney: Monty Miller, 1985.

Mazour, Anatole G. *The First Russian Revolution, 1825: The Decembrist Movement: Its Origins, Development, and Significance*. Stanford: Stanford University Press, 1961.

Mbah, Sam, and I.E. Igariwey. *African Anarchism: The History of a Movement*. Tucson: See Sharp Press, 1997.

McAdam, Doug, John D. McCarthy, and Mayer N. Zald. "Introduction." *Comparative Perspectives on Social Movements: Political Opportunities, Mobilizing Structures, and Cultural Framings*. Ed. Doug McAdam, John D. McCarthy, and Mayer N. Zald. Cambridge: Cambridge University Press, 1996.

McCarthy, John D. "The Globalisation of Social Movement Theory." *Transnational Social Movements and Global Politics: Solidarity Beyond the State*. Ed. Jackie Smith et al. Syracuse: Syracuse University Press, 1997. 243–259.

McKay, Ian. *Reasoning Otherwise: Leftist and the People's Enlightenment in Canada, 1890–1920*. Toronto: Between the Lines, 2008.

McLaren, Angus. "Sex Radicalism in the Canadian Pacific Northwest, 1890–1920." *Journal of the History of Sexuality* 2, 4 (1992): 527–546.

Merithew, Caroline Waldron. "Anarchist Motherhood: Toward the Making of a Revolutionary Proletariat in Illinois Coal Towns." *Women, Gender, and Transnational Lives: Italian Workers of the World*. Ed. Donna Gabaccia and Franca Iacovetta. Toronto: University of Toronto Press, 2002. 217–246.

Merriman, John. *The Dynamite Club: How a Bombing in Fin-de-Siècle Paris Ignited the Age of Modern Terror*. Boston: Houghton Mifflin Harcourt, 2009.

Messer-Kruse, Timothy. *The Haymarket Conspiracy: Transatlantic Anarchist Networks*. Champaign-Urbana: University of Illinois Press, 2012.

———. *The Trial of the Haymarket Anarchists: Terrorism and Justice in the Gilded Age*. New York: Palgrave Macmillan, 2011.

Messer-Kruse, Timothy, James O. Eckert Jr., Pannee Burckel, and Jeffery Dunn. "The Haymarket Bomb: Reassessing the Evidence." *Labor: Studies in Working-Class History of the Americas* 2, 2 (2005): 39–51.

Miller, David. *Anarchism*. London: J.M. Dent and Sons, 1984.

Molinaro, Dennis G. "'A Species of Treason?': Deportation and Nation-Building in the Case of Tomo Čačić, 1931–1934." *The Canadian Historical Review* 91, 1 (March 2010): 61–85.

Molinaro, Julius, and Maddalena Kuitunen, eds. *The Luminous Mosaic: Italian Cultural Organizations in Ontario*. Welland: Soleil Publishing, 1993.

Montgomery, David. *The Fall of the House of Labor: The Workplace, the State, and American Labor Activism, 1865–1925*. Cambridge: Cambridge University Press, 1987.

Morgan, Philip. *Italian Fascism, 1915–1945*. Houndmills: Palgrave Macmillan, 2004.

Moritz, Theresa, and Albert Moritz. *The World's Most Dangerous Woman: A New Biography of Emma Goldman*. Vancouver: Subway Books, 2001.

Mormino, Gary. "The Hill upon a City: The Evolution of an Italian-American Community in St. Louis, 1882–1950." *Little Italies in North America*. Ed. Robert F. Harney and J. Vincenza Scarpaci. Toronto: The Multicultural History Society of Ontario, 1981. 141–164.

Morris, Brian. *Bakunin: The Philosophy of Freedom*. Montreal: Black Rose Books, 1993.

Morrison, Toni. *Playing in the Dark: Whiteness and the Literary Imagination*. Cambridge: Harvard University Press, 1992.

Moya, José. "Italians in Buenos Aires's Anarchist Movement: Gender Ideology and Women's Participation, 1890–1910." *Women, Gender, and Transnational Lives: Italian Workers of the World*. Ed. Donna Gabaccia and Franca Iacovetta. Toronto: University of Toronto Press, 2002. 189–216.

Murray, Robert K. *Red Scare: A Study in National Hysteria, 1919–1920.* New York: McGraw-Hill, 1961.

"Naturalization in Canada." The Quebec History Encyclopedia. http://faculty.marianopolis. edu/c.belanger/quebechistory/encyclopedia/Naturalizationin Canada.htm.

Nettlau, Max. *A Short History of Anarchism.* London: Freedom Press, 1996.

Neville, Peter. *Mussolini.* London: Routledge, 2004.

Nicholson, C. Brid. *Emma Goldman: Still Dangerous.* Montreal: Black Rose Books, 2010.

Nomad, Max. *Apostles of Revolution.* New York: Collier Books, 1961.

Nursey-Bray, Paul. "Malatesta and the Anarchist Revolution." *Anarchist Studies* 3 (1995): 25–44.

"Obituaries: Two Historians of Anarchism – Roland Biard and Carlo Pier Masini." Anarchist Federation, http://www.afed.org.uk/org/issue50/obit.html.

Orleck, Annelise. *Common Sense and a Little Fire: Women and Working-Class Politics in the United States, 1900–1965.* Chapel Hill: The University of North Carolina Press, 1995.

Palmer, Howard. *Ethnicity and Politics in Canada Since Confederation.* Ottawa: Canadian Historical Society, 1991.

———. *Patterns of Prejudice: A History of Nativism in Alberta.* Toronto: McClelland and Stewart, 1982.

Paz, Abel. *Durruti in the Spanish Revolution.* Oakland: AK Press, 2007.

Peck, Gunther. "Reinventing Free Labor: Immigrant Padrones and Contract Laborers in North America." *Journal of American History* 83, 3 (Dec 1996): 848–871.

Peirats, Jose. *The CNT in the Spanish Revolution: Volume I.* Hastings: Meltzer Press, 2002.

———. *Anarchists of the Spanish Revolution.* London: Freedom Press, 1990.

Pennacchio, Luigi G. "Exporting Fascism to Canada: Toronto's Little Italy." *Enemies Within: Italian and Other Internees in Canada and Abroad.* Ed. Franca Iacovetta, Roberto Perin, and Angelo Principe. Toronto: University of Toronto Press, 2000. 52–75.

Pernicone, Nunzio. *Carlo Tresca: Portrait of a Rebel.* New York: Palgrave Macmillan, 2005.

———. "War among the Italian Anarchists: The Galleanisti's Campaign against Carlo Tresca." *The Lost World of Italian-American Radicalism: Politics, Labor, and Culture.* Ed. Phillip V. Cannistraro and Gerald Meyer. Westport: Praeger Publishers, 2003. 78–97.

———. *Italian Anarchism, 1864–1892.* Princeton: Princeton University Press, 1993.

———. "Luigi Galleani and Italian Anarchist Terrorism in the United States." *Studi emigrazione* 30, 111 (1993): 469–488.

Pick, Daniel. *Faces of Degeneration: A European Disorder, 1848–1918.* Cambridge: Cambridge University Press, 1989.

———. "The Faces of Anarchy: Lombroso and the Politics of Criminal Science in Post-Unification Italy." *History Workshop* 2 (Spring 1986): 60–863.

Porter, David, ed. *Vision on Fire: Emma Goldman on the Spanish Revolution.* New Paltz: Commonground Press, 1983.

Potestio, John, and Antonio Pucci, eds. *The Italian Migrant Experience.* Thunder Bay: Canadian Italian Historical Association, 1988.

Powell, T.G. *Mexico and the Spanish Civil War.* Albuquerque: University of New Mexico Press, 1981.

Pozzetta, George E. "The Mulberry District of New York City: The Years before World War One." *Little Italies in North America.* Ed. Robert F. Harney and J. Vincenza Scarpaci. Toronto: The Multicultural History Society of Ontario. 7–40.

Principe, Angelo. "Glimpses of Lives in Canada's Shadow: Insiders, Outsiders, and Female Activism in the Fascist Era." *Women, Gender, and Transnational Lives: Italian Workers of the World*. Ed. Donna Gabaccia and Franca Iacovetta. Toronto: University of Toronto Press, 2002. 349–385.

———. "A Tangled Knot: Prelude to 10 June 1940." *Enemies Within: Italian and Other Internees in Canada and Abroad*. Ed. Franca Iacovetta, Roberto Perin, and Angelo Principe. Toronto: University of Toronto Press, 2000. 27–51.

———. *The Darkest Side of the Fascist Years: The Italian-Canadian Press, 1920–1942*. Toronto: Guernica, 1999.

Proudhon, Pierre-Joseph. *The Principle of Federation*. Trans. Richard Vernon. Toronto: University of Toronto Press, 1979.

———. *What Is Property? An Inquiry into the Principle of Right and of Government*. New York: Dover Publications, 1970.

———. *Selected Writings of Pierre-Joseph Proudhon*. Ed. Stewart Edwards. Trans. Elizabeth Fraser. Garden City: Anchor Books, 1969.

Pucci, Antonio. "Thunder Bay's Italian Community, 1880s-1940s." *The Italian Migrant Experience*. Ed. John Potestio and Antonio Pucci. Thunder Bay: Canadian Italian Historical Association, 1988: 79–102.

Puleo, Stephen. *The Boston Italians: A Story of Pride, Perseverance, and Paesani, from the Years of the Great Depression to the Present Day*. Boston: Beacon Press, 2007.

"Radowitzky, Simon. 1891–1956." libcom.org. http://libcom.org/history/simon-radowitzky-1891–1956

Raeff, Marc. *The Decembrist Movement*. Englewood Cliffs, New Jersey: Prentice-Hall, 1966.

Ramella, Franco. "Emigration from an Area of Intense Industrial Development: The Case of Northwestern Italy." *A Century of European Migrations, 1930–1930*. Ed. Rudolph J. Vecoli and Suzanne M. Sinke. Urbana: University of Illinois Press, 1991. 261–274.

Ramirez, Bruno. *Crossing the 49th Parallel: Migration from Canada to the United States, 1900–1930*. Ithaca: Cornell University Press, 2001.

———. *On the Move: French-Canadian and Italian Migrants in the North Atlantic Economy, 1860–1914*. Toronto: McClelland and Stewart, 1991.

———. "Immigration, Ethnicity, and Political Militance: Patterns of Radicalism in the Italian-American Left, 1880–1930." *From 'Melting Pot' to Multiculturalism: The Evolution of Ethnic Relations in the United States and Canada*. Ed. Valeria Gennaro Lerda. Rome: Bulzoni Editore, 1990. 115–141.

———. *The Italians in Canada*. Ottawa: The Canadian Historical Association, 1989.

———. "Workers Without a Cause: Italian Immigrant Labour in Montreal, 1880–1930." *Arrangiarsi: The Italian Immigration Experience in Canada*. Montreal: Guernica, 1989. 119–134.

Ramirez, Bruno, and Michael Del Balso. *The Italians of Montreal: From Sojourning to Settlement 1900–1921*. Montreal: Les Éditions du Courant, 1980.

Ravindranathan, T.R. *Bakunin and the Italians*. Kingston and Montreal: McGill-Queen's University Press, 1988.

"Revolutionary Radicalism: Its History, Purpose and Tactics with an Exposition and Discussion of the Steps Being Taken and Required to Curb It." *Report of the Joint Legislative Committee Investigating Seditious Activities*. Vol. 1. Albany: J.B. Lyon, 1920.

Riall, Lucy. *Risorgimento: The History of Italy from Napoleon to Nation-State*. Houndmills: Palgrave Macmillan, 2009.

———. *Sicily and the Unification of Italy: Liberal Policy and Local Power 1859–1866*. Oxford: Clarendon Press, 1998.

Riccio, Anthony V. *The Italian American Experience in New Haven*. Albany: State University of New York Press, 2006.

Richards, David A.J. *Italian American: The Radicalising of an Ethnic Identity*. New York: New York University Press, 1999.

Richards, Robert J. *The Tragic Sense of Life: Ernst Haeckel and the Struggle over Evolutionary Thought*. Chicago: The University of Chicago Press, 2008.

Ricketts, Aidan. *The Activists' Handbook: A Step-by-Step Guide to Participatory Democracy*. London: Zed Books, 2012.

Roberts, Barbara. *Whence They Came: Deportation from Canada, 1900–1935*. Ottawa: University of Ottawa Press, 1988.

Rocker, Rudolph. *Anarcho-Syndicalism: Theory and Practice*. Oakland: AK Press, 2004.

Roediger, David R. *The Wages of Whiteness: Race and the Making of the American Working Class*. London: Verso, 2007.

———. *Colored White: Transcending the Racial Past*. Berkeley: University of California Press, 2002.

———. "Afterword: Du Bois, Race, and Italian Americans." *Are Italians White?: How Race Is Made in America*. Ed. Jennifer Guglielmo and Salvatore Salerno. New York: Routledge, 2003. 259–263.

Salerno, Salvatore. "No God, No Master: Italian Anarchists and the Industrial Workers of the World." *The Lost World of Italian-American Radicalism: Politics, Labor, and Culture*. Ed. Phillip V. Cannistraro and Gerald Meyer. Westport: Praeger Publishers, 2003. 171–188.

———. "*I Delitti della Razza Bianca* (Crimes of the White Race): Italian Anarchists' Racial Discourse as Crime." *Are Italians White?: How Race Is Made in America*. Ed. Jennifer Guglielmo and Salvatore Salerno. New York: Routledge, 2003. 111–123.

——. *Red November, Black November: Culture and Community in the Industrial Workers of the World*. Albany: State University of New York Press, 1989.

Sangster, Joan. *Dreams of Equality: Women on the Canadian Left, 1920–1950*. Toronto: McClelland and Stewart, 1989.

Scarpaci, Vincenza. "Walking the Colour Line: Italian Immigrants in Rural Louisiana, 1880–1910." *Are Italians White?: How Race Is Made in America*. Ed. Jennifer Guglielmo and Salvatore Salerno. New York: Routledge, 2003. 60–76.

———. "Observations on a [sic] Ethnic Community: Baltimore's Little Italy." *Little Italies in North America*. Ed. Robert F. Harney and J. Vincenza Scarpaci. Toronto: The Multicultural History Society of Ontario, 1981. 105–122.

Schmidt, Michael, and Lucien van der Walt. *Black Flame: The Revolutionary Class Politics of Anarchism and Syndicalism*. Oakland: AK Press, 2009.

Sensi-Isolani, Paola A. "Italian Radicals and Union Activists in San Francisco, 1900–1920." *The Lost World of Italian-American Radicalism: Politics, Labor, and Culture*. Ed. Phillip V. Cannistraro and Gerald Meyer. Westport: Praeger Publishers, 2003. 189–204.

Singer, Peter. *A Darwinian Left: Politics, Evolution and Cooperation*. London: Weidenfeld and Nicolson, 1999.

Smith, Carl. *Urban Disorder and the Shape of Belief: The Great Chicago Fire, the Haymarket Bomb, and the Model Town of Pullman*. Chicago: University of Chicago Press, 1995.

Smith, Jackie, and Hank Johnston. "Globalization and Resistance: An Introduction." *Globalization and Resistance: Transnational Dimensions of Social Movements.* Ed. Jackie Smith and Hank Johnston. Lanham: Rowman and Littlefield Publishers, 2002. 1–12.

Solomon, Martha. *Emma Goldman.* Boston: Twayne Publishers, 1987.

Spada, Antonino V. *The Italians in Canada.* Ottawa: Riviera Printers, 1969.

Spriano, Paolo. *The Occupation of the Factories: Italy 1920.* Gwyn A. Williams, trans. London: Pluto Press, 1975.

Stack, John F. *International Conflict in an American City: Boston's Irish, Italians, and Jews, 1935–1944.* Westport: Greenwood Press, 1979.

Steele, Melchior [Raffaele Schiavina]. "1931: Michele Schirru and the Attempted Assassination of Mussolini." *Man!* 1, 5–6 (May–June 1933) http://libcom.org/ history/articles/murder-michael-schirru.

Stirner, Max. *The Ego and His Own: The Case of the Individual Against Authority.* Trans. Steven T. Byington. Ed. James J. Martin. New York: Libertarian Book Club, 1963.

Sturino, Franc. *Forging the Chain: A Case Study of Italian Migration to North America, 1880–1930.* Toronto: Multicultural Historical Society of Ontario, 1990.

——. "Italian Immigration: Reconsidering the Links in Chain Migration." *Arrangiarsi: The Italian Immigration Experience in Canada.* Montreal: Guernica, 1989. 63–90.

Temelini, Walter. "Italian Cultural Presence in Windsor, 1920–1990." *The Luminous Mosaic: Italian Cultural Organizations in Ontario.* Ed. Julius Molinaro and Maddalena Kuitunen. Welland: Éditions Soleil Publishing, 1993. 205–221.

Temkin, Moshik. *The Sacco-Vanzetti Affair: America on Trial.* New Haven: Yale University Press, 2009.

Thistlethwaite, Frank. "Migration from Europe Overseas in the Nineteenth and Twentieth Centuries." *A Century of European Migrations, 1930–1930.* Ed. Rudolph J. Vecoli and Suzanne M. Sinke. Urbana: University of Illinois Press, 1991. 17–49.

Thomas, Matthew. *Anarchist Ideas and Counter-Cultures in Britain, 1880–1914: Revolutions in Everyday Life.* Aldershot: Ashgate Publishing, 2005.

Thompson, John Herd. *Ethnic Minorities During Two World Wars.* Ottawa: Canadian Historical Association, 1991.

——. "The Enemy Alien and the Canadian General Election of 1917." *Loyalties in Conflict: Ukrainians in Canada During the Great War.* Ed. Frances Swyripa and John Herd Thompson. Edmonton: Canadian Institute of Ukrainian Studies at the University of Alberta, 1983. 25–46.

Tolstoy, Leo. *Government Is Violence: Essays on Anarchism and Pacifism.* Ed. David Stephens. London: Phoenix Press, 1990.

Topp, Michael Miller. "'It's Providential that there are Foreigners Here': Whiteness and Masculinity in the Making of Italian American Syndicalist Identity." *Are Italians White?: How Race Is Made in America.* Ed. Jennifer Guglielmo and Salvatore Salerno. New York: Routledge, 2003. 98–110.

——. *Those without a Country: The Political Culture of Italian American Syndicalists.* Minneapolis: University of Minneapolis Press, 2001.

Tresca, Carlo. *The Autobiography of Carlo Tresca.* Ed. Nunzio Pernicone. New York: The John D. Calandra Italian American Institute, 2003.

Turcato, Davide. *Making Sense of Anarchism: Errico Malatesta's Experiments with Revolution, 1889–1900.* London: Palgrave Macmillan, 2012

———. "Italian Anarchism as a Transnational Movement, 1885–1915." *International Review of Social History* 52 (2007), 407–444.

Tyrrell, Ian. *Transnational Nation: United States History in Global Perspective Since 1789.* New York: Palgrave Macmillan, 2007.

United States Military Intelligence Reports: Surveillance of Radicals in the United States: 1917–1941. Frederick: University Publication of America, 1984.

Un Trentennio di Attività anarchica, 1914–1945. Forli: del gruppo "L'Antistato," 1953.

Vecoli, Rudolph J., and Suzanne M. Sinke, eds. *A Century of European Migrations, 1830–1930.* Urbana: University of Illinois Press, 1991.

———. "Luigi Galleani." *Encyclopedia of the American Left.* Ed. Mari Jo Buhle et al. Chicago: St. James Press, 1990. 251–253.

———. "'Primo Maggio' in the United States: An Invented Tradition of the Italian Anarchists." *May Day Celebration.* Ed. Andrea Panaccione. Venice: Marsilio Editori, 1988. 55–83.

———. "The Italian Immigrants in the United States Labour Movement from 1880 to 1929." *Gli italiani fuori d'italia: gli emigrati italiani nei movimenti operai dei paesi d'adozione 1880–1940.* Ed. O. Bayer et al. Milan: Franco Angeli Editore, 1983. 257–306.

Ventresca, Robert, and Franca Iacovetta. "Virgilia D'Andrea: The Politics of Protest and the Poetry of Exile." *Women, Gender, and Transnational Lives: Italian Workers of the World.* Ed. Donna Gabaccia and Franca Iacovetta. Toronto: University of Toronto Press, 2002. 299–326.

Weikart, Richard. *Socialist Darwinism: Evolution in German Socialist Thought from Marx to Bernstein.* San Francisco, London and Bethesda: International Scholars Publications, 1999.

Wellman, Barry, ed. *Networks in the Global Village: Life in Contemporary Communities.* Boulder: Westview Press, 1999.

Wexler, Alice. *Emma Goldman in Exile: From the Russian Revolution to the Spanish Civil War.* Boston: Beacon Press, 1989.

———. *Emma Goldman: An Intimate Life.* New York: Pantheon Books, 1984.

Whelehan, Niall. "Political Violence and Morality in Anarchist Theory and Practice: Luigi Galleani and Peter Kropotkin in Comparative Perspective." *Anarchist Studies* 13, 2 (2005): 147–168.

Whitaker, Reg. *Canadian Immigration Policy since Confederation.* Ottawa: Canadian Historical Association, 1991.

Woodcock, George. *Anarchism: A History of Libertarian Ideas and Movements.* Peterborough: Broadview Press, 2004.

Woods, Ellen Meiksins. *The Retreat from Class: A New 'True' Socialism.* London: Verso, 1998.

Woodsworth, J.S. *Strangers Within Our Gates or Coming Canadians.* Toronto: University of Toronto Press, 1972.

Yans-McLaughlin, Virginia. *Family and Community: Italian Immigrants in Buffalo, 1880–1930.* Ithaca: Cornell University Press, 1977.

Zeilig, Martin. "Emma Goldman in Winnipeg." *Manitoba History* 25 (Spring 1993): 23–27.

Zucchi, John. *A History of Ethnic Enclaves in Canada.* Ottawa: The Canadian Historical Association, 2007.

———. "Cultural Constructs or Organic Evolution? Italian Immigrant Settlements in Ontario." *The Luminous Mosaic: Italian Cultural Organizations in Ontario.* Ed. Julius Molinaro and Maddalena Kuitunen. Welland: Éditions Soleil Publishing, 1993. 19–37.

————. *Italians in Toronto: Development of a National Identity 1875–1935*. Kingston and Montreal: McGill-Queen's University Press, 1988.

Film

Emma Goldman. Dir. Mel Bucklin. 2004. 90 min.

Emma Goldman: The Anarchist Guest. Dir. Coleman Romalis. 2000. 42 min.

The Free Voice of Labor: The Jewish Anarchists. Dirs. Steven Fischler and Joel Sucher. 1980. 50 min.

INDEX

A

Abate, Erasmo, 141

L'Adunata dei Refrattari: attitude to fascism, 153–54, 155, 156–57; and Bortolotti-Confalonieri deportation, 169, 171–79, 181–84, 185; circulation of, 225n95; collaborates with Road to Freedom, 102; feud with C. Tresca, 148–51, 172–76; fundraising by, 87–90, 181–84; importance as a source, 11, 59; international reporting, 84–85; mastheads, 79–80; office of, 74–75; political illustrations, 81; use of post office by, 83; and V. D'Andrea, 123, 124; and women writers, 113, 117–18, 120

AFL (American Federation of Labor), 19, 139

Aguggini, Ettore, 145

Alleanza Antifascista del Nord America (AAFNA), 152, 154–55

Allegra, Pietro, 109–10, 125, 152

Alleva, Aurora, 58, 113, 119, 220n70

Ambrosi, G.B., 156

Amalgamated Clothing Workers' Union (ACWU), 145–46, 152, 184

American Federation of Labor (AFL), 19, 139

Amoroso, Nicola, 155

anarchism: C. Tresca's view of, 144–45; and citizenship, 7–8; classical, 14–15; culture, 6–7, 8; defined, 13–14; difficulty in finding information on, 1–2, 12; gender roles in, 113–19; ineffectiveness of national studies of, 1–2, 8–11; L. Galleani's view of, 141–43; legacy of, 189–91; misrepresentation of, 28–30; newspapers, 6–7, 11; periodization of, 14–15; philosophy of, 17–28; and religious belief, 2, 24–25; use of violence, 30–31, 130. *See also* Italian anarchist movement; Italian anarchists in North America; transnationalism

anarcho-syndicalism, 18–19, 19–20, 139–41

Angel, Mario, 165

Antolini, Gabriella 'Ella,' 126

Antonini, Luigi, 174–76

Arcos, Federico, 12

Argentina, 84

Artico, Egidio, 54

L'Avvenire (newspaper), 137, 140

B

Bakunin, Mikhail: background, 35–37; and C. Cafiero, 20; collectivist position of, 18; on equality, 114, 125; retirement, 42; and Risorgimento, 33, 37–39

Balabanoff, Angelica, 114

Baldi, Ugo, 95, 214n88

Barra, Antonio, 156

Bava-Beccaris, General, 30

Beduz, Pietro, 12

Bellanca, Augusto, 184

Benvenuti, Giuseppe, 167